The Glenmorangie
Fly Fisher's Guide

The Glenmorangie Fly Fisher's Guide
to the waters of mainland Britain

Andrew Graham-Stewart
Paul McNichol

Regional editors
Bill Howes (ENGLAND)
Bill Currie (SCOTLAND)
Moc Morgan (WALES)

Foreword by Wilson Stephens

Robson Books

published in association with
THE FIELD

FIRST PUBLISHED IN GREAT BRITAIN IN 1984 BY
ROBSON BOOKS LTD., BOLSOVER HOUSE, 5-6 CLIP-
STONE STREET, LONDON W1P 7EB. COPYRIGHT©
1984 THE HARMSWORTH PRESS LTD.

British Library Cataloguing in Publication Data
  The Glenmorangie fly fisher's guide.
    1. Salmon-fishing—Great Britain—Handbooks,
    manuals, etc.   2. Trout fishing—Great Britain—
    Handbooks, manuals, etc.   3. Fly fishing—Great
    Britain—Handbooks, manuals, etc.   I. Graham-
    Stewart, Andrew   II. McNichol, Paul   III.
    Howes, B.   IV. Currie, B.   V. Morgan, M.
    799.1'1755   SH685

    ISBN 0-86051-312-2

    Designed by : Keith Johnson
    Cover Design: Tim Epps (Busy Lizzy Design) and
               Keith Johnson

Printed in Great Britain by
Redwood Burn Ltd., Trowbridge.

◈ Contents

FOREWORD		13
INTRODUCTION		15
REGIONAL EDITORS		16
KEY		16
PLATFORM PIECE — Angler's Cooperative Association		19
PLATFORM PIECE — Salmon and Trout Association		21
ENGLAND	INTRODUCTION	25
AVON	The Barrows Fishery	29
	Blagdon Lake	30
	Chew Valley Lake	31
BERKSHIRE	Horton Fishery	32
	River Kennet	33
BUCKINGHAMSHIRE	Church Hill Farm	34
	Latimer Park Lakes	35
	Queen Mother Reservoir	36
	Vicarage Spinney Fishery	37
CAMBRIDGESHIRE	Grafham Water	39
CORNWALL	Argal and College	40
	Crowley Reservoir	41
	Porth Reservoir	42
	Siblyback Reservoir	43
	Stithians Reservoir	44
	River Tamar	45
	Upper Tamar Lake	48
CUMBRIA	Blencarn Lake	49
	River Derwent	50
	River Eden	52
	River Kent	53
	River Lune	54
DERBYSHIRE	River Derwent	56
	Foremark Reservoir	57
	Ladybower Reservoir	58
DEVON	River Avon	60
	Bellbrook Valley	61
	Burrator Reservoir	62
	River Dart	63
	River East Lyn	64
	River Exe	65
	Fernworthy Reservoir	66
	Kennick and Tottiford	67
	River Otter	68
	Slade Fishery	69
	Stafford Moor Fishery	70
	River Tavy	71
	River Taw	73
	River Torridge	74
	Wistlandpound	77
DORSET	Flowers Farm	78
	Kingsbridge Lakes	79
	White Sheet Farm	80

DURHAM	Derwent Reservoir	81
	River Tees	82
	River Wear	83
ESSEX	Ardleigh Reservoir	84
	Chigboro Fisheries	85
	Hanningfield Reservoir	86
GLOUCESTER	Horseshoe Lake	87
	Lechlade Farm	89
	Rainbow Lake	90
HAMPSHIRE	Avington Fisheries	91
	Bridge Farm Trout Fishery	92
	Damerham Fisheries	93
	Eversley Cross Fishery	94
	Hucklesbrook Lake	95
	River Itchen	96
	Ladywell Lakes	97
	Leominster	98
	Rooksbury Mill	99
	Stratfield Saye Fishery	100
	River Test	101
HERTFORDSHIRE	Croxley Hall Waters Fishery	103
KENT	Bayham Fishery	104
	Bewl Bridge Fishery	105
	River Teise	107
LANCASHIRE	Pennine Fishery	108
	River Ribble	109
LEICESTERSHIRE	Eyebrook Reservoir	110
	Rutland Water	111
	Thornton Fishery	112
LINCOLNSHIRE	Toft Newton Reservoir	113
LONDON	Barn Elms Fishery	114
	Walthamstow Reservoirs	115
NORTHAMPTONSHIRE	Pitsford Reservoir	116
	Ravensthorpe Reservoir	117
	Ringstead Grange	118
NORTHUMBERLAND	Bakethin Water	120
	River Coquet	121
	Kielder Water	122
	River Tyne	123
NOTTINGHAMSHIRE	Colwick Lake	125
OXFORDSHIRE	Farmoor No 2	126
	Linch Hill Fishery	127
SOMERSET	Clatworthy Reservoir	128
	Durleigh Reservoir	129
	Hawkridge Reservoir	130
	Otterhead Fishery	131
	Sutton Bingham	132
	Wimbleball Reservoir	133
STAFFORDSHIRE	Gailey Fishery	134
	Patshull Fishery	135

	Tittesworth Reservoir	136
SURREY	Runfold Fishery	137
	Rushmoor Lakes	138
	Willinghurst Fishery	139
SUSSEX	Ardingley Reservoir	140
	Darwell Reservoir	142
	Furnace Brook Fishery	143
	Lakedown Fisheries	144
	Peckhams Copse	145
	Powdermill Lake	146
WARWICKSHIRE	Bishops Bowl	147
	Draycote Water	149
	Packington Fisheries	150
	Shustoke Fishery	151
WILTSHIRE	River Avon	152
	Lower Moor Fishery	154
	Wroughton Reservoir	155
WORCESTERSHIRE	Black Monk Fishery	156
YORKSHIRE	River Aire	158
	Cod Beck Reservoir	159
	Damflask Reservoir	160
	River Derwent	161
	River Esk	162
	Farmire Fishery	163
	Leighton Reservoir	164
	Morehall Reservoir	166
	River Nidd	167
	Ulley Reservoir	168
	Underbank Reservoir	169
	Washburn Valley Fishery	170
	River Wharfe	171
SCOTLAND	INTRODUCTION	173
TWEED AND DISTRICT		178
	Upper Waters	182
	Upper Middle Tweed	183
	Middle Tweed	184
	Lower River	186
	Ettrick, Yarrow and Leader	187
	Whiteadder System	188
	Teviot	190
	Stillwaters	192
THE LOTHIANS		194
LOCH FITTY		196
LOCH LEVEN		197
THE FORTH SYSTEM		198
THE TAY SYSTEM		201
	The Dochart and Lochey	204
	The Upper Tay and Tummel	205
	Middle Tay	209
	Lower Tay	210

	The Earn	211
	Tay Stillwaters	212
ANGUS AND THE MEARNS		215
	South Esk System	216
	North Esk System	217
THE DEE AND THE DON		218
THE MORAY-BUCHAN AREA		223
	The Ythan, Ugie and other waters	225
	The Deveron and other waters	226
	The Findhorn and Lossie	229
THE SPEY		230
	The Upper Spey	232
	The Lower Spey	235
INVERNESSSHIRE		236
	Inverness and The Great Glen	237
	Northern Invernessshire	240
	Fort William, Lochaber and Ardnamurchan	242
EASTER AND WESTER ROSS		245
LOCH MAREE		250
SUTHERLAND		251
	The Kyle of Sutherland	253
	The Forsinard and Badanloch areas	256
	The Naver and Borgie districts	257
	Kylesku, Lochniver and Inchnadamph	259
LOCH STACK		261
LOCH HOPE		262
CAITHNESS		263
ARGYLL		267
LOCH LOMOND AND ASSOCIATED WATERS		272
THE CLYDE		275
THE SOUTH WEST		277
	The Ayr, Doon, Girvan and Stinchar	279
	The Cree, Dee, Urr, Fleet and Nith	281
ANNAN AND BORDER ESK		283
WALES	INTRODUCTION	288
SOUTH EAST WALES		289
	Beacon Reservoir	290
	Cantref Reservoir	291
	Clwywedog Reservoir	292
	Dolygaer Reservoir	293
	Eglwys Nunydd Reservoir	294
	Llandegfedd Reservoir	295
	Llanishen and Lisvane Reservoirs	296
	Llwyn-On Reservoir	297
	Lower Neuadd Reservoir	298
	Pontsticill Reservoir	299
	River Severn	300
	Talybont Reservoir	301
	Upper Neuadd Reservoir	302
	Usk Reservoir	303

Wentwood Reservoir	304
River Usk	305
River Wye	307
Ynysyfro Reservoir	311
Ystradfellte Reservoir	312
SOUTH WEST WALES	313
River Aeron	314
Eastern Cleddau	315
River Cothi	316
Elan Valley Reservoirs	317
Llanllawddog Lake	318
Llysyfran Reservoir	319
Rosebush Reservoir	320
River Taf	321
Teifi Pools	322
River Teify	323
River Towy	325
NORTH EAST WALES	327
Alwen Reservoir	328
Llyn Brenig	329
Llyn Celyn	330
River Dee	331
River Rheidol	332
Lake Vyrnwy	333
NORTH WEST WALES	334
Llyn Alaw	335
River Conway	336
Dinas Reservoir	338
River Dovey	339
River Dysynni	341
River Erch	342
River Glaslyn	343
River Gwyrfai	344
River Llyfni	345
Nantymoch Reservoir	346
Penrhyncoch Lakes	347
Lyn Trawsfynydd	348
Trisant Lakes	349
River Vyrnwy	350
River Ystwyth	351
INDEX TO ADVERTISERS	352

 FOREWORD

For years, fly fishers have needed a guide in the fullest sense to the waters, flowing and still, which give them their sport. Other directories have listed them to the extent of saying where they are and how access may be arranged. This book provides in addition a frank character sketch to each separate fishery.

What makes fly fishing different is the rich variety of its own internal differences. These are not only the obvious ones between the various quarry - those peerless sporting fish the salmon, sea trout, brown trout, rainbow trout, brook trout and grayling; nor between the contasting terrains - rugged Scotland, lush English chalk country, Welsh valleys bright and green or dark and brooding, the wild windscapes in which anglers drift the big lakes. To the fly fisher every river, stream and still water is a world of its own; every beat a separate scene with its own atmosphere, tradition, subtlety and approach.

In giving a portrait of available fly fishing the Glenmorangie Fly Fisher's Guide does not claim to be exhaustive, although it is not far off it. It does not, for example, list fisheries for which an eclectic fisherman has no hope of obtaining permission. It does claim that the facts and comments which it contains are accurate at the time of writing. Fishery fortunes wax and wane; those included are described on their present form, not past reputation.

This has been achieved by appointing three regional editors. Their essential qualification is that each is in love with the fish, the waters and the flies of his homeland, travels much, sees them often, knows how their demands alter with the seasons.

Bill Howes for England, Bill Currie for Scotland, Moc Morgan for Wales have something else in common. This is deep regard for the immaterials which make fly fishing the great sport it is - the courtesies between fishermen, the regard for wildlife of all kinds, the enjoyment of local company, the uplift of scenery. This is not a book which stops at locations, species, weights and fees. It transmits the underlying spirit.

Wilson Stephens

Wilson Stephens.
Former Editor of 'The Field'.

GLENMORANGIE
10 YEARS OLD
SINGLE HIGHLAND MALT
SCOTCH WHISKY

4. JOHNNY URQUHART, Head Cooper, practises his patient craft in the low, whitewashed cooperage at the Glenmorangie Distillery. Here, under the watchful eye of 'Tiger,' the hogsheads are checked, tightened, made sound. Bungholes are reamed to a perfect fit. Johnny well knows that, during the ten years needed to bring the spirit to the peak of its excellence, much will inevitably be lost 'to the angels.' But why, he reasons, should they receive more than their due share?

Handcrafted by the Sixteen Men of Tain.

THE GLENMORANGIE DISTILLERY CO. TAIN, ROSS-SHIRE

INTRODUCTION

Fly fishermen are by nature nomadic. This book, conceived and compiled by two anglers diverse in tactics and travel, aims at filling the existing vacuum for an up-to-date, illustrated guide, to alleviate the pre-trip problems of where to fish, and hopefully supply enough information to make the resultant venture more successful and enjoyable.

Our three regional editors, who have stuck doggedly to their demanding briefs, are experts on their own territories, and have compiled a catalogue of those rivers, lochs, lakes and reservoirs, accessible on the purchase of a day or week ticket. These waters, many of them well known, also include stretches of renowned rivers which might otherwise have been considered exclusive, and also remote stillwaters which might have remained unrecorded in fishing terms. Maps illustrate most waters discussed. It should however be noted that still-water diagrams can only be as good as the material which has been supplied or been made available to the editors. The appropriate seasonal flies have been gleaned from return books, to provide at least a sporting chance. We were anxious not to present a file of computerised data and have, wherever possible, sought local knowledge, candid opinion and hints on the fisheries included.

Fishing in England, Scotland and Wales is as disverse as the terrains themselves; no strict format could honestly be presented – the ratio of rivers to lochs, lakes to streams and reservoirs is fundamentally different in each region. England therefore is catalogued alphabetically by County; Wales is divided roughly into four compass quadrants and Scotland is basically covered anti-clockwise from the South East. Rivers are followed from their source. In England rivers are generally included under the County where they are most prevalent.

Prices have been based on the 1984 season and are obviously likely to vary according to a variety of economic influences. All of our information is, we believe, correct as we go to press, but as the book is neither encyclopaedic nor infallible, the publishers would appreciate any faults to be pointed out for subsequent editions. These subsequent editions will hopefully be expanded to include Northern Ireland, Eire and the islands of Scotland.

Telephone numbers have been supplied for contacts; however, we would ask the reader to use these within reasonable hours. Local restrictions and regulations are generally well thought out aids to conservation. We have included them to prevent the reader from supplying ammunition to the misguided who would seek to banish our sport.

Our sincere thanks must go the John Wilshaw of Salmon and Trout Magazine, Allen Edwards of the Anglers Cooperative Association, Don Thompson of the Salmon and Trout Association, Michael Ruvigny and former Field Editor, Wilson Stephens. Their help and enthusiasm towards the prospect of two keen lay anglers compiling the Glenmorangie Fly Fishing Guide has been invaluable.

A. G.-S.
P. M.   August 1984.

REGIONAL EDITORS

BILL HOWES (ENGLAND)

Author of 15 books on angling, and a contributor to several more. Also a prolific photographer with a library of over 50,000 black and white, and colour pictures. Has illustrated many books with his photographs. Contributes to most of the angling magazines in England, and some abroad. First started fishing almost 50 years ago, and has a list of specimen fish to his credit. An all-round angler, who fishes for trout, salmon, sea and coarse fish both in Britain and overseas.

BILL CURRIE (SCOTLAND)

Bill Currie is a Scot, living in Edinburgh and seldom at home because he is always somewhere fishing for salmon, sea trout or trout. He is well known as a writer on fishing and has written over a dozen books on game fishing and has edited a monthly fishing magazine. He sits on various angling bodies, – ACA and Salmon and Trout Association committees among them. When asked about the future of game fishing in Scotland he is optimistic. He points out that management is better than ever and access is easier. He is keenly in support of more fly fishing throughout the game fishing range and believes that Scotland is poised to enter a period of expansion of fishing facilities for fly fishers.

MOC MORGAN (WALES)

Moc has fished his native Wales since infancy. He contributes regularly to many fishing journals and his fishing and shooting programme 'Living in the Country' has been transmitted for over six years on Radio Wales. Twice winner of the Welsh Fly Fishing Championship and three times Captain of the Welsh Fly Fishing Team, he is currently President of the International Fly-Fishing Association of G. B., President of International Fly Fishing for the Disabled, Chairman of the Welsh A.C. and Director of Coaching for Wales.

General Key

MAPS NOT TO SCALE		
◳ LODGE	○	ESTATES
▪ TOILETS	◢	NO FISHING
◎ PERMIT BOXES	——	ROAD ACCESS
● MAJOR TOWNS	----	FOOTPATH
• MINOR TOWNS	P	PARKING

**The Fishing Tackle Shop in Pall Mall that offers so much more.
Fishing Tackle, Shooting Accessories and Appropriate clothing.**

Platform Piece–Allen Edwards
Anglers Co-operative Association

POLLUTION, ANGLING'S FORGOTTEN WAR

To use the word war in connection with angling may seem strange but this is not the case. Wars fall into many categories, from what is little more than a skirmish through to horrific slugging matches where the casualties are legion. Angling's war against pollution is just such a one. It is a war of attrition. The victims are numbered in millions as fish, insects and birds succumb to water-borne clouds of noxious pollutants of various kinds. Anglers too suffer. They lose their enjoyment, the value of their fishery is greatly reduced. They face the prospect of a long, up-hill, struggle to restore the water to its former glory.

The struggle has been going on for more than one hundred years as nearly all river pollution has been illegal under Criminal Law since the Rivers Pollution Prevention Act of 1876. This may be invoked by the Regional Water Authorities which have the necessary power to prosecute an offender. If the offence is proved in court the polluter can be fined, but the fine is not paid to the fishery owner. The fines often bear little relationship to the scale of the pollution. In one recent incident nineteen miles of a prime northern river were wiped out. The business concerned was fined just £2,000.

Since 1948 anglers have been carrying the battle a stage further by invoking Common Law. Every riparian owner or tenant is entitled to have the water flowing past his land in its natural state of purity. If there is any infringement of this right, the owner or tenant can apply to the Courts for an injunction to restrain the polluter. If the offender disobeys the injunction and continues the pollution he is guilty of contempt of court and can be imprisoned. Where riparian owners or tenants have suffered damage, such as financial loss, loss of enjoyment of their fishing or amenities, then damages can be awarded. These are usually substantially higher than the fines imposed under stautory actions.

But, until the Anglers Co-operative Association was formed by John Eastwood in 1948, hardly anyone took this course of action, for the simple reason that, if the action was unsuccessful, it could cost the person who brought it thousands of pounds. The formation of the ACA provided a simple and effective answer to this problem. By contributing a small sum of money each, thousands of anglers shared, and minimised, the risk of losing an action against the polluters. Since that time the Association has fought hundreds of cases losing only one in the process. The ACA has teeth and polluters know it.

Within months of its formation the ACA applied for an injunction against a polluter. The case was won and damages obtained. In 1951 the ACA fought its most famous case on behalf of members, the Pride of Derby Angling Club and Derby Angling Association. The River Derwent was being grossly polluted by a combination of untreated sewage from the Derby Corporation sewage works, trade effluents from British Tar Distillers and British Celanese. The problem was compounded by the fact that the Central Electricity Generating Board was using water from the river for cooling purposes and returning it as a kind of hells-broth. The case lasted thirteen days in the High Court and six days in the Court of Appeal. The case was won with costs and damages against the defendants. Today the River Derwent from Derby to the River Trent offers some of the finest chub fishing to be found in the country.

In 1953 the ACA fought a long legal battle against the giant steel firm John Summers Ltd who were polluting the estuary of the Dee. Again the case was won.

In 1954 the ACA's legal right to bring cases on behalf of members was disputed by the Consett Iron Company. They lost, went to the Appeal Court and lost again. Not long after that the ACA fought Monsanto Chemicals and again won the case. There have been many smaller cases where injunctions were obtained. One of these was against Sevenoaks Council which was polluting a river with sewage. After six months the ACA took the matter to the Court again because nothing had been done about it. The defendants' Counsel was unwise enough to tell the Judge that he could hardly send the whole Council to jail; the Judge assured him that he not merely could but he would unless steps were taken to build a new sewage works. The Council built one very shortly afterwards.

It is rare, these days, for polluters to go into Court against the ACA so the struggle goes on unpublicised. The battle, however, is not over. In the first six months of 1984 cases were settled on the Rivers Onny, Ewenny, Afon Llwyd, Claydon Bridge Lodges, Pickering Beck and the Blackwater. Damages totalling £20,000 were obtained on behalf of members. The ACA never has less than two dozen cases in the hands of solicitors at any given time, some of which are very complex indeed.

In the early days of the Association the majority of pollutions stemmed from industry and poorly treated sewage. Today it is different. Intensive farming practises and the difficulty of disposing of waste material means that a pollution is as likely to take place in the country as it is in an industrial town. The intensive farming of trout is another source with which the ACA is wrestling.

Think not, by the way, that these actions on behalf of anglers are mounted with the full force of a large organisation. The ACA has just two full time members of staff to furnish material upon which solicitors can act and to generate the funds to finance the cases. The Association has just over seven thousand individual members and nine hundred Clubs and Association; it is in need of the reinforcements which an increase in the number of concerned anglers would bring.

The Anglers Co-operative Association will continue to struggle against polluters with its resources strained to the limit. To those engaged in the effort it really does appear that pollution is angling's forgotten war.

ACA,
Midland Bank Chambers,
Westgate,
Grantham,
Lincs

Platform Piece – T. D. Thompson
The Salmon and Trout Association

The British have always had an ability to spot a dark cloud behind every silver lining. Despite this reputation for pessimism let us pause to consider that in these small and crowded islands, we have managed to achieve something rather wonderful – and rather rare. Nowhere else in the world is there such a variety of good game fishing made easily available to so many people.

Although some may seek to dispute it, it is nevertheless a fact that we really have got something of great value. The clouds are there too however, because it is taking every bit of effort we can muster to keep what we have.

No matter which branch of the sport is considered, there is always a threat somewhere in the background. Think for a moment about the essential elements of fishing. Three things are needed before the fly can be cast with some hope of success. First, the need for water; enough water of sufficiently high quality for fish to live in. Other people want water too. Everyone needs water just to sustain life. Still more water is needed to support a reasonable quality of life, to supply the industries on which jobs depend and to grow the food we eat. Our rivers are the main source of water and each year more and more is taken out of them. In some parts of the country the process of water abstraction has gone so far that rivers which were once prime game fisheries can no longer support sufficient fish to be of interest to the angler.

Secondly, the need for fish. As the number of anglers steadily grows so does the demand for fish. Wild stocks have to be supplemented by fish from farms and the growth of these farms in itself can pose problems. They have been known to pollute the rivers they are situated on. They can also become infected with diseases that are not fully understood. Unless the controls placed upon these farms are intelligently and carefully thought out, the supply of fish needed could diminish with the result that all would lose.

There is still an enviable supply of wild fish, in particular the good runs of salmon and sea-trout into our rivers – or at least into our estuaries. However, anglers are not the only people who want them. One of the major problems of fisheries administration today is that of ensuring that available supplies of fish can be eqitably allocated to give fair shares to all the legitimate claimants and still ensure that the stock will be maintained or, better still, increased.

Thirdly, it is preferred to conduct our sport in peace and quiet, as Izaak Walton long ago urged. Even on the excellent stillwaters which are helping to solve the basic problem of water supply, there are those who quite rightly want to use them for other purposes. The yachtsmen, the water-skiiers, the sail-boarders, the canoeists; all of whom have claims and rights that must be accommodated.

Also, there are those who would deny our right to fish for pleasure at all, and who use violence to prevent us from doing so. These people must be resisted with vigour within the law they themselves defy.

In short there is an ever-growing need for conservation. With an increasing number of bodies representing the many interests involved it all would seem very remote from the rod and line. Because conservation has gone on in the past there is still quality game fishing today. It must go on in the future, fighting old menaces and indentifying new ones, if the sport and the people who enjoy it are to keep what they now have.

The Salmon & Trout Association exists to protect these basic and essential elements of the sport of game fishing. It is the only national body devoted full-time to this purpose and is recognised by Government as such.

The Association is represented on all Fisheries Advisory Committees throughout England and Wales. It has voluntary officers looking after local game-fishing interests in fifty-eight branches throughout the United Kingdom. Above all, it has a powerful lobby comprised of members of both Houses of Parliament and both sides of those Houses. They can and do represent our interests at the very seat of Government.

If game fishing is to survive in the face of all those who want our water, our fish and our right to fish, its devotees cannot take these things for granted. If you are not already a member please turn to our advertisement and give us your support. Not only will you be helping us to protect your sport but there are direct benefits of membership also to enhance your personal enjoyment of all that fly-fishing entails.

THE FIELD
bedside book

This charming and delightful book – a rich miscellany from the pages of *The Field*, Britain's foremost country-interest magazine – portrays a countryman's year with all its varied interests and pursuits. It covers serious subjects, seriously, but there are also the grave, the festive and the humorous... From looking after a newt to organizing the village fete; from mastering the complexities of fly-fishing to the art of budding roses.

Beautifully illustrated, *The Field Bedside Book* will give great pleasure not only to those who live in villages up and down the country, but also to city-dwellers who long for a breath of fresh country air.

£3.95

ROBSON BOOKS
BOLSOVER HOUSE
5—6 CLIPSTONE STREET LONDON W1P 7EB

 ENGLAND
AN INTRODUCTION

England is a comparatively small and over-populated country. Within it, however, there is a tremendous variety in terrain from high wind-swept and hostile uplands (the Pennines and the lake District), wild moorlands (Dartmoor, Exmoor, the Peak District, and the Yorkshire Moors), to gentle rolling hills, and fat fertile plains, with every possible configuration in between. This panorama affords the fly-fisher a very wide choice indeed of water and sport.

Whilst salmon and sea trout runs in England are nothing like as prolific as those carried by the great rivers north of the Border, given sufficient water reasonable influxes can still be expected. Migratory fish are catered for particularly in the West Country, South Coast, Durham, Northumbrian, Lancashire, and Cumbrian rivers. The problems of overfishing at sea and in the estuaries, and organized poaching are in part being counter-balanced by the extensive stocking of salmon fry in the upper reaches of established or suitable rivers, and the cleaning up of rivers (e.g. the Tyne and the Tees) which were until recently so totally polluted in their lower reaches as to be impassable to salmon and sea trout; indeed before too long the taking of salmon from the Thames may be more than a novelty.

The South of England, of course, features legendary chalk "streams" such as the Test, Avon and Itchen. The fishing on these Wiltshire and Hampshire rivers is largely but by no means exclusively preserved; they offer superb sport with the dry fly for trout that are able to feast and grow very large in the marginally alkaline water. The latter condition does not encourage spawning, and this necessitates considerable stocking, which has been a feature on these waters for may decades, to meet their ever-growing popularity. Long gone are the days when Victorian gentlemen only bothered to fish the Test during the Mayfly season!

The rugged trout rivers of the North of England such as those of the Yorkshire Dales are not as bountiful as their gentler southern cousins, but they provide challenging upstream wet or swift water dry fly fishing for vigorous wild fish. It is perhaps a sign of the times that many Yorkshire rivers have been the subject of an extensive release programme of brown trout fry in 1984, causing more than the occasional set of raised eyebrows in certain localities!

The above-mentioned rivers, together with a few stillwaters (with the noted exception of the Lake District, England is largely bereft of natural stillwaters) comprise the main **traditional** game fishing waters. A long tradition of good and often excellent angling-orientated hotels and inns serve these areas. However, extensive though this traditional and largely wild (in terms of fish) fly fishing is, it could never have absorbed without dire consequences the proliferation of interest in this section of angling that has developed in the last quarter of a century or so.

Fortunately, this period has also seen a tremendous increase in the use of established and new reservoirs throughout England for game fishing. Some of these reservoirs, for instance many of those in Devon and Cornwall, are run very much as "natural" fisheries, with the only stocking being that of surplus fry; for this approach to work, the reservoir must have adequate feeder streams that are suitable for spawning. However, the majority of today's game fishing reservoirs are operated on a "put and take" basis, a system that first evolved in the Midlands some 100 years ago. Fish are basically stocked to meet demand, or in other words to match the catch rate; the required density (and also weight) of fish per acre can thus be maintained.

Parallel to this development in reservoirs, there has been a great growth in the use of small stillwaters, which are either exploited or excavated specifically as game fisheries. Often they take the form of ex gravel-pits, or lakes fashioned into natural river valleys. Frequently these fisheries are run in conjunction with a fish-farm enterprise, with the latter supplying the catering trade's demand for trout, as well as the fishery's stocking requirements. Ironically, with supplies of trout for the table having reached almost glut proportions, the fishery, which was usually conceived as a sideline within the enterprise, has often become the mainstay of the business. Fish on these smaller specialised waters have quite simply become a direct commercial crop; the charges at several of these waters are in part at least related to the weight of fish taken.

This new generation of English stillwaters, from the massive reservoirs such as Grafham or Rutland down to the very intimate fisheries of just two acres or so, have a great deal in common, which sets them apart from natural upland lakes. These waters are generally low-lying with fertile beds and a profusion of plant life – the perfect environment for very extensive small animal and insect life. In these conditions the fish have rich and almost unlimited food sources, producing spectacular growth rates amongst brown and in particular rainbow trout, which are slightly more suited to these English fisheries, with their comparative lack of oxygen and warmer water. Rainbows only occasionally spawn naturally in this country, and this lack of diversion in turn assists the growth rate of this very adaptable species.

Both rainbow and brown trout thrive in today's reservoirs and fisheries, even in the midst of conurbations; indeed, there is very good fishing to be had within London itself. The end result of all this is that the angler now has a wealth of quality fly-fishing available almost throughout the land, with fish plentiful around the two pound mark and considerable numbers very much heavier (even into the high teens) indeed. Some of the large lures, which are used particularly to attract very large trout, may appear as heresy to the purist fly-fisher; this is simply a personal matter of preference for the individual. Despite very occasional misgivings, one must conclude that England's modern stillwaters constitute a vast and beneficial angling resource, where the partially controlled environment can ensure that supply meets demand.

Fish breeders are constantly evolving new quick-growing strains, and consequently fish over ten pounds are no longer such a rarity. Some interesting hybrids are also being produced including the "Triploid"; this is a sterile Hen rainbow, which will appeal to the increasing number of fisheries who are extending their seasons, with some even staying open all year round. A further development which is still in its infant stage is that of put and take salmon stillwater fisheries, whereby Scottish farm-bred salmon are imported, released and then sought with sinking lines and large lures.

A game fish that has been the subject of a great change of attitude in the last few years is the grayling. This attractive fish used to be widely and actively discouraged from so many rivers, as it competed for the same food as the trout.

Today, however, the grayling is generally accorded considerable respect as a sporting quarry in its own right, and one that allows a major extension to the fly-fishing season on many of England's rivers.

Wherever the angler pursues his sport in England, it is essential that he is in possession of the relevant water authority rod licence. The latter is necessary in addition to any fishing permit that is required for a particular water. "Free" fishing is available on certain waters (for instance in the Lake District) but often it is still obligatory to obtain a (free) permit; if in doubt, make local enquiries.

Given that the country does not divide up easily into especially meaningful regions, and that Water Authority areas are often confusing, the English section is split into traditional counties, as are featured on most modern atlases and maps. Where rivers cross county lines, they are featured in the county in which they are most prevalent. This catalogue of English waters is not intended to be utterly exhaustive, but rather a fair and detailed cross-section of the great wealth of fly-fishing available.

The Barrows Fishery

Barrow Gurney, Avon.
Tel: Chew Magna (027589) 2339.

Controlled by the Bristol Waterworks
Company.

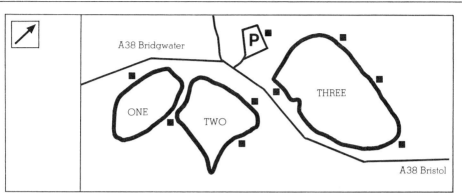

Three man-made concrete reservoirs known as The Barrows No 1 (26 acres), No 2 (39 acres), and No 3 (60 acres) situated off the A38 about five miles south of Bristol. The reservoirs are known among local anglers as the Barrow Tanks Aquatic life includes sedges, midge, snails and shrimps.

Facilities:	Several shelters, with toilets, provided around the reservoirs. A self-service permit kiosk in the park.
Season:	April 5th to October 15th. Hours: from one hour before sunrise to one hour after sunset.
Charges:	Full season £105, OAPs and disabled (Monday to Friday inclusive) £55, juniors (under 17 years) and full-time students £45. A special 'C' season permit costing £230 also includes fishing at Chew Valley Lake. Day ticket £4, OAPs and disabled £2.50, and juniors £2. A Wessex Water Authority rod licence is required, and issued on site.
Day catch limit:	8 fish, evening 4 fish (over 12 inches).
Boats:	Yes.
Restrictions:	Fly fishing only. No spinning. No trolling. Because of the steep banks wading or standing in the water is prohibited. No dogs or portable radios allowed.
Stocking policy:	Large pre-season stocking with yearling fish, then at regular intervals.
Annual catch rate:	(1983) 4,343 fish, at an average weight of 1 lb 5 oz. Catches include 12 fish over 4 lb, with the largest a 5 lb 14 oz rainbow.
Recommeded flies:	Early season—Amber Nymph, Greenwell's Glory, Invicta, Dunkeld, March Brown, Teal & Green, Wickhams Fancy. Mid to late season—Peter Ross, Zulu, Viva, Watson's Fancy, Teal & Black, Mallard & Claret, Dunkeld, Black Pennell, Butcher, White Chenille, Baby Doll, Marabou.
Local knowledge:	There is no wading, so to achieve distance a shooting line is often used, and a lightly weighted nymph makes a popular combination. But generally almost any pattern of fly, lure or nymph is worth trying.

Blagdon Lake

Blagdon, Avon.
Tel: Blagdon (0761) 62527.   Owner: Bristol Waterways.

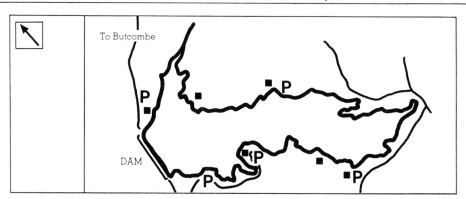

This flooded valley reservoir extends to 440 acres, and is situated in picturesque surroundings about 12 miles from Bristol. It was formed by damming the River Yeo and opened for fishing in 1901. The lake is rich in aquatic life, corixa, damselfly, sedges, midge, olives and shrimp.

Facilities:	Comfortable lodge adjacent to car park. Permit issuing kiosk. There is a small tackle shop, and Wessex WA rod licences are available from the office.
Season:	March 31st to October 15th. Hours: 7 a.m. to 1 hour after sunset until April 5. Then the starting time changes to 1 hour before sunrise.
Charges:	Season: Bank—£300 also includes Chew Valley and Barrows. Day: £5.50, evening (after 3 p.m.) £3 May onwards. Concessions: OAPs, disabled, juniors, full-time students.
Day limit:	8 fish, evenings 4 fish.
Boats:	Rowing – day £11.50, evening (after 3 p.m.) £7.50. Advance booking advisable.
Restrictions:	Fly fishing only. Trolling, trailing and spinning pro-hibited.
Annual catch rate:	(1983) 17,366 fish. This included 97 over 4 lb, with 13 of these over 6 lb. Largest fish a rainbow of 9 lb 14 oz.
Recommended flies:	
Early season:	Amber Nymph, Green Nymph, Buzzer Nymph, Invicta, Mayfly Nymph, Pheasant Tail Nymph, Baby Doll, Sedge Pupa, Viva.
Mid-to-late season:	Black Lure, Dunkeld, Mayfly Nymph, Midge Pupa, Orange Sedge Pupa, Muddler Minnow, Persuader, Peter Ross, Black/White Chenille, Zulu, Viva.
Local knowledge:	Boat fishing is very popular, and any of the traditional patterns can be effective. Most successful throughout the season is floating line, long leader and a pattern like Dunkeld on the point, with one small wet fly on a single dropper.

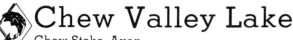

Chew Valley Lake

Chew Stoke, Avon.
Tel: Chew Magna (027589) 2339. Owner: Bristol Waterworks Company.

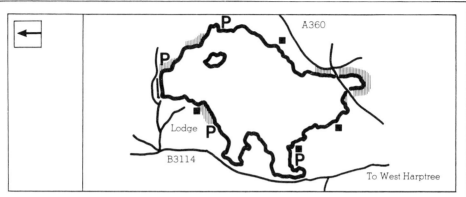

A vast flooded valley reservoir of some 1,200 acres. It is attractively situated to the south of Bristol, in the Mendip Hills. It is a well established reservoir fishery. Rich in aquatic life, with sticklebacks, shoals of coarse fish fry, corixa, tadpoles, snails, shrimps, sedges, gnats, midges, Pond Olives and Alder Fly.

Facilities: There is a permit issuing machine on site, and Wessex Water Authority rod licences also issued. Also available are car parks at various points around the reservoir area.

Season: April 5th to October 15th. Hours: from one hour before sunrise to one hour after sunset.

Rods per day: No limit to bank fishing.

Charges: A full season permit for bank costs £300 and includes Blagdon Reservoir and The Barrows. Day permit £5.50, evening (after 3 p.m. from May 1) £3. Concessionary permits available for OAPs, disabled, juniors and full-time students.

Day catch limit: 8 fish, evening 4 fish.

Boats: Hire charge – day £14, evening £9.50 per rod. Concessionary charges also available to season permit-holders.

Restrictions: Fly fishing only. Bait, trolling, trailing, spinning, trouser waders, chest waders, and dogs prohibited.

Stocking policy: Early pre-season stock, then at regular intervals throughout the season. Trout stocked are from the Bristol Waterworks own hatchery.

Annual catch rate: (1983) 19,475 fish, including 133 fish over 4 lb, with 21 of these over 6 lb. Largest fish: rainbow 9 lb 6 oz, brown 6 lb 3 oz.

Recommended flies:

Early season: Black Lure, Viva, Dunkeld, Grenadier, Mallard & Claret, Silver Invicta, March Brown

Mid to late season: Mayfly Nymph, Damselfly Nymph, Pheasant Tail Nymph, Black & Peacock Spider, Dunkeld

Local knowledge: In early season the shelving bank areas fish well. Suggest floating or sink-tip lines with long leaders to fish nymphs.

Horton Fishery

Horton, Berkshire.   Proprietor: Kingsmead
Tel: Colnbrook (02812) 4858.   Fish Farms Ltd.

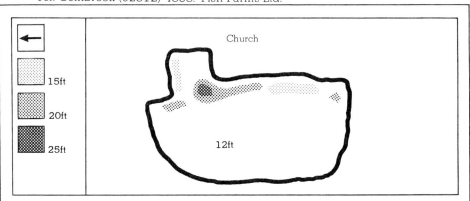

This landscaped ex-gravel pit lake of 14 acres, is one of a group of lakes in the area. It is rich in aquatic life with Pond Olives, Damselfly, Dragonfly, Mayfly, Sedge, Caenis, Snails, Shrimp, perch and roach fry.

Facilities: Fishing lodge (coffee etc), toilet, car parking. Permits issued on site.

Season: Open all year round. Hours: 8.30 a.m. to dusk.

Rods per day: 45 maximum.

Charges: Day £6 weekdays, £5.50 weekends, evening £3.50 (after 4 p.m.), evening weekends £4. Winter part-day from 1.30 p.m.

Day limit: No catch limit. All trout caught to be paid for at approximately £1 per 1 lb.

Boats: 3 (fly only) £3.50 for 1 or 2 anglers. £2.50 part-day.

Restrictions: Fly fishing (limited worm and spinning). No wading. No loose feeding. No keepnets.

Stocking policy: Regularly to maintain catch rate. Mostly with rainbows.

Annual catch rate: 2.5 per rod average.

Recommended flies:

Black Chenille, Baby Doll, Viva, Zulu and Blue Zulu, Muddlers and Dog Nobblers. Pheasant Tail Nymph, Olive Nymph, Green Nymph, Mayfly Nymph.

Local knowledge: Kevin Gardener: Nymphs are most effective all year round. Use a sink-tip or floating line to fish an Olive nymph or Pheasant Tail nymph just below the surface. Suggest a greased leader of at least 9 feet in length.

River Kennet
Wiltshire and Berkshire

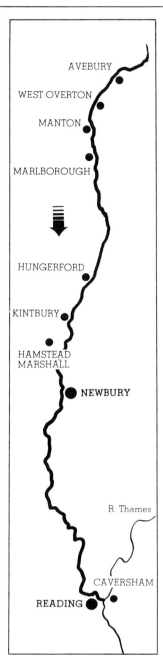

AVEBURY

WEST OVERTON

MANTON

MARLBOROUGH

HUNGERFORD

KINTBURY

HAMSTEAD
MARSHALL

NEWBURY

R. Thames

CAVERSHAM

READING

The Kennet rises near Marlborough Downs, and takes an easterly course for 44 miles to join the Thames at Caversham. The lower reaches are a combination of river and canal, and as such are of little interest to the fly-fisherman. The upper reaches, however, from above Marlborough to the Hungerford area, have a very fine reputation for excellent trout and grayling.
Rod licence: Thames Water Authority, Nugent House, Vastern Road, Reading, Berks. RG1 8DB. Tel: (0734) 593538.

Seasons: Trout – April 1st to September 30th; Grayling – June 16th to March 14th.

Marlborough. Manton Weir Fishery. Mainly Brown Trout, which are stocked throughout the season according to catch rate. Season opens on April 15th. Booking enquiries to Malcolm Hassam – Tel: Marlborough (0762) 54219.

Hungerford. The Denford Fisheries comprises two miles of main river and carriers. The fishing is dry fly and nymph with a limit of six rods per day. Stocked with Rainbows on a regular basis; there are also quality Wild Browns and Grayling. Catch limit is four trout per day, with no limit on grayling. Fishing is by season permit on a nominated day basis. Full rod £200, half rod £115, with day tickets for members' guests. Enquiries to Hungerford (0488) 84179.

Kintbury. Barton Court Fishery has 3½ miles of first-class trout fishing. 9 a.m. till dusk, with day limit of six fish. A full weekday season permit costs £300, half rod £150, and day tickets £15. Bookings and further details from Edward Hill – Tel: (0488) 58226.

Hamstead-Marshall. The Craven Estate has 3½ miles of river and canal. Trout, Grayling and coarse fish. The river section includes two weir pools, where there is always the chance of a very large trout. Day ticket enquiries to Head Bailiff, Craven Estate, Hamstead-Marshall, Kintbury, Berks.
This area also has the Wilderness Fishery, run as a private trout syndicate, with extensive rights on the main river, several carriers and feeder streams. Enquiries to local tackle shops.

Recommended flies: Dry – Olive Quill, Claret Dun.

Local knowledge: Dry fly is the usual method on most of the trout fisheries. However, upstream nymphing may also be very effective after early July.

Church Hill Farm

MURSLEY, BUCKS.
Tel: Mursley (029672) 524. Proprietor: Tim Daniels.

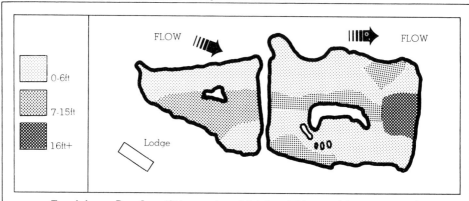

Two lakes – Dog Leg (2½ acres) and Jubilee (7½ acres) in open country near Bletchley. Specifically built as fishery in 1976. Clay soil. Rich aquatic life including minnow, tadpoles, sticklebacks, shrimp, mayfly, sedge. Weed is not a problem.

Facilities:	Comfortable lodge with tackle shop. Cooked or ploughman's lunches available daily ex Sunday.
Season:	April 1st to October 31st. Hours: 9.00 a.m. – 9.00 p.m. or dusk (whichever earlier).
Rods per day:	25—weekdays. 30—weekends. Reservations recommended.
Charges:	Season—£285. Day—£12. Evening—£6.50. Permits and Anglian Water Authority Licences available from Lodge.
Day limit:	4—(excluding fish under 1 lb).
Stocking policy:	Daily to match catches. 20% Brown and 80% Rainbow and Gold (rainbow strain).
Annual Catch rate:	2.2 (average size 2.2 lb). 67 fish over 5 lb. Largest rainbow 9 lb 11 oz. Largest brown, 6 lb 2 oz (1983).

Recommended flies:

April	Dog Nobbler, Viva, Jack Frost, Black Lure, White Lure
May	Dog Nobbler, Zulu, Green Nymph, Black Buzzer
June	Invicta, Pheasant-Tail Nymph, Shrimp
July	Sedge, Invicta, Black Nymph, Damselfly Nymph
August	Viva, Black Chenille, Daddy Longlegs, Muddler
September	Muddlers, Black & Peacock Spider, Green Nymph, Sedge, Viva, Shrimp, Black Gnat.
October	Muddlers, Black Lure, Pheasant-Tail Nymph, Baby Doll.
Local knowledge:	Arthur Cove – Of all the fisheries I go to, Church Hill Farm gives me the most pleasure to fish, not only for the high average size of fish there to be caught, but also the variety of ways in which they can be tempted to take both lures and nymphs. In all a very civilized place to fish with a minimum of rules.

Latimer Park Lakes

Latimer,
Chesham, Bucks.

Tel: (02404) 2396.
Manager: C. W. Cansdale.

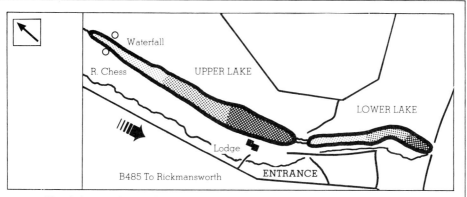

The fishery is located on a private estate in Buckinghamshire, and it consists of Upper Lake (8 acres) and Lower Lake (4 acres) fed by the River Chess. Aquatic life is prolific, with shrimp, Corixa, snails, midge, Damselflies, Olives and a small Mayfly hatch. There is also ½ mile of river and sidestream for members only.

Facilities:	A comfortable fishing lodge with free tea and coffee making facilities. Light refreshments, flies and Thames Water Authority rod licence available. Washroom and toilets. Car park.
Season:	April 2nd to September 30th inclusive. Hours: 9 a.m. to dark. Members from 6 a.m. Closed on Sundays.
Rods per day:	Strictly limited, so prior booking essential.
Charges:	Season membership permits cost £280 for one day per week. £150 for one day per two weeks. Day ticket £12 (bookable max 1 week in advance), evening (4 p.m. onwards) £6 (bookable max 1 month in advance).
Day catch limit:	4 fish, evening 2 fish (excluding fish under 1 lb).
Boats:	Four on Upper Lake. Hire charge: £2.50, or £1 for a four hour period.
Restrictions:	Traditional fly fishing only. No wading. No shooting head lines. Maximum hook size 8. Maximum hook length 1 in. Maximum dressing overall 1¼ in.
Stocking policy:	Daily with rainbows and brown trout reared on site.
Annual catch rate:	Average weight of fish caught 2 lb 2 oz. With a 2.6 fish per rod average.
Recommended flies:	Nymphs: Pheasant Tail, Mayfly, Damselfly, Green and Black Nymphs, Amber and Caenis Nymph. Lures, small: Viva, Zulu, Missionary, Appetiser, Mini-dog Nobblers, Baby Doll, Muddlers (various colours). Wet flies: Bloody Butcher, Coachman, Dunkeld, Gold Ribbed Hare's Ear, Greenwell's Glory, Invicta
Local knowledge:	The fishery has produced some large fish, with a rainbow of 10 lb 13 oz, and in 1983 a superb brown of 8 lb 2 oz. Floating lines are generally best, but when fish are close to the bottom a sink-tip line and weighted nymph is often successful.

Queen Mother Reservoir

DATCHET, BUCKS.
Tel: Colnbrook (02812) 3605.   Fishery owner: Roger Haynes.

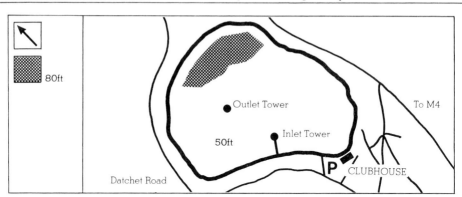

This popular reservoir of 475 acres, adjacent to Heathrow Airport, has built up a big-fish reputation by producing some very large rainbow and brown trout. Aquatic life includes Midge, Daphnia, Shrimp, roach and perch fry, and a small mayfly hatch.

Facilities: A large clubhouse with toilets, changing room. It also has a bar for snacks and refreshments daily in summer. It is only open at weekends from October. Fishery office issues permits and Thames Water rod licences, and has a variety of tackle for sale. Tackle may also be hired, and lessons are available.

Season: Summer, March 1st to November 1st.
Winter, November 1st to end of January.

Charges: Season permit, details available on request. Bank – day £8.50, part-day £6.25, evening (from 5 p.m.), £4.25. Boat (single) – day £11.50, part-day £8.50, evening £5.50. Boat (double) – day £18, part-day £13, evening £8.50.

Catch limit: 8 fish, part-day 5, evening 3.

Boats: 30.

Restrictions: No wading, no persons under 8 years allowed on reservoir.

Stocking policy: 10,000 pre-season, then about 1,000 per week during March and April, dropping in numbers in October.

Recommended flies: Jack Frost, Invicta, Appetizer, White Ghost, Zulu, Black Chenille, Viva, Damsel nymph, Green nymph.

Local knowledge: Roger Haynes: I now have 53 casting platforms constructed around the concrete banking of the reservoir. In January 1983 one of my guests fishing from the bank caught seven rainbows totalling 40 lb 6 oz, including 9 lb 2 oz, 7 lb 3 oz, 7 lb 1 oz and 6 lb.

There have been four rainbows over 10 lb, and a record brown of 9 lb 2 oz. Many of the big fish are taken from a boat, on the drift, and by using lead core lines to fish a lure deep. Often during evenings fish come in close on the sloping bank, when various nymphs can be very effective.

Vicarage Spinney Fishery

Little Linford, Bucks.
Tel: (0908) 616534.   Proprietors: M. D. & S. A. Sando.

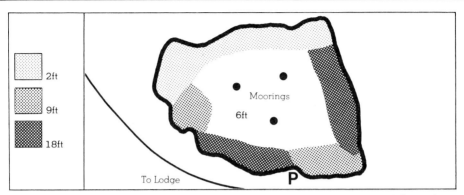

This consists of a six acre ex-gravel pit lake near Newport Pagnell. It was first opened for trout fishing in 1982. Aquatic life includes Sedges, Damselfly, Dragonfly and Midge. Also present are caddis larvae, shrimp and plentiful bleak and roach fry.

Facilities: Fishing lodge, with facility for making tea and coffee. Permits issued on site. Car park, toilets.

Season: April 1st to October 29th inclusive. Hours: 9 a.m. to one hour after sunset.

Rods per day: 20 maximum.

Charges: Full season permit £280, half-season £140. Day ticket £10, half-day £5. There are concessionary permits for juniors, OAPs and disabled. Advance bookings by post to 6 Kipling Drive, Newport Pagnell.

Day catch limit: 4 fish, half-day 2 fish.

Boats: 3. Two-man boats cost £6, half-day £3.

Restrictions: Fly fishing only. No wading.

Stocking policy: At weekly intervals with rainbows and browns.

Annual catch rate: (1983) 3.5 fish per rod average.

Recommended flies:
Traditional wet flies to include March Brown, Silver March Brown, Cinnamon & Gold, Teal & Green, Orange Sedge, Peter Ross, Greenwell's Glory, Invicta, Black & Peacock Spider, Grenadier.
Nymphs: Hatching Nymph, Green Pupa, Amber Nymph, Damsel Nymph, Chomper, Buzzer Nymph, Corixa, Pheasant Tail Nymph.
Lures: Sweeney Todd, Muddler Minnow, Appetizer, Perch Fry, Church Fry, Matuka, White Baby Doll, Chinelle (white, black), Marabou (white, black), Viva.

Local knowledge: During the early part of the season almost anything will take fish. Preference is for floating and sink-tip lines. Early in the season the trout show a preference for white coloured patterns. A weighted nymph is effective at finding deep swimming fish at most times.

PIG OVERBOARD!

...and other strange but true letters to THE FIELD

Compiled and illustrated by
MERRILY HARPUR

Cartoonist Merrily Harpur has delved among the archives of *The Field*, Britain's foremost country magazine, and selected unusual letters from the gimlet-eyed observers of such curiosities. To many she has added her own highly individual cartoons and the result – *Pig Overboard!* – is an entertaining view of the natural world which proves that, if you look *closely enough*, all is never quite as it seems.

£6.95

ROBSON BOOKS
BOLSOVER HOUSE
5—6 CLIPSTONE STREET LONDON W1P 7EB

Grafham Water

NEAR HUNTINGDON, CAMBS.

Tel: Huntingdon (0480) 810531.
Controlled by Anglian Water Authority.

↑

35-50ft

51-60ft

Tower

Reserve

P

P

DAM

Tower

Lagoon

P

A vast landscaped reservoir of 1,500 acres, formed by flooding a valley. It was opened in 1966. The dam end is the deepest, dropping to about 70 feet. A rich water life, including coarse fish and their fry (roach, perch). There are also snails, shrimps, sedges, daphnia, chironomids etc.

Facilities:	Several car parks and toilets. Day ticket vending machine on site. Fishing lodge where permits, artificial flies and small items of tackle may be purchased
Season:	23/4 to 23/10. Hours: one hour before dawn to one hour after sunset.
Charges:	Full season permit £195, mid-week permit £168. Day ticket £6.50, evening £4, juniors half-price. Seven day holiday permit £31.
Day catch limit:	8 fish, evening three fish.
Boats:	40. Motor boat hire charge day £14.50, evening £9. Pulling boat, day £8, evening £4.50. Drogues supplied, but no anchors.
Restrictions:	Fly only. No wading at the dam. Trolling only allowed with oars, in a restricted area.
Stocking policy:	Rainbow and brown trout of 12 to 13 inches minimum length. Stocking is carried out at regular intervals up to the end of August.
Annual catch rate:	(1983) 3.6 fish per rod average. Total 41,752 fish, including 5,132 browns. Biggest brown 8 lb 6 oz, rainbow 5 lb 8 oz.
Recommended flies:	Wickhams Fancy, Soldier Palmer, Silver Invicta, Butcher, Dunkeld, Greenwells Glory, Mallard & Claret Nymphs: Pheasant Tail, Buzzers, Sedge Pupa, Damselfly Nymph, Brown Nymph. Lures (recommended for the backend of season): Muddlers (various), Appetizer, Missionary
Local knowledge:	Drifting can be very effective, and each boat is equipped with a drogue for controlling this. A sink-tip line is recommended. A full sinking line can be difficult to manage on a fast drift. A floating line and nymph while standing in the bankside shallows is often productive.

Argal and College

NEAR FALMOUTH,   Tel: Penryn (0326) 72544.
CORNWALL.   Controlled by South West Water Authority.

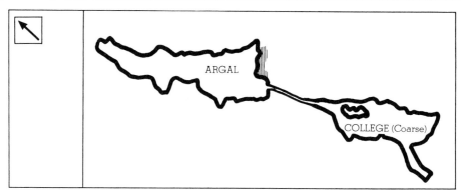

Two adjacent reservoirs, Argal 65 acres and College 38 acres amidst delightful countryside. Argal reservoir offers traditional fly fishing for trout, with good access to banks. College is reserved for coarse fishing.

Facilities: Car park, with adjoining picnic area. Toilets, with facilities for the disabled. Self service kiosk for permits.

Season: 1/4 (or Good Friday, whichever is earlier) to 12/10. Hours: 1 hour before sunrise to 1 hour after sunset.

Rods: No set limit.

Charges: Day £5, evening £3 (after 3 pm).
O.A.P.'s, disabled, and full time students under 18 £4. Juniors under 16 - £1. The Authority issues books of 20 pre-paid permits at 15 per cent discount–for instance, full day price £100, discount price £85. Concessions also for boat bookings. Pre-paid permits may be used at any of the Authority's 'stocked' trout fisheries.

Day catch limit: 5 fish, evening 3 fish, over 10 inches.

Boats: Day £5, half-day £3.50 (from 3 pm). Advance booking advisable.

Restrictions: Fly only. No trolling. No boats on Thursdays and Fridays. No dogs.

Stocking policy: With rainbows.

Annual catch rate: (1982) 3,983 fish.
(1983) 1.7 fish per rod average. 3,929 fish.

Recommended flies:
Sweeney Todd, Black & Peacock Spider, Dunkeld, Invicta, Amber Nymph, Olive Nymph, Black gnat, Viva, Appetizer, and various small lures.

Local knowledge: Although described as a traditional fly fishing reservoir, Argal has yielded rainbows up to 11 lb 8 oz–so various lures and large fish tactics are worthwhile.
Fish caught between 7 and 10 inches may be retained.

Crowley Reservoir

Near Camelford, Cornwall. Controlled by South West Water Authority.
Tel: Camelford (0840) 213396. Warden: Francis Bartlett.

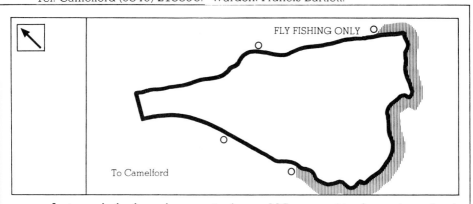

An irregularly shaped reservoir of some 115 acres set in pleasant moorland countryside. Aquatic life includes hatches of sedge, gnats, midege, damselfly, dragonfly, water beetles, snails etc.

Facilities:	Ample car parking. A self-service kiosk for day permits.
Season:	March 15th to October 12th inclusive. Hours: one hour before sunrise to one hour after sunset.
Rods:	No limit.
Charges:	Season permits £21. OAPs, disabled, full-time students (under 18 years) £10.50, and juniors (under 16 years) £5.25. Season permits are available from Information Office, SWWA, 3-5 Barnfield Road, Exeter. Day permits £1.60, concessionary day permit 80p.
Day limit:	4 fish.
Boats:	None available.
Restrictions:	Special zoned areas for fly fishing, spinning and bait. Size-limit seven inches. No fishing in the nature reserve area.
Stocking policy:	With rainbow trout fry.
Annual catch rate:	Catches are not recorded.
Recommended flies:	Teal Blue & Silver, March Brown, Coachman, Peter Ross, Greenwell's Glory, Teal & Green, Wickhams Fancy, Mallard & Claret, Corixa, and various nymphs. Any small lure pattern may be worth trying.
Local knowledge:	Traditional wet fly tactics most effective. Sink-tip and slow sinking lines often successful, but when fish are active at the surface a floating line and greased leader recommended.

Porth Reservoir

NEAR NEWQUAY, CORNWALL. Controlled by South West Water Authority.
Tel: Newquay (06373) 2701.   Warden: Dennis Parkyn.

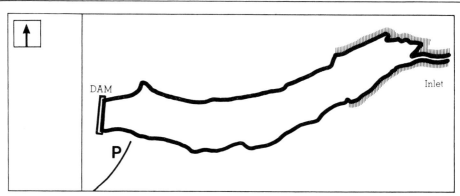

A 40 acre reservoir set in attractive country, offering some interesting and challenging fishing. Aquatic life includes: sedges, dragonflies, midges, snails and tadpoles.

Facilities:	Self service kiosk for permits. Car park.
Season:	1/4 (or Good Friday, whichever is earlier) to 12/10 inclusive. Hours: From one hour before sunrise to one hour after sunset. Boat anglers from 9 am.
Rods:	No set limit.
Charges:	Day permit £5, evening £3 (after 3 pm). O.A.P.'s, disabled, and full-time students under 18 years, £4. Juniors under 16 years £1. The Authority issues books of 20 pre-paid permits at 15 per cent discount–for instance, full day price £100, discount price £85. Concessions also for boat bookings. Pre-paid permits may be used at any of the Authority's 'stocked' trout fisheries.
Day catch limit:	5 fish, evening three fish over 10 inches. Fish between seven inches and 10 inches taken while achieving a limit may be kept.
Boats:	Day charge £5, half-day £3.50 (after 3 pm). Advance booking advisable. Boats must keep well clear of bank anglers.
Restrictions:	Fly fishing only. No spinning. No trolling. No dogs allowed. No boats on Tuesdays or Wednesdays. No trouser waders. All fish under seven inches to be returned.
Stocking policy:	With rainbows, occasionally.
Annual catch rate:	1983–3,112 fish. 2.0 fish per rod. 1982–3,411 fish. 2.1 fish per rod.
Recommended flies:	Peter Ross, Mallard & Claret, Wickhams Fancy, Black & Peacock Spider, Butcher, Greenwells Glory, Butcher, Black Gnat, various small lures.
Local knowledge:	Fish up to 4 lb 8 oz taken. Floating and sink-tip lines most effective when bank fishing.

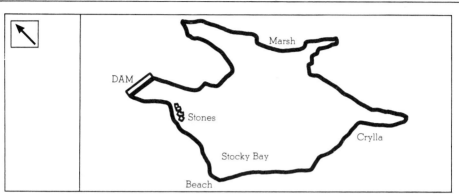Siblyback Reservoir

Near Liskeard, Cornwall. Controlled by South West Water Authority.
Tel: Liskeard (0579)42366. Warden: Reg England.

This very attractive reservoir of 140 acres offers fly fishing for rainbow trout up to 8 lb 9 oz, and brown trout to 7 lb. Rich in aquatic life. This is one of the Authority's 'stocked' reservoir fisheries.

Facilities:	Car park, refreshment kiosk, self service permit kiosk.
Season:	April 1st to October 31st inclusive. Hours: 1 hour before sunrise to 1 hour after sunset.
Charges:	Day £5, evening £3 (after 3 pm). OAP's disabled and full time students under 18 £4. Juniors under 16 – £1. The Authority issues books of 20 prepaid permits at 15 per cent discount – for instance, full day price £100, discount price £85. Concessions also for boat bookings. Pre-paid permits may be used at any of the Authority's 'stocked' trout fisheries.
Day limit:	5 fish, evening 3 fish, over 10 inches.
Boats:	Day £5, half-day £3.50 (after 3 pm). Advance booking advisable.
Restrictions:	Fly fishing only. No dogs allowed. No boats Thursdays or Fridays.
Stocking policy:	At intervals with rainbow trout. Some brook and brown trout.
Annual catch rate:	(1982) 6,646 fish. 1.8 fish per rod average. (1983) 6,876 fish. 2.1 fish per rod average.
Recommended flies:	Black Gnat, Damselfly nymph, Green nymph, Black & Peacock Spider, Alexandra, Wickhams Fancy, various small lures.
Local knowledge:	Most patterns of the popular lures, in the smaller sizes, are successful fished on sink-tip or sinking line. In the late evening period, during summer months, a dry fly can be most effective.

Stithians Reservoir

NEAR REDRUTH, CORNWALL. Controlled by South West Water
Tel: Truro (0872) 3541.   Authority.

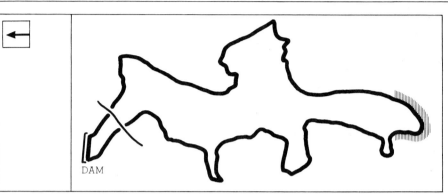

DAM

An irregularly shaped moorland reservoir of 274 acres, which offers interesting fishing for wild brown trout. Water life includes fair hatches of sedge, midge, dragonfly, snails, and water beetles.

Facilities: A self-service kiosk situated by the dam for day permits. Car parking areas.

Season: 15/3 to 12/10 inclusive. Hours: one hour before sunrise to one hour after sunset.

Rods: No limit.

Charges: Season permit £21, O.A.P.'s, disabled, and full-time students (under 18 years) £10.50. Juniors (under 16 years) £5.25.
Day permit £1.60, concessionary day permits 80p.

Day catch limit: All fish of seven inches or more may be taken.

Boats: One boat operated by the Stithians Trout Fly Fishing Association.

Restrictions: Fly only. No trolling. No dogs. No trouser waders. Size limit 7 inches. Fishing with more than one rod and line at any one time is prohibited.

Stocking policy: With rainbow trout fry.

Annual catch rate: Catches are not recorded.

Recommended Flies:
Traditional patterns such as Butcher, Alexandra, March Brown, Wickhams Fancy, Peter Ross, Mallard & Claret, Sedge patterns, Black & Peacock Spider, Damselfly Nymph, Green Nymph, Mayfly and other Nymph patterns.

Local knowledge: The irregular shape of the reservoir can aid casting in strong winds. Traditional wet fly methods are effective most of the season. Leaded nymphs fished on floating lines take fish 'on the drop'. Wading can be dangerous. No fishing in the nature reserve area.
The Stithians FFA organises competitions and other events. Details from Mr E. Williams, Middle Boswin, Nine Maidens Road, Porkellis, Helston, Cornwall.

River Tamar
Cornwall and Devon

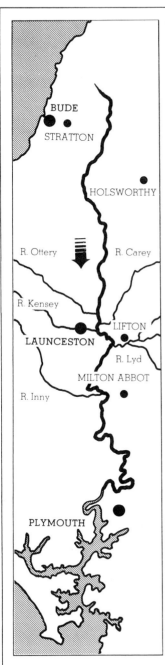

The Tamar rises very near the North Coast, and flows 60 miles south-east to Plymouth Sound. For much of its length it is the boundary between Devon and Cornwall. This renowned game fishing water is gentler in character than most south-western rivers as it traverses rich farmland for most of its course. The Tamar is fed by five main tributaries – the Ottery, Lyd, Kensey, Carey and Inny: all offer productive trout fishing.

Rod licence required: Fisheries and Recreation Office, SWWA, 3-5 Barnfield Road, Exeter EX1 1RE. Tel: (0392) 50861.

Seasons: Salmon – March 1st to October 14th; Sea Trout – March 3rd to September 30th; Brown Trout – March 15 to September 30th.

West Clawton, near Holsworthy. $6\frac{1}{2}$ miles of <u>Brown Trout</u> water. Day £1, week £3 – from Beare Sports, Belle View, Bude or DIY Centre, The Square, Holsworthy.

Lifton. <u>Salmon, Sea Trout, Trout.</u> 20 miles of the Tamar, Lyd, Carey, Wolf and Thrushel are controlled by the Arundell Arms, one of Britain's premier angling hotels. The tributaries are clear water streams, generally shallow with gravelly runs and long pools, and they all join the Tamar about a mile from the hotel. The 1983 season saw a record 627 sea trout (to over 4 lb) taken, mostly from the Lyd. Priority for permits goes to hotel residents, but some day tickets are often available to non-residents. Charges: Salmon and Sea Trout day permits – £5.75 (March, April); £8 (May); £9.50 (June, July, August); £10.50 (September, October 1st to 14th). Sea Trout night only £5. Brown Trout £5.75 and lake trout fishing (on 3 acre Tinhay Lake) £8. There are full-time bailiffs, as well as instructors available for tuition. For full details contact the Proprietor – Mrs. Anne Voss-Bark, The Arundell Arms, Lifton, Devon. Tel: (0566) 84666.

Launceston. <u>Salmon, Sea Trout, Brown Trout.</u> Launceston A.A. controls water on the Tamar and Ottery. Week and day tickets from Kennedy Sports, Church Street, Launceston. Membership details from Hon. Sec., M. Jones, 16 Highfield Park Road, Launceston, Cornwall. Tel: (0566) 2422. The Association also has a limited number of permits available for the Barnham Water.

Lydford. <u>Brown Trout.</u> A short stretch available from March 16th to September 7th. Permits from Forestry Commission, Southern House, Lydford, Nr. Okehampton.

River Tamar
Cornwall and Devon

Milton Abbot. <u>Salmon, Sea Trout, Brown Trout.</u> The Endsleigh F.C. has 5 beats, with a limit of 2 rods per beat. The fishery extends for 9 miles downstream of Greystones Bridge. The annual average salmon catch is nearly 250 fish. Spinning for salmon is allowed until April 30th, thereafter fly only. Endsleigh season – March 1st to October 10th. Day rod fee – £11 March to May; £13 June to August; £15 September and October. Hotel enquiries to the Manager, Endsleigh House, Milton Abbot. Tel: (082287) 248. Fishing enquiries and rod bookings to Dr. W. Medd, Peterswood House, Ruxley, Crescent, Claygate, Esher, Surrey.

Recommended flies: Salmon – Yellow Torrish tube, and standard patterns on single or small double hooks – Blue Charm, Shrimp, Thunder & Lightning, Hairy Mary, Stoat's Tail.
Sea Trout – Peter Ross, Butcher, Coachman, Silver Invicta, Black Pennell, Stoat's Tail.
Trout – Pheasant Tail nymph, Mayfly nymph, Stickfly, Greenwell's Glory, Grey Duster, Black Spider, Peter Ross.

Local knowledge: For salmon on the Tamar and Lyd fly rods of 10 to 14 ft, depending on the river section, are needed. Generally conditions dictate a floating or sink-tip line, with a leader of 12 to 14 lb bs. Yellow and black combinations feature regularly in the most successful patterns. Sea trout are best sought at night with floating line and wet fly. For brown trout use a floating line and size 12, 14 or 16 patterns; upstream dry fly fishing can be very good in this area.

Upper Tamar Lake

NEAR BUDE, CORNWALL.   Controlled by South West Water Authority.
Tel: Kilkhampton (028882) 262.   Resident Warden: Ken Spalding.

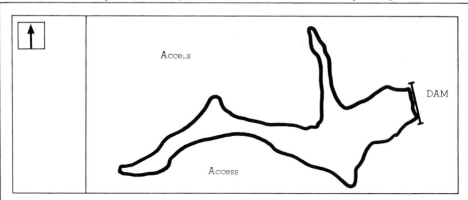

Consists of two lakes, Upper and Lower. Upper is reserved for fly fishing. Recently constructed yet holds rich water life, including sedge, black buzzers, midge, shrimps etc.

This reservoir, one of the Authority's stocked fisheries, has yielded trout to over 12 lb.

Facilities:	Ample car parking. Self service kiosk for day permits. Refreshment kiosk.
Season:	1/4 to 31/10. Hours: 1 hour before sunrise to 1 hour after sunset. Before 9 am anglers should use lower car park.
Charges:	Day £5, evening £3 (after 3 pm). O.A.P.'s, disabled, and full time students under 18, £4. Juniors under 16 – £1. The Authority issues books of 20 pre-paid permits at 15 per cent discount–for instance, full day price £100, discount price £85. Concessions also for boat bookings. Pre-paid permits may be used at any of the Authority's 'stocked' trout fisheries.
Day limit:	5 fish, evening 3 fish, over 10 inches. Anglers achieving a limit may purchase a second permit. Fish caught between 7 inches and 10 inches do not count towards limit, but may be retained.
Boats:	Day £5, half day £3.25 (after 3 pm). Advance booking usually advisable.
Restrictions:	Fly fishing only. No boats on Thursdays or Fridays. No fish under 7 inches to be retained.
Stocking policy:	Mainly rainbows, but some browns and brook trout.
Annual catch rate:	(1982) 7,935 fish. Average catch 1.8 fish per rod. (1983) 1.8 fish per rod average. 7,384 fish.
Recommended flies:	Traditional wet fly patterns always effective. But for the larger fish, generally lying deep, any of the popular lure patterns are recommended.
Local knowledge:	The record for this water is held by a 12 lb 12½ oz rainbow taken in 1982. Previously, in 1977, a rainbow of 12 lb 7 oz was caught.

Blencarn Lake

Blencarn, Penrith,   Tel: Culgaith (076888) 284.
Cumbria.   Proprietor: J. K. Stamper.

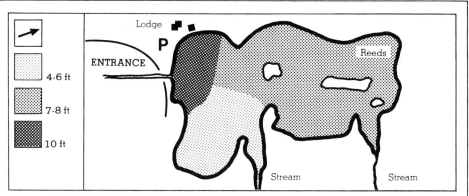

A 15-acre lake lying in farmland in the Eden Valley. This young fishery was man-made, naturally landscaped, and stocked with trout in 1981. It has a depth of about 12 ft, and there are two islands. The banks are clear which aids backcasting. Aquatic life is maturing annually, with sedge, mayfly, damselfly, lake olives and buzzers.

Facilities: A fishing lodge, toilets, and car parking area close to the lakeside. Permits issued on site. North West Water Authority rod licence required.

Season: April 1st to September 30th. Hours: 9 a.m. to one hour after sunset, half-day rods from 5 p.m. to one hour after sunset.

Rods per day: 10 maximum.

Charges: Day permit £8, evening £5.

Day catch limit: 4 fish, half-day two fish.

Boats: None.

Restrictions: Fly only. No wading. All sizeable fish must be killed. When bag limit is reached fishing must cease; an additional ticket may be purchased. No dogs.

Stocking policy: Heavy pre-season stock, then regularly with brown and rainbow trout.

Recommended flies: Black Pennell, Red Sedge, Peter Ross, Greenwell's, Dunkeld, Mallard & Claret, Baby Doll, Mickey Finn, Zulu, Viva, Missionary, Ace of Spades, plus Mayfly, Pheasant Tail and various other nymph patterns.

Local knowledge: Blencarn already has a reputation for free rising fish. Dapping the mayfly in June, and later the Daddy Long Legs can be productive. Many brown trout are taken on dry fly, while the larger rainbows tend to fall to lures. The record limit catch is four rainbows weighing 12 lb 1 oz, and the heaviest individual fish taken is a 7 lb rainbow.

River Derwent
Cumbria

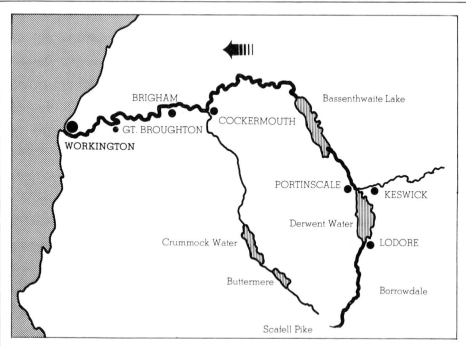

The Derwent rises in Styhead Tarn, near Scafell Pike, and flows north for 33 miles through Derwentwater and Bassenthwaite Lake to Cockermouth and on into the Solway Firth. Game fish are present everywhere through the Derwent system, except for certain sluggish sections of the lower reaches. Rod licence required: North West Water Authority, Rivers Division, P.O. Box 12, New Town House, Buttermarket Street, Warrington WA1 2QF.

Seasons: Salmon – February 14th to October 31st; Sea Trout – May 1st to October 15th; Brown Trout – March 15th to September 30th.

Borrowdale. Trout fishing available – enquire locally or at Scawfell.

Derwentwater. Trout numerous (as well as perch, pike and eels), although it is not ideal fly-fishing water. Permits – enquire locally.

Keswick. Keswick A.A. has 3 miles downstream of Portinscale, as well as 2½ miles of the Greta above its confluence with the Derwent. Permits from Temple Sports, 9 Station Street, Keswick.

Brigham. The Broughton Working Men's A.A. has 1 mile to Broughton Cross (members only). A further stretch of the Derwent and of the tributary Cocker is held for members of the Cockermouth and District A.A. Local tackle shops issue trout day tickets (£2).

River Derwent
Cumbria

Cockermouth. Castle Fisheries own and control several stretches down to the estuary. Mainly for members, but some permits are available for visitors. Contact the Manager, Castle Fisheries, Cockermouth Castle. The town waters can be fished; permit enquiries to the Town Hall.

Recommended flies: Dunkeld, Teal and Blue, Alexandra, Peter Ross, Zulu, Greenwell's.

Local knowledge: The Derwent offers a long season of varied and often excellent fishing in spectacular surroundings. The trout are game, and plentiful around the half-pound level. Sea trout run from July onwards. For salmon, this is generally a latish river, with August to October being the best period.

River Eden
Cumbria

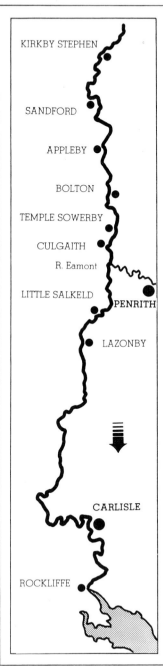

The Eden rises near Wild Boar Fell and flows north-west for some 65 miles through Kirkby Stephen, Appleby and Carlisle to enter the Solway Firth near Rockcliffe. This is a fine system for game fish, with salmon, sea trout, brown trout and grayling; for migratory fish the Eden has a reputation for being a latish river, although there is a run of early spring salmon.

Rod licence required: North West Water Authority

Season: Salmon – January 15th to October 14th; Sea Trout – May 1st to October 15th; Brown Trout – March 15th to September 30th.

Kirkby Stephen. 20 miles of excellent Trout and Grayling water controlled by the Kirkby Stephen and District Angling Association. Contact Mr. B. Owen, Church House, Long Marton, Appleby.

Appleby. Trout, Grayling. The Tufton Arms Hotel has five miles of the main river and becks. 4 rods limit per day. Fly only. Day permits £5 (£6 high season). Tel: (0930) 51593. Permits for grayling between October and January from Shoe and Sports Supplies, Market Place, Appleby. Prior to October 1st this section is reserved for Appleby A.A. members.

Upper Appleby. Five miles, fly only. Day £4 (£5 – July and August), week £24 (£30 July and August) – from Shoe and Sports Supplies, Market Place, Appleby.

Lazonby. Salmon, Trout. Bracken Bank Lodge Hotel has stretches on the Eden for residents. Occasionally permits issued to non-residents. Tel: Lazonby (076883) 241.

Penrith. Salmon, Trout, Grayling. Penrith A.A. has considerable fishing on the Eden and Eamont. Enquiries to R. Allinson, 7 Scaws Drive, Penrith. Day tickets £5, season £30 from Sykes Sports Shop, Great Dockray, Penrith. Tel: (0768) 62418.

Brampton. Trout fishing on the tributary Irthing controlled by the Brampton Angling Association. Permits from Brampton Sports Shop.

Carlisle. Salmon, Sea Trout, Brown Trout. 7 miles held by Carlisle A.A. Day tickets – £2.50 (Salmon) and £1 (Trout) – from R. Raine, 21 Warwick Road; McHardy's, South Henry Street;

Recommended flies: Dunkeld, Watson's Fancy, Black Pennel, Peter Ross, Coachman, Sweeney Todd

River Kent
Cumbria

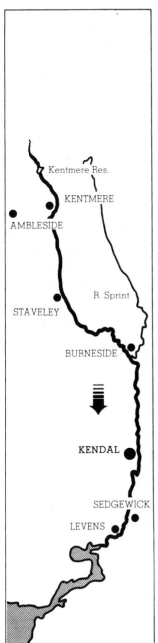

The Kent rises on the south-east side of High Street Mountain. In the 15 miles before it reaches Morecambe Bay after a southward journey through Kendal, the river descends from over 2,500 feet. Accordingly it is a very swift-flowing water. The Kent used to be noted for salmon, but pollution has taken its toll; happily the situation is now slowly improving.

Rod licence required: North West Water Authority, Dawson House, Great Sankey, Warrington WA5 5LA. Tel: (092572) 4321.

Seasons: Salmon – February 1st to October 15th; Sea Trout – May 1st to October 15th; Brown Trout – March 15th to September 30th.

Staveley. Seven miles controlled by the Staveley & District Angling Club. Weekly tickets (£4) issued. The club also has fishing on the 24 acre Kentmere Tarn (£6 weekly). Contact Permit Secretary, D. Taylor, 18 Rawes Garth, Staveley. Tel: (0539) 821002.

Burneside. An excellent stretch from Eggholme Wood to Cowan Head held by the Burneside & District A.A., who also have fishing on the tributary Sprint. The Jolly Anglers' Arms issues permits to visitors.

Kendal. Salmon, Sea Trout, Brown Trout. Kent A.A. have 9 miles with very good brown trout. Some day tickets issued up to August 31st (8 a.m. to 10 p.m.). Size limit – 9 inches. Contact J. Parkin, 11a Blea Tarn Road, Kendal.

Sedgewick. Salmon, Sea Trout, Brown Trout. National Trust water. Day tickets from Manager, Low Park Wood Caravan Site, Sedgwick.

Recommended flies: Silver Sedge, Invicta, Peter Ross, Black Gnat, Butcher, Mallard & Claret, Alexandra, Gold Muddler, Jock Scott.

Local knowledge: The main influx of salmon and sea trout is from late July onwards. The main river holds quite sizeable trout and the tributaries offer good sport for smaller fish. The Sprint has a very good reputation for sea trout.

River Lune
Cumbria

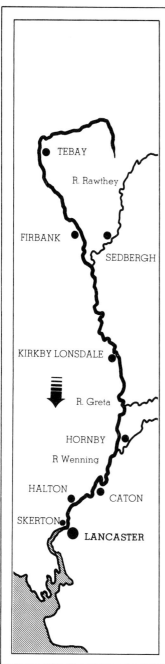

The Lune has its source near Ash Fell and takes a southerly course for 45 miles to Lancaster and the Irish Sea. The river has a fine reputation for salmon, sea trout and brown trout. The main runs of migratory fish are in August and September.
Rod licence required: NWWA.

Seasons: Salmon – February 1st to October 15th; Sea Trout – May 1st to October 15th; Brown Trout – March 15th to September 30th.

Tebay. The Tebay Fishing Club has very extensive rights near Penrith. Good sport for free rising trout, and occasional salmon and sea trout. Weekly permits from Sec., H. Riley, White Cross House, Tebay. Tel: Orton (05874) 376. Permits also from the George Hotel.

Howgill. Salmon, Sea Trout, Brown Trout. Sedbergh & District A.A. has 7 miles from Rawthey to Gibbet Hill. Weekly tickets from E. Lowis, Main Street, Sedbergh. The Club also has trout fishing on the River Rawthey – season permit £50, week £15 and day £5.

Kirby Lonsdale. Salmon, Sea Trout, Brown Trout. Kirby Lonsdale A.A. has 3 miles of first-class water, particularly for sea trout and sizeable trout. Weekly permits issued to anglers staying locally in guest houses and hotels.

Caton. 6 miles held by Lancaster A.A.; fly only if water level below 1 ft 6 in. Day tickets for one section issued by Station Hotel.

Halton. Salmon, Sea Trout, Brown Trout. The NWWA runs the Halton Fishery. Salmon – day (8 a.m. to 8 p.m.) ticket £4 before July 31st (thereafter £5.50) – from Darwen and Gough, 6 Moor Lane, Lancaster. 8 rods – lower beat, 12 rods – top beat. Sea Trout – May 1st to October 15th (8 p.m. to 4 a.m.) – £2.80 per permit from Mrs. Curwen, Greenup Cottage, Hornby Road, Caton, Nr. Lancaster. 12 rods – lower beat, 15 rods – top beat. Brown Trout (8 a.m. to 8 p.m.) – £1.10 per day from Darwen and Gough. All NWWA prices are halved for juniors, OAPs and disabled.

Skerton. NWWA runs the Skerton fishery. Salmon – £5.50 per day (5 a.m. to 10 p.m.), £4 before July 31st. Sea Trout – £2.80 per permit (8 p.m. to 3 a.m.). Tickets from Darwen and Gough (see Halton above).

Recommended flies: Salmon – Hairy Mary, Munro Killer, Jock Scott, Thunder and Lightning. Trout – Silver Sedge, Alexandra, Dunkeld, Peter Ross, Sweeney Todd, Coachman, Black Gnat.

Meet the Specialist.

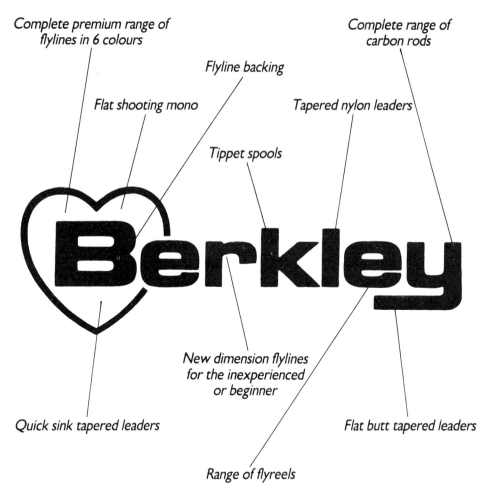

Complete premium range of
flylines in 6 colours

Complete range of
carbon rods

Flyline backing

Flat shooting mono

Tapered nylon leaders

Tippet spools

Quick sink tapered leaders

New dimension flylines
for the inexperienced
or beginner

Flat butt tapered leaders

Range of flyreels

River Derwent
Derbyshire

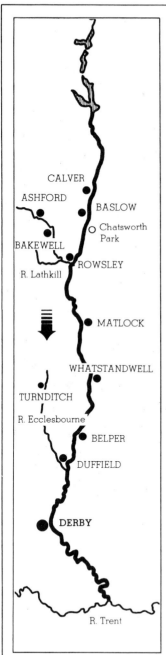

The Derwent rises on High peak in the very North of the County, and flows South and South-East for 60 miles to join the Trent. Trout and Grayling predominate in the headwaters, but coarse fish take over as the river flows closer to Derby. The upper Derwent and important tributaries, Wye, Lathkill and Ecclesbourne, are esentially stream, glide and pool waters offering the angler the opportunity to switch methods of attack between wet and dry fly.

Rod Licence required: Severn Trent Water Authority – from Fisheries Manager, S.T.W.A., Trent Area Laboratories, Meadow Lane, Nottingham. Tel: (0602) 865007.

Seasons: Brown Trout – March 18th to October 15th, Rainbow Trout – May 16th to November 13th, Grayling – June 16th to March 14th. (Local variations).

Baslow. Cavendish Hotel has 6 miles from Calver to Rowsley. Brown Trout re-stocked annually. Rainbows and Grayling also breed naturally. Residents only. Tel: (024688) 2311. The Hotel also has an exclusive stretch of 4½ miles upstream of Ashford on the Wye. Good clear chalk-stream fishing for Browns and Rainbows. The Cavendish Hotel waters are leased from the Chatsworth Estate.

Rowsley. Brown Trout, Rainbow Trout, Grayling. Peacock Hotel has fishing for residents only on Derwent (£10.50 per day) and Wye (£14 per day). Tel: Matlock (0629) 733518.

Matlock. Brown Trout, Rainbow Trout. 1 mile of water. Tickets (£2 per day) available from Midland Hotel, Matlock Bath. Tel: (0629) 2630.

Whatstandwell. Grayling, Trout. Quarter mile. Day tickets (£1) available from Derwent Hotel – Tel: Ambergate (077385) 2077.

Duffield. Trout, Grayling amongst predominance of coarse fish. Bridge Inn has 5 miles stretch at £1 per day. Tel: Derby (0322) 841073.

Turnditch. Trout. 3 miles of River Ecclesbourne. Earl of Harrington Angling Club, Derby issues day tickets for this fly only water.

Recommended flies: Dry (small sizes) – Greenwells Glory, Black Gnat, March Brown, Olives
Wet – Butcher, Greenwells Glory, Spiders

Local knowledge: The Derwent offers particularly varied fly-fishing. Fine and far-off tactics are often needed, with flies no larger than 16.

Foremark Reservoir

NEAR BURTON-ON-TRENT, DERBY. Controlled by Severn Trent Water
Tel: Burton-on-Trent (0283) 702352.   Authority, Soar Division.

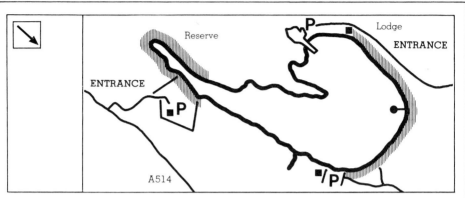

A large, irregularly-shaped water of some 230 acres, about four miles east of
Burton-on-Trent. This storage reservoir, with steeply sloping banks, was first
opened to anglers in 1979. Water life includes sedge, corixa, midge, shrimps,
snails, and fish fry.

Facilities:	Fishing lodge. Toilets. Car park. Telephone. Day permits available from Mrs V. Lawrence, Brookdale Farm, Milton, near the fishing lodge entrance.
Season:	5/4 to 15/10 inclusive. Hours: 7 am to half-hour after sunset.
Rods per day:	150.
Charges:	Full season £140, and £100 weekdays only. Half-price seasons £70 and £50 for children (under 16 years) of adult season permit-holders. Season permits from Administration Section, Severn Trent Water Authority, Leicester Water Centre, Anstey, Leicester. Tel: Leicester 352011 ext 265.
	Day permits £5, evening £3.20 (from 6 pm until August–then from 5 pm, in September 4 pm, and 3 pm in October.) Concessionary permits £2.50 for juniors (under 16), O.A.P.'s and registered disabled.
Day catch limit:	6 fish, three fish (evening) and six fish (concessionary).
Boats:	10 rowing boats. Hire charge day £4.30, evening £2.90.
Restrictions:	Fly fishing only. No walking on the dam. No fishing in the nature reserve area.
Stocking policy:	Large pre-season stocking, then at monthly intervals throughout the season. Annually some 20,000.
Recommended flies:	Small lure patterns, such as Appetiser, Whiskey, Sweeney Todd, Viva, Church Fry, Muddler Minnow. Nymphs, including Hatching Midge Pupa, Sedge Pupa, Pheasant Tail, Westward Bug. Traditional wets: Brown Sedge, Peter Ross, Watson's Fancy, Wickhams Fancy. Teal & Green.
Local knowledge:	Boat anglers often do well along the edge of the dam wall (out of bounds to bank anglers). Slow and fast sink lines generally used to best effect.

Ladybower Reservoir

Bamford, North Derbyshire.
Tel: (043351) 254.

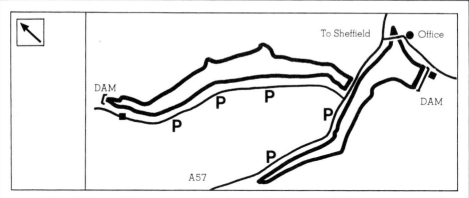

This 504 acre lake is of irregular shape which is useful when a strong wind is blowing. The natural banks and forestry plantations make it extremely picturesque. Water life includes a good hatch of mayfly, sedge, shrimp, and snails.

Facilities:	Fishing lodge. Permits issued at office.
Season:	April 1st to October 15th inclusive. Hours: 1 hour before sunrise to 1 hour after sunset.
Rods per day:	No limit.
Charges:	Season £94. Weekday £70. Day: high season, £4.80 (up to June 1). Low season: £4.30, evening £2.90 (after 4 p.m.). Concessionary: OAPs, disabled, juniors (under 16) £2.40. Severn Trent W.A. rod licence required.
Day limit:	4 fish to end of May, 6 fish after June 1.
Boats:	20. Day £4.10.
Restrictions:	Fly fishing only.
Stocking policy:	Pre-season, then weekly. A total of some 25,000 of rainbows and browns each season.
Annual catch rate:	17,584 fish.
Recommended flies:	Damselfly Nymph, Green Nymph, Green Beast, Mayfly Nymph, Sedge (various patterns), Corixa, Baby Doll (various colours), Ace of Spades, Viva, Black Chenille, White Chenille, Alexandra, Peter Ross.
Local knowledge:	Early season fishing from bank best with slow sinking or sink-tip lines, using a long leader. The regulars often use two droppers and a point lure. Record fish, a rainbow of 10 lb 2 oz.

DEBRETT'S

Salmon Stories

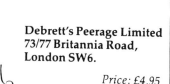

Debrett's Peerage Limited
73/77 Britannia Road,
London SW6.

Price: £4.95

By Jack Chance

Illustrated by Fred Banbery

Introduction by His Grace
The Duke of Devonshire MC, PC.

River Avon
Devon

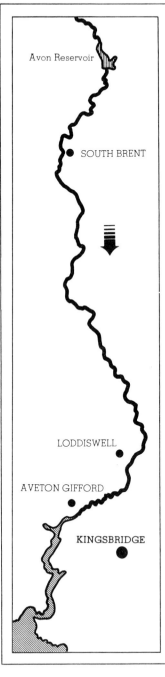

The Avon flows from its source on Dartmoor down through the Avon Valley into the channel at Bigbury Bay. It is generally fast-flowing over its length of some twenty miles, and is tidal below Aveton Gifford. The Avon is good fly-fishing water for both trout and migratory fish.

Rod licence required: Fisheries and Recreation Office, SWWA, 3-5 Barnfield Road, Exeter EX1 1RE. Tel: (0392) 50861.

Seasons: Salmon – April 15th to November 30th; Sea Trout – April 15th to September 30th; Brown Trout – March 15th to September 30th.

South Brent. Sea Trout, Brown Trout, Salmon. An attractive stretch of 1,000 yards. Permits from Mrs. J. Theobalds, Little Aish Riding Stables, South Brent.

Loddiswell. Salmon, Sea Trout, Brown Trout. Mostly both banks of a near-mile long stretch divided into two beats. Season permits only issued. Enquiries to local tackle shops, and Post Office. Enquiries also to D. M. Blake (Sports), 73 Fore Street, Totnes, and O'Neil's, 55 Church Street, Kingsbridge.

Aveton Gifford. Salmon, Sea Trout, Brown Trout. Several miles (mostly both banks) controlled by the Avon Fishing Association. No day tickets. Permits – week £15, fortnightly £20, monthly £30. Enquiries to Hon. Sec., E. Coombes, 19 Stella Road, Preston, Paignton. Permits from Post Office at Loddiswell.

Recommended flies: Soldier Palmer, March Brown, Wickhams Fancy, Alder, Hackled Greenwell, Gold Ribbed Hare's Ear, Blue Variant, Teal Silver and Blue, Alexandra, Kingfisher, Blue Terror, Dunkeld (tandem), Jock Scott, Stoat Tail.

Local knowledge: Excellent sport on light tackle for trout (to 3 lb). Sea trout are most prolific from late May to early July. On the Association water it is fly only, except after October 1st when spinning for salmon is allowed on the stretch below Silveridge. Wading is necessary on much of the Avon because of overhanging foliage.

Bellbrook Valley

NEAR OAKFORD,   Tel: Oakford (03985) 292
DEVON.   Proprietor: Mrs. Braithwaite.

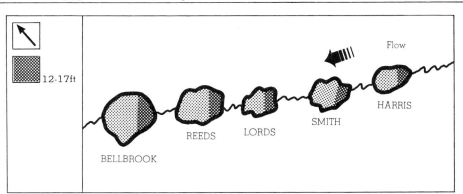

12-17ft

Flow

HARRIS

SMITH

LORDS

REEDS

BELLBROOK

Five lakes in a series down a valley. The fishery was created by the late John Braithwaite who named the pools Harris, Smith, Lords, Reeds and Bellbrook. Idyllically set near Bampton off the A361.

Facilities: Car park on site. Fishing hut for shelter
Season: All year round.
Rods per day: 20 maximum.
Charges: Day £6, half-day £3, plus catch to be paid for at £1.20 per 1 lb.
Day limit: 8 fish, half-day 4 fish. A second permit may be purchased.
Restrictions: No wading. Returns card must be completed and handed in to office for weighing of fish. No spinning or bait.
Stocking policy: Hen fish, Rainbows only, from stock grown in the fishery's own stew ponds.
Recommended flies: Throughout the year traditional patterns of wet flies. Also dry flies on summer evenings. Various nymphs such as Damselfly, Mayfly, Green Nymph, Sedge Pupa etc. Amber Nymph, Demoiselle, Iron Blue Nymph, Lake Olive Nymph, Pheasant Tail Nymph, Buzzer Nymph, Corixa and Shrimp.
Wet flies: Cardinal, Mallard & Blue, Mallard & Claret, Wickham's Fancy, Coachman, Invicta, Pennell, Fancy, Peter Ross,
Dry flies: Mayfly, Adult Midge, Pond Olive, Greenwell's, Brown Sedge, Hawthorn, Black Gnat.
Various lures, in the small sizes, are always worth trying.
Local knowledge: Floating or sink-tip lines are most useful on these small pools. Best tactic is floating line and greased cast, with most fish taken on small patterns just below the surface. In adverse conditions when the fish are down–or when one wishes to fish the deep section– then apply the same outfit without greasing the nylon. Nymph patterns most successful. Summer evenings dry fly worth trying.

Burrator Reservoir

Near Yelverton, Devon.   Controlled by South West Water Authority.
Tel: Yelverton (082285) 2564. Warden: Robin Armstrong.

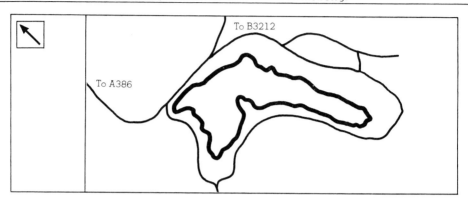

An irregular-shaped reservoir of 150 acres, attactively set on Dartmoor. As
well as fly fishing, spinning is also allowed in particular areas. Aquatic life:
dragonfly, sedge, midge, shrimp, snails etc.

Facilities:	Self-service kiosk for day permits. Car parking area.
Season:	March 15th to September 30th inclusive. Hours: sunrise to midnight.
Rods per day:	No limit.
Charges:	Season permit £21. Concession for OAPs, disabled, and full time students (under 18 years) £10.50. Juniors (under 16 years) £5.25. Day ticket £1.60, concessionary 80p. Season permits available from the Information Office, SWWA, 3-5 Barnfield Road, Exeter. SWWA rod licence required.
Day catch limit:	4 fish.
Boats:	None.
Restrictions:	Fly fishing (restricted area for spinning). No dogs allowed. Size limit 7 inches.
Stocking policy:	Rainbow and brook trout stocked as fry. Natural brown trout.
Annual catch rate:	Catches not recorded.
Recommended flies:	Black & Peacock Spider, Coachman, Coch-y-bon-ddu, Pheasant Tail Nymph, Mayfly Nymph, Damselfly Nymph, Leaded Shrimp, Amber Nymph, Stickfly, Silver Invicta, plus various small lures such as Missionary, Viva, Zulu, Chenille, Baby Doll, Muddler.
Local knowledge:	Try a floating line with long leader here and fish a nymph fairly deep. Also a slow sinking line with a small lure is effective in early season. Some late evenings are worth fishing with dry fly.

River Dart
Devon

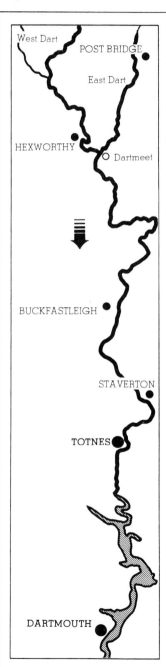

The Dart rises at the centre of Dartmoor, and flows for some 36 miles to Totnes and then into a long estuary to reach the sea at Dartmouth. The river starts as two separate streams, the East Dart and West Dart, which tumble crystal clear, fast and shallow across the moor to join forces at Dartmeet. The Dart and its tributaries, including the Swincombe, Blackbrook and Wallabrook, comprise a prolific game fishing system

Seasons: Salmon – February 1st to September 30th; Sea and Brown Trout – March 15th to September 30th.

East and West Dart. Salmon, Sea Trout, Brown Trout. Salmon best from early May to early September, and sea trout from midsummer onwards. Proprietor for most of the water is the Duchy of Cornwall. Salmon and Sea Trout permits – season £30, week £12, and day £3. Brown Trout permits – season £12, week £2.50, day 60p. All fish under 6 inches to be returned. Permits from Post Offices at Princetown and Postbridge; Tuckerman's Tackle, Torquay; Bowden & Son, Chagford; Barkers, Buckfastleigh; The Rod Room, Coryton; Arundell Arms, Lifton; Forest Inn, Hexworthy.

Buckfastleigh. Salmon, Sea Trout, Brown Trout. Buckfast Blue Fishery has permits available – from Sports Shop. 35 Fore Street, Buckfastleigh.

Staverton. Salmon, Sea Trout, Brown Trout. Stretch of fly only along west bank from Staverton Weir to Austin's Bridge. Salmon and brown trout permits (week and day) and sea trout permits (week only) from Sports Shop, Buckfastleigh; Hodge Sports, Newton Abbot; Dart A.A., Hon. Sec., Moorlands House, Marldon Cross, Paignton.

Totnes. Salmon, Sea Trout. The weir pool is available from Tuesday to Friday – day ticket £5. Limited to one rod per day, and fly only. Contact Blake's Sports Shop

Details on other opportunities for fishing the Dart can be obtained from the Dart A.A. Secretary (see Staverton above).

Recommended flies: Salmon – small tube flies (size 10 & 12 doubles or trebles) like Hairy Mary, Torrish, Silver Wilkinson. Trout – Greenwell's, Coachman, Pheasant Tail, Peter Ross, Wickhams, Alder, Dark Sedge.

Local knowledge: The lower reaches are primarily salmon and sea trout (very good) waters, with floating or sinking lines used according to water conditions.

River East Lyn
Somerset and Devon

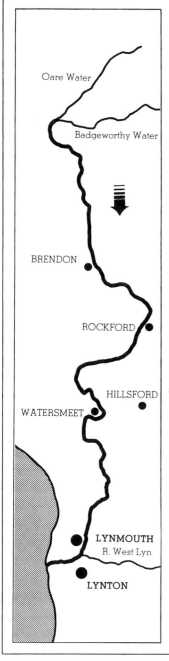

The East Lyn flows down from Exmoor Forest through exquisite countryside to the sea at Lynmouth Bay. It is joined at Lynmouth by the West Lyn, but the fishing on the latter is almost exclusively preserved.

Rod licence required: Fisheries and Recreation Office, SWWA, 3-5 Barnfield Road, Exeter EX1 1RE. Tel: (0392) 50861.

Seasons: Salmon – February 1st to October 31st; Sea and Brown Trout – March 15th to September 30th.

Badgworthy and Oare. Some 4 miles of trout fishing. Approximate price – day £2.50, season £25. Permits from Parsonage Farm. Tel: Brendon 234.

Brendon. Salmon, Sea Trout, Brown Trout. Stretch available at £2 day, £25 season from Mrs. Lester, Glebe House, Brendon. Brown trout fishing on the Oare Water (1 mile) and Badgworthy Water (3 miles) is available for £2 per day from Doone Valley Riding Stables, Malmsmead, Brendon. The Rockford Inn, Brendon (Tel: 05987 214) has a short stretch of water with sea and brown trout.

Hillsford. The Hoarock Water (half mile from Hillsford Bridge to Watersmeet) is reserved by the SWWA for children to fish for trout.

Watersmeet. The SWWA controls both the Watersmeet Fishery (downstream of Rockford) and the Glenthorne Fishery (upstream to Brendon Bridge). Water Authority permits cover both fisheries. Salmon and Sea Trout – season £90; March 1st to June 30th £25; 28 days £25; week £14; day £4.50; evening (8 p.m. to 2 a.m.) £1.20. Brown Trout – season £10.50; week £3.75; day 75p. Permits from – The Warden, Combe Park Lodge, Hillsford Bridge, Lynton; Mrs. Pile, Oakleigh, 4 Tors Road, Lynmouth; Mr. Lynn, Ironmongers, High Street, Porlock; Anglers Corner, Imperial Buildings, Castle Hill, Lynton; or by post from Information Office, SWWA, 3-5 Barnfield Road, Exeter. Fishing times 8 a.m. to sunset, except from June 1st to September 30th, when sea trout fishing is allowed until 2 a.m.

Recommended flies: Hawthorn, March Brown, Grey Duster, Wickham's, Greenwell's, Sedge, Black Gnat, Alder, Pheasant Tail nymph, Stickfly, Mayfly nymph.

Local knowledge: The East Lyn is generally a fast and shallow river flowing over a rocky bed. Rain can thus produce very quick and substantial changes in the water level, allowing large and sudden influxes of migratory fish. There is a good salmon run from July.

River Exe
Somerset and Devon

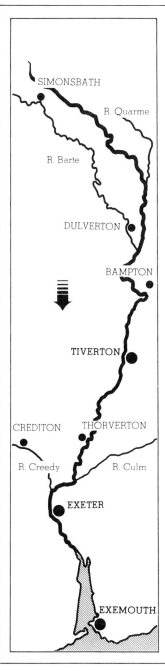

SIMONSBATH

R. Quarme

R. Barte

DULVERTON

BAMPTON

TIVERTON

CREDITON   THORVERTON

R. Creedy   R. Culm

EXETER

EXEMOUTH

The Exe rises high on Exmoor and flows across the moor and through a wooded valley to reach Tiverton. In this area the river widens considerably, as it continues on a southerly course to Exeter, and on to the sea at Exmouth after a long estuary. From March, salmon enter the lower reaches, which also hold grayling and coarse fish. Major tributaries include the Barle, Creedy, and Culm: these rivers are mainly shallow and stream-like, and offer brown trout fishing, with occasional salmon.

Rod licence required: Fisheries and Recreation Office, SWWA, 3-5 Barnfield Road, Exeter EX1 1RE.

Season: Salmon – March 15th to October 31st; Sea Trout – April 15th to October 31st; Brown Trout – March 15th to September 30th.

Dulverton. <u>Salmon, Brown Trout.</u> The Exmoor Forest Hotel has water for guests, and the salmon beat contains some excellent pools. The hotel has has rights on 8 miles of the Barle. Enquiries to the Proprietor, T. G. Woodward, Exmoor Forest Hotel, Simonsbath, Somerset. Tel: Exford (064383) 341. The Carnarvon Arms Hotel has 7 miles of the Exe, Barle and Haddeo reserved for guests. Tel: Dulverton (0398) 23302. Local residents have fishing on the Exe and Barle for an annual £2.10. Permits from L. Nicholson, Fishing Tackle, High Street, Dulverton. The Tarr Steps Hotel, Hawkridge, Dulverton, holds 3 miles of water – free to hotel residents. Non-residents day tickets – £10 (Salmon) and £5 (Trout). Tel: Winsford (064385) 293.

Tiverton. <u>Salmon, Trout, Grayling</u>. Hartnoll Country House Hotel at Bolham has rights, with day tickets £5, and season £20. Tel: Tiverton (0884) 25777.

Thorverton. Fly only <u>Brown Trout</u> fishing (4 fish limit) – £2 day. Enquiries: Mr. T. Mortimer, High Banks, Latchmore, Thorverton. Tel: Exeter (0392) 860241.

Exeter. Salmon. Water on Exe and Creedy – £2 day, £30 season. Day tickets from Exeter Angling Centre, Smythen Street, off Market Street, Exeter. Tel: (0392) 36404. Season permits from SWWA.

Recommended flies: Brown Trout – Coachman, Grey Duster, Greenwells, Black Spider, Pheasant Tail, Sea Trout – Alexander, Teal & Silver, Coachman.

Local knowledge: Brown Trout (many over the pound) move well to dry fly in the upper reaches. For grayling in the lower reaches, the use of leaded nymphs can be rewarding.

Fernworthy Reservoir

Near Chagford, Devon.   Controlled by South West Water
Tel: Chagford (06473) 2440.   Authority.

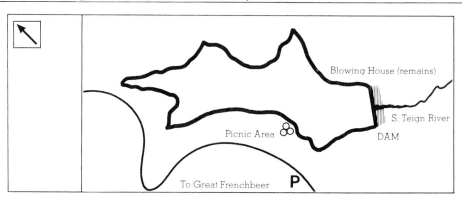

This 76 acre reservoir, nearly one mile long, is situated amid some of the best of Dartmoor countryside. Construction was completed in 1942. Lies off the A382, near Moretonhampstead.

Facilities:	Car parking. A picnic area on the bank. Self service kiosk for permits.
Season:	April 1st to October 31st inclusive, depending on water conditions. Hours: 1 hour before sunrise to one hour after sunset.
Charges:	Day £5, evening £3 (after 3 p.m.). OAPs, disabled and full time students under 18 £4. Juniors under 16—£1. The Authority issues books of 20 prepaid permits at 15 per cent discount—for instance, full day price £100, discount price £85. Concessions also for boat bookings. Pre-paid permits may be used at any of the Authority's 'stocked' trout fisheries.
Day catch limit:	5 fish, evening, 3 fish, over 10 inches. A second permit may be purchased. Any fish between 7 inches and 10 inches caught while achieving bag limit may be retained.
Boats:	Day (from 9 a.m.) £5, half-day £3.50 (after 3 p.m.). Advance booking advisable.
Restrictions:	Fly fishing only. No spinning. No dogs. All fish under 7 inches to be returned.
Annual catch rate:	(1982) 6,344 fish. Average catch 2.1 fish per rod. (1983) 1.9 fish per rod average. 6,354 fish.
Recommended flies:	Alder, Black Gnat, Alexandra, Black Zulu, Dunkeld, Butcher, Coachman. Lures: Appetizer, Missionary, Baby Doll, Viva, Dog Nobblers (various), Orange Marabou, Church Fry, Badger Matuka, Mickey Finn.
Local knowledge:	Traditional wet flies fished on floating line are recommended. Sinking line around the dam end of the reservoir (to 60 ft), and also elsewhere when using lures.

Kennick and Tottiford

NEAR BOVEY TRACEY,   Tel: Bovey Tracey (0626) 833199.
DEVON.   Controlled by South West Water Authority.

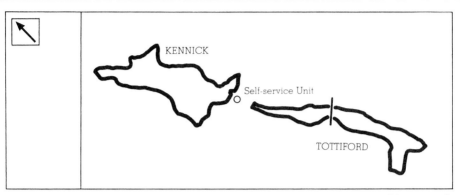

These two reservoirs, Kennick 45 acres and Tottiford 35 acres, set like natural-looking lakes in delightful country surroundings, off the A382. Interesting waters that have rainbows up to 11 lb.

Facilities: Ample car parking. Self service kiosk for permits.

Season: 1/4 to 31/10 inclusive. Hours: 1 hour before sunrise to 1 hour after sunset.

Charges: Day £5, evening £3 (after 3pm), O.A.P.'s, disabled and full time students under 18 £4. Juniors under 16 - £1. The Authority issues books of 20 pre-paid permits at 15 per cent discount–for instance, full day price £100, discount price £85. Concessions also for boat bookings. Pre-paid permits may be used at any of the Authority's 'stocked' trout fisheries.

Day limit: 5 fish, evening 3 fish. Anglers achieving a limit may purchase a second permit. Fish between 7 inches and 10 inches do not count towards limit, but may be retained.

Restrictions: Fly only. Size limit 7 inches/. (no fish under this to be retained.).

Stocking policy: Rainbows and browns as necessary.

Annual catch rate: (1982) 10,402 fish. Average catch 2.0 fish per rod. (1983) 1.9 fish per rod average. 10,639 fish.

Recommended flies:
Early season: Mallard & Claret, Greenwells Glory, Wickhams Fancy, March Brown, Olive nymphs, Damselfly nymphs, Mayfly nymph.
late season: Various sedges, Shrimp Invicta, Jersey Herd, Whiskey, Butcher, Black Lure, Black Chenille, Sweeney Todd, Dunkeld, various small lures.

Local Knowledge: In 1983 Kennick reservoir yielded rainbows of 10 lb 8 oz on a Black Lure, and 8 lb 3 oz on a Black Chenille.

River Otter
Devon

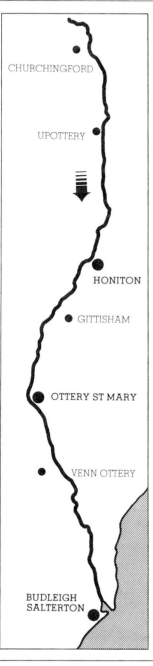

The Otter rises on the east end of the Blackdown Hills, and flows south-west through 24 miles of fine scenery to its estuary at Budleigh Salterton. This attractive little river offers good brown trout fishing, and reasonable sea trout (particularly in the lower reaches). Much of the water is controlled by local hotels for the benefit of their guests, with some opportunities for non-residents. Rod licence required: SWWA, Fisheries and Recreation Office, 3-5 Barnfield Road, Exeter. Tel: (0392) 31666.

Season: Sea and Brown Trout – March 15th to September 30th.

Honiton. Brown Trout. 5 miles of the river is held by the Deer Park Hotel, Weston, Nr. Honiton. Tel: (0404) 41266. Dry fly only. Permit costs: Season £50, week £25. Day tickets – residents £5, non-residents £7.50. The Combe House Hotel, Gittisham, Nr. Honiton (Tel: 0404-2756) has a stretch at £3.50 per day; permits only issued to non-residents if not taken by hotel guests. A short section is held by the Otter Inn, Weston, Nr. Honiton. Tel: (0404) 2594. Permits and cost by arrangement with hotel proprietor. A further stretch of water, wet and dry fly only, is available for 50p per day from Mr. C. May, Bridge House, Weston, Nr. Honiton.

Venn Ottery. 1,000 yards below Gosford Bridge is held by the Venn Ottery Barton Hotel. Tel: Ottery St. Mary (040481) 2733. Good wet and dry fly water with some fine pools. Charges: hotel residents – day £5, half-day £3; juniors – day £4, half-day £2.50. Non-residents – day £6, half-day £3.50; juniors – day £4.50, half-day £2.75. Fishing chalet also available for hire. Catch limit: 4 fish, half-day 2 fish.

Budleigh Salterton. Sea Trout and Brown Trout. A free stretch is controlled by the SWWA – rod licence only required. Season April 1st to September 30th.

Recommended flies: Coachman, Wickhams Fancy, Greenwells Glory, Alder, Stonefly, March Brown, Hawthorn, Black Gnat, Kingfisher Butcher, and various sedge patterns.

Local knowledge: The Otter has a good head of wild brown trout in the one pound and upwards range. Traditional dry and wet fly tactics (with floating line) should be adopted. The weir pools on some sections offer fine sport with sea trout.

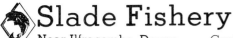

Slade Fishery

Near Ilfracombe, Devon.   Controlled by South West
Tel: Ilfracombe (0271) 62870.   Water Authority.

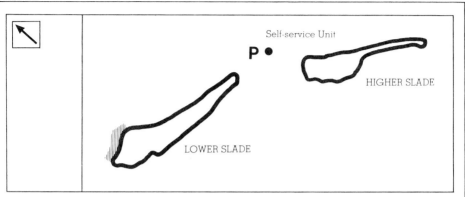

Two small reservoirs known as Lower, 6 acres, and Upper, 4 acres, situated about 1½ miles from Ilfracombe. The Upper Lake is operated as a traditional fly-only trout fishery. The Lower is an 'any method' water, including fly fishing, for coarse fish as well as trout. Water life is extensive with sedge, gnats, midge, dragonfly, damselfly, daphnia, shrimp, snails, and coarse fish fry.

Facilities: Car parking area, and a self-service kiosk for day permits.

Season: March 15th to October 12th inclusive for brown trout. All year for rainbows. Hours: one hour before sunrise to one hour after sunset.

Rods: 12 maximum for both reservoirs.

Charges: No season permits. Day ticket £1.60. A concessionary 80p permit for OAPs, juniors (under 16 years) and disabled. Permits are available at the Post Office, Lee Road, Slade. Monday-Saturday 8 a.m. to 8 p.m.

Day catch limit: 3 trout, over 10 inches.

Boats: None.

Restrictions: Fly only on Upper. Only one permit per day/rod. All undersized fish to be returned immediately. Wade with caution, as some sections of bank are steep. All coarse fish hooked to be returned to the water.

Stocking policy: Mainly rainbows.

Annual catch rate: Not recorded.

Recommended flies:
            Peter Ross, Blue Zulu, Bloody Butcher, Kingfisher Butcher, Coachman, Damselfly Nymph, Amber Nymph, Pheasant Tail Nymph, Green Nymph, Westward Bug, various sedge patterns. Most traditional patterns and some lures worth trying.

Local knowledge: Most fly fishing methods will take fish, when conditions are favourable. A slow sinking line is generally most effective. Depending on weather and water, when fish are deep, a weighted nymph can be successful.

Stafford Moor Fishery

Dolton, North Devon.
Tel: Dolton (08054) 371. Proprietor: Mr. A. Joynson.

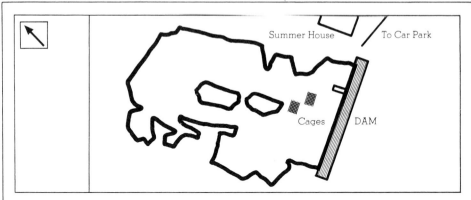

This is a man-made lake of some 14 acres, attractively landscaped and set in farmland surroundings. Aquatic life is abundant and includes sedges, midges, pond olives, snails and daphnia.

Facilities:	Comfortable clubhouse.
Season:	March 26th to November 13th inclusive. Hours: 9 a.m. to dusk.
Rods per day:	26.
Charges:	Day £8, and £4.60 (evening after 4 p.m.).
Day limit:	4 fish, evening 2 fish.
Boats:	None.
Restrictions:	Fly fishing only. No wading. No fish to be returned to the water.
Stocking policy:	Fish reared on site, from 2 lb to over 10 lb.
Annual catch rate:	1.83 per rod average.
Recommended flies:	
	Olives, Black Gnats, Damselfly Nymphs, Mayfly Nymphs, Green Nymph, various small lures.
Local knowledge:	With this fishery noted for double-figure trout, it pays to use a slightly heavier leader than normal. Records are: rainbow 14 lb 2 oz, brown 10 lb 2 oz. An additional 7 acres lake expected to be opened for exclusive use of floating lines and small patterns and mainly for dry fly and nymph.

River Tavy
Devon

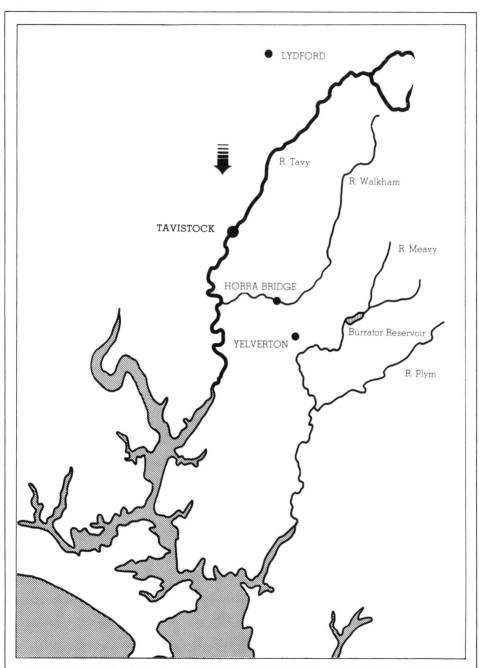

LYDFORD

R. Tavy

R. Walkham

TAVISTOCK

R. Meavy

HORRA BRIDGE

Burrator Reservoir

YELVERTON

R. Plym

River Tavy
Devon

The Tavy rises between Great Kneeset and Little Kneeset on Dartmoor, and then flows south-west for 20 miles to enter the Tamar estuary above Plymouth. It is a first-rate salmon and sea trout water, with brown trout as well in most reaches. The Tavy descends swiftly along a rocky bed for much of its length, and is rewarding fly water. The main tributary is the Walkham which also provides interesting trout fishing in moorland surroundings.
Rod licence required: Fisheries and Recreation Office SWWA, 3-5 Barnfield Road, Exeter EX1 1RE. Tel: (0392) 50861.

Seasons: Salmon – April 1st to December 15th; Sea Trout – March 3rd to September 30th; Brown Trout – March 15th to September 30th.

Tavistock. Salmon, Sea Trout, Brown Trout. A limited number of permits are available for a three mile stretch of the Tavy, and also a short section of the Walkham. The fishery includes 3 noted pools for salmon and sea trout. Trout fishing also available. Permit applications to Messrs. Barkells, 15 Duke Street, Tavistock. Tel: (0822) 2198. Or Jeffrey's Ltd., 19 Old Town Street, Plymouth.

Horrabridge. Salmon, Sea Trout, Brown Trout. Fishing opportunities on the Tavy and Walkham. Most of the water is controlled by the Tavy, Walkham and Plym Fishing Club. Permits issued by local tackle shops. Further details from G. Gay, 29 Whiteford Road, Mannamead, Plymouth.

Yelverton. Salmon, Sea Trout, Brown Trout. Extensive local waters on the Rivers Tavy, Walkham, Plym and Meavy are run by the Tay, Walkham & Plym Fishing Club (see Horrabridge above). Permist are issued to non-members: season £16, week £6, day £3. For brown trout only: season £8, week £3, day £1. Concessions for juniors. Permits may be obtained from tackle shops in Tavistock, Plymouth and Yelverton.

Recommended flies: Salmon – Stoat's Tail, Silver Doctor, Yellow Torrish, Blue Charm. Trout – Greenwell's Glory, Coachman, Peter Ross, Teal & Blue, Mallard & Claret, Grey Duster.

Local knowledge: The Tavy is a fine small game river with migratory fish and trout providing almost year round sport. Much of the fishing is inexpensive by national standards, and with good runs of sea trout (mainly from late June) and salmon represents remarkable value.

River Taw
Devon

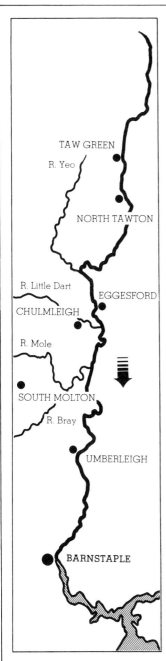

TAW GREEN

R. Yeo

NORTH TAWTON

R. Little Dart

EGGESFORD

CHULMLEIGH

R. Mole

SOUTH MOLTON

R. Bray

UMBERLEIGH

BARNSTAPLE

The Taw rises on Okement Hill on the north edge of Dartmoor. It flows for some 50 miles first north-east through moorland to Lapford, and then north-west through fertile farmland to Bideford Bay. This is an important salmon and sea trout river, with plentiful good brown trout in the upper reaches

Seasons: Salmon – March 1st to September 30th; Sea and Brown Trout – March 15th to September 30th.

Taw Green. Trout. Half-mile private stretch. Week £2.50, day 60p. Contact Mr. French, Davencourt, Taw Green, Okement. Tel: Sticklepath (083 784) 325.

North Tawton. Trout. 1 mile stretch, fly only owned by K. Dunn, The Barton, North Tawton. Tel: (083782) 230.

Eggesford. Salmon, Sea Trout, Trout. The Fox and Hounds Hotel has 7 miles of the Taw (3½ of single bank and 3½ of double bank), plus a stretch of the Little Dart. Ten beats on the Taw, including some very productive salmon and sea trout lies and pools. In 1983 over 300 sea trout were taken. The Hotel offers 7 day Rover tickets at £50 (March and April) and £40 (May–September). Day rods cost from £6 to £10 according to beat and season. The Rover ticket puts the holder on to a rota for the best beats. Brown trout fishing costs £4 per day. Permits are available to non-residents. Enquiries to Fox and Hounds, Eggesford, Chulmleigh, N. Devon. Tel: (0769) 80345.

South Molton. Salmon, Sea Trout, Brown Trout. South Molton A.C. has water on the Taw and the Mole. Fly only. Tickets from Tackle Shop, 6 The Square, South Molton.

Umberleigh. Salmon, Sea Trout, Brown Trout. The Rising Sun Inn has 3½ miles, divided into 8 beats. Fine spring salmon run, and very good sea trout from mid-summer. Fly only after April 15th. Permits for hotel residents – week £48, day £8. Occasionally permits available to non-residents. Enquiries to the Rising Sun Inn, Umberleigh, N. Devon. Tel: High Bickington (0769, 60447.

Newbridge, Barnstaple. Salmon, Sea Trout, Brown Trout. Double bank stretch run by Barnstable & District A.A. Mainly for members, but a limited number of visitors' permits are issued. Day ticket – salmon £5, trout £2. Contact Mrs. B. Parkin, 6 Gribble Close, Barnstaple (Tel: 0271 42352) or local tackle shops.

Recommended flies: Salmon – Gary, Silver Wilkinson, Brown Trout – Wickhams, March Brown, Grenadier.

River Torridge
Devon

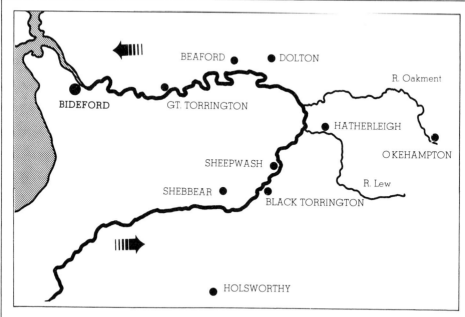

The Torridge rises in north-west Devon, and flows first in a south-easterly and then in a north-westerly direction to the Taw estuary at Barnstaple Bay. This noted game river is generally smooth-flowing, as it undulates through a gentle landscape. The Torridge can attract good migratory fish runs, and carries sporting brown trout especially in the upper reaches. The main tributary is the Okement.
Rod licence required: Fisheries and Recreation Office, SWWA, 3-5 Barnfield Road, Exeter EX1 1RE. Tel: (0392) 50861.

Seasons: Salmon – March 1st to September 30th; Sea and Brown Trout – March 15th to September 30th.

Okement. <u>Brown Trout</u> on Okement and Torridge (2 miles of water) for £1 per week. Contact Mr. Pennington, Hill Barton Farm, Okehampton. Tel: (0837) 454.

Hatherleigh. <u>Salmon, Sea Trout, Brown Trout</u> – on Torridge, Okement and Lew. George Hotel has fishing for guests, with occasional day tickets for non-residents.

Torrington. The Town Mills Hotel has 9 miles of very good water, split into 9 beats, with 25 named pools. Details and prices from Proprietor, Town Mills Hotel, Torrington. Tel: (08052) 2114.

Weare Giffard. <u>Salmon, Sea Trout, Brown Trout.</u> Day tickets issued by Post Office, Weare Giffard. Tel: Bideford (02372) 2479.

Shebbear. First-class fly fishing water, held by Devil's Stone Inn.

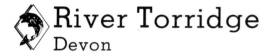

River Torridge
Devon

Sheepwash. <u>Salmon, Sea Trout, Brown Trout.</u> The Half-Moon Inn has seven miles. Day tickets – salmon £5.50, sea and brown trout £4.50. Regular stocking with brown trout. Contact Charles Inniss, Half-Moon Inn. Tel: Black Torrington (040923) 376.

Dolton. <u>Salmon, Sea Trout, Brown Trout.</u> Union Inn Fishery and Lower Torridge Fishery – details from R. Cusden, Union Inn. Tel: Dolton 244.

Beaford. Little Warham Fishery (1½ miles) – fly only. Occasional day tickets (£7.50) from P. Norton-Smith. Tel: Beaford 317.

Holsworthy. Four mile stretch of both banks of the Upper Torridge for <u>Brown Trout</u> fishing, held by the Woodford Bridge Hotel. This is fly fishing only, and free to hotel guests. The hotel also has 2½ miles, both banks, of the Lower Torridge for <u>Salmon, Sea Trout and Brown Trout.</u> Plus a further three miles of single bank. Both the lower beats free to guests. Fly only from May 1. Each beat has a fishing lodge with calor gas etc. Season March 1st to September 30th. Day tickets £7 to non-residents. The hotel fisheries have 40 named pools. Wading essential. Hotel has well-stocked shop, ghillies, and tuition by arrangement. Roger Vincent, Woodford Bridge Hotel, Milton Damerel, near Holsworthy, Devon. Tel: (040926) 481.

Recommended flies: Salmon – Yellow Torrish, Jock Scott, Green Highlander, Black Doctor, Silver Doctor, Stoat's Tail.
Sea Trout – Peter Ross, Teal & Red, Teal Blue & Silver, Invicta, Mallard & Claret, Butchers.
Brown Trout – most of the above sea trout patterns, plus March Brown, Pennell, Watson's Fancy, Zulu.

Local knowledge: Some sections are heavily wooded, and the areas around noted pools are often cleared to facilitate casting. Nevertheless, wading is often necessary to cover the water adequately.

Wistlandpound

NEAR BARNSTAPLE, DEVON. Controlled by South West Water Authority.
Tel: South Molton (07695) 2429. Warden: Gordon Rogers.

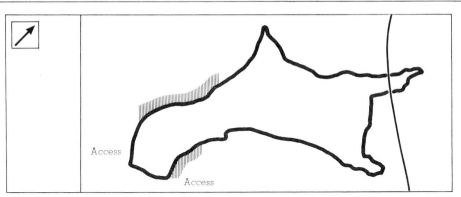

This 41 acre reservoir in attractive surroundings is reached via the A39 from Barnstaple. Steep banks, prolific water life.

Facilities:	Self service kiosk for permits.
Season:	1/4 to 31/10 inclusive. Hours: 1 hour before sunrise to 1 hour after sunset.
Charges:	Day £5, evening £3 (after 3 pm). O.A.P.'s, disabled, and full time students under 18 £4. Juniors under 16 - £1. The Authority issues books of 20 pre-paid permits at 15 per cent discount–for instance, full day price £100, discount price £85. Concessions also for boat bookings. Pre-paid permits may be used at any of the Authority's 'stocked' trout fisheries.
Day limit:	5 fish, evening 3 fish, over 10 inches. Anglers may purchase a second permit.
Boats:	None.
Restrictions:	Fly fishing only. No spinning or bait. No wading. Undersized fish of 7 inches to 10 inches taken whilst achieving a limit may be kept. All fish under 7 inches to be returned.
Stocking policy:	Rainbows, as necessary.
Annual catch rate:	(1982) 4,229 fish. Average catch 1.9 fish per rod. (1983) 1.9 per rod average. 3,946 fish.
Recommended flies:	Most of the lure patterns do well on this water. Zulu, Viva, Whisky, Black Chenille, White Ghost, Muddlers, Baby Dolls, etc.
Local Knowledge:	Slow sinking line to fish a lure early in the season. Alternatively, sink-tip or floating line with long leader to fish a weighted pattern. Largest fish in 1983 a 5 lb 10 oz rainbow, which fell for a Black Lure.

Flowers Farm

Hilfield, Dorset.
Tel: Cerne Abbas (03003) 351.   Proprietor: Alan Bastone.

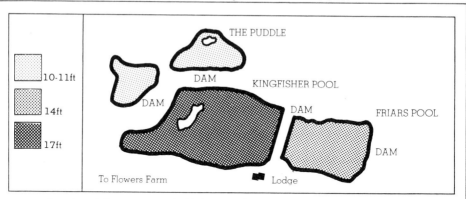

A series of three spring-fed lakes totalling 3½ acres at different levels down a small valley, some four miles from Cerne Abbas, and overlooking Blackmore Vale. Water life includes good hatches of mayfly, and there are large numbers of shrimp.

Facilities:	Small lodge, weighing room, toilets, car parking down to lakeside. Fishing tuition by arrangement.
Season:	March 3rd to December 31st inclusive. Hours: 5.30 a.m. to half-hour after sunset. Part-day from 1 p.m. to half-hour after sunset. Evening fishing begins at 4 p.m.
Charges:	Day £9, half-day £7, evening £5. Advance booking advisable. Additional permit may be purchased.
Day limit:	4 fish, half-day 3 fish, evening 2 fish.
Boats:	None.
Restrictions:	Fly fishing only. No wading. Single hook flies, maximum hook size 10. All fish caught to be killed. No dogs allowed.
Stocking policy:	Weekly. Rainbows and browns from minimum 12 inches up to 7 lb.
Annual catch rate:	(1983) 2,040 fish by 1,175 anglers.
Recommended flies:	
	Early season: Black Chenille, Sweeny Todd, Ace of Spades, Viva.
	Other times: as above, plus Baby Doll, Stickfly, Silver Invicta, Pheasant Tail Nymphs, Pennell and traditional wet flies.
Local knowledge:	Black coloured patterns do best early in the season. Mayfly patterns during hatch, and always worth using is a shrimp pattern fished deep. Biggest fish of 1983 rainbow 6¾ lb, and the best three fish limit 11¼ lb. Top lake 17½ feet deep at deepest point, other lakes vary from 11 ft to 14 ft at their deepest points, which are at the overflow points.

Kingsbridge Lakes

Organford, Dorset.
Tel: Lytchett Minster (0202) 622220. Proprietor: Chris Lees.

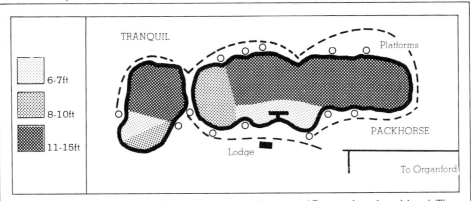

The fishery consists of two lakes set in 50 acres of Dorsetshire heathland. The lakes are 'Packhorse' (5 acres) and 'Tranquill' (1½ acres). Among the water life is a good early season rise of sedges, plentiful tadpoles in late spring, with midge, corixa, Alder, and damselflies in summer. The fishery also has 3 miles of the River Sherford (part tidal), which provides sport for sea-trout from the end of July.

Facilities: A comfortable fisherman's lounge, with ample car parking close by. Flies suitable for the water, and small items of tackle for sale.   Permits and Wessex Water Authority rod licences are issued on site.

Season: Summer – March 22nd to October 22nd inclusive. Hours: 8.30 a.m. (7.30 a.m. for season permit holders) to dusk or 9 p.m., whichever is earlier. Winter – October 23rd to November 30th. The fishery is closed from December 1st to December 25th. Open December 26th to January 8th inclusive. Hours: 9 a.m. to dusk.

Rods per day: 20 maximum.

Charges: A full season permit costs £220. Day tickets (summer) £9.50, half-day £6.50, and evening £4. Sea trout (River Sherford) – season £45, day £4.

Day limit: 4 fish, half-day 2, evening 1. Plus the catch and release arrangement.

Restrictions: Fly fishing only. Single hooks to a maximum size 8. No wading. Barbless hooks only. Note – for sea trout any legal method is allowed.

Stocking policy: Regularly with rainbows and brown trout. All sizes to over 10 lb.

Annual catch rate: (1983) 3.5 fish per rod average. Heaviest fish a 13½ lb rainbow.

Recommended flies: Damselfly Nymph, Mayfly Nymph, Green Nymph, Silver Invicta, weighted shrimp, Dunkeld

Local knowledge: A minimum of 5 lb breaking strain leader is recommended. Fish caught over the authorised bag limit may be returned to the water, or taken and paid for at the current rate.

White Sheet Farm

Wimborne, Dorset.
Tel: (0202) 884504.   Proprietor: Phil Cook.

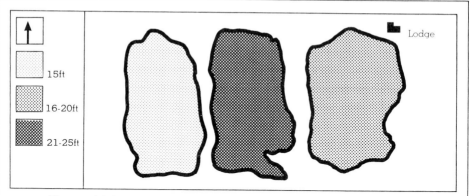

15ft

16-20ft

21-25ft

Lodge

This established trout fishery has three lakes that are generally 15 ft to 20 ft deep. The lakes are known as Spring Lake, Upper Lake, and Lower Lake, totalling six acres. The fishery has a woodland setting. There is an abundance of aquatic life, with good hatches of mayfly, sedge, Olives, damselfly, dragonfly, plus numerous shrimp and snails. There is extensive bankside cover, which adds to the attractiveness of the fishery.

Facilities: A fishing lodge, tackle shop, toilets, and washroom. Day permits and Wessex Water Authority rod licences are available on site.

Season: March 25th to October 14th. Hours: 8 a.m. to sunset, but not later than 9.30 p.m. Half-day rods from 2 p.m., evening from 4.30 p.m.

Rods per day: 20 maximum.

Charges: Day permit £10.50, half-day £8.50, evening £6.

Day catch limit: 4 fish, half-day 3 fish, evening 2 fish.

Boats: None.

Restrictions: Fly fishing only. No tandem hooks or droppers. No wading. All fish caught must be killed.

Stocking policy: Daily with browns and rainbows of weights ranging from 1½ lb up to 9 lb.

Annual catch rate: Average weight 1 lb 12 oz. 2.1 fish per rod average.

Recommended flies: Pheasant Tail Nymph, Mayfly (dry), Mayfly Nymph, (weighted and unweighted), Damselfly Nymph, Green Nymph, Amber Nymph, Sedge (wet and dry), Alder, Hawthorn, Buzzers, Midge Pupa, shrimp and floating snail.

Local knowledge: Ted Andrews: My first choice is for nymphs in small sizes, like Pheasant Tail, Mayfly or Amber. Green nymphs are firm favourites and definitely use a floating line. For most of the season the trout are generally free rising, and success can best be achieved by using artificials which are good imitations of natural insects.

Derwent Reservoir

Edmondbyers, Co. Durham. Owner: Sunderland & South Shields
Tel: Consett (0207) 55250. Water Co.

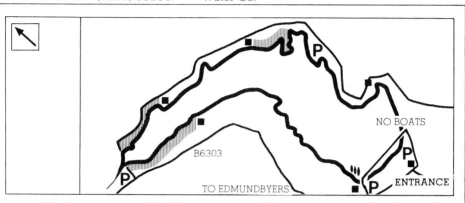

This is a reservoir of 1,000 acres (when full), constructed and landscaped in 1967. It was formed by damming the River Derwent. There is some seven miles of bank fishing. Aquatic life includes midge, sedges, Olives, shrimp and minnows.

Facilities:	Fishing lodge, toilets, car parking (offers access to both ends of the dam), self-service unit for day tickets.
Season:	May 1st to October 14th inclusive. Hours: from 1 hour before sunrise to 1 hour after sunset until end of August. September and October – the finishing time is half-hour after sunset.
Rods per day:	No limit.
Charges:	Season, by application to Sunderland & South Shields W.C., 29 John Street, Sunderland. Day – £4, half-price for juniors and OAPs.
Day catch limit:	8 fish (reduced to 4 for a 72-hour period immediately after stocking).
Boats:	Motor boats £13, rowing £6.50.
Restrictions:	Fly fishing only. No fishing in the nature reserve. Size limit 10 inches.
Stocking policy:	At intervals. Season total (approx) 10,000 rainbows, 2,000 browns. Over 12 inches.
Annual catch rate:	1.4 per rod average.
Recommended flies:	Baby Doll, Muddlers (various colours), Butcher, Alexandra, Invicta, Dunkeld, Peter Ross, Cinnamon & Gold, Black Pennell, Teal & Green, Woodcock & Yellow, Black & Peacock Spider, various nymph patterns.
Local knowledge:	In early season, if still cold, fish deep with sinking line and small lure or weighted nymph. During mid-season regulars to the water switch to floating line and nymphs nearer the top, or traditional wet and dry flies. Boat anglers tend to drift-fish, using a team of three in loch style. Later in the season Daddy Long Legs can be very successful.

River Tees
Durham

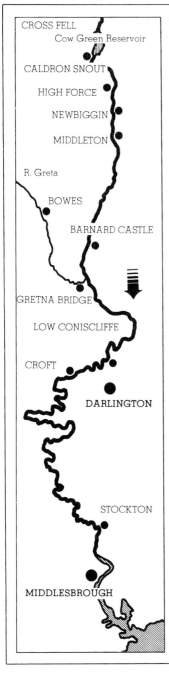

CROSS FELL
Cow Green Reservoir
CALDRON SNOUT
HIGH FORCE
NEWBIGGIN
MIDDLETON
R. Greta
BOWES
BARNARD CASTLE
GRETNA BRIDGE
LOW CONISCLIFFE
CROFT
DARLINGTON
STOCKTON
MIDDLESBROUGH

The Tees rises on Cross Fell in the Pennines and flows east for 70 miles to the North Sea below Middlesbrough. Very recently, salmon have been running the river again in reasonable numbers, after decades of virtual absence. There is also trout and grayling fishing in the boulder-strewn upper reaches and also the major tributary Greta.

Rod licence required: Northumbrian Water Authority, Northumbria House, Town Centre, Cramlington, Northumberland NE23 6UP. Tel: Cramlington (0670) 713322.

Seasons: Salmon – February 1st to October 31st; Sea Trout – April 4th to October 31st; Brown Trout – March 22nd to September 30th.

Middleton-in-Teesdale. Stretch from Broken Way to the ford below Newbiggin, and from the footbridge at Newbiggin to the foot of Cauldron Snout. Fly only. Permits – season £12, week £5, day £2.50 – from Raby Estate Office, Middleton-in-Teesdale, and from High Force Hotel and Langdon Beck Hotel, Forest-in-Teesdale. Upper Teesdale Estate also has water.

Barnard Castle. The local Fly Fishing Club and Darlington F.F.C. have water in the area. Trout and large Grayling. At Balder Foot, about 80 yards downsteam on the Yorkshire bank, the brown trout fishing is free.

Gainford. Half-mile held by Raby Estates Office, Staindrop (permits issued).

Darlington. Darlington A.C. has rights to a useful stretch – members and guests. Darlington Brown Trout A.A. has fine stretch at low Coniscliffe. Enquiries to local tackle shops.

Croft. Darlington A.C. has an upstream section, and Thornaby A.A. has downstream stretch.

Stockton. Stockton A.A. has some 10 miles of river from Gainford to Middleton-on-Row, near Darlington.

Recommended flies: Blue Winged Olive, Gold Ribbed Hare's Ear, Alder Fly, Black Gnat, Greenwell's Glory.

Local knowledge: In October 1983, a disastrous oil spillage near High Force decimated fish and water life (just as the salmon spawning was commencing) as far downstream as Darlington. A major re-stocking programme has been undertaken, but it will be some time before the upper and middle Tees reaches are fully recovered.

River Wear
Durham

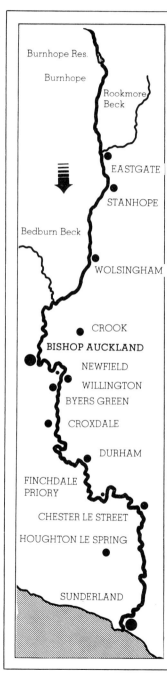

The Wear rises on Burnhope Seat to the West of the County. It flows East for some 65 miles past Stanhope, Bishop Auckland and Durham to reach the North Sea at Sunderland. Salmon and Sea Trout have been steadily re-establishing following anti-pollution measures and re-stocking. Major tributaries include the Rookhope and the Browney.

Rod Licence required: Northumbrian Water.

Season: Brown Trout – March 22nd to September 30th, Sea Trout – April 4th to October 31st, Salmon – February 1st to October 31st.

Stanhope. Sea Trout, Brown Trout. 2 miles of water controlled by the Stanhope AA – permits available. A stretch of river at Eastgate is controlled by the NWA. Day tickets from West End Filling Station, Stanhope.

Wolsingham. Sea Trout, Brown Trout. Stretch of water available on day ticket issued at Post Office.

Willington. Sea Trout, Brown Trout, Salmon. Stretch from Sunnybrow to Page Bank held by Willington & District AC. Day £1.50, Week £6. Permits from Bonds Tackle, High Street, Willington; A. Coates, Sports & Tackle, Hope Street, Crook; Angler's Services, Claypath, Durham.

Bishop Auckland. Salmon, Sea Trout, Brown Trout. The local Angling Club has water at Newfield, Page Bank, Croxdale, West Mills Dam, Willington and Byers Green, and also on two stretches of the River Browney. Details on day permits from D. Naisbett, Windrow Sports, Bondgate, Bishop Auckland.

Durham. Salmon, Sea Trout, Brown Trout. In the City there is free fishing from Milburngate Bridge on the left bank to the Sewage Works, and from the Ice Rink on the right bank to Kepler Priory Farm.
Day tickets (for mainly Trout) are issued for a 2 mile stretch of the South bank at Finchale Abbey caravan site. Apply to The Farmhouse shop – Tel: Durham (0385) 66528. Season £10, Day 75p.

Chester-Le-Street. Salmon, Sea Trout, Brown Trout. Local club controls one mile of water on which fly and other legal methods are allowed. Contact T. Wright (Hon. Sec.), 156 Sedgeletch Road, Houghton-Le-Spring.

Recommended Flies: Grouse & Claret, Blue Zulu, Peter Ross, Silver Sedge, Alexandra, Sweeney Todd.

Local knowledge: There is a good run of Sea Trout from mid-June onwards, given sufficient head of water.

Ardleigh Reservoir

Nr. Colchester, Essex. Run by Ardleigh Estates Ltd.
Tel: (0206) 230642.   Fisheries Officer: Richard Connell.

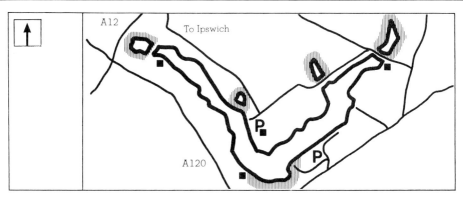

Ardleigh Reservoir, 130 acres of East Anglia, offers top quality fly fishing which some claim to be due to the long, irregular shape of the reservoir. This obviously favours the bank angler – and indeed there are some 5½ miles of bank. Aquatic life includes plentiful coarse fish fry.

Facilities:	Fly tying and casting instruction by arrangement.
Season:	April 1st to September 30th.
Rods per day:	About 50.
Charges:	Day £5, evening (after 5 p.m.) £4. Juniors half price. A second permit may be purchased.
Day limit:	8 fish.
Boats:	18 pulling boats, £5 day, £3 half-day.
Restrictions:	All under-sized fish caught to be returned. No spinning during fly fishing season. Trolling only in October.
Stocking policy:	10,000 to 12,000 early season. Rainbows and browns then at intervals.
Annual catch rate:	(1983) Average per rod 2.75. A record 29,000 fish.
Recommended flies:	
	Greenwell's Glory, Partridge & Orange, Black Chenille, Missionary, Appetizer, Dunkeld, Marabou, Muddlers (various), Black & Peacock Spider, Pheasant Tail Nymph, Ardleigh Nymph.
Local knowledge:	The best fish of the 1983 season were a brown trout of 6 lb 12 oz and a rainbow of 6 lb 2 oz. New to the fishery is an 8 acre water for brown trout fishing. There is a 4 rod limit, £8 per session. In addition there is a smaller water holding large fish. There is a 2 rod limit, £10 per session.

Chigboro Fisheries

HEYBRIDGE,
MALDON, ESSEX.

Tel: Maldon (0621) 57368.
Proprietor: Dave Weston.

Map legend:
- 5-6ft
- 9ft
- 12ft

Map labels: Island, Sandbar, P

A 16 acre ex-gravel pit lake, landscaped to blend with its farmland situation. The fishery is located on the B1026. Water life is extensive with Sedge, daphnia, Caenis, Shrimp, caddis larvae and heavy concentrations of sticklebacks.

Facilities:	Restaurant, open from 12 to 2 pm. Huts. Toilet. Car park. Permits issued on site. Flies and small items of tackle available.
Season:	1/4 to 29/10 (to end of November in 1984). Hours: 7 am to sunset.
Rods per day:	50 maximum.
Charges:	Season: £285 (50 days), £175 (25 days), mid-season (mid-May to mid-September) £115. Day £9.
Day limit:	4 fish, part-day 2 fish. 12 inch minimum.
Boats:	4, £5 per boat.
Restrictions:	Fly fishing only.
Stocking policy:	Rainbow, brown and brook. Over 10,000 stocked, from fish reared on site. Maintaining a density of 100 per acre. Average size 15 to 16 inches.
Annual catch rate:	2.35 per rod average. 3,502 rods returned 8,228 fish.
Recommended flies:	
	Early season: Buzzers, Shrimp, Pheasant Tail nymph, leaded Shrimp, traditional patterns such as Invicta, Hare's Ear.
	Lures: White Muddler, White Chenille, Black Chenille, Whiskey, Ace of Spades, Missionary, Viva.
Local knowledge:	A few casting platforms at one end of lake, ideal for disabled in wheelchairs. Grassy banks, with a minimum of 30 feet clear for back cast. Largest fish (1983): rainbow $8\frac{3}{4}$ lb, brown 5 lb 1 oz, brook 3 lb 12 oz. Best 4 fish limit $17\frac{1}{4}$ lb.

Hanningfield Reservoir

Near Chelmsford, Essex.   Controlled by Essex Water Co.
Fishing Lodge Tel: (0268) 710101. Tel: Chelmsford (0245) 400381.

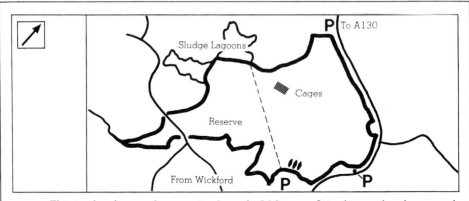

This is a landscaped reservoir of nearly 900 acres. It is of irregular shape, and situated in pleasant country surroundings amid coniferous forestation, south of Chelmsford and easily reached via the A130. There is a variety of aquatic life, including sedges, buzzers, snails, shrimps, dragonfly larvae, and small fish, particularly roach fry.

Facilities:	A fishing lodge, toilet and washroom facilities, and car parks situated at convenient places.
Season:	April 15th to October 29th inclusive. Hours: bank fishing from 6 a.m., boat from 8 a.m., to one hour after sunset.
Rods per day:	470 maximum.
Charges:	Full season permit £253, and £184 Monday to Friday inclusive. First time season ticket holders must pay a joining fee of £50. Day tickets (issued in 1984 for the first time) cost £8, and must be booked in advance. Anglian Water Authority rod licence essential.
Day catch limit:	6 fish.
Boats:	26 pulling boats. Hire charges are day £7, half-day £4, evening £2.25. Advance booking advisable.
Restrictions:	Fly fishing only. No fishing in area reserved for wild fowl.
Stocking policy:	Pre-season stock is with about 20,000. Then at regular intervals throughout the season. Rainbows and browns.
Annual catch rate:	A 2.2 fish per rod average, and 1¾ lb average weight.
Recommended flies:	
Wet flies:	Mallard & Claret, Peter Ross, Watson's Fancy, Bloody
Nymphs:	Footballer, Amber Nymph, Pheasant Tail Nymph,
Lures:	Most patterns do well. Muddlers, Black Lure, Beastie,
Local knowledge:	Geoff Bucknall finds it preferable to use a boat, and to use a drogue to drift fish a floating or slow sinking line. A team of three wet flies, such as Mallard & Claret on the point, Black & Peacock Spider on the middle dropper, and an Invicta at the top. A particularly successful pattern is a Sweeny Variant.

Horseshoe Lake

South Cerney, Glos. Managed by Jeremy Kemp for
Tel: Cirencester (0285) 861034. Gerrard Cross Fish Farms Ltd.

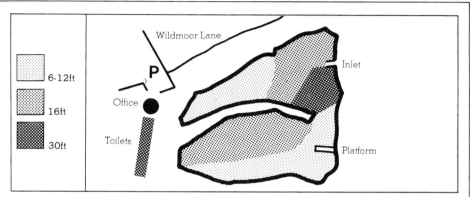

Horseshoe is an attractively landscaped ex-gravel pit of 15 acres. The lake is shaped as its name implies, and this can aid casting on days when strong winds prevail. The water is generally clear, and has a good mayfly hatch, as well as plentiful sedge and midge.

Facilities: Car park, office, flies and small items of tackle may be purchased. Toilet.

Season: March 19th to January 31st inclusive. Hours: 7 a.m. to dusk.

Charges: Day £10.50, part-day £8.50, and £5 for 2 fish ticket. Juniors and OAPs – £4.50. Advance booking advisable.

Day limit: 6 fish, half-day 4 fish, plus a special 2 fish permit.

Boats: One – rowing.

Restrictions: Fly fishing only.

Stocking policy: About 20,000 mainly rainbows from 1 lb to over 10 lb. Stock reared on site.

Annual catch rate: 2.5 per rod average.

Recommended flies: Mayfly Nymph, Pheasant Tail Nymph, Damselfly Nymph, Olive Nymph, Buzzers, Suspender Buzzers, Whisky, Viva, Baby Doll, Jack Frost, Grey Ghost and Dog Nobblers.

Local knowledge: Alan Pearson: Usually nymphs fish best. A dry sedge can be effective, especialy in the evening. There is a good number of large fish in the 5 to 6 pound range. They spend most of the time down deep; sunk line and lures are required to attract them.

Lechlade Farm

Tel: (0367) 52754.
Proprietor: John Taylor.

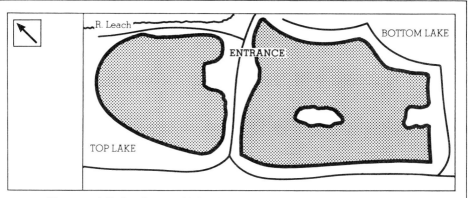

Two carefully landscaped lakes known as Top Lake and Bottom Lake totalling 10 acres, and located amidst pleasant woods. On the A361 Burford-Lechlade road. Opened for fishing in 1982. Extensive water life, including abundant mayfly and sedge hatches.

Facilities:	Large car park. Lodge offers refreshments.
Season:	1/4 to 31/12. Hours: 8.45 am to dusk, booking advisable for evenings.
Rods per day:	25.
Charges:	Season permit: (on application). Day ticket £9.75, half-day £6. All fish over the catch limit to be paid for at approximately £1.20 per 1 lb.
Day catch limit:	5 lb weight of fish (free), half-day 2½ lb weight of fish (free).
Boats:	Two Aquapeche boats, Day £5, half-day £3.
Restrictions:	Fly fishing only. All fish caught to be killed.
Stocking policy:	Heavy stocking rate with trout from the fishery's own farm. Fish of 1¼ lb to around 10 lb stocked, with most in the 2 lb to 3 lb range.
Annual catch rate:	3½ fish per rod average.
Recommended flies:	
	early season: traditional wet flies always worth using. mid-season: Mayfly nymph, Pheasant Tail nymph, Damselfly nymph, Green nymph, Suspender buzzer. late season: small lures, including Zulu, Viva, mini-dog nobblers, whiskey etc.
Local knowledge:	Most artificials fished on floating or sink-tip lines take fish. In warmer weather a slow sinking line often more effective. The fishery record brown of 10½ lb was taken in 1983 on a Mayfly nymph. Largest rainbow weighed 7½ lb.

Rainbow Lake

South Cerney, Glos.
Tel: Cirencester (0285) 86113.   Proprietor: Dave McPherson.

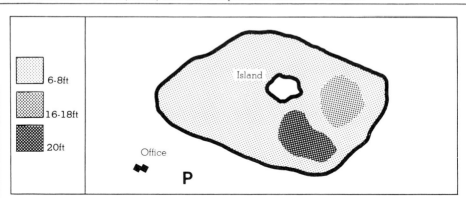

An attractive lake of some 10½ acres comprises this 'put and take' fishery that is located near Cirencester, Glos. Fishery reached by way of Wildmoorway Lane. Abundance of natural flies to be seen on the water. Aquatic life includes damselfly, midge, sedge, mayfly, olives, dragonfly, daddy longlegs, snails and shrimps.

Facilities: Car park adjacent to the water. Range of flies suitable for the lake available at the office. Clubhouse.

Season: Open all the year round. Hours: summer—half-hour after sunrise until sunset. Winter—7.30 a.m. to sunset.

Rods per day: 40 maximum.

Charges: Day £10.50 for a 4 fish limit, or £5 for 'catch and return', paying £1 per 1 lb for all fish killed.

Boats: Three, cost per day £5 or £6 for two sharing.

Restrictions: No wading. Fly only fishing.

Stocking policy: 110 fish to the acre. Weekly with rainbows to match catches. Including fish over 10 lb.

Annual catch rate: 1983 Average 4 fish per rod. Largest fish 15 lb rainbow.

Recommended flies: Pheasant Tail Nymph, Mayfly Nymph, Damselfly Nymph, Green Nymph, Muddlers, Black Ghost, White Ghost, Christmas Tree, Buzzers, Grey Duster, Dog Nobbler, Invicta, Whisky, Appetizer.

Local knowledge: Dave McPherson: the water in this lake is so clear that when the wind drops the resulting calm makes fishing difficult. It is necessary to scale down to a 1½ lb leader and very small flies. Alternatively use a long leader and fish the bottom with small lures and nymphs. From about the end of Autumn the trout start chasing the coarse fish fry—then employ a sinking line or sink-tip line with 12 ft to 15 ft long leader and fry imitations fished fairly deep, fast and jerkily. An experimental stock of salmon (12 oz to 4 lb) were introduced in 1983.

Avington Fisheries

Itchen Abbas, Hampshire.   Proprietors: Sam Holland.
Tel: Itchen Abbas (096278) 312.   Fishery Manager: Roy Ward.

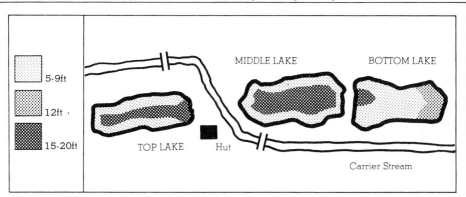

This well-known fishery near Winchester, Hants, consists of three waters: Top Lake (1¾ acres), Middle Lake (2½ acres) and Bottom Lake (2 acres). The fishery is set in rich farm land, and located in the attractive valley of the River Itchen. It was opened originally as a trout farm and, by selective breeding, very large rainbows were produced, as well as hybrids known as Cheetah and Tiger. A 20 lb 5 oz rainbow trout was caught from Middle Lake on rod and line, the heaviest rainbow ever recorded. Aquatic life is prolific, and varied, including pond olives, Dragon and damsel flies, caddis, shrimp, louse, snail, crayfish, newts and tadpoles. At times weed does become a problem.

Facilities:	Ample car parking, WC, washroom. Office on site for permits, but advance booking is requested. Artificial flies suitable for the water are available at the office.
Season:	April 3rd to October 3rd. Hours: 9 a.m. to sunset, or not later than 8.30 p.m. whichever is earlier.
Rods per day:	20 maximum.
Charges:	Full season permit £375 (one day per week) half season £195 (one day per fortnight). Day £13.85 including VAT. Half-day £7.00 including VAT.
Day catch limit:	4 fish from lake, plus two from the stream.
Restrictions:	Fly fishing only. Artificial flies and lures to measure no more than one inch including the dressing. No wading. No spinning. No non-fishing guests. No dogs.
Stocking policy:	Daily with rainbows. A few browns also stocked. All fish of a 2 lb minimum. 10 lb plus rainbows also stocked.
Annual catch rate:	Not available. Only the large fish are counted. In 1982 about 120 fish over 10 lb were caught.
Recommended flies:	Proven patterns are: Polystickle, Jersey Herd, Church Fry, Westward Bug, Sweeney Todd, Black Matuka
Local knowledge:	This fishery is noted for the size of its fish. Best rainbow: 20 lb 5 oz, best brown: 12¼ lb, and best cheetah trout: 9½ lb. The best fish of 1983 season 16 lb 12 oz and the heaviest four fish limit from the lakes 41½ lb.
	Floating and sink-tip lines are best, and weighted flies and nymphs are more effective than unweighted ones.

Bridge Farm Trout Fishery

Old Basing, Hants.
Tel: (0256) 65939.   Owners: P. A. and H. J. Herring.

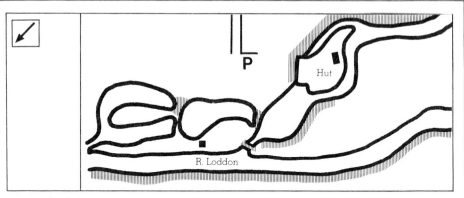

This fishery, situated amid farmland, consists of five spring-fed and connected lakes of some 4½ acres near Basingtoke. There is also a useful fishing strech of the River Loddon. Aquatic life is fairly abundant, and includes Mayfly, Olives, sedge, Black Gnats, Damselfly, buzzers, midge, snails and shrimp.

Facilities:	A shelter and weighing-in room. Toilets. Car parking area.
Season:	April 1st to October 31st inclusive. Hours: 8 a.m. to 9 p.m., or sunset if earlier.
Rods:	18 to 20 maximum.
Charges:	Day ticket £12, half-day £6.90 (8 a.m. to 1 p.m. or 1 p.m. to 6 p.m.). Thames Water Authority rod licence is required (not available on site).
Boats:	None.
Restrictions:	Dry fly and nymph fishing only. No wading. Hook size 10 maximum. All fish caught to be killed.
Stocking policy:	Starting with a pre-season stock – then daily with rainbows and browns of 1 lb upwards – fish reared on the fishery's own farm.
Annual catch rate:	3.1 fish per rod average.
Recommended flies:	Any of the standard patterns such as Pheasant Tail Nymph, Corixa, various buzzer nymphs, Amber Nymph, Greenwell's Glory, Wickhams Fancy, Black & Peacock Spider, Mayfly and various sedge patterns.
Local knowledge:	Floating line most generally used. Long leader with a fine point – about 3 lb breaking strain – because of the crystal clear water. This outfit, with a damselfly nymph, is a very successful combination. Heaviest fish of 1983 season were a 7 lb 8 oz rainbow and a 6 lb 13 oz brown. There is a one-mile length of chalk stream fishing, for brown trout only. Upstream nymphs and dry fly only allowed during April, August and September. Dry fly fishing only during May, June and July.

Damerham Fisheries

Near Fordingbridge, Hants.
Tel: Rockbourne (07253) 446.   Directors: A. English and J. English.

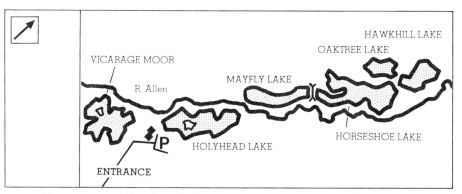

There are six lakes from half an acre to 3 acres, situated in a picturesque valley some three miles from Fordingbridge. The lakes are spring fed and rich in aquatic life. There are good hatches of Hawthorn fly, Mayfly, Iron Blues, Olives, Sedge and Alder flies, and plentiful snails, shrimps and tadpoles.

Facilities:	Office and clubhouse with washroom. Large car park. Bookings must be made in advance by telephone or post.
Season:	March 26th to October 31st inclusive. Hours: 9.30 a.m. to dusk.
Rods per day:	40 maximum.
Charges:	Full season permit £365, half-season £200 (16 visits). Day ticket £13.20, half-day £7.50 (afternoons only).
Day catch limit:	4 fish. Half-day two fish.
Boats:	None.
Restrictions:	Fly fishing only. One fly per cast only. No spinning. No dogs. Maximum hook size No 8 long shank.
Stocking policy:	Daily with rainbows, plus a few browns. Some 15,000 fish stocked per season.
Annual catch rate:	2.74 fish per rod average. 2.75 lb weight average. 10,669 fish totalling 28,242 lb caught. Heaviest fish 12 lb 4 oz (1983).
Recommended flies:	Damsel Nymph, Olive Nymph, Mayfly Nymph, Green Nymph, Alder Fly, Black Gnat, Blue Winged Olive, Teal Blue & Silver, Teal & Green, Black & Peacock Spider, Mallard & Claret, Walkers Sedge, Dunkeld and Greenwells. Most of the popular lures in varying colours.
Local knowledge:	The most effective combination on these lakes is a floating line with a fairly long leader to fish nymphs. Alternatively grease the leader and fish dry flies. The waters are clear and therefore ideal for spotting and stalking particular fish.

Eversley Cross Fishery

Near Eversley, Hants.
Tel: Yateley (0252) 878704. Proprietor: Kingsmead Fish Farms Ltd.

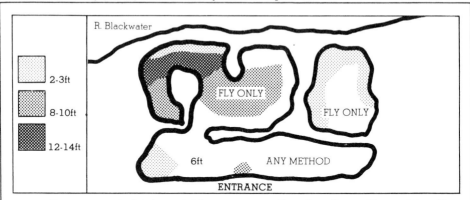

Two connected lakes of 11 acres near Eversley Cross, Hampshire. The irregular shape of the fishery creates many small bays. Aquatic life includes shrimps, daphnia, snails, pond olives and damselflies.

Facilities: Car park. Toilets. Permits issued on site.

Season: Open all year. Hours: 8.30 a.m. to sunset. In winter it is advisable to check by phone that fishery is open before travelling.

Charges: Day £4.50 weekdays, £5 weekends, evening £3 weekdays, £3.50 weekends, from 4 p.m.

Day limit: No catch limit. All trout caught to be paid for at £1 per 1 lb approx.

Boats: None.

Restrictions: Mainly fly fishing. Limited bank section for worm and spinning.

Stocking policy: Stocked to maintain at least 140 fish per acre with rainbows up to 5 lb, reared by the fishery.

Annual catch rate: 1.83 per rod average.

Recommended flies: Black Dog Nobblers, Marabou (various colours), Viva, Christmas Tree, Zulu, Baby Doll (various patterns), Whisky, Badger Matuka, Missionary, Appetizer.

Local knowledge: Floating line and a leader of over 10 ft to fish a Dog Nobbler lure has been a highly successful method. It pays to ring the changes on the colour patterns of the lure.

Hucklesbrook Lake

Fordingbridge, Hants.
Tel: Ringwood (04254) 78997.

Proprietors: Steve Hare and
Bob Morey.

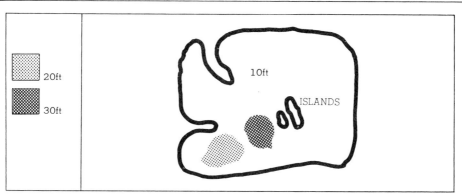

This is an attractively landscaped ex-gravel pit of some 30 acres, situated alongside the A338 between Fordingbridge and Ringwood. Aquatic life in this new lake is increasing all the time. It includes shrimps, snails, corixa, midge, sedge, pond olives, damselflies and a hatch of mayfly.

Facilities:	Office and shop on site for permits. In addition to flies and small items of tackle, there is a very large selection of fly-tying materials for sale. Casting and fly tying tuition is also available, by arrangement.
Season:	April 1st to September 30th inclusive. Hours: from 9 a.m. to sunset.
Rods per day:	40 maximum.
Charges:	Full season £230 for one day per weekend. £205 for one day per week. Day permit £9, half-day £6 (all permits include Wessex Water Authority rod licence).
Day catch limit:	Four fish. Half-day two fish.
Boats:	Four. Hire charge, day £3 and £4.
Restrictions:	Fly fishing only. No spinning. No wading.
Stocking policy:	Species are rainbows, browns and American brook trout. Frequent stocking to maintain density.
Annual catch rate:	1¼ lb per fish average. 2,373 fish up to 6¼ lb, and the record a rainbow of 8 lb.
Recommeded flies:	Damselfly Nymph, Mayfly Nymph, Black & Pea-cock Spider, Stickfly, Silver Invicta, Bloody Butcher, King-fisher Butcher, Alexandra, Viva, Mallard & Claret, March Brown, Soldier Palmer, Teal & Green, Peter Ross, Greenwell's Glory and most other traditional wet-fly patterns.
Local knowledge:	Steve Hare—A Viva is always effective, and towards the end of the season Butcher and Alexandra. Short-lining from boat or bank, loch style with a team of three flies – using Zulu, Black Pennell, Alexandra, Mallard & Claret, Butcher etc. When fishing from the bank keep moving to cover the water.

River Itchen
Hampshire

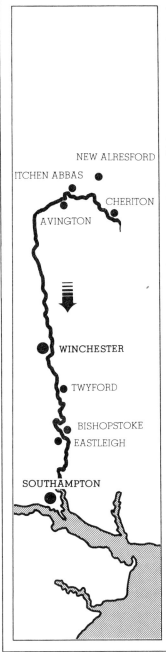

NEW ALRESFORD
ITCHEN ABBAS
CHERITON
AVINGTON
WINCHESTER
TWYFORD
BISHOPSTOKE
EASTLEIGH
SOUTHAMPTON

The Itchen rises near Alresford, and flows through Winchester and then southwards to empty into Southampton Water after a journey of some 25 miles. This renowned chalk stream has excellent trout fishing throughout its length; salmon and sea trout are also present in the lower reaches. The Itchen has abundant weed growth and extensive insect life. Prolific fly hatches, including Mayfly, Olives, Hawthorn, Damselfly and Sedges provide a very rich diet.

Rod licence required: Southern Water Authority, Guildbourne House, Chatsworth Road, Worthing, Sussex. Tel: (0903) 205252.

Seasons: Salmon – January 17th to October 2nd; Sea Trout – May 1st to October 3rd; Brown and Rainbow Trout – April 3rd to October 31st; Grayling – June 16th to March 14th.

Itchen Abbas. A carrier stream flows through well-known Avington Trout Fishery. Fly only for <u>Browns</u> and <u>Rainbows</u>. Day tickets (including three lakes) £13.85. 9 a.m. to sunset or 9.30 p.m. whichever is earlier. Roy Ward – Fishing Manager – Tel: Itchen Abbas (096278) 312.

Winchester. Section of river known as The Weirs is controlled by City Council: free fishing. A further stretch (fly only) is run by Winchester Angling Club. Enquiries to local tackle shops.

Bishopstoke. A stretch of river, and the lakes at Hiltingbury, run for under 16-year-olds, and also some physically handicapped adults. Enquiries to Civic Offices, Leigh Road, Eastleigh. Tel: (0703) 614646.

Eastleigh. The Manor Fishery offers excellent fly fishing, as do the Segars Carrier Fishery and the Kanara Beat. Fly only. Day and season permits issued by the Rod Box, 52 St George's Street, Winchester. Tel: (0962) 713458.

Recommended flies: Ginger Quill, Red Quill, Caperer, March Brown, Greenwell's, Yellow Dun, Mayfly, Alder, Hawthorn. Nymphs – Partridge and Orange, Mayfly, Damselfly, Stickfly, Westward Bug, Pheasant Tail.

Local knowledge: Although dry fly is generally the rule, wet fly can also be effective, particularly if fish are seen to be nymphing. When using a nymph, grease part of the leader as this will help when fish cannot be seen clearly; movement of the greased part will indicate a taking trout.

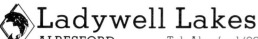Ladywell Lakes

ALRESFORD,
HANTS.

Tel: Alresford (096273) 2317.
Proprietor: B. Dening.

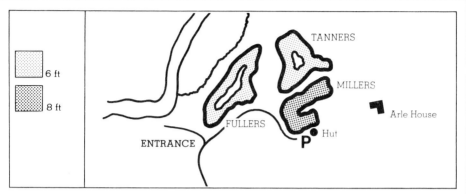

6 ft

8 ft

TANNERS

MILLERS

Arle House

FULLERS

ENTRANCE

P Hut

Three lakes totalling 2½ acres, with length of chalk stream, near Winchester, Hants. Aquatic life includes a small hatch of mayfly, with plentiful sedge, damselfly, buzzers, corixa, shrimps, snails, tadpoles etc.

Facilities:	Fishing hut. Flies suitable for the fishery are available. Fly fishing tuition by arrangement.
Season:	3/4 to 30/9. Hours: 9 am to dusk.
Rods:	limited.
Charges:	Day £10, half-day £5.75. Additional day ticket available.
Day catch limit:	4 fish, half-day 2 fish.
Boats:	None.
Restrictions:	Fly fishing only. No wading. Maximum fly size 8, and one inch overall length including the dressing.
Stocking policy:	Rainbows and browns, of 12 inches and over. One lake stocked with browns only.
Catch rate:	2.7 per rod average.
Recommended flies:	
	Green Nymph, Brown Nymph, Pheasant Tail Nymph, Black Buzzer, Damselfly Nymph, Corixa, Westward Bug, Lake Olive Nymph, Buzzer Nymph, Mayfly Nymph, Sedge Pupa, Hatching Midge Pupa.
	March Brown, Coachman, Dunkeld, Alexandra, Greenwell's Glory, Silver Invicta, Grenadier, Soldier Palmer, G & H Sedge.
Local knowledge:	The lakes have grassy and fishable banks, with an average depth of around six feet, with the occasional 12 ft hole. Early season white coloured patterns are recommended, while later in the season small dark patterns are effective.

Leominstead

EMERY DOWN, HANTS.

Tel: Lyndhurst (042128) 2610.
Proprietor: Leo Jarmal.

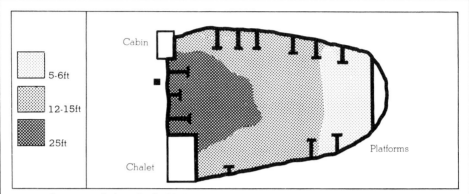

5-6ft

12-15ft

25ft

Cabin

Chalet

Platforms

A stream-fed secluded lake of about 8 acres in the wooded surroundings of the New Forest. Because the banks are left to grow wild with trees right to the bank edge, casting platforms have been introduced. Abundant water life, including sedges, midge, snails, shrimps, daphnia, coarse fish fry.

Facilities:	Ample car parking space. An office selling permits, Southern Water rod licence, and a selection of flies
Season:	3/3 to 31/10 inclusive. Hours: 9 am to 9 pm or sunset (whichever is earlier).
Charges:	Season permit (30 days, one day per week). £327. Half-season (15 days, one day per fortnight) £170. Day ticket £12.50, half-day £7.50 (from 3 pm). A second permit may be purchased when limit has been taken. Advance booking is always advisable.
Day catch limit:	4 fish, half-day 2 fish.
Restrictions:	Fly fishing only. Maximum hook size 10 and fly size no more than one inch overall in length. No fish to be returned–all caught must be killed. No dogs allowed. No tandems, droppers or barbless hooks.
Stocking policy:	Mainly rainbows, stock reared on site. Periodic stocking of up to 10,000 each season with some fish over 10 lb.
Annual catch rate:	(1983) 3 fish per rod average, and average weight 2.8 lb per fish. (1982) 3.7 fish per rod average. Largest fish of 1983–a 12 lb 14 oz rainbow
Recommended flies:	Mayfly Nymph, Damselfly Nymph, Green Nymph, Amber Nymph, Wonderbug, Westward Bug, Persuader, Dunkeld, Black Ghost, Missionary, Polystickle, Jersey Herd, Zulu, Viva, Jack Frost, Whiskey,
Local knowledge:	Alan Pearson, who took the 12 lb 14 oz rainbow at the fishery in 1983 says: 'Because of the excellent casting platforms there is no need to cast a great distance. No need, either, to fish deep. The main food supply appears to be daphnia, and this keeps the trout in the top six feet of the water. So stick to a floating line or a slow to medium sinker. Nymphs always work well, and so do small marabou patterns in various colours.'

Rooksbury Mill

Andover, Hants.
Tel: Andover (0264) 52921.   Manager: Peter Atkinson.

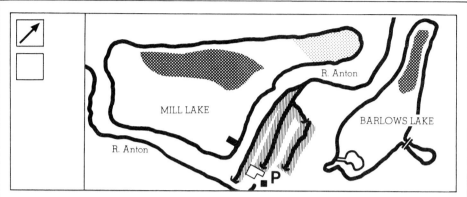

Two lakes, Mill Lake (6.5 acres) and Barlows (2.6 acres) plus one mile of the River Anton. The fishery is situated on the outskirts of Andover, just off the A343. Rich in aquatic life with good hatches of Sedge, Olives, Alders and Buzzers. There are sticklebacks and coarse fish fry.

Facilities:	Comfortable clubhouse with tea and coffee making equipment. Tackle shop stocking a full range of all the popular artificials. Anglers may also have their catch smoked. Large car parking area.
Season:	April 4th to October 31st. Hours: 8 a.m. to dusk.
Rods:	30 per day maximum.
Charges:	Season: full rod (one day per week) £275, half-rod (one day per fortnight) £140. Popular is the 'Flexible Ten' season (10 week day visits) £100, and 'Flexible Five' season (5 week day visits) £55. Day £12, half-day £6. All inclusive of VAT. Permits and Southern Water Authority licences available from office on site.
Day limit:	5 fish, half-day 2. An additional permit may be purchased.
Boats:	Two, on Mill Lake. Charge is £5 for two anglers, £3 for one. Half price for half-day. Advance booking advisable.
Restrictions:	Wet or dry fly by orthodox methods only. Double-hooks not allowed. No spinners. No wading. All fish to be recorded. River: dry fly and upstream nymph only. Maximum hook size 12 on river, 8 on lake.
Stocking policy:	Rainbows and browns several times a week, maintaining a minimum of 100 fish per acre.
Annual catch rate:	Average weight 2½ lb. There were 66 fish over 6 lb. Total catch 4,054 fish (1983).
Recommended flies:	Damsel Nymph, Mayfly Nymph, Green Nymph
Local knowledge:	Peter Atkinson – Sinking and floating lines can be used all season, much depends on the day. But during evenings when there is plenty of surface activity, obviously the floater is best.

Stratfield Saye Fishery

Stratfield Turgis,   Tel: Basingstoke (0256) 882543.
near Basingstoke, Hants. Proprietor: Duke of Wellington.

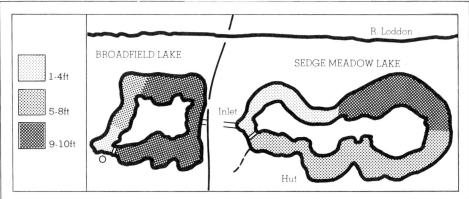

This interesting fishery consists of two lakes, Broadford of 9 acres, and Bridge Meadow 5 acres, situated on a private estate (Wellington Country Park) in the picturesque Loddon Valley. Water life includes Mayfly, Sedge, shrimps, snails, Corixa, Caenis and Damselfly.

Facilities:	Fishing lodge. Artificial flies available. Car park.
Season:	April 1st to October 15th inclusive. Hours: 8.30 a.m. to dusk.
Rods:	12 maximum.
Charges:	Full season £250 (one day a week), £130 for half season permit. A Thames Water rod licence is required.
Day catch limit:	4 fish, and two fish.
Boats:	None.
Restrictions:	Dry fly and nymph fishing only. No lures. No droppers. No wading. Maximum hook size 8.
Stocking policy:	Weekly consignments of rainbows, plus some browns from the fishery's own hatchery.
Annual catch rate:	1 lb 13 oz average weight of fish caught per visit.
Recommended flies:	
	Pheasant Tail Nymph, Black & Peacock Spider, Alder Larva, Amber Nymph,, Mayfly Nymph, Damselfly Nymph, Olive, Dry Sedge, Corixa, Silver Invicta, Coachman, Greenwell's Glory, Black Pennel, Woodcock & Green, Kingfisher, Butcher, Dunkeld, Grenadier.
Local knowledge:	Generally floating line, yet a slow sinker can be most effective when fishing a damselfly nymph. When fish are rising it often pays to grease the leader and fish a dry pattern, or a small nymph. Largest fish of 1983 a rainbow of 11½ lb.

River Test
Hampshire

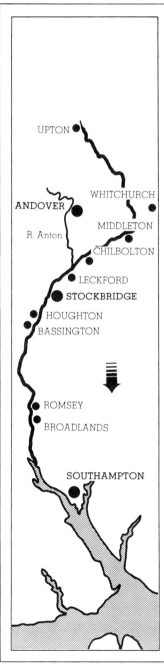

From its source near Upton, the Test flows south via Stockbridge and Romsey to enter Southampton Water at Totton. This chalk 'stream' is world-renowned for its superb trout fishing. In keeping with this legendary status, most of the fishing on the main river and its tributaries is privately owned and very strictly preserved. Despite this, there are opportunities for the visiting angler: prices tend to be high, but this only reflects the excellence of the sport to be had. Species are brown trout, rainbow trout, and grayling, with sea trout and heavy salmon in the lower reaches.
Rod licence required: Southern Water Authority, Guildbourne House, Chatsworth Road, Worthing, Sussex. Tel: (0903) 205252.

Seasons: Salmon – January 17th to October 2nd; Sea Trout – May 1 to October 31; Brown and Rainbow Trout – April 3rd to October 31st; Grayling – June 16th to March 14th.

Middleton. Two exclusive stretches – one at Middleton and the other known as Lower Mill Water. Fly only, with 4 fish catch limit. Enquire – Rod Box, 52 St George's Street, Winchester. Tel: (0962) 713458.

Chilbolton. Dry fly fishing permits available from May to September. Weekday tickets £35, weekends and Bank Holidays £40. Enquiries during office hours to Chilbolton (026474) 243.

Andover, River Anton. Rooksbury Mill Fishery has one mile of this important tributary (plus two lakes) stocked with Browns and Rainbows. Dry fly and upstream nymph fishing only. No wading. Hours: 8 a.m. to dusk. Tel: Andover (0264) 52921.

Stockbridge. Half-mile, well-stocked with Browns and Rainbows (to over 7 lb), held by Greyhound Hotel. Day ticket £15, or £25 for exclusive beat. Tel: Andover (0264) 810833.

Bossington. Eight beats on this estate water, offering excellent fly fishing. No wading. Three fish day limit. Day permit £40. Enquire to Rod Box (see under Middleton above).

Romsey. Stretch of river in Memorial Park with Salmon, Sea Trout and Browns run by Test Valley Council. Day tickets £7.60, limited to two rods per day, by post from Council Offices (Fishing Permits), Dutton Road, Romsey. Tel: (0794) 515117. Very occasionally permit opportunities arise for the Broadlands Estate water below the town. Apply to Estate Office for further information.

River Test
Hampshire

Recommended Flies: March Brown, Gold Ribbed Hare's Ear, Alder, Hawthorn, Mayfly, Greenwell's Glory, Houghton Ruby, Dark Olive Quill, Ginger Quill, Caperer, Iron Blue, Yellow Dun, Red Palmer. Most nymphs and variants are useful.

Local knowledge: Very alkaline water, thick bankside and underwater weed growth combines to give the perfect environment for the great variety and richness of insect life. Fly hatches can indeed be spectacular on this generally swift and silent river. A very cautious approach is needed, and wading is rarely advisable, even if allowed. Especially on bright days, it is necessary to literally stalk a particular trout. Polaroid glasses can be worthwhile. The Test so often provides the ultimate in chalk stream fishing.

Croxley Hall Waters Fishery

Rickmansworth, Herts.   Tel: Rickmansworth (0923) 778290.
Proprietors: Mr. and Mrs. Sansom-Timms.

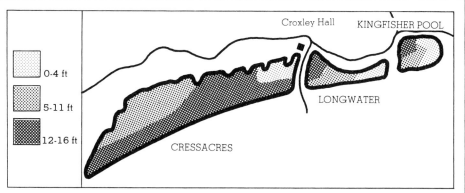

There are three lakes, Cressacres (7½ acres), Longwater (2 acres) and Kingfisher (1 acre), set in the country surroundings of Croxley Hall farm. Aquatic life includes shrimps, sticklebacks, damselflies, sedge, buzzers and caenis. Expansive watercress beds.

Facilities: Shelter with tea and coffee-making facility. Car park. Toilets. Permit and Thames Water Authority rod licences issued on site.

Season: March 17th to October 31st (summer). Hours: 9 a.m. to 9.30 p.m. or dusk.
November 1st to November 27th (winter). Hours: 9 a.m. to dusk. Due to an expansion programme in 1984, and into 1985, including the construction of an additional lake, the fishery will only be open at weekends and Bank Holidays (while the work is in progress).

Charges: Day £12. Season permits and other ticket prices to be announced when work is completed.

Day catch limit: 4 fish.

Restrictions: Fly fishing only. No wading or standing in the water. Maximum hook size 10. Single fly only up to July 1. All fish caught to be killed.

Annual catch rate: 2.5 fish per rod.

Recommended flies: Damsel Nymphs, Stickfly, Green Nymph, Viva, Dunkeld, Whisky, Polystickle, Muddlers (various), Dog Nobblers, Ace of Spades.

Local knowledge: The Longwater lake is reserved for dry fly and nymph on floating line – and the damselfly nymph has been most successful. Cressacres Lake fishes well to lures, wetflies, and nymphs.

Bayham Fishery

Lamberhurst, Kent.
Tel: Lamberhurst (0892) 890276. Proprietor: John Parkman.

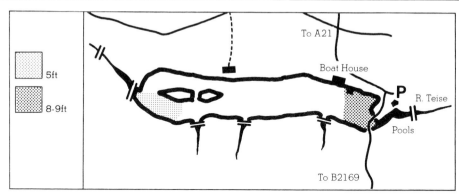

The fishery consists of a lake of 16 acres, and four pools on the RIver Teise. Set in the picturesque surroundings of the Teise valley between Lamberhurst and Tunbridge Wells. The opening of the fishery coincided with the 1980 season, and a large number of quality fish have since been caught. The lake, which is fed by the Teise, is rich in aquatic life; there is a considerable hatch of damselflies, plus mayflies, pond olives (early season), and the great red sedge (late season). In addition, there are plentiful dragonfly, small black midge, and small bleak. The bed of the lake is thick with swan mussel. In the cascade pools on the river there are ample supplies of shrimp, corixa and snails.

Facilities:	Comfortable lodge, refreshments (tea, coffee, soup). Flies and small items of tackle. Ample car parking space.
Season:	April 3rd to October 31st. Hours: Day tickets 7.30 a.m. till dusk. Season permits: sunrise till dusk.
Rods per day:	35 maximum around the banks of lake and river.
Charge:	Season: £100 to £300, depending on the amount of fishing required. Day £15, half-day £10, and evening £5.
Day limit:	Full day 5 fish, half-day 3 fish, evening 2 fish.
Boats:	6 rowing. Cost: £7 full day double, £5 half-day double, £5 full day single, £3.50 half-day single.
Restrictions:	Fly fishing only. No wading. Maximum hook size a long-shanked 10. Dog nobblers and similar large lures are not encouraged.
Stocking policy:	Mainly rainbows, over 1½ lb (many over 3 lb, with percentage of 8 lb to 10 lb-plus), also some browns.
Annual catch rate:	(1983) 2.7 per rod average. 3,524 anglers caught 9,501 fish. Of this 929 were over 3 lb.
Recommended flies:	Mayfly Nymph, Green Nymph, Olive Nymph, Pheasant Tail Nymph, Black & Claret, Whisky, Damselfly Nymph
Local knowledge:	John Parkman: The fishery is noted for large fish, and most have been taken by anglers employing 'specimen hunting' tactics. When the water is clear, time is spent looking, with polaroid glasses, and once a big fish is spotted, it is concentrated upon.

Enjoy your leisure time

Fishing at Southern Water Trout Fisheries

Providing some of the finest sport in the south, amidst beautiful countryside at:

Bewl Bridge and Ardingly Reservoirs

Season – April to October.

Whole and weekday season and various day permits available. Boats for hire, flycasting courses, tackle and flies, competitions and prizes.

Free information leaflets from:
**The Manager
Bewl Bridge Reservoir
Lamberhurt
Tunbridge Wells
Kent TN3 8JH
Tel: Lamberhurst (0892) 890661**

Bewl Bridge Fishery

Near Lamberhurst, Kent.
Tel: Lamberhurst (0892) 890352. Controlled by Southern Water Authority.

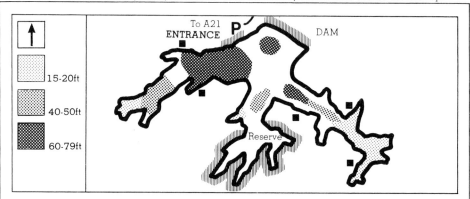

A reservoir of 770 acres located in open country 1½ miles south of Lamberhurst on the A21. Abundant fish fry, sticklebacks, sedge, midge, and buzzers.

Facilities:	Tackle shop stocking flies and lures useful for this water. There is a self-service permit issuing unit. The sailing clubhouse sometimes available for cooked meals and licenced bar.
Season:	April 3rd to October 31st inclusive. Hours: sunrise to 1 hour after sunset or 10 p.m., whichever is earlier.
Charges:	Season £195, weekday season £150. Day £6, juniors £4.50, beginners £3, evening £4.50. Permits include SWA rod licence.
Day limit:	6 fish, junior 4, beginners 2, evening 4.
Boats:	50. Motor-boat – day £8, evening £5.50. Pulling boat – day (double) £6, (single) £4.50. Evening (double) £4.50, (single) £3.50. Available from 9 a.m. Advance booking advisable.
Restrictions:	Fly fishing only. No trolling. No person under 14 years allowed unless accompanied by adult. All fish caught to be killed.
Stocking policy:	Rainbows and browns. 1983 – 32,000 stocked from the fishery's own hatchery.
Catch rate:	49,765 fish by 23,329 anglers.
Recommended flies:	Viva, Buzzers, Black Chenille, Olives, Sedges, Damsel-fly Nymph, Muddlers, Dog Nobblers.
Local knowledge:	The 15-mile perimeter provides extensive interesting bank fishing. Care is needed when wading, as there are a few deep holes around the bank. Because of the irregular shape whichever direction the wind is blowing a sheltered section can be found. During most of the season floating lines and slow sinkers are best, and nymph fishing can be effective throughout the day. The record rainbow is 10 lb 2 oz (1983) taken on a dog nobbler.

River Teise
Kent

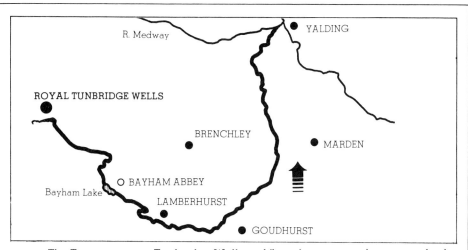

The Teise rises near Tunbridge Wells and flows for twenty miles in a northerly direction through Lamberhurst, to join the Medway near Yalding. The upper reaches are well-stocked with brown and rainbow trout, whereas the more sedate lower reaches are largely populated with coarse fish.

Season: April 1st to September 30th.

Tunbridge Wells. The Hoathley Fishery (including the Bartley Mill stream) is situated between Lamberhurst and Tunbridge Wells. Wild Browns, as well as stocked Rainbows and Browns. Any legal method allowed. Season permit £40, day ticket £2 – issued on site.

Lamberhurst. A long and attractive stretch, including pools and cascades. The river feeds a superb 16 acre lake. The fishery is regularly stocked, and large rainbows are taken. Fly only. 7.30 a.m. till dark. Day ticket (inclusive of river and lake) £15 for a five fish limit; half-day £10 for three fish limit. Further details from John Parkman, Bayham Lake Fishery, Lamberhurst, Kent. Tel: (0892) 890276.

Recommended flies: Traditional patterns of wet flies in smaller sizes, Green Nymph, Pheasant Tail, Sedges, Amber Nymph. Flashy patterns when water is coloured.

Local knowledge: This small river requires a cautious approach. Where the banks are clear, wading should be avoided (wading is prohibited at Bayham). However, there are stretches where the river narrows sharply with high banks, making wading essential for any ease of casting either upstream or downstream. The Teise is inclined to colour very quickly following rain.

Pennine Fishery

Littleborough, Lancashire.   Proprietors: R. Davies
Tel: (0706) 78325.   and C. M. Ditchfield.

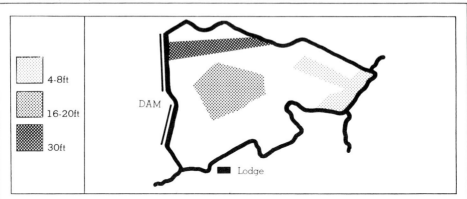

This small reservoir of 2¼ acres, better known as Calderbrook Lake, provides exciting fishing for large trout. This is an old established water, first formed in 1863. It is rich in aquatic life with prolific hatches of the various species of Sedge. There are also Black Gnats, Midges, minnows, sticklebacks, tadpoles, shrimps and the bed of the lake is thick with caddis larvae.

Facilities: There is a lodge for shelter in bad weather. Artificial flies available, and permits on site. Fly fishing tuition by arrangement.

Season: Open all year, except for two weeks in February. Hours – Summer, 5 a.m. to 9 p.m. Winter, dawn to dusk.

Rods per day: 26 maximum at one time during fly season.

Charges: Season, by arrangement. Day – 8 hours £10. Session (4 hours) £6. A Lancashire Water Authority rod licence required.

Day limit: 4 fish, session 2 fish. Fish may be returned. Further permits may be purchased.

Boats: None.

Restrictions: Fly fishing only to end of September. Barbless hooks preferred. No wading (dangerous because of up to 8 feet of water close in). No groundbaiting.

Stocking policy: Daily on put-and-take basis. Always 2,000 fish in the lake. Rainbows, browns, occasional brook trout. Fish from 1½ lb up to 14 lb.

Annual catch rate: 2¾ lb average weight.

Recommended flies:
Black & Peacock Spider, Suspender Buzzer, Partridge & Orange, Baby Doll, Butcher, Marabou (white, black and orange). Most lures work well early in the year.

Local knowledge: The deep water channel extending from the dam wall is best fished with fast sinking line, and there is a good chance of a large fish. In 1982 47 trout over 10 lb caught. In 1983 there were 60 over 6 lb, and 6 over 8 lb. Heaviest fish a rainbow 11 lb 4 oz (record) and the best 4 fish limit 33 lb. Lures, even dog nobblers, on size 8 hooks are effective early in the season. (After September 30 any method fishing allowed for rainbows).

River Ribble
Yorks and Lancs

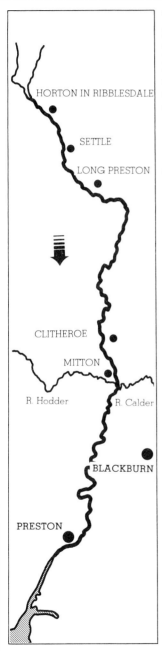

HORTON IN RIBBLESDALE

SETTLE

LONG PRESTON

CLITHEROE

MITTON

R. Hodder   R. Calder

BLACKBURN

PRESTON

The Ribble rises at Ribblehead on Whernside mountain, and flows south for over 50 miles, through Settle and Preston to the Irish Sea. Important tributaries include the Hodder and Calder which join the main river at Hodderfoot and Calderfoot respectively. Below these confluences near Clitheroe, coarse fish predominate, and the main game-fishing waters are upstream with good sport for salmon, sea trout, trout and grayling.
Rod licence required: NWWA, Rivers Division, P.O. Box 12, New Town House, Buttermarket Street, Warrington WA1 2QG.

Seasons: Salmon February 1st to October 15th; Sea Trout – May 1st to October 15th; Brown Trout – March 15th to September 30th.

Ribblehead. From source to Helwith Bridge – 12 miles held by Manchester A.A. for members only. No day tickets. Contact P. Mellow, 126 Boothroyden Road, Blackley, Manchester.

Edisford Bridge. Permit enquiries to the Warden, Edisford Camping Site. Ribble Valley Council also run a short stretch of fishing – tel: Clitheroe 25111. A further stretch of water offers day tickets – enquiries to Ken Varey – tel: Clitheroe 23267.

Long Preston. Trout, Grayling. Long Preston Angling Club has water with permits from local tackle dealers.

Clitheroe. Brown Trout, Sea Trout. Clitheroe A.A. has 3 miles of Ribble and 1 mile of Lune. Visitors only if accompanied by member. Enquiries: J. Hodgson, 83 Sparth Gardens, Clayton-le-Moors, Nr. Accrington.

Mitton. One of the best fishing areas on the river. NWWA controls the Mitton fishery which is very good for Sea Trout. Permits £4 per day (8 a.m. to midnight) until July 31st, and £5.50 thereafter, from Mrs. M. Haynes, Mitton Hall Farm, Mitton, Nr. Whalley. Permits (60p) also issued for further NWWA water, from Mitton to Calderfoot. Brown trout permits (£1.10) available from Mrs. Haynes for stretch from Mitton Bridge to Hodderfoot (4 rod limit).

Recommended flies: Alexandra, Peter Ross, Partridge and Orange, Grouse and Claret, Dunkeld

Local knowledge: Sea trout fishing is usually best as the light fades. The Ribble tends to have a good back-end run of salmon, mostly in the 10 lb range, but with some fish up to 30 lb. The upper reaches of the main river and the Hodder hold good grayling stocks (to 2 lb or more).

Eyebrook Reservoir

Caldecott, Leics.
Tel: Rockingham (0536) 770264.

Run by Corby & District
Water Company.

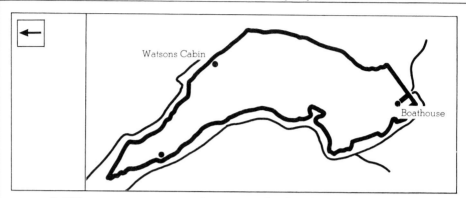

Watsons Cabin

Boathouse

A 400-acre reservoir situated in a natural valley. It is fed by the Eye Brook. A perimeter road runs right round the lake. Extensive weed growth. Aquatic life includes daphnia, Sedge, Midge, Corixa, snails, shrimp etc.

Facilities:	Large car park. Fishing hut. Permits on site.
Season:	April 1st to September 30th inclusive. Hours: from 8 a.m.
Rods per day:	No limit.
Charges:	Season – £135. Weekly – £20. Day – £5. Evening – £2.50.
Boats:	24. £5 per day, £3 evening. For 9 boat bookings paid in advance get one booking free.
Restrictions:	Fly fishing only. No shooting head lines.
Stocking policy:	Regular stocking with mainly rainbows of around 1 lb.
Annual catch rate:	(1982) 22,5000 fish. 1.5 per rod.
Recommended flies:	
	Mallard & Claret, Black & Peacock Spider, Invicta, Ginger Quill, Corixa, Appetizer, Missionary, Whisky, Badger Matuka, Muddlers (various), Viva.
Local knowledge:	Be prepared to ring the changes on tactics. There are times when fish are preoccupied on feeding on roach fry – try a sink-tip line with Missionary or Peter Ross. If the fish are feeding on sedge – then make another change! The records are good: Brown 10 lb 2 oz, rainbow 8 lb 10 oz.

Rutland Water
EMPINGHAM,
LEICS.

Tel: Empingham (078086) 770.
Controlled by Anglian Water Authority.

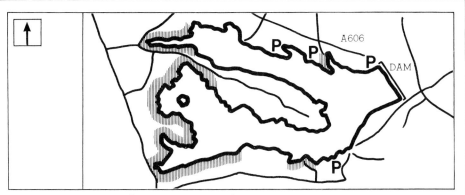

A comparatively new reservoir of some 3,000 acres, created by flooding a valley. The water is pumped in from the Rivers Welland and Nene. Some exceptional brown trout have been caught. Some 24 miles of shore-line, most of which is wadeable.

Aquatic life is varied with snails, shrimps, louse, daphnia, buzzers, extensive hatches of sedge (various), plus roach and perch fry.

Facilities: Fishing lodge situated at Whitwell where day tickets and Anglia Water Authority rod licences may be purchased. There are toilets and changing rooms. There is also a facility for disabled anglers. Several large car parks around the perimeter of the lake.

Season: 1/4 to 29/10. Hours: one hour before sunrise (but not before 4.30 am) to one hour after sunset.

Charges: Full season permit £228, mid-week season £174. Day £6.30, evening £4.20. Half-price for juniors. Seven day holiday permit £30.

Day catch limit: 8 fish. Evening 4 fish.

Boats: Motor boats-hire charge £17 day, £10 evening. Pulling boat – £7.50 day, £4.50 evening. Advance booking is always advisable.

Restrictions: Fly only fishing. Trolling only in one particular area.

Stocking policy: Rainbows and browns. A very large pre-season stock, and further stocking at intervals throughout the season.

Annual catch rate: (1983) 2.75 average per rod. 60,000 fish, which includes some 15,000 browns.

Recommended flies: Soldier Palmer, Whiskey, Missionary, Chenille (black or white), Dog Nobblers, mini-Dog Nobblers (any of the various colour schemes), Baby Doll, Jersey Herd, Muddlers (various), Black Matuka, Badger Matuka, Black Lure, White Marabou, Gold Ribbed Hare's Ear, Pheasant Tail Nymph, Damsel Nymph, Green Nymph,

Local knowledge: Noted for big fish, with a 9 lb 12½ oz brown taken from the Normanton bank, on a yellow dog nobbler on a floating shooting head line. Also in 1983 two browns of 10 lb 5 oz, and a rainbow of 9 lb 6 oz. The record brown of 12½ lb was taken in 1982.

Thornton Fishery

Near Leicester.
Tel: (053021) 7107.   Controlled by Cambrian Fisheries.

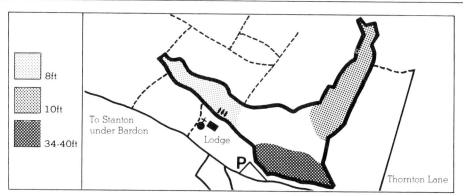

A fairly new trout fishery, though an established reservoir of 75 acres. First opened for trout fishing in 1975, it offers interesting angling with a chance of a large fish. There is ample casting opportunity from the natural banks. Aquatic life includes good hatches of sedge, buzzers, corixa, bloodworm and coarse fish fry.

Facilities:	Comfortable lodge. Large car parking area. Permits issued on site. A perimeter track affords access to most of the fishing bank.
Season:	March 7th to April 1st for boats only. April 1st to October 15th boats and bank. October 16th to November 30th boats only. Hours: 8 a.m. bank, 9 a.m. boats, to 1 hour after sunset.
Rods per day:	60 maximum.
Charges:	Season: £130 (7 days), £90 (5 days Monday to Friday). OAPs concessionary permit £90. Day £5, half-day £3.
Day limit:	6 fish, half-day 4 fish.
Boats:	12 (rowing). £4 per person, half-day £2.50.
Restrictions:	Fly fishing only. No wading. No fishing from the dam.
Stocking policy:	Pre-season, then weekly with rainbows and browns to a season total of up to 15,000.
Annual catch rate:	1.75 per rod average.
Recommended flies:	Missionary, Appetizer, Black Chenille, White Chenille, Sweeny Todd, Viva, Butcher, Mallard & Claret, Silver Invicta, Pheasant Tail Nymph, Green/Brown Nymph, Black Buzzers.
Local knowledge:	Slow sinking line and small lure always worth trying. In summer a floating line and nymph. A shooting head line can be helpful from the bank. With adequate wind, drift-fishing from the boat in traditional loch-style often produces results. Largest fish – 9 lb 2 oz rainbow in 1983.

Toft Newton Reservoir

Market Rasen, Lincolnshire.
Tel: (0673) 7453. Controlled by Anglian Water Authority.

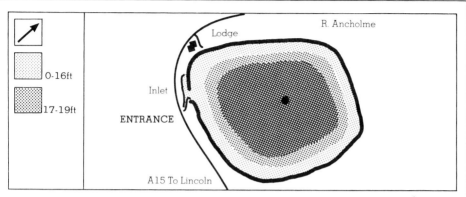

A 41 acre concrete banked reservoir, with a fairly even bottom with a depth of about 20 ft. The reservoir used to be rich in insect life before it was completely drained early in 1983. Various insects are now re-establishing.

Facilities:	Portacabin-style fishing lodge with seats, tables, washing and toilet facility. Tickets are issued on site.
Season:	April 13th to October 29th. Hours: one hour before sunrise to one hour after sunset.
Rods per day:	60 maximum.
Charges:	Season permits – enquire Fisheries Officer, A.W.A., Lincolnshire River Division, 50 Wide Bargate, Boston. Day ticket – Type A £6, Type B £3.80. Juniors half-price.
Day catch limit:	8 fish (type A) and 2 fish (Type B). A further day ticket is available. Anglian Water Authority rod licence required.
Boats:	None.
Restrictions:	Fly fishing only. No wading. No more than three hooks to be used.
Stocking policy:	At regular intervals with rainbows, and a lesser number of brown trout.
Annual catch rate:	(1983) 8,000 trout at an average 2.4 per rod, with fish up to 7 lb.
Recommended flies:	Black Chenille, Muddlers (black and white), Viva, Baby Doll, Appetiser, Missionary, Matuka, Whisky, Sweeney Todd, Amber Nymph, Orange Nymph, Corixa, Sedge Pupa, Gold Ribbed Hare's Ear.
Local knowledge:	In early season a sinking line with small lures is most effective. In mid to late season nymphs are first favourite, and on some late evenings the dry fly is worth fishing.

Barn Elms Fishery

Barnes, London.
Tel: 01-748 3423.   Controlled by Thames Water Authority.

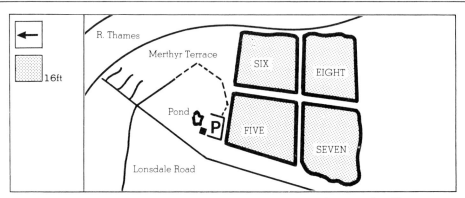

There are four reservoirs in this group, situated near the Thames at Hammersmith Bridge. The reservoirs are numbered '5' (24 acres), '6' (20 acres), '7' (23 acres), and '8' (18 acres). These old established reservoirs are generally square-shaped with concrete banks. Among the aquatic life are snails, sticklebacks, daphnia, sedge and prolific hatches of buzzers.

Facilities: Car park, rest room, toilets, plus a track leading to the reservoirs for the disabled.

Season: March 15th to November 30th inclusive. Hours: 7.30 a.m. to half-hour after sunset.

Rods per day: 200 maximum.

Charges: Season: none. Book of ten day tickets £55.70, ten part-day £43.50 – (which is payment for nine – one free). Day – summer: £6.30, half-day £4.80, evening £2.60. Winter: (from October) – day £4.80, half-day £2.60. There are reduced rates for OAPs, juniors and disabled. Permits and rod licences issued by gatekeeper.

Day limit: 6 fish, part-day 4, evening 2.

Boats: 16, rowing only, but only on No. 5 reservoir.

Restrictions: There are two reservoirs available for fly fishing only – Nos. 5 and 7. Any legal method is permitted on No. 8 (N.B. Check for changes).

Stocking policy: Daily in early season, then at regular intervals for the rest of the season with rainbows and browns.

Annual catch rate: 2.2 on No. 5, 1.7 on No. 7, 2.0 on No. 8.

Recommended flies: Small lures, such as Whisky, Viva, Black Chenille, Appetizer, White Ghost, Muddlers, Suspender Buzzer and various nymphs.

Local knowledge: Chris King: Usually only three of the reservoirs are open for fishing. Early in the season it is best to use a sinking line, or a floater with extra long leader, to fish a lure deep – black lures being favourite. In summer a floater to fish nymphs is most effective. If you have the bank to yourself, try casting along the margin into the corners where the fish tend to concentrate. Occasionally rainbows from 5 lb to 8 lb are taken.

Walthamstow Reservoirs

Tottenham, London.
Tel: 01-808 1527.   Controlled by Thames Water Authority.

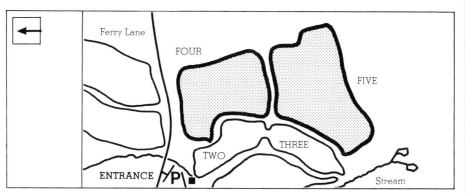

There are several old established reservoirs in this group, in Ferry Lane, London. But only two of the lakes are reserved for trout fishing. These are No. 4 (30 acres), and No. 5 (41 acres). The nearest railway stations are Blackhorse Lane and Tottenham Hale. Aquatic life includes various sedges, Chironomids, Daphnia, snails, sticklebacks and coarse fish fry.

Facilities:	Car parking area, toilets, a self-service permit kiosk. Trout fishing and casting instruction by arrangement. Special concessionary arrangements can also be made for a novice accompanied by an experienced angler.
Season:	March 15th to November 15th. Hours: 6.30 a.m. or sunrise, whichever is the later, to half-hour after sunset.
Rods per day:	Dependent on conditions.
Charges:	Day permit £6.50, part-day £5 from 1 p.m. (2 p.m. from the start of British summer time). Concessions for OAPs, juniors and disabled.
Day catch limit:	6 fish, part-day 4, evening 2.
Restrictions:	Fly fishing only on reservoir No. 5. Catch returns should be submitted before leaving the reservoir site. Permits will not be issued to children under eight years of age.
Stocking policy:	Total for the season 34,000 rainbows, 4,000 browns – on a regular basis.
Annual catch rate:	2.2 fish per rod average by fly fishing. 2.0 any method.
Recommended flies:	Early season – Chironomid Buzzers, Damsel Nymphs, Olive patterns, and such lures as Viva, Baby Dolls and Dog Nobblers. Mid to late season – Wet fly patterns like Mallard & Clareet, Coachman, Wickhams Fancy
Local knowledge:	Neil Harris—'When the fish are feeding on daphnia the most effective "artificial" is a hot orange pattern, fished in the surface film. During summer months a seal's fur body of a sedge pupa pattern is always worth trying. During summer evenings keep a low profile and when possible cast along the bank with a floating line and one of the sedge patterns.'

Pitsford Reservoir

Near Northampton,
Tel: Northampton (0604) 781350. Controlled by Anglian Water Authority.

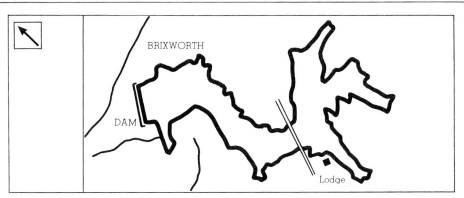

This is flooded valley reservoir, with a water area of some 739 acres. The landscaped banks are convenient for wading, and comfortable to fish from. The water holds varied aquatic life, including various sedges, buzzers and midge, and there are large hatches of pond olives. There are also shrimp, louse, snails, daphnia, minnows, sticklebacks, roach and perch fry.

Facilities: There is a fishing lodge, W.C. and car park. Tickets and rod licences are issued on site.

Season: April 1st to October 29th inclusive. Hours: from one hour before sunrise to one hour after sunset.

Rods per day: No limit.

Charges: Full season £120, mid-week season £100. The seven day holiday permit is £20. Day ticket £4, evening (after 5 p.m.) £2.70 (after 4 p.m. in April and September). Juniors half-price.

Day catch limit: 8 fish.

Boats: Hire charge for motor boat – day £12, evening £8. Pulling boat – day £8, evening £5. All boats must be booked in advance.

Restrictions: Fly fishing only. No additional day ticket issued.

Stocking policy: About 5,000 browns stocked at end of season to over-winter. Then a total of some 20,000 rainbows at regular intervals during the season.

Annual catch rate: (1983 season) 2.22 fish per rod. Recorded total 11,146 fish. Largest rainbow 4 lb 13 oz; brown 4 lb 13 oz.

Recommended flies: Small dog nobblers generally effective. Other lures such as Black Lure, Viva, Sweeny Todd, Zulu, Muddler, Minnow, Badger Matuka.

Local knowledge: During mid-season dry fly fishing often proves effective, especialy during evenings. Also successful are Olives and sedges in small size patterns. Nymphs, weighted and unweighted, are always worth trying. Bank anglers do well with floating line, or sink-tip, and nymphs or small lures – depending on prevailing conditions. Boat anglers often do well fishing the drift with a 'team of three' patterns.

Ravensthorpe Reservoir

Near Northampton.
Tel: Northampton (0604) 781350. Controlled by Anglian Water Authority.

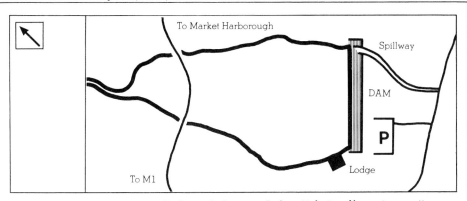

Facilities:	Fishing lodge, and day ticket self-service unit.
Season:	April 1st to October 29th inclusive. Hours: 1 hour before sunrise to 1 hour after sunset.
Rods per day:	No limit.
Charges:	Season – £140. Seven day holiday permit – £20. Day £4.50, evening after 5 p.m. (4 p.m. April and September) £3. Juniors half-price. Season and seven day permits also include fishing at Pitsford Reservoir.
Day limit:	8 fish.
Boats:	8 pulling – day £8, evening £5. To be booked at Pitsford Reservoir. Tel: (0604) 781350.
Restrictions:	Fly fishing only. No additional day tickets issued.
Stocking policy:	About 7,000 fish, mainly rainbows, with small number of browns. Average size 12 inches.
Annual catch rate:	(1983) 2.05 fish per rod.
Recommended flies:	Black Lure, Black Muddler, Sweeny Todd, Appetizer, Baby Doll, Viva, Zulu, Sedge patterns, Buzzers, Pheasant Tail nymph.
Local knowledge:	White Baby Doll, White Muddler, and other white coloured lures often successful. Orange Buzzers, Green Buzzers and Black Buzzers are always consistent. In mid-season all the sedge patterns are worth fishing.

Ringstead Grange

Ringstead, Northants.
Tel: Wellingborough (0933) 622960. Proprietor: Harold Foster.

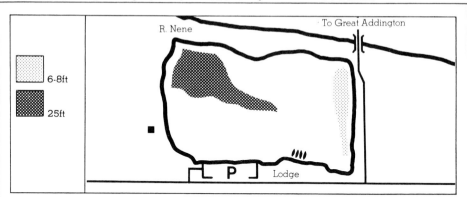

This stream fed ex-gravel pit of 36 acres is located on the A604, just 4 miles from Thrapston. There are large hatches of sedge and buzzers. Thick weed growth in summer.

Facilities:	Fishing Lodge, car park.
Season:	April 4th to October 29th inclusive. Hours: 7 a.m. to sunset.
Charges:	Day £5, evening £3.50.
Day limit:	6 fish, evening 3 fish. Trout caught can be returned.
Boats:	6 rowing. £7 (for 2 persons), evening £3.
Restrictions:	Fly fishing only. The weight of 2 lb plus fish must be recorded. No wading.
Stocking policy:	Over 17,000 annually. Mainly rainbows stocked on a weekly basis. Fish from $1\frac{1}{4}$ lb to 15 lb stocked. Some brown and brook trout.
Annual catch rate:	2.5 per rod average.
Recommended flies:	
	Black Dog Nobblers, Muddler, Viva, Invicta, Wonderbug, Grey Duster, Greenwell's Glory, Pheasant Tail Nymph, Buzzers (various).
Local knowledge:	Floating and sink-tip lines generally most effective to fish nymphs. In summer, dry fly works well, fished close to the weed growth. There are very large fish, and the records are: rainbow – 14 lb 4 oz, brown – 6 lb 11 oz and brook trout – 4 lb 12 oz.

Bakethin Water

Near Bellingham, Northumberland.
Tel: Bellingham (0660) 40398. Controlled by Northumbrian Water Authority.

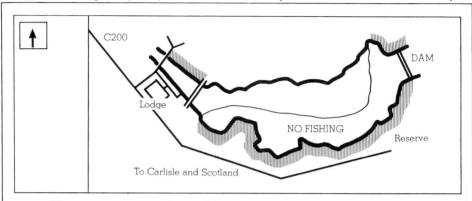

This is a comparatively small reservoir of 168 acres situated at the shallow end of the vast Kielder Water. Both reservoirs are linked, and at certain times there is a free passage of water, and fish, between the two. There is extensive aquatic life, including a huge number of snails, abundant hatches of gnats and midges, plus sedge and fish fry.

Facilities:	Fishing lodge. Car park.
Season:	May 1st to September 30th inclusive.
Rods per day:	50.
Charges:	Weekly permit £7, day £4.50, evening £3. Northumbrian Water Authority rod licence required.
Day catch limit:	8 fish (over 9 inches). Catch and release fishing is allowed.
Boats:	6 (rowing); day charge £5, evening £3.
Restrictions:	Fly fishing only. No wading. No fishing in the nature conservation area.
Stocking policy:	Pre-season with about 6,000 brown trout of 9 inches to 12 inches. Also rainbows, with a few up to 8 lb stocked.
Annual catch rate:	2.5 per rod average. (More browns than rainbows).
Recommended flies:	Invicta, Sweeney Todd, March Brown, Baby Doll, Muddler Minnow, Black Lure, Greenwell's Glory, Pheasant Tail Nymph, various sedges and sedge pupa. Most of the traditional wet flies are worth trying.
Local knowledge:	The area where the River North Tyne enters the reservoir is noted for good fishing. Fishing the drift is the popular style with most boat anglers.

River Coquet
Northumberland

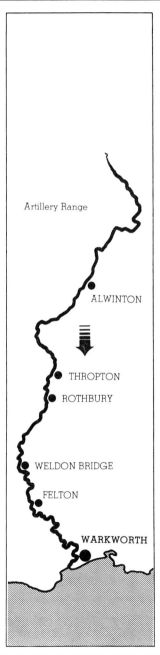

The Coquet rises high in the Cheviot Hills and flows through Rothbury and after some 40 miles reaches the North Sea at Warkworth Harbour. It is a noted game fishing river, with salmon moving up from February onwards. The Coquet is, however, generally regarded as a 'late' river, with a good run of salmon and sea trout well into October. Brown trout average around half a pound, with a reasonable number of much heavier fish. Rod licence required: Northumberland Water Authority, Regent Centre, Gosforth, Newcastle.

Seasons: Salmon – February 1st to October 31st; Sea Trout – April 4th to October 31st; Brown Trout – March 22nd to September 30th.

Rothbury. Salmon, Sea Trout, Brown Trout. The Rothbury and Thropton Angling Club has several miles of excellent water at Rothbury, and a further stretch at Thropton (plus some tributary fishing). Permits from Tackle Shop, High Street, Rothbury. Northumbrian Anglers' Federation also has water; details from Northumbrian A.F. Hon. Sec., Mr. P. Hall, 3 Ridley Place, Newcastle NE1 8JQ.

Whitton. A 2½ mile stretch of single bank fishing for Sea Trout and Salmon is offered free to residents of the Whitton Farmhouse Hotel – tel: (0669) 20811.

Weldon Bridge. Salmon and Trout permits available from the Anglers Arms Hotel.

Felton and Acklington. Salmon and Trout fishing from Felton Bridge down to the dam held by the Northumbrian A.F. (see Rothbury above). Trout permits are issued at Felton Post Office.

Warkworth. Most of the water here is owned by the Duke of Northumberland, and a large section of it is leased to the Northumbrian A.F. (see Rothbury above). Trout permits are issued by several distributors in the area and also in Newcastle.

Recommended flies: Trout – Peter Ross, Butcher, Zulu, Mallard & Claret, and some of the small lure patterns.
Sea Trout – Blue Terror, Alexandra, Silver Sedge, Blue Zulu, Kingfisher Butcher, and small flashy lure patterns. Salmon – Green Highlander, Mar Lodge, Thunder and Lightning, Dunkeld, Stoat Tail, Hairy Mary, and most tube fly patterns.

Local knowledge: There is usually a large run of sea trout in September and October. In 1983 sea trout up to 14 lb were taken.

Kielder Water

Bellingham, Northumberland. Controlled by the Northumbrian
Tel: Bellingham (0660) 40398.   Water Authority.

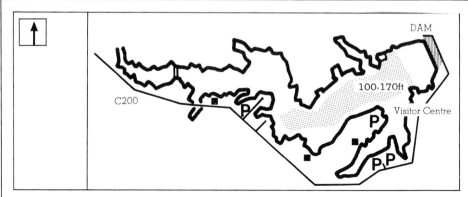

At 2,684 acres Kielder is reckoned to be the largest man-made lake in
Europe. It was opened for fishing in 1982. Kielder is situated in a forest area of
the Cheviots just four or five miles from the Scottish border. There are some 27
miles of shoreline which offers the bank angler a variety of fishing areas. Water
life is rich and varied by way of the five main feeder streams, with sedges,
shrimps, snails, gnat larvae and fish fry.

Facilities: Fishing lodge. Car parks. Toilets. Self-service permit
                        issuing machines.

Season: June 1st to September 30th.

Rods per day: No limit.

Charges: Day ticket £4.50 including Northumbrian Water
                        Authority rod licence. Evening permit £3.

Day catch limit: 8 fish.

Boats: 25. Motor boats, moored at the Matthews Linn centre.
                        Hire charge, day £10, evening £6.

Restrictions: Fly fishing, and worm. No fishing from the dam or valve
                        tower.

Stocking policy: Originally stocked with 250,000 trout. But no set
                        stocking plan. Numbers are expected to be maintained
                        by brown trout spawning in the feeder streams.

Annual catch rate: An estimaed 2.0 fish per rod average.

Recommended flies:
                        March Brown, Invicta, Sweeney Todd, Baby Doll,
                        Muddler, Zulu, Matuka, Black Lure, Viva. Also worth
                        trying are Sedge Pupa, and various nymphs such as
                        Damsel Nymph, Mayfly Nymph, Green Nymph,
                        Corixa.

Local knowledge: The shallows where most of the feeder streams come in
                        are usually most productive and best fished by floating
                        line and nymph. Boat anglers do well on the drift, using
                        the loch style with a point fly and two droppers.

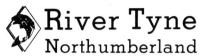

River Tyne
Northumberland

River Tyne
Northumberland

The North and South Tyne rivers descend from the hills to meet near Hexham, and thereafter form the River Tyne itself, which flows on through Corbridge, Prudhoe and Newcastle to the North Sea at Tynemouth. The system provides reasonable sport with trout and grayling, while salmon and sea trout runs have improved in line with pollution controls.

Seasons: Salmon – February 1st to October 31st; Sea Trout – April 4th to October 31st; Brown Trout – March 22nd to September 30th.

Alston. Section of upper reaches of South Tyne controlled by Alston and District Angling Association. Permits from F. Graham (Hon. Sec.), Brownside, Alston, or D. Jackson, High Market Place, Alston, or Struthers, Front Street, Alston.
A four-mile stretch is also available from Defty-Macnaney, The Research and Development Co. Ltd., Garrighill, Alston. Tel: (0498) 81537.

Haltwhistle. Salmon, Sea Trout, Brown Trout. Permits for South Tyne – £5 per week (to July 31st) and £15 per week thereafter – from Greggs Sports, Main Street, Haltwhistle. The local Haltwhistle Angling Association has six miles from Bardon Mill to Featherstone Castle.

Haydon Bridge. Section controlled by South Tyne Angling Association. Visitors' permits issued (up to August 31st) by J. Moore (Hon. Sec.), 24 Strother Close, Haydon Bridge.

Falstone. Trout permits available from Black Cock Inn, Falstone.

Otterburn. Fishing on the tributary Rede can be had with tickets from Percy Arms Hotel and Otterburn Towers Hotel.

Bellingham. 4½ miles of the North Tyne held by the Bellingham Angling Club. Trout (fly only) and Salmon. Six trout limit. Contact – T. Armstrong, 24 Westlands, Bellingham.

Chollerford. George Hotel has stretch of North Tyne for trout for residents at £2 per day. Permits also issued by Percy Arms Hotel, Otterburn.
Hexham. Salmon, Trout, Grayling. Tickets for Tyne Green stretch of main river issued by Tynedale District Council, Prospect House, Hexham.

Ovingham. Northumberland Anglers Federation holds rights from Ovingham to Wylam. Permits from several outlets. Enquiries – P. Hall (Hon. Sec.), 3 Ridley Place, Newcastle NE1 8JQ.

Newburn. 200 yards of tidal water below bridge controlled by Big Water Angling Club. Contact – J. Creighton, 12 Bellister Grove, Fenham, Newcastle.

Recommended flies: Trout – Butcher, Peter Ross, Dunkeld, Watsons Fancy, Coachman, Zulu, various lures.
Salmon – Mar Lodge, Blue Charm, Hairy Mary, Black Mary, Spinning Jenny;

Local knowledge: The South and North Tynes are generally fast stream-like rivers, which favour dry-fly for trout, particularly on warm summer evenings. Deep pools (for instance at Haltwhistle) should be explored with lure patterns in the smaller sizes. It should be remembered that the Tyne holds brown trout up to 5 lb.

Colwick Lake

Colwick, Nottingham.
Tel: (0602) 870787.   Controlled by Nottingham City Council.

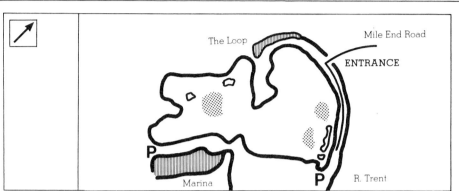

A landscaped reservoir of 65 acres situated in Colwick Park, off the Mile End Road, Nottingham. Aquatic life includes sedge, midge, dragonfly, beetles and coarse fish fry.

Facilities: A lodge, toilets, car parking. Fishing permits and Severn Trent Water Authority rod licences are issued on site.

Season: March 18th to October 15th inclusive. Hours: one hour before sunrise to one hour after sunset. Boats from 8.30 a.m. to sunset or at latest 8.30 p.m.

Rods per day: 110.

Charges: Season permit £125, day ticket £5.10, evening (after 5 p.m.) £3.15, concessionary £2.55 for juniors (under 16 years) OAPs and disabled.

Day catch limit: 4 fish up to end of May, then six fish thereafter. Evening two fish, then three fish.

Boats: Rowing boats—hire charge—full day £3.50, evening (after 6 p.m.) £2.75. Power boats—full day £7.50, evening (after 6 p.m.) £5.50.

Stocking policy: Annually with some 9,000 to 10,000 trout, consisting of mainly rainbows, with some browns and brook trout. These are stocked regularly to maintain density.

Catch rate: In 1983 some 6,775 fish were caught.

Restrictions: Fishing with natural or artificial fly only. No trolling. All fish under 10 ins to be returned.

Recommended flies:
March Brown, Greenwell's, Wickhams Fancy, Dunkeld, Stickfly, Damselfly Nymph, Mayfly Nymph, Amber Nymph, Green Nymph, Pheasant Tail Nymph. Plus lures like Missionary, Appetizer, Ace of Spades, Chenille (white and black), Blue Zulu, Viva, Dog Nobbler, Frog Nobbler, Flashabou.

Local knowledge: Anglers should take care as the banks of this lake are steep in places. Slow sinking and sink-tip lines are effective at most times. Long casting often necessary from the bank. Boat anglers find fishing on the drift with two, sometimes three, flies successful.

Farmoor No.2

FARMOOR,   Tel: Oxford (0865) 863033.
NEAR OXFORD.   Controlled by Thames Water Authority.

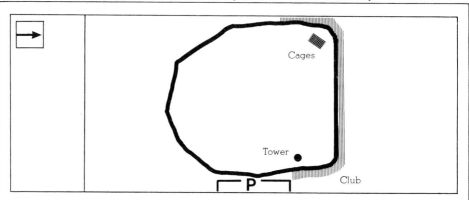

A 240 acres reservoir just five miles from Oxford. Man-made concrete bowl, with steep sloping banks. It was opened for fishing in 1978. Hatches of buzzer and sedge.

Facilities:	Clubhouse shelter, large car park, permits issued on site. Several toilets situated around reservoir perimeter.
Season:	1/4 to 30/11 inclusive. Hours: 9 am to half-hour after sunset.
Rods per day:	150.
Charges:	Day, £6.50, Part-day £4.80 including VAT. Concessionary permits are half-price for juniors (under 16), disabled, and O.A.P.'s.
Day limit:	6 fish, part-day 4.
Boats:	None.
Restrictions:	No wading. Fly fishing only. No fishing from the dam (separating the two reservoirs). Browns caught after October 1 must be returned. Only one concessionary permit per person per day–a second permit may be taken, but at the full price.
Stocking policy:	Large pre-season stock, then twice a week throughout season. Expected total: 6,000 browns, and 29,000 rainbows, mostly 12 ins to 13 ins.
Annual catch rate:	1.7 per rod average.
Recommended flies:	Dog nobblers, (various colours), Viva, Invicta, Green nymph, Sedge, Buzzers, Whiskey, Peter Ross, Appetizer, Jack Frost, Badger Matuka, Pheasant Tail, Greenwell's.
Local knowledge:	In early season the freshly stocked fish are often reckless. Long casting is a distinct advantage in mid-season period. Sinking line and lures generally successful, but summer evenings floating line and nymph effective. Always the chance of a large over-wintered fish.

Linch Hill Fishery

Stanton Harcourt, Oxon. Owners: A.R.C. Ltd.
Tel: Oxford (0865) 882215. Fishery Manager, J. H. Kalicki.

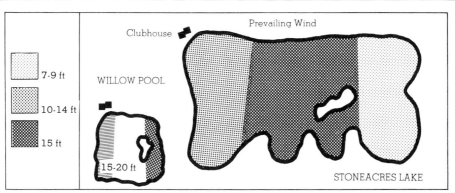

There are two lakes, Stoneacres the largest at 58 acres, and Willow Pool 12 acres. Both attractively landscaped ex-gravel pits. They are run separately with different charges and catch limits. Aquatic life: Sedge, Mayfly, Alder, Damselfly, Black Gnat, shrimp, buzzers.

Facilities:	Large car park. Clubhouse (the one at Willow Pool has a picnic area and barbeque). Permits issued on site. Large selection of artificial flies available. Fly fishing tuition by arrangement.
Season:	March 16th to October 31st. Hours: Season ticket holders from 6 a.m., day tickets from 9 a.m.
Charges:	Stoneacres, full season £135, mid-week season £90, Juniors (under 16) full season £70, mid-week £45. Day £9, evening £6. Willow, full season £300. Day £20, evening £13. Additional day tickets may be purchased.
Day limit:	Stoneacres: 5 fish, evening 3 fish. Willow: 4 fish, evening 2 fish.
Boats:	Stoneacres: 6. Willow: 2.
Restrictions:	Fly fishing only. Stoneacres: undamaged fish may be returned. Willow: all fish caught to be killed. All flies to be tied on single hooks not exceeding size 6. Tandem lures, double and treble hooks not allowed. Size limits: rainbow 12 inches, brown 14 inches. No wading. No trolling.
Stocking policy:	Stoneacres, 100 to the acre with basic stock of 12 inch fish – with some larger specimens. Willow, stocked with extra large rainbows, average weight 4 lb plus.
Recommended flies:	Dog Nobblers (various), Appetizers, Black Leech, Missionary, Sweeny Todd, Viva, Zulu, Black Chenille, White, Chenille, Baby Dolls (various colours).
Local knowledge:	Generally, from bank or boat, it is floating or sink-tip line, with a leader of about 9 ft. Boats are fished from anchor, not drifting.

Clatworthy Reservoir

Near Wiveliscombe (0984) 23549.
Controlled by Wessex Water Authority.

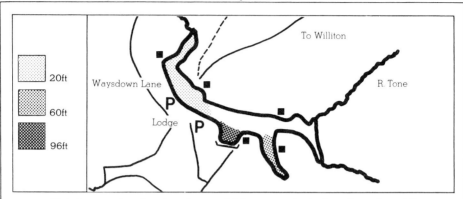

This is an upland water of some 130 acres, situated on the edge of Exmoor, with access from the A361 Taunton-Bampton road. Aquatic life includes Mayflies, Sedges, Damselflies, Olives, Midge, Caenis, snails, shrimps etc.

Facilities: Lodge, toilets. Day tickets available from self-service kiosk on site. Large car park.

Season: March 31st to October 15th. Hours: 8 a.m. to one hour after sunset.

Rods per day: No limit.

Charges: Full season £130. Concession £97.50. Day permit £5. Concession for OAPs, juniors (under 16 years) and disabled £3.50.

Day limit: 6 fish, over 12 inches.

Boats: Hire charge, £10 per person, includes day permit. £8 after 4 p.m., including permit.

Restrictions: Fly fishing only. No spinning. No single boat bookings on opening day.

Stocking policy: Mainly with rainbows, with some browns. Pre-season stocking, then once or twice monthly to maintain density.

Annual catch rate: 5,000 fish approx. A 2.45 fish per rod average. There were five fish over 6 lb, the largest a 9 lb 12 oz rainbow (1983).

Recommended flies:
Most of the traditional wet flies. Short list includes March Brown, Greenwell's Glory, Bloody Butcher, Kingfisher Butcher, Black & Peacock Spider, Footballer, Grenadier, Caenis Nymph, Corixa, Amber Nymph, Green Nymph, Stickfly.
Effective lures are Appetiser, Marabou, Chenille (various colours), Muddlers, Baby Dolls, Viva, Badger Matuka, Dog Nobblers.

Local knowledge: Wading can be an advantage around most of the shoreline, as there are some steep and wooded areas that are almost impossible to fish from the bank. Boat anglers do well when on a slow drift, using floating line and a long leader.

Durleigh Reservoir

Near Bridgwater, Somerset.
Tel: Bridgwater (0278) 424786. Controlled by Wessex Water Authority.

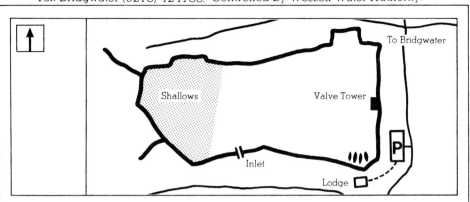

This attractive and very popular reservoir of 77 acres is situated in farmland by the Quantock Hills, and just two miles west of Bridgwater. It is reckoned to be the oldest trout fishery in the Authority's area. There is abundant aquatic life, including shrimp, sedge, hatches of midge, damselflies, dragonflies, snails, sticklebacks and coarse fish fry.

Facilities: Comfortable lodge situated close to the dam wall, and boat moorings. Permits issued at self-service kiosk on site. Artificial flies suitable for the water available from the bailiff's office. Large car parking area.

Season: March 23rd to November 30th. Hours: 8 a.m. to one hour after sunset.

Charges: Full season permit £130, concession £97.50. Day ticket £5. Concessionary for OAPs and juniors (under 16 years) £3.50 – banks only. Permits include Wessex Water Authority rod licence.

Day limit: 6 fish (over 12 inches).

Boats: Hire charge £5 per day, £3 after 4 p.m. There are no concessions on boat charges.

Restrictions: Fly fishing only. No single booking of boats on opening day.

Stocking policy: Stocked with rainbows only. At start of season stocking of some 3,000 fish with frequent additions according to catch returns.

Annual catch rate: In 1983 over 5,000 trout, with nine fish over 6 lb, heaviest 10 lb 9 oz. The rod average is 1.92 fish.

Recommended flies:
March Brown, Peter Ross, Invicta, Greenwell's Glory, Butcher, Whisky, Viva, Chenille, Marabou, Muddler Minnow, Missionary, Appetizer, Black & Peacock Spider, Pheasant Tail Nymph, Green Nymph, Footballer, Stickfly, Suspender Buzzer.

Local knowledge: As this is a comparatively shallow reservoir, most of the shoreline is wadeable. But fishing from the dam wall is very popular, and during opening weeks produces many limit catches.

Hawkridge Reservoir

Spaxton, Somerset.   Controlled by the Wessex Water
Tel: Bridgwater (0278) 4786. Authority.

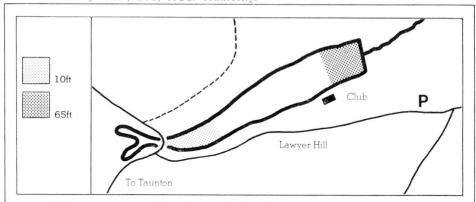

This is an attractively landscaped upland reservoir of 32 acres, and it is set in a small valley in the Quantock Hills, some six miles west of Bridgwater. It has proved a popular trout fishery since it was first opened in 1964. Aquatic life incudes sedges, midge, snail, shrimp, rudd fry, and there are large numbers of sticklebacks.

Facilities: Large car park, toilets. Permits issued on site.

Season: March 31st to October 15th. Hours: 8 a.m. to one hour after sunset.

Rods per day: Limited.

Charges: Full season £100, concession £75. Day ticket £5, concessionary (OAPs and juniors) £3.50. Permits include Wessex Water Authority rod licence.

Day catch limit: 6 fish (over 12 inches).

Boats: None.

Restrictions: Fly fishing only.

Stocking policy: Rainbows and browns. Starting with a pre-season stock, then regular stocking throughout the season, at monthly or twice monthly intervals.

Annual catch rate: (1983) 2,504 fish, heaviest a 5 lb 8 oz rainbow. 2.08 fish per rod average.

Recommended flies:
Dunkeld, Invicta, Peter Ross, Alder Fly, Greenwell's Glory, Spider Palmer, Wickham's Fancy, plus various small lures such as viva, Zulu, Appetizer, Whisky, Ace of Spades, White Muddler and Sweeny Todd. Other patterns worth trying at anything of the season are Black & Peacock Spider, Pheasant Tail Nymph, Mayfly Nymph, Amber Nymph, Stickfly, and various buzzers.

Local knowledge: The reservoir has a steep shelving bottom. But the bank is comfortable to fish from, and a long line is not always necessary during early weeks. There are frequently good rises during the summer months, and a floating line with traditional patterns is often effective.

Otterhead Fishery

Near Churchingford, Somerset.
Tel: (0278) 57333.

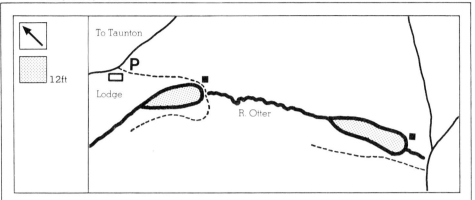

Two small lakes totalling about five acres pleasantly situated on the Blackdown Hills at the head of the River Otter. Located to the south of Taunton, the lakes once formed part of an estate. Aquatic life is rich, with sedge, shrimp, mayfly, olives, midges, damselflies, dragonflies, and caddis larvae.

Facilities:	Lodge and self-service permit kiosk. Car parking.
Season:	March 31st to October 15th. Hours: 8 a.m. to one hour after sunset.
Rods per day:	Limited number.
Charges:	Full season permit £90. Concession £67.50. Day ticket £5, concession for OAPs, juniors (under 16 years) and disabled £3.50. Permits include Wessex Water Authority rod licence.
Day limit:	6 fish, over 12 inches.
Boats:	None.
Restrictions:	Fly fishing only.
Stocking policy:	Mainly rainbows, with smaller percentage of browns. Pre-season stocking, then followed by regular stocks to maintain density throughout the season. All fish from the Authority's own hatchery.
Annual catch rate:	(1983) 1,295 fish caught, largest fish a 3 lb brown. The average catch per rod 1.84.
Recommended flies:	Traditional patterns including Silver Invicta, March Brown, Kingfisher Butcher, Jersey Herd, Polystickle, Gold Ribbed Hare's Ear, Dunkeld, Pheasant Tail Nymph, Stickfly, Buzzer Nymph, Amber Nymph, Midge Pupa. Most of the popular lures, such as Baby Doll, Appetizer, Black/White Chenilles, Muddlers, Sweeny Todd, Zulu, Mickey Finn, Missionary, Jack Frost, Black Ghost, Badger Matuka, Marabou and various dog nobblers.
Local knowledge:	Floating and sink tip lines generally most effective. Most of the season the fish are near the top, when nymphs and occasionally dry flies are most successful. Try not to disturb the water by wading; use a long leader, and a very slow retrieve.

Sutton Bingham

Near Yeovil, Somerset.
Tel: Yetminster (0935) 872389. Controlled by Wessex Water Authority.

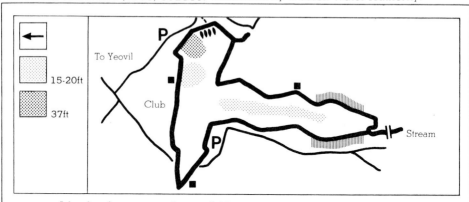

A lowland reservoir of some 142 acres is set in attractive countryside on the Somerset-Dorset border, about four miles south of Yeovil on the A37. There is prolific aquatic life, particularly mayflies, olives, midge, and various sedge, plus shrimp, snails, tadpoles, and water beetles.

Facilities: A comfortable lodge is situated near the dam with a large car park close by. Artificial flies useful for this fishery are available from the bailiff. Permits are available from a self-service kiosk on site.

Season: March 24th to October 15th. Hours: 8 a.m. to one hour after sunset.

Rods per day: No limit.

Charges: Full season permit £130. Concession £97.50 – OAPs, juniors (under 16 years) and disabled. Day ticket £5, concessionary (bank only) £3.50. Permits include Wessex Water Authority rod licence.

Day limit: 6 (over 12 inches).

Boats: Charge – £5.

Restrictions: Fly fishing only. No spinning.

Stocking policy: Mainly rainbows with some browns. Starting with a pre-season stock, then at frequent intervals throughout the season with fish from the Authority's own hatchery.

Annual catch rate: 1.96 fish per rod average. A total of 7,533 fish; largest a 10 lb 10 oz rainbow (1983).

Recommended flies: Most traditional wet flies – Greenwell's Glory, March Brown, Black & Peacock Spider, Invicta, Dunkeld Various lures – Appetizer, White Ghost, Baby Doll, Chenille (black, white), Muddlers, Matuka, Blue Zulu, Viva, Bloody Butcher and Kingfisher Butcher. Plus various nymphs like Damsel, Pheasant Tail, Stickfly.

Local knowledge: Apart from the sailing club area, all of the bank is available and ideal for wading – but fish the margin before wading and disturbing the water. In early season sinking lines, small lures and wet flies are most effective. As the season progresses then use floating line and nymph, or traditional wet fly. Sutton Bingham is noted as a nymph water.

Wimbleball Reservoir

Brompton Regis, Somerset.   Controlled by South West Authority.
Tel: Brompton Regis (03987) 372. Warden: Brian Poole.

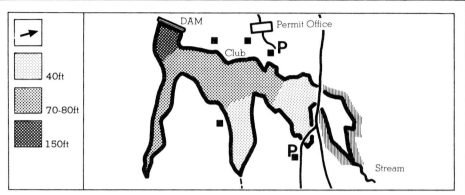

This very attractive reservoir of 374 acres is fairly new, being completed in 1979. It is the largest reservoir in the region, and very popular with anglers. Aquatic life includes Pond Olive, Alder, Hawthorn, Black Buzzers, Midge, Sedges, Shrimp and snail.

Facilities: Clubhouse, toilet and washroom, car parks and picnic area. Self service system in the recreation area, or permits direct from the warden.

Season: April 1st to October 31st inclusive. Hours: one hour before sunrise to one hour after sunset.

Charges: Day £5, evening £3, (after 3 pm).
OAP's, disabled, and full time students under 18 – £4, Juniors under 16 – £1.
The Authority issues books of 20 pre-paid permits at 15 per cent discount – for instance, full day price £100, discount price £85. Concessions also for boat bookings. Pre-paid permits may be used at any of the Authority's 'stocked' trout fisheries.

Day limit: 5 fish, evening 3 fish, over 10 inches. Angler achieving a limit may purchase a second permit.

Boats: 15. Day £5, half-day (after 3 pm) £3.50. Advance booking advisable.

Restrictions: Fly fishing only. No dogs allowed. No fish under 7 inches to be retained.

Stocking policy: Regularly with mainly rainbows. Some browns and brooks.

Annual catch rate: (1982) 19,930 fish. 2.5 fish per rod average.
(1983) 16,154 fish. 2.2 fish per rod average.

Recommended flies: Greenwell's Glory, Olives, Orange Buzzer, Dark Sedge, Black & Peacock Spider, Pheasant Tail nymph, Amber nymph, Viva, Whiskey, Black Chenille, Muddler, Baby Doll, Appetizer, Missionary.

Local knowledge: This vast reservoir has an extensive shore-line, and boats can be useful for fishing different areas. But bank fishing can be good. From May fishing is usually best before lunch and during evening hatches.

Gailey Fishery

CANNOCK, STAFFS.
Tel: Penkridge (078571) 4855

Proprietors: Chris Buxton and
Mrs G. Brassington.

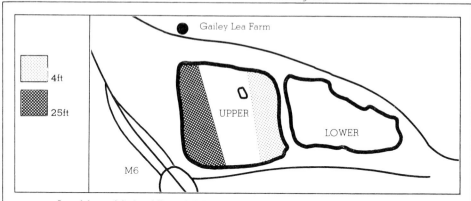

An old established British Waterways reservoir was drained and formed into a trout lake of 35 acres. Although close to the M6 motorway, the fishery is surrounded by fields. Aquatic life is prolific with shrimp, snails, dragonfly, damselfly, buzzers and roach fry.

Facilities:	Fishing lodge, which sells flies and small items of tackle. Casting tuition by arrangement. Car park.
Season:	1/3 to 30/10 inclusive. Hours: 8.30 am to dusk.
Rods per day:	70 maximum.
Charges:	Season permits from £157.50.
	Day tickets £8, morning (weekdays only to 1 pm) £4, evening (April from 3 pm, May from 4 pm) £4.
	Concessions for O.A.P.'s and children. Discount for party booking.
Day catch limit:	6 fish, morning and evening three fish.
Boats:	8 pulling boats, £2.50 per person, morning and evening £2.
Restrictions:	Fly fishing only. All fish caught must be killed.
Stocking policy:	With rainbows and browns to maintain density of 100 fish per acre. All fish over 1 lb, and up to 14 lb.
Annual catch rate:	Two fish per rod average.
Recommended flies:	
	Early season black and green coloured lures–Viva, Sweeney Todd, Undertaker, Black Zulu, Black Chenille, Black Matuka, Green Matuka.
	As season progresses the smaller more traditional patterns such as Mallard & Claret, Cardinal, Silver Invicta, Teal & Blue, Peter Ross, Greenwell's Glory, Black & Peacock Spider, Amber Nymph, Pheasant Tail Nymph.
Local knowledge:	Although this is considered a testing lake to fish, quality rainbows up to a fishery record 13 lb 14 oz have been caught.

Patshull Fishery

Burnhill Green, Wolverhampton.
Tel: Pattingham (0902) 700100.

The Patshull Park Estate trout fishery consists of an irregularly shaped lake known as the Great Pool, and the smaller Church Pool. Natural banks with casting platforms. Aquatic life includes sedges, olives, chironomids.

Facilities: Fishing lodge, for permits, tackle, flies. Also on site is the Lakeside Lodge Hotel.

Season: March 15th to October 31st. Hours: 7.30 a.m. to dusk.

Charges: Day £9, evening £5. Severn Trent W.A. rod licence required.

Day limit: 6 fish, part-day 3 fish.

Boats: For 1, 2 or 3 persons £3.50 and £2. Advisable to book at weekends.

Restrictions: Fly fishing only.

Stocking policy: Mainly rainbows on a regular basis to maintain density. Some 20,000 per year.

Annual catch rate: 3.5 fish per rod average.

Recommended flies:
Lures including Whisky, Sweeny Todd, Appetizer, Black Chenille, White Baby Doll, Jack Frost, Viva, Zulu, and Dog Nobblers in various colours.
During summer, weighted and unweighted nymphs— Damselfly Nymph, Mayfly Nymph, Green Beast, Corixa, Suspender Buzzer, and traditional wet flies – Butcher, Dunkeld, Connemara Black etc.

Local knowledge: In early season black coloured lures are often most productive. Dog Nobblers and Ace of Spades have taken good early season catches. The use of buzzer patterns can take many fish when they are rising. Yet lures can also be effective most of the season.

Tittesworth Reservoir

Near Leek, Staffs.
Tel: (053834) 389.   Controlled by Severn Trent W.A.

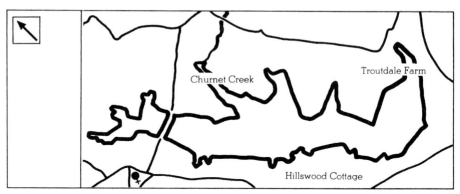

Churnet Creek

Troutdale Farm

Hillswood Cottage

This picturesque 200 acre lake is of an irregular shape and is fed by the River Churnet. There is a good variety of aquatic life.

Facilities:	Fishing lodge. Car park. Permits issued on site.
Season:	April 8th to October 15th inclusive. Hours: 1 hour before sunrise to 1 hour after sunset.
Rods per day:	No limit.
Charges:	Season: by application to S.T.W.A. Day – high season £4.80, low season £4.30 (after June 1). There are reduced rates for evenings, and for OAPs, juniors (under 16), and disabled.
Day limit:	6 fish.
Boats:	20 (approx.). £4.30 (15 ft), £3.80 (12 ft) per day. Reduced rates for evenings.
Restrictions:	Fly fishing only. No spinning. Size limit 11 inches.
Stocking policy:	Mainly rainbows. Regular stockings. Approximate total 15,000.
Annual catch rate:	Not known.
Recommended flies:	
	Mallard & Claret, Black Pennell, March Brown, Invicta, Dunkeld, Connemara & Black, Hare's Ear, Damsel Nymph, Green/Brown Nymphs, Seal's Fur Nymph, Pheasant Tail Nymph, Buzzer Nymph.
Local knowledge:	Boat anglers generally do best by loch-style drifting. Churnet Creek area is a favourite spot for bank anglers. Excellent brown trout – largest taken 9 lb 5 oz.

Runfold Fishery

RUNFOLD,
SURREY.

Tel: Runfold (02518) 2374.
Proprietor: E. G. Sutton.

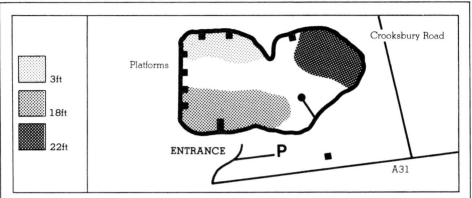

A secluded and attractive spring-fed lake of seven acres sheltered by surrounding woodland on a 12 acres private estate, near Farnham, Surrey. Located just off the A31 Guildford–Farnham road. Water life includes hatches of Mayfly, Damselfly, Dragonfly, Sedge, Black Buzzer, Caenis, plus shrimps and snails.

Facilities: Lodge, washroom, toilets. Car parking. Flies available from the office.

Season: Open all year round.

Rods per day: 25 maximum.

Charges: Day ticket £10, half-day £5.50. Prior booking always advisable. Additional permit available. Thames Water Authority rod licence required.

Day catch limit: 4 fish, half-day two fish.

Boats: 1. Hire charge £2.

Restrictions: Fly fishing only. No wading. No spinning. No large lures.

Stocking policy: On a 'put-and-take' basis in order to maintain a density of 80 fish to the acre. Rainbows up to around 5 lb.

Annual catch rate: Not available.

Recommended flies:
Black Chenille, Black Ghost, Baby Doll, Viva, Missionary, Alexandra, Peter Ross, Wickhams Fancy, Butcher, Dunkeld, Black Gnat, Pheasant Tail Nymph, Caenis Nymph, Mayfly (dry and nymph), Stickfly, Ginger Buzzer, Alder fly.

Local knowledge: Use a sink-tip line, or a floating line with long leader, and work a nymph or small lure about 12 ft down. A good early pattern is a small Viva worked deep.

Rushmoor Lakes

Haslemere, Surrey.
Tel: Haslemere (0428) 2818.   Proprietor: D. Whitehead.

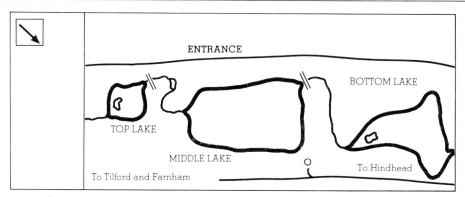

The fishery consists of three spring-fed lakes (about five acres) with an average depth of six feet, set in a picturesque valley. There is rich insect and water life including a good hatch of mayfly, plus Sedge, Olives, Midge, Buzzers, shrimp, snail, minnows and sticklebacks.

Facilities: Two fishing huts for shelter, and anglers to have refreshments. Car park, toilets. Casting tuition by arrangement.

Season: March 1st to October 31st inclusive. Hours: 8.30 a.m. to sunset.

Rods per day: 6 – strictly limited, but more allowed if in private party.

Charges: Season permit price available on application. Day ticket £12.50 including VAT. Prior booking is essential. Thames Water Authority rod licence required.

Day catch limit: 4 fish, but catch and return fishing with barbless hooks allowed after limit has been achieved.

Boats: None.

Restrictions: Fly fishing only. No wading. No dogs. No children. No radios. No lures.

Stocking policy: Rainbows and browns from 1¼ lb up to around 5 lb.

Annual catch rate: 2.36 fish per rod average. Weight average 1½ lb per fish caught. Largest fish of 1983 – a 7 lb 2 oz rainbow.

Recommended flies:
Peter Ross, Wickham's Fancy, Blue Zulu, Coachman, Bloody Butcher, Brown Sedge, Damselfly Nymph, Sedge Pupa, Amber Nymph, Pheasant Tail Nymph, Alder Larva, Mayfly Nymph, Buzzer Nymph.

Local knowledge: David Whitehead: This is not normally a dry fly water, but excellent for fishing a nymph. The mayfly nymph in particular is very effective for about three months of the season. Use a floating line, and depending on the colour of the water, grease about three quarters of the leader.

Willinghurst Fishery

Shamley Green, Surrey.
Tel: (0483) 275048.   Proprietor: Mark Syms.

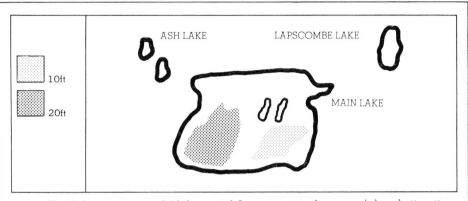

The fishery consists of 4 lakes, total 6 acres, set in the peaceful and attractive surroundings of a private estate. The Main lake is the largest at 4 acres. Others are Ash, Alder and Lapscombe. Another lake is expected to be opened shortly. Aquatic life: Pond olives, sedges, midge, sticklebacks, tadpoles.

Facilities: Large fishing lodge, weight scales and record book in which all fish caught to be entered. Car park and picnic area.

Season: Summer—April 1st to October 31st inclusive. Winter—November 1st to March 31st Fridays, Saturdays, Sundays.
Hours: 9 a.m. to half-hour before dusk (see notice board for exact time).

Charges: Season, by arrangement.
Day £11.50, evening £6. A second permit available – before catching additional fish.

Day limit: 4 fish, evening 2 fish.

Boats: None.

Restrictions: Dry fly, wet fly and nymph only. Only flies tied on single hooks not exceeding No 6 short shank, or No 10 long shank.

Stocking policy: Twice weekly for first three months, then weekly. All rainbows, minimum $1\frac{1}{2}$ lb up to 10 lb.

Annual catch rate: 2.75 per rod average.

Recommended flies: Black is a good colour. Viva, Black Lure, Black Chenille, Sweeny Todd, Baby Doll, Pheasant Tail Nymph, Damselfly Nymph, Mayfly Nymph.

Local knowledge: Lapscombe Lake has trees and rhododendrons around its shores, and a measure of casting skill is required. But the rewards of quality fish can make this most worthwhile. A deep, slow-fished lure is often successful on Main Lake. The two small lakes, Ash and Alder, offer good nymph fishing.

Ardingly Reservoir

Near Haywards Heath, Sussex.
Tel: Ardingly (0444) 892549.   Controlled by Southern Water Authority.

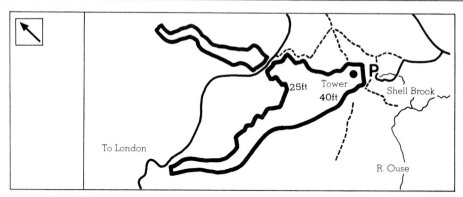

This 190 acre reservoir is situated in pleasant countryside 3 miles north of
Haywards Heath, Sussex. It was first opened for trout fishing in 1979. Aquatic
life includes Sedges, Caenis, midges, buzzers, daddy long legs and coarse
fish.

Facilities:	Fishing lodge. Artificial flies and tackle available. Self-service permit kiosk.
Season:	March 6th to October 16th inclusive. Hours: Sunrise to 1 hour after sunset.
Rods per day:	No limit.
Charges:	Season (full) £175, weekday £135. Day £5.30, 'brace' £3, half-day £4. Permits available at office.
Day limit:	6 fish, 'brace' ticket 2, half-day 4.
Boats:	15 (rowing) single day £4.50, half-day £3.50. Double £6, half-day £4.50. Advance booking advisable. Boats from 9 a.m.
Restrictions:	Fly fishing only. No bank fishing in nature reserve. No trolling or trailing.
Stocking policy:	13,000 for the season. Fortnightly stocking. Some fish to 7 lb.
Annual catch rate:	2.28 per rod average.
Recommended flies:	Invicta, Appetizer, Muddler, Black & Peacock Spider, Viva, Whisky, Dunkeld, Green Nymph, Sweeny Todd.
Local knowledge:	Whether to use floating or sinking line generally depends on conditions, but in early season it is the slow sinker to fish a small lure that scores. Most of the season nymphs, weighted and unweighted, are worth using.

Darwell Reservoir

Near Battle, Sussex.
Tel: Robertsbridge (0580) 880407.

Controlled by the Hastings Fly
Fishers Club Ltd.

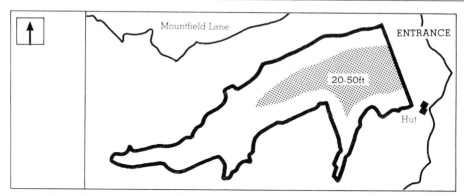

This old established and attractively landscaped reservoir is 170 acres in extent. Located off the A21. Heavily wooded banks. Aquatic life includes a small hatch of mayfly. There are also sedge, Caenis, shrimp, roach and perch fry.

Facilities: A clubhouse, toilets, telephone, car park; flies and tackle available. Permits issued on site (from bailiff or self-service unit). Casting tuition by arrangement.

Season: April 1st to October 30 inclusive. Hours: 8 a.m. to one hour after sunset.

Charges: Season permit £90. This allows 35 days fishing, and concessionary boat hire charge. Day ticket £5, part-day (after 4 p.m.) £4. Juniors under 16 years of age £3. Southern Water Authority rod licence issued on site.

Day catch limit: 6 fish (April 4 fish), and 3 fish for part-day and junior permit holders.

Boats: 13 pulling boats, hire charge £3 per boat, evening £2.

Restrictions: Fly fishing only. No trolling. Restricted to four fish in April and May. Maximum number allowed in a boat is two persons.

Stocking policy: A pre-season stock, then at intervals throughout the season with rainbow and brown trout. There are some wild brown trout in the reservoir.

Annual catch rate: Average just over two fish per rod.

Recommended flies: Early season favourites are Whisky, Viva, Muddler, Appetizer, Church Fry, Amber Nymph, Stickfly, Corixa.

Local knowledge: Philip White: There is a half-mile long steep dam where a sinking line is often an advantage in the deepwater – some 50 ft. There are small clearings around the bank where fishing is possible – but for the remainder it is heavily wooded, mainly willows. Casting from the bank is into an average 8 ft to 10 ft. Fish can be found close in, and a floating line to fish a leaded stickfly can be most effective.

Furnace Brook Fishery

Cow Beech,   Tel: Rushlake Green (0435) 830298.
near Herstmonceux, Sussex.   Proprietor: Lawrence Ryan.

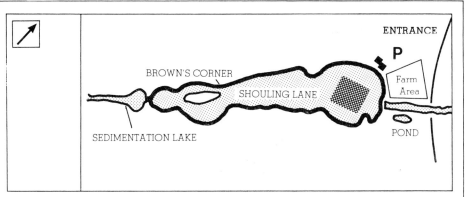

A long and narrow lake of 6½ acres, stream fed, set in a pleasant landscaped valley. This trout farm and fishery is surrounded by woodland, and cornfields, near Hailsham. Rich water life with a mayfly hatch in June, Pond Olives, Sedge, Black Gnat, Daphnia, Shrimp, Water Boatman and damselfly.

Facilities:	A fishing lodge that over-looks the lake, with tea-making facility. There is a drying room, washroom and toilets. Ample car parking. Permits issued on site.
Season:	April 3rd to October 10th inclusive. Hours: negotiable, depending on time of year.
Charges:	Season permit, various grades at prices varying from £150 to £320. Day ticket £10, evening £6. Southern Water Authority rod licence required.
Day catch limit:	4 fish, part-day two fish. On reaching the limit a second permit may be taken.
Boats:	None.
Restrictions:	Fly fishing only. No wading. No tandem, double or treble hooks. Maximum hook size 8 long shank. All fish caught to be killed.
Stocking policy:	On a weekly basis, with brown and rainbow trout up to 14 lb.
Annual catch rate:	Three fish per rod average.
Recommended flies:	Green (and brown) Pheasant Tail Nymph, Amber Nymph, Green Olives, Black & Peacock Spider, Black Marabou, Invicta, Mini-Dog Nobblers, Greenwell's Damsel Nymph, Daddy Long Legs, Brown Sedge, Sedge, March Brown, Soldier Palmer.
Local knowledge:	This is a good nymph and dry fly water. Because of the chance of a really large fish it pays to have a leader of at least 6 lb breaking strain – but in summer, when the water is very clear then it may be necessary to drop to a 4 lb breaking strain point.

Lakedown Fisheries

Burwash, Sussex.
Tel: Burwash (0435) 883449.   Manager: Kevin Hooker.

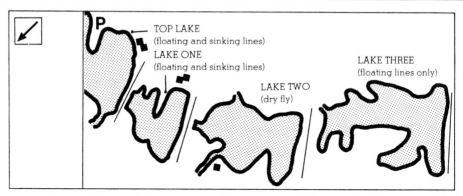

Four landscaped lakes covering 16 acres in rural Sussex. The fishery consists of a 3 acres lake reserved for dry fly fishing. There are three other lakes of about 4 acres apiece for general fly fishing. Aquatic life: Mayfly, Damselfly, Pond Olive, Buzzers, Shrimps, Corixa, snails.

Facilities:	Fishing lodge, hut, toilets. Permits issued on site, advance booking advisable. Car park.
Season:	April 4th to October 31st inclusive. Hours: 9 a.m. to sunset.
Charges:	Season permit (full) £325 for all weekdays and one day at weekend (6 fish limit per week). Day permit £12.50, half-day £7. There are concessions for juniors.
Day catch limit:	4 fish, part-day two fish.
Rods:	40 maximum.
Boats:	None.
Restrictions:	Fly fishing only. No wading. No shooting-head lines. No hooks larger than size 10. No droppers. No fish to be returned.
Stocking policy:	Weekly (on put-and-take basis) to maintain density. Rainbows, browns and tiger trout.
Annual catch rate:	(1983) 3,047 anglers caught 6,629 fish. Including 423 fish over 4 lb.
Recommended flies:	Mayfly Nymph, Amber Nymph, Buzzer Nymph, Pheasant Tail, Stick Fly, Midge Pupa, Corixa, Peter Ross, Black & Peacock Spider, Greenwell's Glory, Dunkeld, Alexandra, Butcher, Black Pennell, Invicta. Small lures like Matuka, worm fly, Marabou, White Ghost, Zulu, Whisky, Baby Doll, etc.
Local knowledge:	Generally use floating line, long leader (some 15 ft) with a 3 lb to 5 lb breaking strain point. Throughout the season suggest damselfly nymphs, black lures and traditional wet flies. The fishery record (1983) of 12 lb 6 oz was taken on a Zug Bug Nymph fished on a floating line.

Peckhams Copse

Near Chichester, Sussex.
Tel: Chichester (0243) 779905. Resident Manager: Tom Chapman.

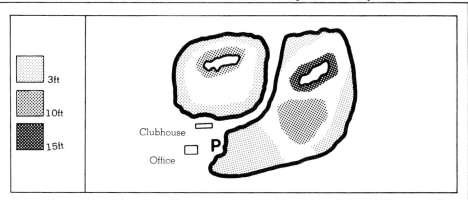

Two ex-gravel pit lakes known as No 1 (18 acres) and No 2 (20 acres). The trout fishery is part of the Southern Leisure Centre which also includes coarse fishing lakes and a large caravan park. The two attractively landscaped trout lakes are rich in aquatic life, including sedge, shrimp, snails, pond olives, mayfly, corixa, and elvers – which enter by way of a small stream.

Facilities:	Snack bar, clubhouse, toilet and washing facilities. Flies and various items of tackle available at the office.
Season:	April 3rd to October 31st. Hours: 7 a.m. to one hour after sunset.
Rods per day:	80 maximum.
Charges:	Season: Monday to Thursday or Friday to Sunday – £345. Season: one day per week – £241.50. Day £13.50. No part-day permits. Tickets and Southern Water Authority rod licences available on site.
Day catch limit:	4 fish.
Boats:	9 pulling boats. Advance booking advisable. Hire charge: £4 per day.
Restrictions:	Fly and nymph fishing only. No tandem hooks, and maximum hook size 10. No Muddler Minnows or Dog Nobbler lures.
Stocking policy:	Weekly with fish over 1½ lb, and up to 10 lb plus. Mainly rainbows. A few browns at intervals.
Annual catch rate:	(1983) 7,111 fish caught by 2,651 anglers. This included 39 fish of 4 lb and over. The largest fish of the season – a 6 lb 9 oz rainbow from Lake No 2. Fishery record 10 lb 1 oz taken in 1982.
Recommended flies:	
Early season:	Green Nymph, Peter Ross, Butcher, Dunkeld, Appetizer, Missionary, Black & Peacock Spider, Baby Doll.
Mid and late season:	Gold Ribbed Hare's Ear, Corixa, Pheasant Tail Nymph, Buzzers (various), Damselfly Nymph. Hawthorn, Alder, Greenwell's Glory, Sedge, Tupps,
Local knowledge:	Tom Chapman prefers a sink-tip or slow sinking line, or even one of the intermediate lines. At the start of the season try any of the early patterns, but never 'over cast'.

Powdermill Lake

Sedlescombe, Sussex. Controlled by Hastings Fly Fishers
Tel: Robertsbridge (0580) 880407. Club Ltd.

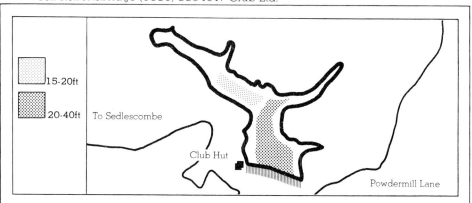

15-20ft

20-40ft

To Sedlescombe

Club Hut

Powdermill Lane

This very attractive established reservoir of 54 acres used to be known as the Great Sanders Reservoir. It is located off the B2089 Rye road. Much of the bank is too wooded to fish from. Aquatic life includes a reasonable hatch of mayfly, sedge (including Grannam), Caenis, Daddy Long Legs, shrimp, roach and perch fry.

Facilities:	A clubhouse, toilets, telephone, car park, flies and tackle available. Permits issued on site. Casting tuition by arrangement.
Season:	April 1st to October 30th inclusive. Hours: 9 a.m. to one hour after sunset.
Charges:	Season permit £90 inclusive of VAT. This allows 35 days fishing, and concessionary boat hire charge. Day ticket £5, part-day (after 4 p.m.) £4, juniors under 16 years £3. Southern Water Authority rod licence required.
Day catch limit:	6 fish (April four fish), and three fish for part-day and junior permit holders.
Boats:	8 pulling boats, hire charge £3 per boat, evening £2.
Restrictions:	Fly fishing only. No trolling. Restricted to four fish in April and May. Maximum number allowed in a boat is two persons.
Stocking policy:	A pre-season stock, then at intervals throughout the season with rainbow and brown trout. There are some wild browns.
Annual catch rate:	Average just over two fish per rod.
Recommended flies:	Stickfly, Corixa, Amber Nymph, Black & Peacock Spider, Pheasant Tail Nymph, Greenwell's Glory, Appetizer, Missionary, Viva, Sweeny Todd, Whisky, Muddlers, Chenille, lures (black, white and orange).
Local knowledge:	Philip White – Because much of the bank is too wooded to fish from, the popular section is the dam. The water is around 40 ft deep, and sinking lines are generally used. During summer a floating line to fish an Amber Nymph is to be recommended. Also a leaded stickfly is worth trying close into the dam. Boat anglers should try dapping.

Bishops Bowl

Bishops Itchington, Warks.
Tel: Harbury (0926) 613344. Proprietor: Chris Poupard.

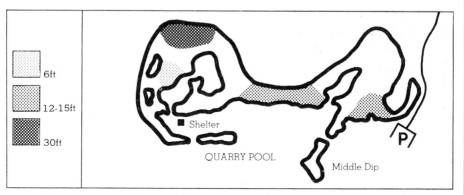

6ft

12-15ft

30ft

■ Shelter

QUARRY POOL

Middle Dip

P

This comparatively new fishery of some 40 acres consists of spring-fed lakes formed from old limestone quarries. Water life includes mayflies, sedges, Olives, midges and damselflies.

Facilities:	Fishing lodge, offering snacks and a place to shelter in poor weather.
Season:	Summer March 22nd to October 22nd. Hours: 6 a.m. to dusk. Winter October 23rd to January 8th (closed December 19th to 25th). Hours: 9 a.m. to dusk.
Rods:	50 maximum.
Charge:	Summer – day £9, half-day £7, evening £5. Winter – day £8, half-day £6.
Day limit:	4 fish, half-day 3 fish, evening 2 fish. Fish caught over the limit may be paid for at current rate per lb.
Boats:	6 boats. Half-day £3, evening £2.
Restrictions:	Fly fishing only. Single hook maximum size 8. No wading. Boats only allowed in a certain area.
Stocking policy:	Mainly rainbows, minimum 1½ lb to over 10 lb. Plus 25% browns. Most of the stock reared on site.
Annual catch rate:	2.5 per rod average.
Recommended flies:	
Early season:	Black Lure, Viva, Zulu, Ace of Spades, Black Dog Nobbler. Mid-May to end of June: Mayfly Nymph.
Mid-summer:	Black coloured nymphs, small lures, Sedge patterns.
Autumn:	Pheasant Tail Nymph, Green Nymph, White Baby Doll, Yellow Dog Nobbler.
Local knowledge:	Chris Poupard: During the mayfly hatch try a large unweighted nymph fished on a floating line and greased leader. Yellow coloured lures during Autumn. Nymphs are best fished from mid-water to the top. There are also good rises when daddy long legs are on the water.

Draycote Water

KITES HARDWICK, Tel: Rugby (0788) 811107.
WARKS. Controlled by Severn-Trent W.A.

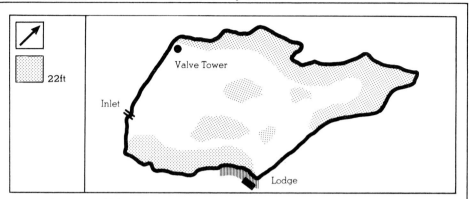

This is a 600 acres reservoir near Rugby. Permits are issued at the Kites Hardwick Filling Station on the A426 road. Water life includes sedges, sticklebacks, and chironomids.

Facilities:	Fishing Lodge. Anglers must sign in.
Season:	1/4 to 23/10. Hours: 7.30 am to 1 hour after sunset.
Charges:	Season. £160, weekdays £130. Day £5.60 (£5 after June 1), half-day £3.30. £2.80 for O.A.P.'s, disabled, and juniors under 16 accompanied by an adult.
Day limit:	8 fish.
Boats:	29. Rowing, £3.80, half-day £2.50 (after 4 pm). Motor, day £8.80, half-day £5.
Restrictions:	Fly fishing only. No trolling. No second permit, no fishing in front of sailing club.
Stocking policy:	Weekly. 40,000 trout, mainly rainbows released in 1983. Fish reared on site.
Annual catch rate:	2.11 per rod.
Recommended flies:	Sweeney Todd, Whiskey, Zulu, Viva, Appetizer, Black Chenille, Dog Nobbler, Green Nymph, Pheasant Tail Nymph.
	Traditional wet: Greenwells Glory, March Brown, Ginger Quill, Invicta, Soldier Palmer.
Local Knowledge:	Method generally depends on weather. Cold windy days favour sinking line and lures. In warmer weather the fish are generally near the surface. Then a floating line with nymphs or traditional wet flies is recommended.

Packington Fisheries

Meriden, Warks.
Tel: Meriden (0676) 22574.

Proprietor: The Lord Guernsey
Packington Estate Sporting Enterprises.

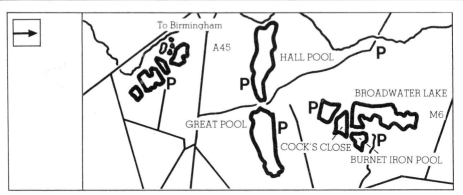

The fishery consists of 6 lakes totalling some 87 acres, in a parkland setting. Three of the lakes are reserved for season members, the other three are open for day ticket fishing. Adjacent club for anglers.

Facilities:	Fishing lodge, with refreshments. Flies and small items of tackle on sale. Fly fishing tuition by arrangement.
Season:	March 18th to November 11th inclusive. Hours: 6 a.m. to 1 hour after sunset.
Rods per day:	54 bank, plus about 30 boat anglers.
Charges:	Season—from £66 to £253. Day—£7.50 (full day), morning £5 (6 a.m. to 1.30 p.m.), afternoon £5.50 (2.30 p.m. to closing). Juniors (under 16 years) £4, half-day £3.
Day limit:	None.
Boats:	On each lake (15 in total). Day £4, afternoon £3, evening £2.
Restrictions:	Fly fishing only. No wading.
Stocking policy:	Regular weekly stocking with rainbows, and browns. 30,000 plus fish, 12 inches minimum.
Recommended flies:	Black Chenille, White Chenille, Baby Doll, Whisky, Whisky Muddler, Orange Marabou, Viva, Black & Peacock Spider, Damselfly Nymph, Dog Nobblers (various colours).
Annual catch rate:	Total number of fish 27,000.
Local knowledge:	Traditional flies, nymphs, most of the lures, used in conjunction with any of the usual fly-fishing methods, will all take fish. Season members' lakes: Hall Pool (19 acres), Great Pool (30 acres) and Park Meadow (6 acres). Day ticket lakes: Broadwater Lake (28 acres), Cock's Close (10 acres) and Burnet Iron Pool (6 acres). Record fish: a 9 lb 15 oz rainbow.

Shustoke Fishery

Near Coleshill, Warks.
Tel: Furnace End (0675) 81702.   Operated by Cambrian Fisheries.

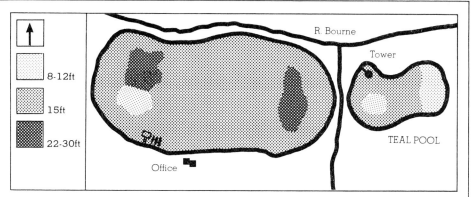

This fishery consists of two old established reservoirs. Lower (95 acres) is 25 ft to 30 ft at the deepest, whereas Teal Pool, a pear-shaped 8 acres is 15 ft at the deepest. The fishery is situated some 10 miles from Birmingham. The aquatic life includes Sedge, Damselfly, Buzzer, the occasional shrimp, and large concentrations of roach fry.

Facilities:	Small fishing hut. Car park. Toilets (including one for disabled). Permits issued on site, and small selection of artificial flies available. Severn Trent rod licence required (not available on site).
Season:	April 8th to November 25th inclusive. Hours: 8 a.m. to one hour after sunset. Teal Pool closes October 31st, 8 a.m. to sunset.
Rods per day:	No limit. Teal pool 8 rods maximum.
Charges:	Season (full) £130, a 120 fish limit, 5 named days (8 fish per day). Part season £65, any two named days, 8 fish per day, with 80 fish season limit. Day tickets £5.50, half-day £3. Juniors and OAPs £3.50, half-day £3. Day ticket on Teal Pool £11.50.
Day catch limit:	8 fish, half-day 4 fish. Concessionary permits 4 fish and 2 fish. Teal Pool 2 fish.
Boats:	7 rowing boats. Hire charge: day £4, part-day £2. No boats on Teal Pool.
Restrictions:	Fly fishing only. No wading. No dogs. Size limit 12 inches. Minimum cast strength on Teal Pool is 5 lb breaking strain.
Stocking policy:	Regularly throughout the season. Some 14,000 rainbows, 2,000 browns, from 12 inches. On Teal Pool stocking with 2½ lb to over 15 lb.
Annual catch rate:	1.5 per rod average.
Recommended flies:	Most lure patterns including Black Chenille, White Chenille, Muddlers, Viva, Jack Frost, all the Marabou patterns, and Dog Nobblers in white and black.
Local knowledge:	Mick Reeves (Manager): Boat anglers often anchor and fish a fast sinking line with a lure where the fry are concentrating. Dry flies and buzzer nymphs work when fish are rising in summer.

River Avon
Wilts and Hants

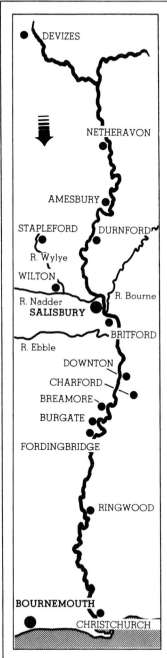

The Avon rises east of Devizes, and flows south for 48 miles to the Channel at Christchurch Bay. It has long been rated one of Britain's greatest angling rivers. The upper reaches are typical chalk stream, with first-class trout. The middle reaches hold trout, grayling, and coarse fish. Below Salisbury, the Avon is greatl swollen by the extra water from its main tributaries – the Nadder, Wylye, Ebble and Bourne. The lower reaches feature migratory fish, and a profusion of coarse fish. Throughout its length, the Avon has abundant weed growth, which harbours particularly rich insect and other water life.

Rod licence required: Wessex Water Authority, 2 Nuffield Road, Poole, Dorset. Tel: (0202) 671144.

Seasons: Salmon – February 1st to September 30th; Sea Trout – April 15th to October 31st; Trout – April 15th to October 15th; Grayling – June 16th to March 14th.

Amesbury. 4 miles of river in two sections held by Salisbury & District A.C. (see Durnford below). Fly fishing for Brown Trout and Grayling. Club has an adjacent lake holding Rainbows. Members only.

Durnford. 3 miles controlled by Salisbury & District A.C. for members only. Excellent water, with Brown Trout of over 6 lb taken in 1984. Applications for membership to the Secretary, Ron Hillier, Club HQ, 29A Castle Street, Salisbury, Wilts. Membership fees are £21 (Juniors £13) annually, plus a £5 (Junior £2) registration fee. The Club also have water on the Wylye at Bapton and Stapleford, and two adjoining stretches of the Bourne at Hurdcott.

Salisbury. Day ticket issued by Salisbury & District A.C. – Salmon £8, Trout £6, and Coarse (Grayling) £3. The Club also has a fine stretch of the Nadder. Day tickets for Salisbury & D.A.C. from Lees Stores, Ashley Road, Salisbury, or Brabon, Newsagents, Wilton Road, Salisbury. A few miles of the Nadder are let by the Rod Box, 52 St. George's Street, Winchester. Tel: (0962) 61561. Day £23.

Britford. The London A.A. fishery consists of a long stretch of the main river, plus a navigation length, and a section known as the main carrier. Plentiful Grayling, plus Trout, and Salmon. Membership of the Association costs £12.50 p.a., plus £2.50 to join the Game Fishing section which allows the purchase of day permits at £6 (salmon) and £3 (trout). The fishery bailiff is Mike Packwood – tel: (0722) 28982. London A.A. HQ (for

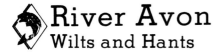
River Avon
Wilts and Hants

membership application) is 183 Hoe Street, Walthamstow, London E17. Tel: 01-520 7477.

Longford. The Longford Estate Water covers a large area with several miles of main river and feeder streams. <u>Salmon, Trout, Grayling.</u> Fishing is by syndicate membership – details from T. Williams, Waterways, Charlton-All-Saints, Nr. Salisbury.

Downton. The Bull Hotel has a fine stretch. Day tickets – <u>Salmon</u> £10, <u>Trout</u> £4 <u>Coarse (inc. Grayling)</u> £2.50, with reduced rates for residents. Tel: (0725) 20374. The Salisbury & D.A.C. have the Charford Fishery of one mile. Day tickets – Salmon £8, Trout £6, Coarse (Grayling) £3 – from Newsagent, Salisbury Road, Downton.

Burgate. Salisbury & D.A.C. has 1¼ miles of water. Day tickets (as in Downton above) available from Burgate Manor Farm. A long section of river is held by the Bat and Ball Hotel at Breamore. Day tickets for <u>Trout, Salmon and Grayling.</u> Tel: Downton (0725) 22252.

Christchurch. <u>Salmon, Sea Trout, Trout.</u> There is superb sea trout fishing in the renowned Bridge Pool; however, this tends to be booked up from year to year. £55 per day for punt (for 2 persons fly-fishing). Best months – August and September. Permits available for the Royalty Fishery – variable prices for trout and salmon. Enquiries and permits for the above – Davis Tackle Shop, 75 Bargate, Christchurch. Tel: (0202) 485169.

Recommended flies: Mayfly, Dark Olive, Blue Winged Olive, Iron Blue Dun, Stratford Sedge, Greenwells, Pheasant Tail, Black Gnat.

Local knowledge: Much of the trout fishing in the upper Avon and tributaries (with many fish well over a pound) is by upstream fly and upstream nymph. There is local concern about the disease which is decimating the crayfish; the latter are a very important food source for the larger trout in the upper reaches. Most salmon (including large springers) are taken in the lower reaches by spinning and prawn. Fly fishing for salmon only really comes into favour in the higher reaches.

Lower Moor Fishery

Oaksey, near Cirencester, Tel: Malmesbury (0666) 860232.
Wilts.   Proprietors: Mr. & Mrs. Geoff Raines.

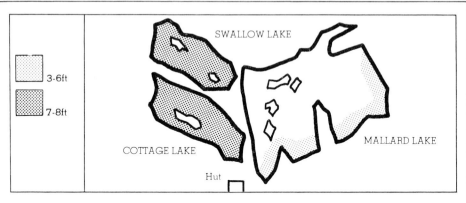

The fishery consists of three ex-gravel pits which have been attractively landscaped. The three waters cover a total of 46 acres. They are known as Mallard Lake (the largest at 30 acres), Swallow Pool and Cottage Pool. There is a prolific mayfly hatch, and an abundance of Sedge, Olives, Damselfly, buzzers, shrimps etc.

Facilities:	A fishing hut with tea and coffee making equipment. Car parking area. Toilets.
Season:	March 21st to January 31st inclusive. Swallow Lake opens May 16th and closes October 15th. Mallard Lake closes December 31st, and Cottage Lake closes January 31st.
Charges:	Day ticket £9, half-day £5.50. Juniors day ticket (for those still at school) £4.50 for a two fish limit.
Day catch limit:	4 fish, half-day two fish.
Boats:	None.
Restrictions:	Fly fishing only. Double and treble hooks not allowed. No wading. All trout caught must be killed.
Stocking policy:	At least 10,000 trout are stocked. The stock consists of rainbows, browns, American brook trout, and tiger trout. Minimum size 12 inches. Stocking continues regularly to maintain a density of 80 to 100 fish per acre.
Annual catch rate:	A 2.8 fish per rod average.
Recommended flies:	Lures: Black Lure, Muddler, Baby Doll, Appetizer, Whisky, Viva, Blue Zulu, Matuka, White Chenille, Flies: March Brown, Stickfly, Teal & Black, Silver Invicta, Brown Sedge, Pond Olive, Mayfly, Greenwell's Glory, Grenadier. Nymph: Sedge Pupa, Red Pupa, Sinfoils Fry, Corixa,
Local knowledge:	Although officially the fishery is open until the end of January, the brown trout fishing ends on October 15th. There are quality fish to be caught, with browns to over 5 lb, and rainbows up to 8 lb. Swallow Lake has 90 per cent brown trout. Cottage Lake is stocked with mainly rainbows.

Wroughton Reservoir

Wroughton, Wilts. Controlled by Thames Water
Tel: Swindon (0793) 24331 ext. 234. Authority (Cotswold Div.).

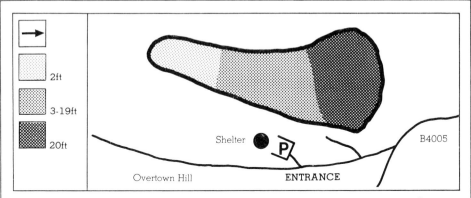

This is an old established (over 50 years) 3 acre reservoir in a pleasant country setting, with natural banks. Located about 3 miles from Swindon. Aquatic life includes tadpoles, mayflies, snails, shrimp, and sedges. Extensive weed in shallow end in summer.

Facilities: Comfortable shelter, car park, toilet.

Season: April 1st to November 30th inclusive. Hours: 8 a.m. to 1 hour after sunset.

Rods per day: 8 maximum.

Charges: Season: not available. Day £5.20, part-day £4.20. During November day ticket £4.20. Tickets on day or in advance from TWA, 17 Bath Road, Swindon.

Day limit: 6 fish, part-day 4 fish.

Boats: 2 punts. 60p per punt (2 anglers).

Restrictions: Fly fishing only. No wading. Size limit 13 inches.

Stocking policy: Throughout the season with rainbows and browns.

Annual catch rate: (1983) 555 fish by 359 rods. Heaviest fish: 5 lb 14 oz – rainbow, 5 lb 12 oz – brown.

Recommended flies:

Early season: Jack Frost, Dog Nobblers, Muddlers, Viva, Zulu.

Mid-to-late season: Pheasant Tail Nymph, Green Nymph, Westward Bug.

Local knowledge: Deep end is more productive, and the favourite area for boat anglers. In early season the Jack Frost does well fished deep. A floating line with a 10 ft to 15 ft long leader is favourite. Shallow end becomes thick with weed, which restricts it to dry fly and nymph.

Black Monk Fishery

Lenchwick, Worcestershire.
Tel: Evesham (0386) 870180. Proprietor: Hywel Morgan.

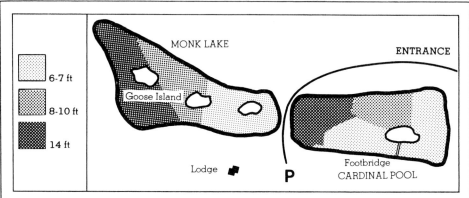

Cardinal Pool and Monk Lake (around five acres each) are spring-fed waters, located in a sheltered and attractive valley just two miles north of Evesham on the edge of the Cotswolds. Aquatic life includes Mayfly, Damselfly, Pond Olives, Buzzers, shrimp and snails.

Facilities: A comfortable lodge where hot lunches, teas etc. can be obtained. Toilets, car park. Flies and small items of tackle also available.

Season: March 19th to December 31st inclusive.

Charges: Season permit details on application.
Day ticket £10, allows fishing on both lakes, with a two fish catch allowed from Cardinal Pool or six fish from Monk Lake. An £8 ticket for Monk only allows four fish, £5 for just two fish.

Boats: None.

Restrictions: Fly fishing only. No wading. No fish caught to be returned. Maximum hook size No 10 long shank.

Stocking policy: Regularly with rainbows, including fish to 10 lb plus.

Annual catch rate: From Cardinal Pool a $3\frac{1}{2}$ lb average weight of fish caught, and from Monk Lake $2\frac{1}{2}$ lb average. weight.

Recommended flies:
Viva, Chenille, Muddlers, Whisky, Buzzers (green and black), Daddy Long Legs, Pheasant Tail Nymph, Corixa, Green Tag Stickfly, Amber Nymph.

Local knowledge: Average depth on these lakes is 7 ft with deep areas of about 14 ft near the outlets. For most of the season a floating line with long leader is most effective. Weighted nymphs do well in the deep water.

River Aire
Yorkshire

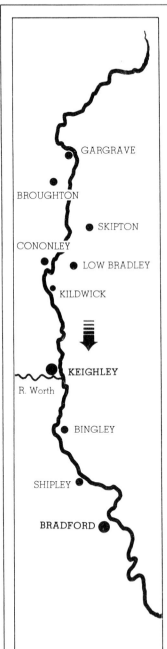

The Aire rises at Airehead to the east of Settle, and flows 70 miles south-east to join the Ouse at the latter's estuary. In its upper reaches, it is a typical tumbling Dales river, holding good trout and grayling. From around Keighley downstream, coarse fish are increasingly prevalent. Below the start of the industrial conurbations at Shipley only a few coarse fish survive the very high pollution levels.

Rod licence required: Yorkshire Water Authority, Fisheries and Recreation (Rivers Division), 21 Park Square South, Leeds LS1 1QG. Tel: (0532) 440191.

Seasons: Trout – March 25th to September 30th; Grayling – June 1st to February 27th.

Gargrave. Trout. Aire Fishing Club has a fine stretch – members only. Bradford City A.A. also has a good stretch downstream of Gargrave to the railway bridge. Enquiries to local tackle shops. Gargrave Council issues permits to local residents and their guests.

Broughton. Trout. 1 mile of single bank held by Bradford No 1 A.A. Rods per day limited. Enquiries: D. Arnett, 49 Templars Way, Bradford.

Skipton. 3 miles held by Skipton A.A. Reserved on Sundays for members and holders of a weekly permit. Weekday tickets (concessions for OAPs and juniors) from J. Preston, 18 Beech Hill Road, Carleton, Skipton. Tel: (0756) 5435.

Bradley. Trout, Grayling. Section held by Bradford No 1 A.A. – for ticket enquiries see Broughton above.

Cononley. Trout, Grayling. Bradford City A.A. has most of the fishing in this area. Day tickets from Railway Inn or tackle shops.

Kildwick. Keighley Angling Club has a long stretch, but with coarse fish largely predominant. The Club also has trout water on the River Worth at Oakworth. Permits from Willis Walker Ltd. Sports & Tackle, 105-109 Cavendish Street, Keighley. Tel: (0535) 602928.

Bingley to Shipley. 3 miles run by the Saltaire A.A. Hours 6 a.m. to 11 p.m. during the trout season. Contact W. Troman. Tel: Bradford (0274) 583088.

Recommended flies: Buzzer Nymph, Black and Peacock Spider, Sweeney Todd, Zulu, Viva

Local knowledge: Heavy brown trout and good bags are taken consistently in the Aire, particularly downstream of Gargrave and in the Skipton area.

Cod Beck Reservoir

Osmotherley,   **North Yorkshire.**
near **Northallerton,**   Tel: (0532) 440191.

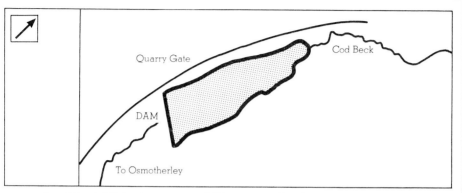

An old established reservoir of 25 acres, and with a maximum depth of over 70 feet. It is attractively set in the Cod Beck Valley. Aquatic life includes snails, water boatmen, sedge, midge, fish fry.

Facilities: Car parking at each end of the dam. Permits from Osmotherley Post Office. Advance booking advisable. A Yorkshire Water Authority rod licence required.

Season: March 25th to September 30th inclusive. Hours: 8 a.m. to 8 p.m. (March to May), 10 p.m. (June to July), 9 p.m. (August) and to 8 p.m. (September).

Rods per day: 12 maximum.

Charges: Season permits not available. Day ticket £3.

Day catch limit: 4 fish, size limit 10 inches.

Boats: None.

Restrictions: Fly fishing only. No wading. Landing net to be of knotless material. All under-sized fish to be returned.

Stocking policy: Pre-season, mainly with browns. At intervals with rainbows.

Annual catch rate: Not available.

Recommended flies:

March Brown, Mallard & Claret, Peter Ross, Butcher, Invicta, Black & Peacock Spider, Muddlers, Baby Doll, Appetizer, Viva, Chenille (black, white), and various nymphs – Pheasant Tail, Amber Nymph, and midge pupa.

Local knowledge: Most of the traditional patterns of wet flies are used with success, and at almost anytime of the season some of the popular lures – in smaller sizes on sinking line – also useful. Any of the nymph patterns fished on floating line.

Damflask Reservoir

Low Bradfield, Yorkshire.
Tel: Leeds (0532) 440191. Controlled by Yorkshire Water Authority.

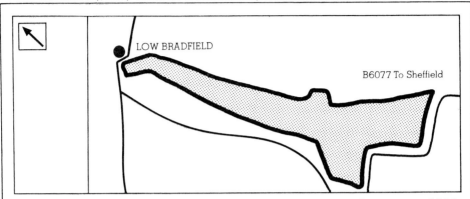

Situated in the Peak District National Park is the Damflask reservoir of 115 acres. It is a long and attractive water that was constructed in 1896 and situated off the B6077 near Sheffield. This is a mixed trout and coarse fish water. Aquatic life: midge, sedge, shrimp, snails and coarse fish fry.

Facilities: Self-service permit issuing machine on site. Car park.

Season: March 25th to September 30th inclusive. Hours: 7 a.m. to 8 p.m. until the end of April and during September, then 7 a.m. to 9 p.m. in May and August, then from 7 a.m. to 10 p.m. in June and July.

Rods per day: No limit.

Charges: Day ticket £2, half-day £1. Juniors, OAPs and disabled a concessionary day ticket £1, half-day 50p. A Yorkshire Water Authority rod licence required.

Day catch limit: 2 fish. 11 inches size limit.

Restrictions: Fly fishing and other legal methods. No wading. No groundbaiting. No undersized fish to be retained. No dogs.

Stocking policy: Pre-season with browns and rainbows, then at intervals throughout the season.

Recommended flies:
Traditonal wet flies and nymphs. Any of the modern lure patterns may be used effectively.

Local knowledge: When fish are deep a long leader and weighted nymph, or a brightly coloured lure pattern on a sinking line is usually successful.

River Derwent
Yorkshire

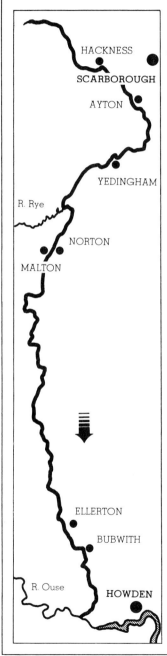

The Derwent rises on Fylingdales Moor near Whitby. It then flows basically South past Scarborough, Malton and York, for some 57 miles, to join the Ouse just above the latter's estuary. In its upper reaches, the Derwent can be excellent for Trout and Grayling. As with so many Yorkshire rivers, fly-fishing water becomes more occasional as the Derwent crosses the Plain of York, and coarse fish tend to predominate.

Rod Licence required: Fisheries and Recreation Office, Yorkshire Water Authority (Rivers Division), 21 Park Square South, Leeds LS1 2QG. Tel: (0532) 440191.

Seasons: Trout – March 25th to September 30th, Grayling – June 1st to February 27th.

Hackness. Derwent Anglers Club has the rights to a ten mile stretch – mainly both banks down to Ayton Road bridge. The river is well stocked with Trout, and there are some fine Grayling. Day tickets (prices vary with the season) from Pritchards Tackle, 56 Eastborough, Scarborough Tel: (0723) 374017, and Hackness Grange Hotel. Enquiries to Sec. J. Martin, 26 Linghill, Newby, Scarborough.

Yedingham. Whilst there are considerable numbers of coarse fish along this stretch, it also includes good Trout and Grayling. Details from Leeds Amalgamated Society of Anglers, Beckett Street, Leeds. Tel: (0532) 499721.

Nunnington. Trout. This is a fly only stretch of the River Rye with a four fish limit. Permits from Estate Office, Nunnington.

Malton. Some Trout and fine Grayling among the coarse fish in this area. Malton and Norton Angling Club controls water on the Derwent and Rye. Enquiries: M. Foggin, 123 Welham Road, Norton, Malton. Tel: (0653) 3208.

Recommended flies: Wet – Peter Ross, Butcher, Dunkeld, Whisky, Wickhams, Black Gnat, Mallard & Claret, Sweeney Todd, Zulu, Chenilles and Baby Dolls. Dry – Wickhams, Black Gnat, Orange Quill, Greenwell, and various sedge patterns.

Local knowledge: On the Derwent club water the point fly must be a wet or dry pattern only. There is a day limit of 4 fish (minimum ten inches).
The tributary Rye is well noted for its Trout and Grayling, and much of the fishing is fly only. Thigh waders and short rods are recommended on this water.

River Esk
Yorkshire

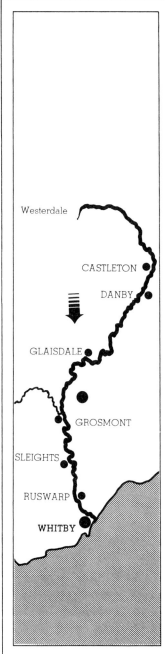

The Esk rises high on Westerdale Moor in the Cleveland Hills, and flows East through beautiful scenery for some 24 miles to reach the North Sea at Whitby. Now re-established (after a re-stocking programme) as a notable Salmon water, this fast and fairly shallow river also provides interesting sport with Sea Trout, Brown Trout and Grayling.

Rod Licence required: Fisheries and Recreation Office, Yorkshire Water Authority (Rivers Division), 21 Park Square South, Leeds LS1 2QG. Tel: (0532) 440191.

Seasons: Salmon and Sea Trout – April 6th to October 31st, Brown Trout – March 25th to September 30th, Grayling – June 1st to February 27th.

Castleton. Trout, Grayling. 3 stretches held by Danby and District Angling Club, including section from Six Arches Bridge to Castleton Road Bridge. Tickets available from Ward Thompson, Borough Road, Middlesborough.

Danby. Salmon, Sea Trout, Brown Trout. Weekly permits issued by Danby Post Office and the Duke of Wellington Inn.

Glaisdale. Salmon, Sea Trout, Brown Trout. Generally preserved by Esk Fishery Association. Occasionally there are opportunities through the Anglers Rest Hotel.

Ruswarp. Salmon, Sea Trout, Brown Trout, Grayling. Esk Fishery Association has two miles; permits from local tackle shops. Esk Fishery Association also has stretches at Grosmont, Goathland, and Sleights. For tidal water between Ruswarp and Whitby apply for tickets to Mr. Hall, Boatyard, Riverside, Ruswarp.

Whitby. Upstream to Glaisdale – enquiries re. day and week tickets to Angling Supplies, 5 Haggersgate, Whitby.

Recommended flies: Salmon – Munro Killer, Hairy Mary, Jock Scott, Silver Wilkinson. Trout (wet) – Greenwells Glory, Black and Peacock Spider, Butcher, various Nymphs.
Trout (dry) – small sizes of March Brown and Greenwells Glory.

Local knowledge: For Trout, small flies (maximum size 16) should be used. However, the Esk is not generally regarded as a very reliable fly fishing water for Trout, which tend to be numerous but small.
When there is sufficient flow, Salmon run up as far as Danby Beck.

Farmire Fishery

Farnham, North Yorkshire.
Tel: Harrogate (0423) 866417.   Proprietors: B. & V. Morland.

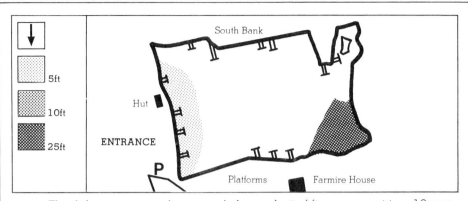

This fishery consists of a spring-fed gravel pit of five acres, set in a 12 acre reserve near Knaresborough. The lake itself has a varying depth, with a fairly clean gravel bottom. There are specially constructed casting platforms for bank fishing. Aquatic life includes Sedge, Daphnia, Midge, snails and shrimp.

Facilities: A fishing hut overlooking the lake. Flies, casts and small items of tackle for sale. There are seats on each of the casting platforms.

Season: April 1st to November 3rd inclusive. Hours: 8 a.m. to 8 p.m., or dark, whichever is earlier.

Rods: 10 per day maximum.

Charges: Season permit £200 (one named day per week). Day ticket £8. A Yorkshire Water Authority rod licence required.

Day catch limit: 2 fish, but trout can be returned.

Boats: None.

Restrictions: Fly fishing only. No barbed hooks allowed on the fishery. No wading. Fishing only from the platform. Micromesh landing nets only to be used.

Stocking policy: Generally at weekly intervals. Rainbows, browns and brook trout.

Catch rate: 22,757 trout at an 8 fish per rod average. Fishery record 12 lb 5 oz rainbow.

Recommended flies: Black Lure, Viva, Black & Peacock Spider, Green-backed Baby Doll, Polystickle, Whisky, Church Fry, Damselfly Nymph, Amber Nymph, Stickfly, Daddy Long Legs, Squirrel & Silver.

Local knowledge: Brian Morland: 'An excellent dry fly water, superb in May and June – when the mayfly hatch – and again in late August, September and October. All patterns of dry fly will catch, but the larger bushier flies seem to be more successful: sedges, daddy long legs etc. Of the smaller patterns, Black Gnats, Tups and Greenwell's are popular. White dry flies seem to work very well. Best fish 1983 – rainbow 11 lb 5 oz, and brown 8 lb 2 oz.

 Leighton Reservoir

Near Masham,   Tel: Ripon (0765) 89224.
North Yorkshire. Controlled by Swinton Estate.

To Masham

R. Burn

Inflow from Roundhill Reservoir

This reservoir, 100 acres in extent, was built in 1926. It is situated on the edge of Masham Moor. The reservoir is fed by a few small streams. There is a variety of aquatic life, including sedge, shrimps and minnow.

Facilities:	Fishing hut, toilets, and a permit issuing machine located in the car park.
Season:	April 7th to October 14th inclusive. Hours: from 6 a.m. to 10 p.m.
Charges:	Season permits available, apply to Estate Office, Swinton, Masham, Ripon, N. Yorks, HG4 4JH. Day ticket £6, evening ticket £3. Half-price juniors (under 14 years) and disabled. Yorkshire Water Authority rod licence essential.
Day catch limit:	6 fish, evening 3 fish.
Boats:	None.
Restrictions:	Fly fishing only. No wading.
Stocking policy:	Total of about 10,000 annually, mainly rainbows, and released at regular intervals. Fish up to 5 lb have been stocked.
Annual catch rate:	Two fish per rod average. In 1983 season 333 fish over 3 lb taken, with the heaviest 9½ lb.
Recommended flies:	
Early Season:	Mostly small lures: Black Lure, Whisky, Appetizer, Missionary, Zulu, Greenwell's Glory, March Brown, Pheasant Tail Nymph, Green Nymph, Amber Nymph.
Mid-to-late season:	Muddlers (various), Viva, Black Matuka, Badger Matuka, Appetizer, Baby Doll, Chenille (black, white), Dog Nobblers, Grey Ghost, plus various nymph patterns weighted and unweighted.
Local knowledge:	Because of the no wading rule the trout often move in close to the bank, so it pays to fish the bank ara before starting to make longer casts. Fry patterns are generally effective because the fish often concentrate on feeding on the minnows.

165

Morehall Reservoir

Stocksbridge, South Yorks.
Tel: Leeds (0532) 440191. Controlled by Yorkshire Water Authority.

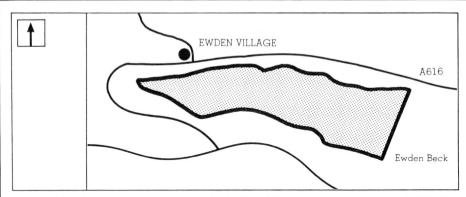

A landscaped and grassy banked lake of 65 acres. Constructed in 1930, the reservoir is situated in the Ewden Beck valley, off the A616, north west of Sheffield. Water life includes sedge flies, gnats, midge, caddis grubs, snails and fish fry.

Facilities:	A self-service permit issuing machine on site. Car park.
Season:	March 25th to September 30th inclusive. Hours: 7 a.m. to 8 p.m., with extension to 10 p.m. during June and July.
Charges:	Season permits £25. Day tickets, from April 8 to September 30, £2. No half-days. Concessionary permits for juniors, OAPs and disabled. A Yorkshire Water Authority rod licence required.
Day catch limit:	2 fish (11 inches minimum size).
Boats:	None.
Restrictions:	Fly fishing only. No wading. No dogs. No fishing from boats.
Stocking policy:	Monthly throughout the season. Main species is brown trout.
Recommended flies:	Most of the traditional patten of wet flies and nymphs, especially March Brown, Dunkeld, Sedge, Mallard & Claret, Pheasant Tail, and various lures.
Local knowledge:	Floating line or sink-tip on most occasions. When fish are deep a long leader and weighted nymph is usually effective. Small lures on slow sinking line usually worth trying. Black & Orange Marabou has proved very successful.

River Nidd
Yorkshire

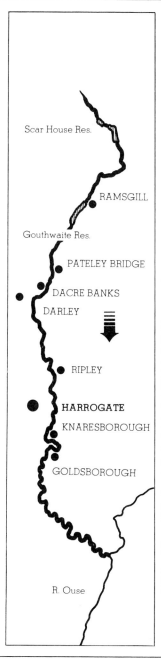

Scar House Res.

RAMSGILL

Gouthwaite Res.

PATELEY BRIDGE

DACRE BANKS

DARLEY

RIPLEY

HARROGATE

KNARESBOROUGH

GOLDSBOROUGH

R. Ouse

The Nidd has its source on Great Whernside mountain, and from there it flows down Nidderdale, past Pateley Bridge and Knaresborough to join the Ouse at Nun-Monkton. In its early upper reaches it provides good fishing, although local angling associations control most of the water, with only limited opportunities available to the visitor. Species are Trout and Grayling; below Ripley, coarse fish tend to take over except in the faster-flowing sections.

Rod Licence required: Fisheries and Recreation Office, Yorkshire Water Authority (Rivers Division), 21 Park Square South, Leeds LS1 2QG. Tel: (0532) 440191.

Seasons: Trout – March 25th to September 30th, Grayling – June 1st to February 27th.

Ramsgill. Fishing controlled by Bradford No. 1 Angling Association. Above Ramsgill a double-bank stretch is controlled by A.W. Hainsworth & Sons Ltd., Spring Valley Mills, Farsley, Pudsey, Leeds. Leeds and District Amalgamated Society of Anglers also have water.

Wath. Nine mile stretch from Gouthwaite Reservoir to Dacre Banks held by The Nidderdale Angling Club. No day tickets issued before June. Mainly reserved for members and their guests. No fish under 10 inches to be taken. Day tickets £2.50, season Permit £38, from local Post Office, and public house.

Darley. Excellent <u>Trout</u> and <u>Grayling</u> on a 2½ miles stretch held by the Harrogate Fly Fishers Club. Members and guests only. Enquiries to T.D. Tredger, 18 St. Catherine's Road, Harrogate.

Knaresborough. 900 yards stretch available for dawn to dusk fishing from April 1st. Tickets from Lido Caravan Park, Wetherby Road, Knaresborough. Tel: (0423) 865169. Knaresborough Anglers also have water.

Goldsborough. The Greenfishers Angling Club have fishing for members and their guests from April 1st. Secretary – Frank Holt, 7 Primrose Walk, Oldham OL8 1HJ. Knaresborough Piscatorials have fishing near Grimbald Bridge, with a limit of two trout. Tickets from Tackle shop, High Street, Knaresborough.

Recommended flies: Coachman, Mallard & Claret, Dunkeld, Zulu, Appetizer, Black Chenille, Viva.

Local knowledge: The stream fishing for Trout in the upper reaches can be very rewarding. There is a Mayfly hatch on some sections of the river.

Ulley Reservoir

Near Rotherham, Yorkshire. Controlled by the Yorkshire
Tel: Leeds (0532) 440191   Water Authority

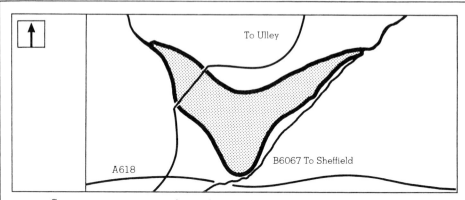

Set in country surroundings this 30 acre water, constructed in 1874, offers
mixed trout and coarse fishing. The reservoir is located east of Sheffield, and
reached via the A618 and B6067. Aquatic life includes sedge, gnat, midge
and fish fry.

Facilities: Permit issuing machine on site. Ample car parking.
                   Toilets.

Season: March 25th to September 30th inclusive. Hours: 7 a.m.
                   to 8 p.m. until end of April, and during September.
                   Then 9 p.m. closing in May and August, and 10 p.m.
                   closing in June and July.

Charges: Day £2, half-day £1. Concessions to juniors (under 15
                   years), OAPs and disabled, day £1, half-day 50p.

Catch limit: 2 fish. 11 inches size limit. Yorkshire Water Authority
                   rod licence required.

Restrictions: Fly fishing, and other legal methods. No wading. No
                   undersized fish to be retained. No dogs.

Stocking policy: Pre-season with browns and rainbows. Then at intervals
                   throughout the season.

Recommended flies:
                   Traditional wet flies, nymphs, and most of the modern
                   lure patterns, like Ace of Spades, Missionary, Appetizer,
                   and any of the Muddler patterns.

Local knowledge: When trout are seen chasing the coarse fish fry then a
                   sinking line and an imitative lure fished deep is most
                   effective. Try using a short, jerky retrieve.

Underbank Reservoir

Near Stocksbridge, Yorkshire. Controlled by Yorkshire Water
Tel: Leeds (0532) 440191 Authority.

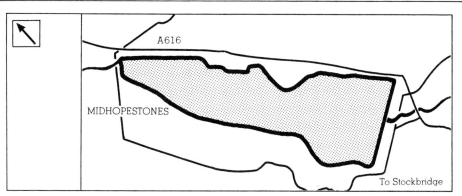

This pleasant lake of 105 acres was built in 1970 and is situated off the A616, north west of Sheffield. It offers mixed trout and coarse fishing. Water life includes sedge, snails and coarse fish fry.

Facilities:	Permits from self-service machine on site. Car park.
Season:	March 25th to September 30th inclusive. Hours: 7 a.m. to 8 p.m. until the end of April and during September. Then 7 a.m. to 9 p.m. in May and August, 7 a.m. to 10 p.m. in June and July.
Rods per day:	No limit.
Charges:	Day tiket £2, half-day £1. Concessionary permits for juniors, OAPs and disabled – day ticket 80p, half-day 50p. A Yorkshire Water Authority rod licence required.
Day catch limit:	2 fish. Size limit 11 inches.
Boats:	None.
Restrictions:	Fly fishing, and other legal methods. No wading. No undersized fish to be retained. No fishing from boats.
Stocking policy:	Pre-season with browns and rainbows, then at intervals throughout the season.
Recommended flies:	
	Traditional wet flies and nymphs. Also most of the modern lure patterns like Black Chenille, Viva, Marabou, Appetizer, Ace of Spades, Sweeny Todd, Baby Doll.
Local knowledge:	To achieve distance from the bank a shooting head line is often used. Lures that are fry imitations are most successful, used on a sinking line.

Washburn Valley Fishery

Otley, Yorkshire.
Tel: 0532-440191 Fisheries Office.

Controlled by the Yorkshire Water
Authority.

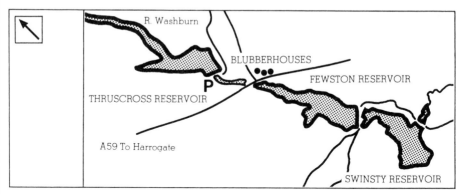

This fishery consist of three old established (1879) reservoirs known as Fewston (156 acres), Swinsty (156 acres) and Thruscross (142 acres). Located in country surroundings and reached via the A59, between Skipton and Harrogate. Water life includes sedge, snails, shrimp, beetles and fish fry.

Facilities:	Fishing lodges at Swinsty and Fewston. Car parks. Permit issuing machines – 50p coin operated – at the reservoirs.
Season:	March 25th to September 30th inclusive. Hours: 8 a.m. to one hour after sunset, but not later than 9 p.m.
Charges:	Season permits not available. Day ticket £3. Yorkshire Water Authority rod licence required.
Day catch limit:	4 fish. Size limit 10 inches.
Boats:	None.
Restrictions:	Fly only except for Thruscross. Chest waders prohibited. The use of bubble float to fish a fly is not allowed. Prohibited fishing areas are indicated. No dogs.
Stocking policy:	Pre-season with mainly browns. Regular intervals with rainbows.
Annual catch rate:	Not known.
Recommended flies:	Most of the traditional patterns of wet flies and nymphs may be used successfully on floating and sink-tip lines. Dark coloured lures generally effective, and mainly fished on sinking line.
Local knowledge:	Lures and sunk lines are best in early season, changing to floating line and traditional patterns thereafter.

River Wharfe
Yorkshire

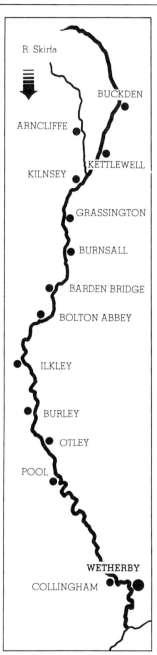

The Wharfe rises on Langstrothdale, and flows for some sixty miles in a South-Easterly direction. It passes and often rushes through dramatic upland country, before gradually becoming a more tranquil water, particularly after Otley. Thereafter, coarse fish are increasingly prevalent, as the river traverses the Plain of York to enter the Ouse near Cawood.

Seasons: Trout – March 25th to September 30th, Grayling – June 1st to February 27th.

Buckden. A two mile stretch controlled by The Bradford City Angling Association. Day tickets from the Buck Inn.

Arncliffe. Interesting fishing for wild <u>Brown Trout</u> on The Skirfare, available to residents of The Falcon Hotel.

Kettlewell. Double bank fishing for <u>Trout</u> and <u>Grayling</u>, both upstream and downstream of Kettlewell, held by the Kilnsey Angling Club. The Club also has a stretch on The Skirfare. Fly only, with a size limit of nine inches for Trout. Day tickets from The Tennants Arms, Kilnsey.

Grassington. <u>Trout and Grayling</u> fishing in the main river and in nearby becks, controlled by The Linton, Threshfield and Grassington Angling Club. Day tickets £4, weekly £16, dawn to dusk, fly only fishing. Size limit nine inches. Day tickets (limited) from Devonshire Hotel, Grassington. Tel: (0756) 752525.

Burnsall. <u>Trout, Grayling</u>. From Stepping Stones to Barden Bridge. Day tickets – Red Lion Hotel or Fell Hotel, Burnsall, and tackle shops.

Bolton Abbey. <u>Trout and Grayling</u> for five miles downstream from Barden Bridge to just below Bolton Bridge. Stocked with Trout on regular basis. Day limit – 4 Trout, minimum 10 inches. Season opens April 1st. Fly only.
Permits: Trout – day £5, week £20; Grayling – day £2, week £10. Juniors half-price, or 50p per day if accompanied by an adult. Bolton Abbey Estate, Skipton.

Ilkley. <u>Trout, Grayling</u>. 1½ miles from Pack Horse Bridge to Stepping Stones, run by Ilkley and District Angling Assoc: Hon. Sec. – J.A. Cockerill, 31 Grange Estate, Ilkley. Permits from Crees Pet Store, or Runnymede News, Ilkley.

Recommended flies: All standard patterns, but particularly those with a bushy hackle, or a Palmered body.

GLENMORANGIE

10 YEARS OLD
SINGLE HIGHLAND MALT
SCOTCH WHISKY

1. KENNY WHITE leaves the Cooperage every year to tame the whins and broom that sprout around
the Tarlogie Springs *(whose hard waters, rich in mineral content, are the source of Glenmorangie)*.
With the leaves turning and the sea-breeze gusting from the Dornoch Firth, the scything marks
the true beginning of the "malt whisky season."

Handcrafted by the Sixteen Men of Tain.

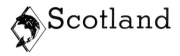 # Scotland

GENERAL INTRODUCTION

It would be easy, but very misleading, to think of Scotland as one fishing region of the United Kingdom. Scotland has, to begin with, the majority of the game fishing waters of Britain. It has, far and away, the major share of waters in which migratory game fish – salmon and sea trout — are found. Its trout lochs, while varying in quality, offer anglers a vast array of fishing – far more than even the most committed anglers could cover in a lifetime. The parish of Scourie in Sutherland, for example, has over three hundred trout lochs. On another scale, the River Tweed, a remarkable river which is now recovering its good spring run of salmon and is showing a good recovery of its autumn salmon and sea trout, can produce a total harvest (to rods and nets) of 40,000 salmon and a similar number of sea trout in a fairly good year. A great year, like 1969, produced nearly 100,000 salmon in the Tweed. The great rivers of the east coast contrast with the shorter rivers of the west coast to give a choice of salmon fishing which runs the gamut of the whole year, from January to November. A multitude of rivers and smaller waters offer pleasant trout fishing, some of it of good quality, in wonderful settings. If you can embrace a country like this in one single category you must be missing something of the variety and quality of sport available.

It is best, I find, to think of the gamefishing of Scotland in landscape terms and the three broadest regional divisions of Scotland are quite helpful, initially at least. The Southern Uplands, covering the Border Hills and the gentler rolling lands between Dumfries and Galloway has good stillwater fishing in the west where there are also several short spate rivers carrying salmon and sea trout. I think of the Luce, the Cree, the Bladenoch, and the Urr in this category. Beside them lie the larger rivers of the western half of the region – the impressive Nith, with its late runs of good salmon and excellent summer sea trout, the Annan, with good summer and autumn migratory fish and the Border Esk with its excellent summer sea trout fishing. These rivers, flowing into the Solway, form a group of waters which have a gentler character, matching the fertile plains they drain, yet they can be memorable fishing waters. They are, however, dependent on summer and autumn rain for their sport and summer drought can ruin them.

The Central Lowlands of Scotland have some interesting small rivers flowing west to the Firth of Clyde. I think of the productive River Stinchar, the Girvan, the Doon and the Ayr in Ayrshire. They are summer and autumn rivers with fair runs of migratory fish (The Stinchar is best), and, like the Solway rivers, they are gentle waters, flowing through good agricultural land, for much of their courses, and near market towns, seaside resorts and nice, open vistas. The interior of the central belt has numerous trout stillwaters and they can lend interesting variety of a holiday in the area. The trouting, and good grayling fishing, on the middle and upper Clyde can be splendid, and can be demanding in terms of skills with dry fly or nymph. On the east side of the central lowlands lies the good reservoir fishing of the Lothians.

Stillwaters in Fife and Kinross, including Loch Fitty and Loch Leven, are waters of considerable note. Loch Leven, with a very long history of flyfishing, may, indeed be the most famous loch in Scotland for the trout angler. It has suffered setbacks of late, but is now recovering. A new stocking programme may well bring it back to its former glory. Finally, in this broad look at the Lowlands, we must not forget the Lake of Menteith, set near the upper waters of the Forth not far from Loch Lomond. This is a stillwater of quality in a fine low valley looking on to the most southern of the Highlands. Nor must we forget Loch Lomond itself, even if it is at least half set above the Highland line and is not really a lowland water. Lomond, with its main tributary the Endrick and its outlet, the River Leven, provides central Scotland with its most interesting game fishery. The sea trout of Loch Lomond are of good size and they can fish well in the island-rich loch, especially out from Balmaha. In autumn, the Endrick carries good runs and can produce fine fish, mainly sea trout, up to ten pounds in weight.

The Highlands of Scotland form a great reach of land, some of it according with the romantic picture of mountain moor and loch and some of it quite different in character. I hesitate to include the lower Tay and the Earn in the Highland bracket, yet both rivers flow from fine mountain territory. The Tay is a fine salmon river, famous for its spring runs and its autumn bounty. It has lost much of its spring clout in recent years, however, but has produced huge September and early October runs of salmon. The Tay and the Earn are good trout rivers in spring also.

I also hesitate to classify the Dee and Don in Aberdeenshire as Highland waters. They are in a sense, because they flow through fine high glens from mountain masses, but their lower reaches grace fine farming valleys with rich estate land. Dee is the best spring river in Scotland for the fly fisher at the time of writing. Its fast clear waters form productive pools and streams. It has excellently organised fishings and it is supervised well as a whole. I doubt whether there is any salmon fishing, no matter how prolific, which can match the Mayfly fishing of the middle Dee. Naturally, water of this quality is difficult to get on to. Most good fishing on Dee is let by the estates to tenants, but it is well worth while making wide enquiries and getting your foot in the door there, if you are seriously interested in fine salmon fly fishing.

In contrast, the neighbourhood Don is not a brilliant spring river for salmon but it is our finest trout fishing in Scotland. Fish up to five or six pounds in weight are taken there on dry fly in May. It is not a duffer's river, however. I know no trout fishing which so cruelly weeds out the skilled fisher from the unskilled. But it is a good tutor too and rewards its fans.

My idea of a great Highland river is the Spey. It has its slow upper reaches with Loch Insh marking the end of its moorland reaches. The river gradually picks up pace and provides fine fly fishing pools above and below Grantown on Spey and produces a river from Grantown down through Aberlour, Craigellachie, Rothes and Fochabers which cannot be faulted for the excellence of its pools and glides and streams. I have to say that the Spey has suffered a loss of spring stock of late, but I also must say that a vigorous management initiative, involving the curtailment of estuary netting and careful stocking have already shown good results. I have no doubt that the Spey, properly managed, and less netted at its mouth, will again become a prime salmon water with tremendous fly fishing. It is already a most notable sea trout water in June and July and is strongly on the ascendancy now.

A very interesting group of rivers flows north and north east, near the Spey, and entering the Moray Firth east of Inverness. They include the Deveron and the Findhorn, both fine waters with salmon and sea trout in them but smaller than the Spey. At Inverness itself the short, heavy Ness drains the vast lochs of the Great Glen -including Loch Ness. This is a salmon river of note and the inland rivers flowing into Loch Ness and Loch Oich above it have good spring salmon fishing. I refer mainly to the Morriston and the Garry. North and west the Great Glen lie numerous large and small lochs, set in impressive hill country and the trout fishing on some of them can be first class – for instance Quoich, Affric, Monar, Mullardoch. To the west of these lochs, in a region of fine peaks and marvellous seascapes, lie some good sea trout lochs and streams. I name a few only – Shiel, Morar, Eilt – and this wild area also provides some good trout loch fishing, as can the islands off the west coast.

The northern Highlands run spectacularly for hundreds of coastal miles of fjords and sea lochs and bays into many of which flow spate rivers carrying sea trout and salmon. Often the salmon of the north west, which are principally summer and autumn fish, run up into lochs and are best fished in stillwater. This is particularly true also of sea trout. Think of the fine sea trout of Loch Maree in Wester Ross, of the Fionn Lochs, of Assynt and Stack and many other waters of the north west. There summer dapping for sea trout is a main pursuit and it can be memorable sport on these wind-swept waters of the north west.

The north east all the way up from Inverness to Wick has its own character. It is not mountainous and is often (for example the Black Isle) very fertile. The rivers of the east, Beauly, Conon, Carron, Oykell and Shin, and above them the Brora and Helmsdale, share in the early spring run of salmon. The most northern of these waters, the Helmsdale and its near neighbour the Brora are best in spring, and, indeed, as far as the Helmsdale goes, it far outstrips anything else in the area throughout the season. These eastern river have good sea trout too, and the waters which flow into the Kyle of Sutherland provide good brackish fishing in that lovely estuary. Brora has sea trout in river and loch.

North of the northern Highlands lie the moors of Caithness, which like northern Sutherland nearby are rich in lochs and famous for trout fishing. I cannot do more than name a sample of the many lochs the area boasts – Watten, St John's loch, and the fine moorland waters round Altnabreac – in which some grand trout rise to the fly. The moors of Caithness also have the spring and summer salmon fishings of the river Thurso and the lesser Wick to attract anglers. Short of taking the ferry to Orkney, where there is also excellent loch trout fishing, or going to the far-flung Shetland isles where there is loch trouting and fly fishing for sea trout in the voes, Caithness makes the most northerly contribution to gamefishing in Scotland.

It is worth reflecting that Scottish trout fishing all needs some form of angling permission. It might be club ticket water, where there is a ticket facility for visitors. It may be hotel water, open for guests or others with permission. It may be that proprietors grant access to visitors, etc, etc. It is not true that trout fishing is free in Scotland, although some fishings are not charged for. Some trout fishings have become known as free, because no proper management and development of the fishings has been arranged. It is, therefore, important that visiting anglers arrange their trout fishing, paying the sums asked for access and the hire of boats. In several places – the Tweed, the Upper Spey and several other areas, the law has now changed. A Protection Order has been granted by the Secretary of State forbidding trout fishing except by those holding written permits. The new protection orders are designed to regularise trout fishing, to encourage development and to provide access and they are working well. Most of us see the decade ahead as one in which good trout fishing will be easier to find and will be a steadily improving asset as a result of these protection orders. Visiting anglers should be careful to establish how proper permission might be obtained to avoid being on the wrong side of the law.

Grouse, Pheasant and Partridge
Walked up or driven
Duck and Goose decoying or flighting
Roe, Red and Fallon Deer Stalking
Pigeon and Rough Shooting
Trout and Salmon Fishing
Hotel and Self Catering

Safari Scotland has the only
Stock Salmon Loch in Scotland
at Carbnui Estate, Dunkeld.

Suppliers of Fresh or Smoked Salmon

Duncan Clark
Safari Scotland
Ardargie Hotel, Forgandenny
Bridge of Earn, Perthshire
Tel: Bridge of Earn (073-881) 2234/2995

The Tweed and its Tributaries

AN INTRODUCTORY NOTE

The Tweed and its tributaries form a most important trout and salmon resource in Scotland. It is a lowland river rising in the moors above Tweedsmuir not far from the source of the Clyde. It takes a great northerly sweep, gathering water as it goes from the Lyne and other smaller streams and turns south to flow through Peebles, Innerleithen and Walkerburn, providing in that area some excellent club trout and salmon fishings. The Leithen and Traquair burns bring volume to this section.

The river receives a very important tributary just about Galashiels where the Ettrick, and its tributary the Yarrow, join from the west not quite doubling the volume of the river in normal water but often swamping the Tweed with floods from the moorland hills of their upper regions. Both Ettrick and Yarrow are interesting salmon and trout waters in their own right. The Gala joins from the left bank two miles below the meeting with the Ettrick and the Leader a few miles below that. With this volume the Tweed flows through its productive middle section, embracing such well known salmon beats as Boleside (just above the Gala), Pavilion, Gattonside, Tweedswood, Gledswood, Bermersyde and Dryburgh. The fattest beats of the river lie immediately below this, roughly between St. Boswells and Kelso, Mertoun, Rutherford, Makerstoun, Upper Floors, Lower Floors and Junction. The junction referred to here is with the Teviot, bringing a substantial flow of water in from the west, roughly parallel to the Ettrick, but flowing for much of its length, through well farmed country.

From Kelso downstream, the Tweed takes on a slower flow as it traverses the Merse of Berwick. There are some very productive waters in this area too, often outstandingly good in early spring and at the beginning of the autumn run in September. I need only mention Sprouston, Birgham, Wark and Coldstream with Lennel below to establish the point.

In all, the Tweed is a most productive autumn river, with an extended season which allows fly fishing for salmon until the end of November and produces far and away the best rod caught autumn catch in Scotland. The Tweed also has a well established spring run from February onwards, and in some years it offers excellent fly fishing on its middle reaches in May and June. Summer fish run according to weather and water and keep rods going in July and August, unless drought ruins the sport. The estuary nets come off in mid-September and a fly-only rule is established. After that date it becomes the apple of every fly fisher's eye since it brings in run after run of large fresh fish which seem to promise sport not only to the end of the fishing season on November 30th but, if we were allowed to fish, throughout the entire winter.

As a trout water, Tweed has an excellent reputation. In its lower and middle reaches wide pools and deep dubs harbour some fine trout which take great skill to catch, after the surge of free rising in April and early May comes to an end. There is excellent fly fishing right up through the middle Tweed, offering fishing on smaller scale waters. There are grayling in Teviot and parts of lower Tweed. The tributaries Leader, Gala, Leithen and Lyne offer hill stream trouting for trout in some marvellous country. Some of the best fish come from the Lyne, which traverses rich farmland between West Linton and its junction with the Tweed above Peebles.

Access to the river for its salmon fishing, especially at peak season is, like other major salmon rivers, something which repays study. The major salmon waters are let by the estates and fishery owners normally on a weekly basis, although one or two have a daily letting arrangement, for example Fairnilee above the junction with Ettrick. There are club salmon fishings on the upper river, which fish best in autumn and the Peeblesshire Salmon Fishing Association manages about sixteen miles of river which, although heavily fished in autumn, holds a considerable stock of salmon and can be generous to visitors.

Access to the river, to upper and middle and lower fishings can also be obtained though hotels and one or two sources listed below which offer day permits for spring and autumn. In summer, from June to the end of August, several major beats on the middle river offer day tickets for salmon fishing which can be productive and offer access to famous water difficult to rent in autumn.

In the details given below the river and its tributaries has been divided into sections from Tweedsmuir in the hills to Berwick on the estuary. The stillwaters in the Tweed area are listed separately in the final section.

The Tweed and its tributaries are covered by a special Protection Order, first issued in 1980, under the Freshwater and Salmon Fisheries (Scotland) Act 1976. Under this order much stricter control of trout fishing has been made possible and all trout fishers on Tweed must ensure that they are in possession of a valid permit before starting to fish. In return for this stricter control, fishery proprietors have made access to the fishings easier.

OPINIONS OF LOCAL EXPERTS

Mr. Ian Fraser: the fishing tackle dealer in Peebles, says that although the upper Tweed does not benefit much from the spring run of salmon, which goes mainly up the Ettrick, from the first floods of summer there is a good chance of a fish from Walkerburn to Manor Bridge. From the Lammas Floods (early August) onwards and especially from late September to the end of the season excellent salmon fishing is available on the upper river. He especially pointed out that the upper river is the only locality on the Tweed where the general public can have ticket access to fishing at reasonable cost and in the best months on the season. He speaks highly of the trout fishing in the area of Peebles. After some years of decline the river is coming back strongly and some remarkable catches were made on fly in April and May 1983 with the best fish over 5 lb., two over 4 lb. and many in the 3-3½ lb. class – surprisingly large trout for the size of water.

Mr. Tom Hardy: proprietor of J & A Turnbull, the fishing tackle shop in Galashiels, said that from Galashiels down to Kelso visitors have some excellent spring fishing available for salmon as well as summer and autumn sport of the highest quality. He has growing optimism about the trout fishing in his area since the protection order was granted (A protection order, giving access to trout fishings with written permission, and protecting that fishing against unauthorised angling was granted in 1980 to the Tweed System under the Salmon and Freshwater Fisheries Act (Scotland) 1976. The Order was renewed in 1983), giving local clubs a measure of security for their trout fishing and constructive stocking policies have been implemented. There are real benefits already apparent and the trout fishing in the district represents excellent value for money. Consistent sport is being enjoyed by ticket holders and visitors.

TACTICS AND TACKLE FOR SALMON ON TWEED

The Tweed season begins in February with two weeks of fly-only fishing and from September 15th until the end of the rod season on November 30th there is a further period of fly-only fishing. Both early spring and autumn fishings on Tweed are periods of long rods – carbon 15 and 16 ft. glass 14 ft. or spliced cane 14 ft. fished with sinking fly lines, usually AFTM 10 S. Some anglers on the lower river have experimented with sinking heads and with heavily weighted tube flies, but these items of tackle are forbidden on the association waters of the upper and middle river and their use is often held to be unsporting. Most anglers on Tweed in spring and autumn use ordinary sinking lines and tube flies or waddingtons of an inch and three quarters to three inches in length.

Best Flies for spring and autumn: Yellow and Black Hair, Garry Dog, Orange and Black Hair, White Wing.

As the spring heats up, floating lines come into use with a selection of smaller tube flies or with conventional greased line doubles in sizes from 4 to 8.

Best Floating Line Flies: Small Garry, Stoat's Tail, Blue Charm, Thunder and Lightning.

Careful attention should be paid to local club regulations. Because of misuse of heavy tackle, strict rules have been enforced by the Peeblesshire Salmon fishing Association. No double or treble hooks above size 4 may be used and no single hooks from 4/0. One swivel only may be used on a salmon cast and that no less than 3 ft. from the fly. (Using a swivel on a fly cast is a rig unique to the Tweed and in most cases it is a thinly disguised attempt to add weight to the tackle. It is often abused.) Wire casts and bubble floats are forbidden. Gaffs are not allowed. No lead-cored lines are permitted. Most of these regulations have been introduced to keep abuse down and they would not normally affect sporting anglers.

TROUT TACKLE AND TACTICS FOR TWEED AND ITS TRIBUTARIES

Spring: Downstream wet fly. A cast of two or three is used
Examples: Tip: Greenwell's Glory No 12 or No 14
        Mid: Red Tag, 12 or 14
        Bob: Butcher, 12
     Or: March Brown, 12; Iron Blue Dun 12
        Blae and Black, 12; Hare's Ear, 12
        Dark Olive, 10 or 12
Late Spring and Summer:
Downstream or upstream wet fly, two or three on cast. Add to above list Mid Olive, Woodcock and Yellow, Woodcock and Hare's Ear (Hare Lug) Snipe and Purple, Badger Quill, Iron Blue spider, Grey Hen, All 14 or in low water 16.

Dry Fly: Fine tackle and small flies used especially on Middle and upper Tweed and tributaries, which are very clear and sometimes difficult streams to fish.

Patterns: Greenwell spider, 14 and 16; Badger Spider, Badger Quill, Black Spider or Black and Silver (Priest), Partridge or Yellow, Partridge and Orange, All 14 or 16.
Parachute patterns (hackle dressed at right angles to hook bend, usually on a little spike on the back of the shank – strongly recommended).

Tweed – The Highest Reaches
Tweedsmuir to Manor Bridge

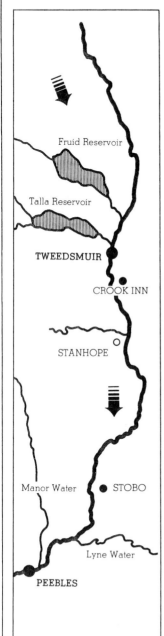

Tweedsmuir. <u>Salmon.</u> **P.** Crook Inn, Tweedsmuir. Tel: 08997 272.
£10 per day inc. VAT. £50 per week.

Tweedsmuir, Lanarkshire. The Crook Inn, Fishing in River Tweed and Lochs Talla, Fruid and St. Mary's (200 yds – 12 miles from hotel). <u>Salmon, Sea Trout, Trout.</u> **P.** Crook Inn, Tweedsmuir. Tel: 08997 272.
Boats: £2 per day. <u>Salmon/Sea Trout</u> £6 per day, <u>Trout:</u> £1-£1.50 per day.

Manor Bridge-Rae Burn. <u>Salmon</u> **P.** I. Fraser, 1 Bridgegate, Peebles. Tel: 20979. Restricted to 20/day. No season for visitors.
21 Feb-14 Sept £2.50 per day inc. VAT, 15 Sept-30 Nov £7 per day inc. VAT.

Stanhope-Peebles (30 miles of river). <u>Trout.</u> **P.** Peeblesshire Trout Fishing Association. D.G. Fyfe, 39 High Street, Peebles. Tel: 20131.
Post Office, Stobo.
I. Fraser, Tackle Dealer, High Street, Peebles.
Sonny's Sportshop, 29 High Street, Innerleithen.
The Luckenbooth, High Street, Innerleithen.
John Dickson & Son, 21 Frederick Street, Edinburgh.
F & D Simpson, 28 West Preston St., Edinburgh.
Tweed Valley Hotel, Walkerburn, Tel: 220.
Crook Inn, Tweedsmuir.
£2 per day, £7 per week, £10 per fortnight, £24 per season or £8 per stretch per season. Prices subject to review.

Lyne Water 5 miles Tweed Junction to Flemington Bridge. <u>Trout.</u> **P.** Peeblesshire Trout Fishing Association,- D.G. Fyfe, 39 High Street, Peebles. Tel: 20131.
I. Fraser, Bridgegate, Peebles. Tel: 20979.
J. Dickson & Son, 1 Frederick Street, Edinburgh.
F & D Simpson, 28 West Preston St., Edinburgh.
Sonny's Sport Shop, 29 High Street, Innerleithen.
Post Office, Stobo.
The Luckenbooth, High Street, Innerleithen.
£2 per day, £7 per week, £10 per fortnight, £24 per season or £8 per stretch per season. Prices subject to review.

Tweed – The Upper Middle
Peebles to the Junction with Ettrick

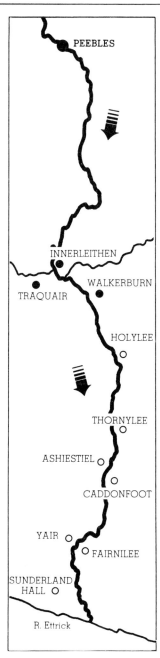

PEEBLES

INNERLEITHEN

WALKERBURN

TRAQUAIR

HOLYLEE

THORNYLEE

ASHIESTIEL

CADDONFOOT

YAIR

FAIRNILEE

SUNDERLAND HALL

R. Ettrick

Wire Bridge Pool (1 ml. below Peebles) – to Caberston/ Holylee march on N. Bank and Juniper Bank/Elibank march on S. Bank. <u>Salmon</u>. **P.** Peeblesshire Salmon Fishing Association.
Seasons: Blackwood & Smith W.S., 39 High Street, Tel: 20131.
Days: I. Fraser, Bridgegate, Peebles. Tel: 20979.
Season: £40 – apply only to odd or even dates and not to Saturdays after 14 Sept.
Days: £7 – payable on reservation for period 14 Sept. to 30 Nov.

Walkerburn 10 miles from Holylee to Peebles. <u>Salmon, Sea Trout, Trout</u>. **P.** Tweed Valley Hotel, Walkerburn. Tel: 089687 220.
From £1.80 per day depending on season and beat.

Traquair <u>Salmon, Sea Trout</u>. **P.** J.H. Leeming ARICS, Chartered Surveyor, Stichill House, Kelso, Roxburghshire. Tel: Stichill 280 24 hr. answering service.
Feb 1-Sept. 30 £5 per day, £30 per week, Oct 1-Nov 30 £15 per day, £90 per week VAT extra.

Peebles – Thornylee (30 miles of river) <u>Trout</u>. **P.** Peeblesshire Trout Fishing Association, D.G. Fyfe, 39 High Street, Peebles, Tel: 20131.
I. Fraser, Tackle Dealer, High Street, Peebles.
Post Office, Stobo.
Sonny's Sportshop, 29 High Street, Innerleithen.
Tweed Valley Hotel, Walkerburn. Tel: 220.
The Crook Inn, Tweedsmuir.
£2 per day, £7 per week, £10 per fortnight, £24 per season or £8 per stretch per season.

Peel ½ mile <u>Salmon, Sea Trout</u>. **P.** Tweed Valley Hotel, Walkerburn, Tel: 089687 220.
Salmon: Downstream Peak £180 & VAT per rod per week (inc. ghillie service). Other private beats £75-£120 per week. Association Permits for guests £35 Mon-Fr. Trout: £1.50 per day, £5.00 per week. Subject to increase.

Fairnilee <u>Salmon, Sea Trout</u>. **P.** J.H. Leeming ARICS, Chartered Surveyor, Stichill House, Kelso, Roxburghshire. Tel: Stichill 280.
Also available through Tweed Valley Hotel, Walkerburn.
1 Feb-30 Sep. £12.50 per week. 1 Oct-30 Nov. £30 per day, £180 per week.

Galashiels Sunderland Hall <u>Salmon, Sea Trout</u>. **P.** R. Smyly, Sunderland Hall, Galashiels, Tel: Selkirk 21298.
Feb-May £8 per day, £40 per week. June-Aug £9 per week. Sept. £60 per week. Oct-Nov £112 per week.

Tweed – Middle Tweed

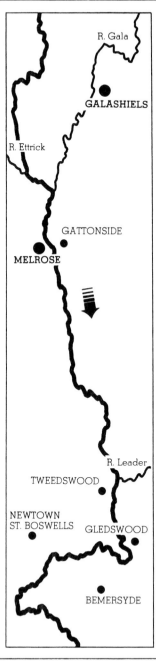

R. Gala

GALASHIELS

R. Ettrick

GATTONSIDE

MELROSE

R. Leader

TWEEDSWOOD

NEWTOWN
ST. BOSWELLS GLEDSWOOD

BEMERSYDE

Galashiels Boleside Beat (Ettrickfoot to Galafoot) Salmon **P.** L. Bald, Fishermans Cottage, Boleside. Tel: Galashiels 2792. Also available through the Tweed Valley Hotel.
1-30 June £30 and VAT daily. £75 and VAT weekly. 1 July-10 Sept £8.50 and VAT daily, £50 and VAT weekly.

Melrose. 2 miles: Pavilion to Tweedswood. (Old Leaderfoot bridge Leader) Salmon, Sea Trout. **P.** Anglers Choice, High Street, Melrose. Tel: 3070.
Cost on application.

Melrose ½ mile North Bank, from suspension bridge to end of the haugh at Friar's Hall: South bank from upper limit St. Helens water downstream to Mill Lade Newstead. Trout. **P.** Melrose & District Angling Association. Anglers Choice, High Street, Melrose. Tel: 3070.
Water Bailiff, Caravan/Tent Site.
I.P. Graham, Dunfermline House, Buccleuch St. Melrose. Tel: 2148.
£1 per day, £3 per week, £5 per season.

Melrose (Ravenswood & Tweedswood) Brown Trout. **P.** Anglers Choice, High Street, Melrose.
50p per day. For Melrose A.A. Season permit holders only irrespective of age.

Melrose. Brown Trout. **P.** The Brother Superior, St. Aidans, Gattonside.
Donation towards the work at St. Aidans: care of mentally handicapped.

Tweed River. Brown Trout. **P.** Melrose & District Angling Association: J. Broomfield, Secretary 'Ravensbourne', Douglas Road, Melrose. Tel: Melrose 2219.
Fishing Tackle Shop 'Anglers Choice' High St., Melrose.
Caretaker, Caravan/Tent Site, Gibson Park, Melrose.
£1 per day, £2.50 per week, £4 per season.

Lowood Bridge, nr Melrose. Right Bank. Trout. **P.** Mr. L.B. Smith, Darnlee, Darnick, Melrose. Tel: 2261.
50p per day, £1 per week, £2 per season.

Galashiels Thornielee to Junction of Tweed and Ellwyn Burn – 12 miles. Trout. **P.** Gala Angling Association: R. Watson, 41 Balmoral Avenue, Galashiels. Tel: 56330.
Messrs J & A Turnbull, 30 Bank Street, Galashiels. Tel: 3191.
Kingsknowes Hotel, Galashiels. Tel: 3478.
Clovenfords Hotel, Clovenfords. Tel: 203.
£1.50 per day, £2 per week, £5 per season.

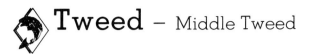 Tweed – Middle Tweed

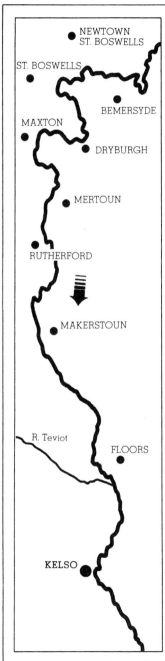

Gala Water Whitelee to Tweed Junction (excluding Torwood Golf Course) Trout. **P.** Gala Angling Association: R. Watson, 41 Balmoral Avenue, Galashiels. Tel: 56330.
£1.50 per day, £2 per week, £5 per season.

Gledswood Estate Water Drygrange Stretch. Trout. **P.**
Drygrange: Mr. W. Lothian.
Gledswood: Mr. S. Herdman.
£1 per day, £3 per season.

Gala Water. Stow, Ferniehurst. Trout. **P.** Royal Hotel, Stow, Tel: 226.
Post Office, Stow.
£1 per day, £2 per week, £4 per season.

Tweed River, 3 miles. Trout. Salmon (by arrangement only) **P.** Dryburgh Abbey Hotel, St. Boswells Tel: 22261.
£1 per day, £3 per week, £5 per month.

St. Boswells, 3 miles. Trout. **P.** Dryburgh Abbey Hotel, St. Boswells. Tel: 0835 22261.
£1.50 per day, £3.50 per week.

St. Boswells. S. Bank: Monksford House to Benrig. N. Bank: Dryburgh Suspension Bridge to Mertoun (other than where marked private). Brown Trout. **P.** Mr. Law, Main Street, St. Boswells.
R. Black, Secy, Kilgraden, Springfield Terrace, St. Boswells.
C.D. Grant, Newsagent, Newtown St. Boswells.
Mr. Geddes, Fishermans House, Mertoun Mill.
Mr. E. Cockburn, Fishermans House, Dryburgh.
Dryburgh Abbey Hotel.
W. Brown, 49 Springfield Terrace, St. Boswells.
Anglers Choice, Melrose.
Miss A. Laing, Newsagent, Newtown. St. Boswells.
£1.50 per day, £3.50 per week, £6.00 per season.

Tweed River. Salmon. **P.** Redpath & Co., 55 Horsemarket, Kelso.
On application.

Tweed – The Lower Reaches

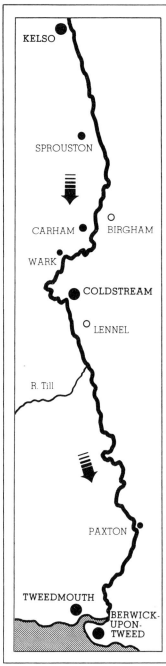

KELSO

SPROUSTON

CARHAM   ○ BIRGHAM

WARK

COLDSTREAM

○ LENNEL

R. Till

PAXTON

TWEEDMOUTH

BERWICK-
UPON-
TWEED

Birgham Dub. <u>Salmon.</u> **P.** Douglas & Angus Estates per The Hon. Caroline Douglas-Home. The Hirsel, Coldstream.
From £25 per day.

Kelso. Junction, Sprouston & Upper Hendersyde. <u>Salmon.</u> **P.** Redpath & Co., 55 Horsemarket, Kelso. Cost on application.

Kelso. S. Side: Junction Pool to Kelso Bridge and Mellendean Burn to top of Broase St.
N. Side: Kelso Cauld to top of Broase St. (Except private water) <u>Trout.</u> **P.** Kelso Angling Association, C. Hutchison, 53 Abbotseat, Kelso.
Forrest & Son, The Square, Kelso.
Redpath & Co, 55 Horsemarket, Kelso.
Sportswise, 43 The Square, Kelso.
River Watchers, Border Temperance Hotel.
Springwood Caravan Park.
£1 per day, £3 per week, £6 per season.

Coldstream. N. Bank to main road bridge. <u>Trout.</u> **P.** Coldstream Angling Association, Market Square, Coldstream. Tel: 2719.
£1 per day, £5 per week.

Milne Graden. <u>Salmon, Sea Trout, Brown Trout.</u> **P.** The Manager, Milne Garden, Coldstream.
Also available through Houndwood House, Reston, Berwickshire. Tel: Reston 232.
£1 per day, £5 per week.

Cornhill. 4 miles: Coldstream Bridge to Dreeper Island. <u>Salmon, Sea Trout, Brown Trout.</u> **P.** Tillmouth Park Hotel, Tel: Coldstream 2255.
£30-£45 Salmon/Sea Trout per day, Brown Trout £2 per day.

Ladykirk. Norham Bridge – Horncliffe. <u>Trout.</u> **P.** Ladykirk and Norham Angling Association, Masons Arms, Norham. Tel: (0289) 82326.
Victoria Hotel, Norham. Tel: (0289) 82237.
£1 per day, £2.50 per week, £5 per season.

Norham. <u>Trout.</u> **P.** Farm House, West Bewbiggin, Norham.
No charge.

Horncliffe. Tidal waters to Berwick. Trout. **P.** N/A.
No charge.

Lennel Beat, Birgham, Wark and Lees Beats.
Coldstream (Town waters). <u>Brown Trout.</u> **P.** Coldstream Angling Association, Market Square, Coldstream. Tel: 2719.

Tweed – Tributaries
Ettrick – Yarrow – Leader

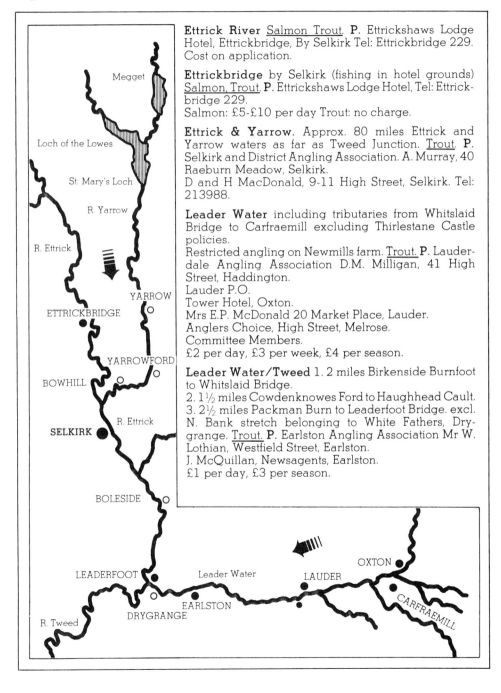

Ettrick River <u>Salmon Trout</u>. **P.** Ettrickshaws Lodge Hotel, Ettrickbridge, By Selkirk Tel: Ettrickbridge 229. Cost on application.

Ettrickbridge by Selkirk (fishing in hotel grounds) <u>Salmon, Trout</u>. **P.** Ettrickshaws Lodge Hotel, Tel: Ettrickbridge 229.
Salmon: £5-£10 per day Trout: no charge.

Ettrick & Yarrow. Approx. 80 miles Ettrick and Yarrow waters as far as Tweed Junction. <u>Trout</u>. **P.** Selkirk and District Angling Association. A. Murray, 40 Raeburn Meadow, Selkirk.
D and H MacDonald, 9-11 High Street, Selkirk. Tel: 213988.

Leader Water including tributaries from Whitslaid Bridge to Carfraemill excluding Thirlestane Castle policies.
Restricted angling on Newmills farm. <u>Trout</u>. **P.** Lauderdale Angling Association D.M. Milligan, 41 High Street, Haddington.
Lauder P.O.
Tower Hotel, Oxton.
Mrs E.P. McDonald 20 Market Place, Lauder.
Anglers Choice, High Street, Melrose.
Committee Members.
£2 per day, £3 per week, £4 per season.

Leader Water/Tweed 1. 2 miles Birkenside Burnfoot to Whitslaid Bridge.
2. 1½ miles Cowdenknowes Ford to Haughhead Cault.
3. 2½ miles Packman Burn to Leaderfoot Bridge. excl. N. Bank stretch belonging to White Fathers, Drygrange. <u>Trout</u>. **P.** Earlston Angling Association Mr W. Lothian, Westfield Street, Earlston.
J. McQuillan, Newsagents, Earlston.
£1 per day, £3 per season.

Tweed – Tributaries
Whiteadder and Dye and Watch Waters

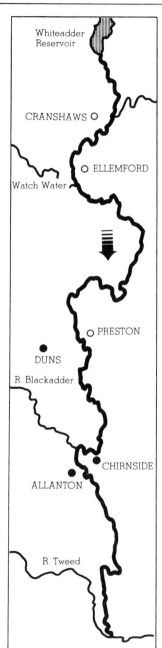

Whiteadder & Dye Tributaries 30 miles Whiteadder from source to Ninewells (Chirnside), excl. private stretches. Dye: from confluence with Whiteadder to Byrecleugh-Horsecupcleugh March, excl. private stretches. <u>Brown Trout</u>. **P.** Whiteadder Angling Association.
James Boyd, St. Leonard's Polwarth, Greenlaw.
Mr. Cowan, Crumstane, Duns.
Black Bull Hotel, Duns.
Mr. Speedy, Whitchester, Ellemford.
Red Lion Hotel, Allanton.
White Swan Hotel, Duns.
£1 per day, £4 per season.

Whiteadder 7 miles: Canty's Bridge to Allanton Bridge, excluding private stretches. <u>Trout</u>. **P.** Berwick & District Angling Association. per. J. Moody Hon Secy. 12 Hillcrest, East Ord, Berwick.
Messrs Jobson, Marygate, Berwick.
Messrs Game Fair, Berwick.
Red Lion, Allanton.
£1.50 per day, £3 per week, £4 per season.

Watch Reservoir <u>Brown Trout, Rainbow Trout</u>. **P.** Whiteadder Angling Association J. McLean, The Row, Longformacus, Berwickshire Tel: Longformacus 272.
Boat: £4 per day, Bank: £1 per day.

Whiteadder Water and tributaries <u>Brown Trout, Rainbow Trout</u>. **P.** Whiteadder Angling Assoc. R. Welsh, Abbey Street, Bathans, Duns. Berwickshire Tel: Abbey St. Bathans 210.
T. Speedy, Ellemford.
D. Young, Elba.
A. Murray, Home Ave. Duns.
£3 per season.

Whiteadder River <u>Brown Trout.</u> **P.** The Bungalow Hotel, Blanerne, Duns. Tel: Chirnside 286.
Free to residents.

Duns Berwickshire Fishing in Whiteadder River 200 yds from hotel. <u>Brown Trout</u>. **P.** The Bungalow Hotel. Tel: Chirnside 286.
Free to residents.

Tweed – Tributaries
Blackadder

Blackadder and Tributaries 13 miles. <u>Trout.</u> **P.** Greenlaw Angling Club.
A. Lamb, Waterford, Wester Row, Greenlaw.
Doigs Stores The Cafe Greenlaw.
Post Office, All Hotels.
75p per day, £3 per season.

Blackadder Kimmerghame Mill to Mouth Bridge <u>Trout</u> **P.** C,. McCosh, Kimmerghame Mill.
A. Bigger, Kimmerghamme Heugh.
R. Welsh & Son, 28 Castle Street, Duns.
50p per day, £2 per week.

Blackadder Whitelaw stretch, South Bank <u>Trout</u> **P.** Whitelaw Farmhouse, Duns, Berwickshire.
£1 per day, £3 per week.

Blackadder Blackadder Mains to Allanbank both banks. <u>Trout</u> **P.** W.P. Harrower, Tofthill, Allanbank, Duns. Tel: Chirnside 302.
50p per day, £2 per week.

GREENLAW

FOGO

DUNS

KIMMERGHAME

ALLANBANK

ALLANTON

CHIRNSIDE

R. Whiteadder

Tweed – Tributaries
Teviot

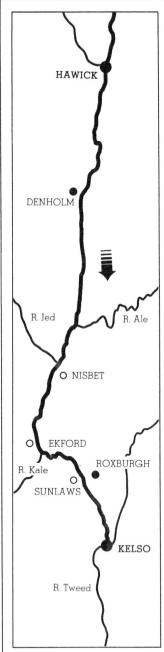

Teviot River, Eckford <u>Salmon, Sea Trout</u>. **P**. Gamekeeper, Keepers House, Eckford, Roxburghshire. Tel: Crailing 255.
£2.50 per day.

Teviot River, Eckford. <u>Salmon, Brown Trout</u>. **P**. Hawick Angling Club 6 Sandhead, Hawick, Roxburghshire, Tel: Hawick 3771.
Trout: £1 per day, £2.50 per week, Salmon: £5 per day.

Teviot 1 mile: Eckford (Buccleuch Estates Waters) <u>Salmon, Sea Trout, Brown Trout</u>. **P**. Gamekeeper, Keepers Cottage, Eckford- Tel: Crailing 255.
Salmon: £5 per day, Trout: £1 per day.

Tweed and Teviot Rivers <u>Salmon, Trout</u>. **P**. Redpath and Co., Kelso, Tel: Kelso 2578.
From £1 per day.

Teviot 2½ miles Oxnam Mouth – Nine Wells, both banks in places. <u>Salmon, Trout</u>. **P**. Jedforest Angling Association, A. Whitecross, 42 Howden Road, Jedburgh. Gun Shop, Kenmore Toll, Jedburgh (trout permits only).
W. Shaw, Cannongate, Jedburgh.
Salmon: £5 per day Trout: £1 per day £4 per week £8 per season.

Teviot N. Side: Ormiston March to Teviot Bridge. S. Side: Teviot Bridge to the junction. <u>Trout</u>. **P**. Kelso Angling Association, C. Hutchison, 53 Abbotseat, Kelso.
Forrest & Sons (Tackle) The Square, Kelso.
Redpath & Co., Horsemarket, Kelso.
Sportswise, 43 The Square, Kelso.
Border Temperance Hotel, Springwood Caravan Park.
£1 per day, £3 per week, £6 per season.

Teviot Hawick to top of Chesters. <u>Salmon, Sea Trout</u>. **P**. Stotharts, Tackle Shop, 6 High Street, Hawick. Tel: 2331.
£5 per day.

Teviot inc. tributaries – Ale, Borthwick, Rule and Slitrig. <u>Brown Trout</u>. **P**. Stotharts, 6 High Street, Hawick.
Club Premises, 5 Sandbed, Hawick.
Dickman (Saddler) Denholm.
Pet Shop, 1 Union Street, Hawick.
£1 per day, £3 per week, £6 per season.

Map labels:
HAWICK
DENHOLM
R. Jed
R. Ale
O NISBET
O EKFORD
ROXBURGH
R. Kale
O SUNLAWS
KELSO
R. Tweed

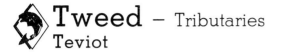 # Tweed – Tributaries
Teviot

Jed Water 1 mile left bank. <u>Trout</u>. **P.** Jedforest Country House Hotel, Camptown. Tel: Camptown 274.
No charge.

Jed/Oxnam Waters Jed – Mossburnfoot Jedfoot Oxnam Water – large part <u>Trout</u>. **P.** Jedforest Angling Association
Gunshop, Kenmore Toll, Jedburgh.
W. Shaw, Cannongate, Jedburgh.
75p per day, £2.50 per week.

Kale Water 1½ miles from junction with Teviot upstream Trout. **P.** Mr. A. Graham, Gamekeepers House, Eckford.
R. B. Anderson W. S., Royal Bank Buildings, Jedburgh. Tel: 3202.
£1 per day.

Kale Water (above Easter Wooden, **Bowmont** (above Primside Mill), **Oxnam** (above Bloodylaws). Trout **P.** Mr. H. Fox, Orchard Cottage, Morebattle.
75p per day, £1.50 per week, £4 per season.

Kale River Brown Trout **P.** Gamekeeper, Keepers House, Eckford, Tel: Crailing 255.
£1 per day.

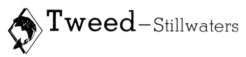 Tweed–Stillwaters

Coldingham Loch. Brown Trout, Rainbow Trout. **P.** Dr. E. J. Wise, West Loch House, Coldingham, Berwickshire. Tel: Coldingham 270.
Cost on application.

Whiteadder Reservoir. Brown Trout. **P.** Lothian Regional Council, Department of Water Supply Services, Alderston House, Haddington, East Lothian. Tel: Haddington 2109.
Cost on application.

Ackerknowe Reservoir. Brown Trout. **P.** Hawick & District Angling Club, 5 Sandbed, Hawick, Roxburghshire. Tel: Hawick 3771.
Pet Store, 1 Union Street, Hawick, Roxburghshire. Tel: Hawick 3543.
David Dickman, Main Street, Denholm, Hawick, Roxburghshire. Tel: Denholm 320.
Horse & Hounds Inn, Bonchester, Hawick, Roxburghshire. Tel: Bonchester 645.
Cost on application.

Acremoor Loch. Brown Trout. **P.** Hawick & District Angling Club, 5 Sandbed, Hawick, Roxburghshire. Tel: Hawick 3771.
Stotharts, 6 High Street, Hawick, Roxburghshire. Tel: Hawick 2231.
David Dickman, Main Street, Denholm, Hawick, Roxburghshire. Tel: Denholm 320.
Pet Store, 1 Union Street, Hawick, Roxburghshire. Tel: Hawick 3543.
Horse & Hounds Inn, Bonchester, Hawick, Roxburghshire. Tel: Bonchester Bridge 645.
Cost on application.

Alemoor Loch. Brown Trout. **P.** Hawick & District Angling Club, 5 Sandbed, Hawick, Roxburghshire. Tel: Hawick 3771.
Stotharts, 6 High Street, Hawick, Roxburghshire. Tel: Hawick 2231.
Pet Store, 1 Union Street, Hawick, Roxburghshire. Tel: Hawick 3543.
David Dickman, Main Street, Denholm, Hawick, Roxburghshire. Tel: Denholm 320.
Horse & Hounds Inn, Bonchester, Hawick, Roxburghshire. Tel: Bonchester Bridge 645.
Cost on application. Bank fishing only.

St. Mary's Loch. Brown Trout. **P.** Rodono Hotel, Yarrow, Selkirk. Tel: Cappercleuch 232.
Glen Cafe, St. Mary's Loch, Yarrow, Selkirk. Tel: Cappercleuch 241.
Tibbie Shiels Inn, St. Mary's Loch, Yarrow, Selkirk. Tel: Cappercleuch 226.
Gordon Arms Hotel, Yarrow, Selkirk. Tel: Yarrow 222.
Cost on application.

Loch of the Lowes. Brown Trout. **P.** Rodono Hotel, Yarrow, Selkirk. Tel: Cappercleuch 232.
Glen Cafe, St. Mary's Loch, Yarrow, Selkirk. Tel: Cappercleuch 241.
Tibbie Shiels Inn, St. Mary's Loch, Yarrow, Selkirk. Tel: Cappercleuch 226.
Gordon Arms Hotel, Yarrow, Selkirk. Tel: Yarrow 222.
Cost on application.

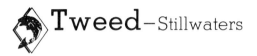 **Tweed**–Stillwaters

Talla Reservoir. <u>Brown Trout.</u> **P.** Lothian Regional Council, Department of Water Supply Services, Comiston Springs, 55 Buckstone Terrace, Edinburgh. Tel: Edinburgh (031) 4454141.
Cost on application.

Fruid Reservoir. <u>Brown Trout.</u> **P.** Lothian Regional Council, Department of Water Supply Services, Alderston House, Haddington, East Lothian. Tel: Haddington 2109.
Cost on application.

The Lothians

AN INTRODUCTORY NOTE

Although there are several fly fishing streams available in the Lothians, and Edinburgh anglers fish them, the region is primarily thought of as a place for good loch fishing. The lochs are in fact nearly all reservoirs, part of the region's supply services. Perhaps the best known of the stillwater fishings of the Lothians is Gladhouse about twelve miles from Edinburgh and nicely set in the Moorfoot hills. It is a trout water of some note, stocked by the Region and fished by arrangement with them. It is a rewarding water in spring and early summer, provided the winds are not too high and it offers varied drifts for trout along its attractive shores and among its islands. Fish up to two pounds can be expected with the average fish about three quarters of a pound.

Near Gladhouse lies Portmore, a hill reservoir of quality stocked with browns and rainbows. Some of its rainbows are large and some seasons show fish of seven or eight pounds. It can be fished from the bank or by boat and is a popular and delightful place to spend an evening.

Other lochs in the region offer a range of trout fishing from bank and boat in stocked waters which vary from those ideal for family picnic trouting to more serious waters with large fish. Full details of each can be had from the Lothian Regional Council, who have a booklet describing all their fishing waters open to the public. One special water in West Lothian should be mentioned, Linlithgow Loch. This water has, in the recent past, produced some very large trout and it still has this aura about it. It is now stocked with rainbows and browns and sizes have tended to stabilise at a nice catchable level. Its richness, however, ensures that substantial fish will be taken there from time to time and the water has greater appeal because of this possibility. It is, however, most nobly set, lying beside a ruined palace with associations with Mary Queen of Scots – a memorable place of fine atmosphere.

LOCAL EXPERT KNOWLEDGE

Drew Jamieson, Water Activities Officer with Lothian Regional Council says: 'One of the most exciting features about fly fishing in the Lothians is the great variety of waters within reach of Scotland's Capital City. One day you can be drifting in a boat for wild brown trout on Gladhouse Reservoir – the next you can be wading for rainbows on Rosebery or Portmore or chasing brook trout at Crosswood or Glencorse. You can choose to follow bigger stockies in Clubbiedean or Morton or lose yourself among the moorlands at Harperrig or Whiteadder after wild half-pound brownies. There is river trouting, sea trout and even the occasional salmon.'

 # The Lothians

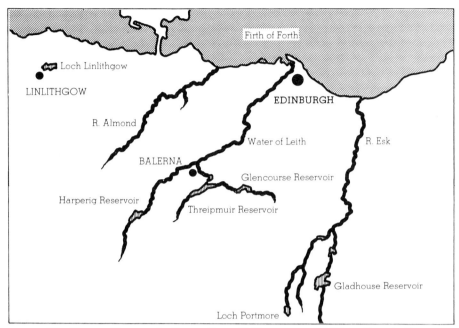

Gladhouse Reservoir. <u>Brown Trout.</u> **P.** Department of Water Supply Services, Comiston Springs, 55 Buckstone Terrace, Edinburgh. Tel: 031-4454141. £5.50 per session (2 rods).

Glencorse Reservoir. <u>Brown Trout.</u> **P.** Lothian Regional Council, Department of Water Supply Services, 55 Buckstone Terrace, Comiston Springs, Edinburgh. Tel: 031-4454141.
3 boats –£5.50 each (incl. 2 rods).

Harperrig Reservoir. <u>Brown Trout.</u> **P.** Department of Water Supply Services, Comiston Springs, 55 Buckstone Terrace, Edinburgh. Tel: 031-4454141.
Bank fishing £1.40. 4 boats, £5.50 (incl. 2 rods).

Linlithgow Loch. <u>Brown Trout.</u> **P.** Garden Shop, The Cross, Linlithgow High Street, Linlithgow. Tel: Linlithgow 5882.
Boat permit £7 (incl. 3 rods). Bank fishing £1.50.

Loch Portmore. <u>Brown Trout, Rainbow Trout.</u> **P.** The Portmore estate changed hands in 1982 and the Company who had leased and run the fishing for several years were unable to negotiate a further lease. Further information is not available at present.

Threipmuir Reservoir. <u>Brown Trout.</u> **P.** Obtainable by post from Leuchold, South Queensferry, West Lothian, by enclosing stamped addressed envelope and fee. Mark letters "Fishing Permit".
Flemings, 42 Main Street, Balerno.
Permits include bank fishing at Harlaw Reservoir.
£8 one day per week throughout the season, £18 full season, £7 per week, £1.25 per day.

 # Loch Fitty

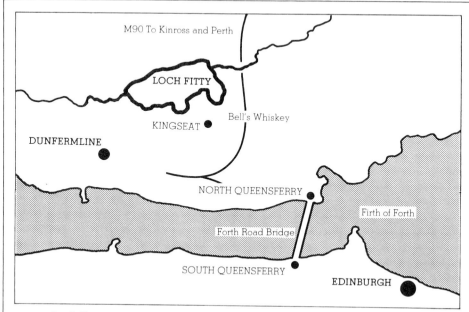

Loch Fitty is a water which for many years lay full of coarse fish, but, through the efforts of Game Fisheries Ltd. was turned into a good rainbow and brown trout water offering fine sport for both bank and boat anglers. Fitty fish can be big and some of the browns and the rainbows have reached seven pounds and more. Its average fish, however, is just over a pound, but many much larger fish show to the fly and provide great sport.

Boats are available for day or evening sessions and bank fishing may be had similarly.

Boat fishing: Session: 10-5 p.m., £14.10 per boat (up to 3 anglers). 5.30 p.m. – dusk, £15-£16 per boat (according to length of evening).

Bank fishing: Session: 10 a.m.-5 p.m., £5.90. 5.30 p.m.-dusk, £5.90.

Access to Loch Fitty from Edinburgh is across the Forth Road Bridge, up the M90 (towards Perth) to the roundabout at the Bell's Whisky Bond, turn off left towards Dunfermline and immediately turn right to Kingseat. The loch is less than a mile from Kingseat, leaving the village by the right and finding the track to Fitty on your left. In all, Fitty is about twenty minutes from Edinburgh.

LOCAL OPINION

It's marvellous having Loch Fitty on the doorstep of Edinburgh and the Fife towns. It has a long season, giving, for example, first class sport well into the autumn. Also having a loch with good mixed trout and rainbow fishing is good fun. There is a chance of a really big fish in Fitty too.

Loch Leven Kinross

The Pier, Kinross.   Controlled by Loch Leven Fisheries.
Tel: (0577) 63407.

This is a very famous loch fishery lying approximately midway between Edinburgh and Perth near the M90 motorway. It is a very rich 'green' water of just over 4,000 acres with attractive drifts among island and along wooded and farmland shores. The loch, once famous for free-rising trout of a pound average has suffered from over-enrichment of the water and it now produces small bags of large trout (three pounders are fairly common) but there are signs that it's stock of smaller trout is recovering. A new stocking policy has been introduced.

Facilities: A good pier with many large clinker-built boats with outboards. Local hotels and shops.

Season: Mid-April to end of September. Day and evening sessions.

Charges: Day (8 hours) 10 a.m.-6 p.m.—£11.50.
Afternoon only (4 hours) 2 p.m.-6 p.m.—£7.50.
Evening (5 hours) 6.30 p.m.-11.30 p.m.—£15.00.

Restrictions: Fly only. No bank fishing.

Stocking: Commencing 1984 70,000 fish per annum.
Average weight (1981): 1.5 lbs. Best fish: 4 lb 15 oz.

Recommended flies:
Early season—Blae & Black Size 12, Dark Greenwell, Butcher.
Summer—Partridge and Orange Sizes 14 and 16, Malloch's Favourite, Hardy's Gold Butcher, Dunkeld (small doubles also used).
Success is also being reported with English reservoir lures fished deeply.

The Forth and Teith Waters
Stirlingshire

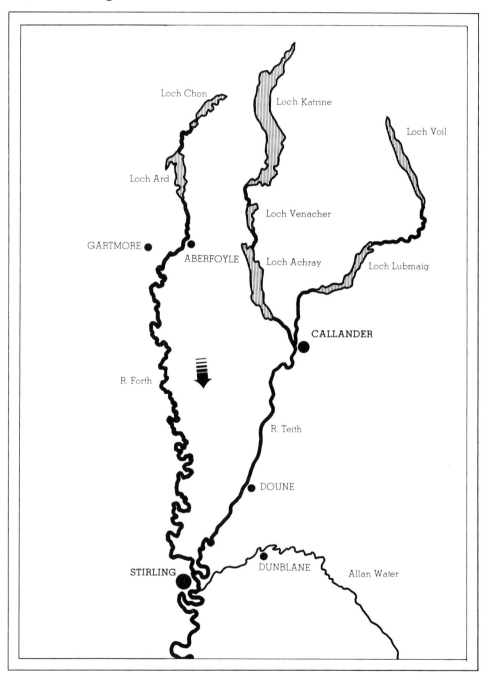

The Forth and Teith Waters
Stirlingshire

AN INTRODUCTORY NOTE

The river Forth, with a great arm of the sea named as its Firth, might well seem to be a major river of Scotland. It is, however, not itself a significant salmon river, although salmon run into it. Its major tributary, the Teith is a far more important salmon and sea trout river with a spring run and good summer and autumn sport in the right conditions. The small but productive Allan Water, which drains the valley between Stirling and Blackford is worth a mention as a water of trout, sea trout and occasional salmon.

The Forth and the Teith both have interesting trout lochs in fine scenery in their hinterlands. The Lake of Menteith, for example, lying in the upper Forth valley, is a fine rainbow and brown trout fishery with boats available to the public. The Teith, and its tributary the Leny, open up the Trossachs lochs, principally Achray and Ard where trout fishing is available in fine countryside and Venachar in the next valley north. These are Highland lochs set between rolling hills with good timber and with high peaks behind. Loch Lubnaig, which lies beside the road from Callander to Lochearnhead is a loch with considerable potential as a trout water and tourist fishing is available.

Allan Water. <u>Sea Trout, Brown Trout, Grilse.</u> **P.** D. Crockart & Son, King Street, Stirling, Stirlingshire.
Allanbank Hotel, Greenloaning, Dunblane, Perthshire. Tel: Braco 205.
McLaren Fishing Tackle & Sports Equipment, Bridge of Allan, Stirlingshire.
£1.50 per day, £2.50 per day after July 31.

Carron Valley Reservoir. <u>Brown Trout.</u> **P.** The Director of Finance, Central Regional Council, Viewforth, Stirling. Tel: Stirling 3111.
£6 per day inc. boat. Saturdays £6.60.

Loch Coulter. <u>Loch Leven Trout, Brown Trout, Rainbow Trout.</u> **P.** Larbert and Stenhousemuir Angling Club, Alex McArther, "Lynewood", 11 Bellsdyke Road, Larbert, Stirlingshire. Tel: Larbert 2581.
£2-£3 per day inc. boat (2 rods).

River Devon. Harviestoun Estate Water upwards to Caldron Linn. <u>Salmon, Sea Trout.</u> **P.** Devon Angling Association, Mr. Br. Breingan, 33 Redwell Place, Alloa, Clackmannanshire. Tel: Alloa 215185.
Arthur West Emporium, Alloa, Clackmannanshire.
Scobie Sports, Primrose Street, Alloa, Clackmannanshire.
£2.50 per season, £1 per day.

River Forth. 6½ miles downstream from Gartmore Bridge to Bucklyvie. <u>Salmon, Brown Trout, Sea Trout.</u> **P.** A. E. Billet, Glenhead, Gartmore, Stirlingshire.
Tackle Shops – Glasgow, Kirkintilloch, Stirling and Falkirk.
75p per day, £5 per season.

River Forth. from Gartmore Bridge upstream. <u>Salmon, Sea Trout, Brown Trout.</u> **P.** Glasgow Telephones & Civil Service Angling Association: T. G. Farmer, Secretary, 27 Brenfield Avenue, Glasgow G44 3LR.
Mrs. Ferguson, Station Buildings, Aberfoyle, Perthshire.
50p per day.

River Forth. <u>Salmon, Brown Trout.</u> **P.** Messrs. D. Crockart & Son, 15 King Street, Stirling. Tel: Stirling 3443.
£2.50 per day, £12.50 per season.

River Teith (Blue banks). <u>Salmon, Trout.</u> **P.** Messrs. D. Crockart & Son, 15 King Street, Stirling. Tel: Stirling 3443.
£5.00 per rod per day, 8 rods.

River Teith. Cumbusmore Estate Waters, $3\frac{1}{2}$ miles (3 beats). <u>Salmon, Trout.</u> **P.** J. Bayne, Tackle Shop, Main Street, Callander. Tel: 0877 30218.
£6 per day, limit 3 rods per beat.

River Teith. Callander Town Water, $1\frac{1}{2}$ miles. <u>Salmon, Trout.</u> **P.** J. Bayne, Tackle Shop, Main Street, Callander. Tel: 0877 30218.
£3 per day, no rod limit.

Loch Achray. <u>Trout.</u> **P.** Loch Achray Hotel, The Trossachs, by Callander, Perthshire. Tel: Trossachs 229.
£1 per day, free to residents.

Lake of Menteith. <u>Rainbow Trout, Brown Trout.</u> **P.** Lake Hotel, Port of Menteith, by Stirling, Stirlingshire. Tel: Port of Menteith 258.
20 boats: £8.50 per day.

Loch Lubnaig. <u>Trout, Salmon.</u> **P.** J. Bayne, Tackle Shop, Main Street, Callander. Tel: 0877 30218.
£1 per day – Trout. £3 per day – Salmon.

Loch Venachar. <u>Salmon, Trout.</u> **P.** J. Bayne, Tackle Shop, Main Street, Callander. Tel: 0877 30218.
£1 per day – Trout. £3 per day – Salmon.

Loch Ard. <u>Trout.</u> **P.** Forest Hills Hotel, Aberfoyle, Perthshire. Tel: Kinlochard 277.
Post Office, Kinlochard, Aberfoyle, Perthshire. Tel: Kinlochard 261.
Cost on application.

LOCAL OPINION

The Teith is a water well worth cultivating a relationship with. It offers a very fair chance to take an early spring salmon and its sea trout fishing is showing good sport in June.

The Tay System

AN INTRODUCTORY NOTE

The Tay system is one of the three great river-and-loch systems which dominate the geography of the Highlands – the others being the Ness-Great Glen system and the Spey. The Tay carries the largest volume of fresh water in the British Isles and from its sources in the hills in the west of the country near Tyndrum on the road to Oban to the ultimate merging with the north sea at Dundee, below a long estuary, the river offers a very varied and productive range of fisheries in both flowing and still water.

In its highest reaches above Loch Tay, the system carries the name of Dochart: a slowish river system with lochs on its course, offering good trout fishing and, from late spring onwards, salmon fishing. The Dochart flows into Loch Tay near Killin and the first of the important Tay salmon fisheries is located there. Loch Tay, an interesting if difficult trout water, offers little fly fishing for salmon. Most of its fish are taken very early from January 14th onwards and are caught by trolling spoons and other baits. Fish have been taken in Loch Tay on fly later in the spring, but the normal practice both in Kenmore (the Eastern end) and Killin (the western end) is trolling.

Most anglers think of the Tay from Kenmore, where it leaves the loch, to Logierait, where it is joined by the Tummel, as the upper river, although many miles of fishing lie above this. The river picks up pace below Aberfeldy where the Lyon joins it – itself a salmon and trout river with interesting sport from late spring on. Reasonably priced, but often productive beats follow in succession down through Weem and Grandtully to Logierait.

The beats of Tay which lie below Logierait – the Kinnaird beats, Dalguise, and other waters down to Dunkeld House water, are usually regarded as the upper middle, with spring fishing from the opening date in January and good sport holding through the months of June, when smaller summer runs of grilse and larger fish appear, and subject to weather and water, keep the anglers busy throughout the summer. These upper middle beats can be extremely productive at times and can carry large fish. Both the upper waters and the upper middle are excellent trout waters with first class fly fishing in spring with olives, march browns and iron blue duns.

From Dunkeld down to Perth the river embraces a series of famous beats, known both for their early spring fishing and for their sustained summer sport followed by a growing autumn run of salmon taking sport right up to the closing date in mid-October. Here you will find names to conjure with – Murthly Castle, Burnbane, Meikleour, Islamouth, Catholes, Stanley (with the Pitlochry Pool), Benchil, Redgorton, Waulkmill, Almondsmouth and Scone. At their best, these Tay fishings can be outstanding and year after year, produce some very large salmon in the forty and fifty pound class along with more likely fish of ten to twenty pounds in weight. Trout fishing on this section is also good and fly fishing can be memorable.

The Tay is not fished by fly nearly enough for its salmon. There is a tradition of spinning it, partly because of its size and partly because it is an early spring river and spun baits seem to get down better to fish in icy water. But there are anglers who fish the fly for preference on the Tay and they have some very exciting scores to report, from the earliest spring fishing on. If streams and pools can be covered by fly, Tay is a splendid water for the method. There is excellent fly water on many beats, but Islamouth and Benchil come to mind as outstanding. there is more than a grain of truth in the claim that the Islamouth beat, with its long glides below the junction, offers fly fishing for salmon without many rivals in Scotland.

The Tributaries of the Tay are often large rivers in their own right. Tummel, for example, although, in its modern form, cut down from its former glory by Faskally hydro-electric dam, is a fine, open Highland river with good fly fishing on it for salmon and with legendary rises of trout to olives in April. I have already mentioned the Lyon as a late spring river. The Isla is not of much interest to the salmon fly fisher but there is some sport in its tributary headwaters later in the season. Almond is a smallish stream, joining the Tay near its mouth just above Perth. It carries fish in autumn, mainly, but lacks flow in summer. The Earn, joining the Tay well down its estuary below Perth, is a salmon and sea trout water of some note. It is a slowish river for the lower part of its length, wandering circuitously from the Auchterarder area down to Bridge of Earn and the tidal reaches. Upstream of Kinkell bridge at Strathallan, however, the Earn is a nice streamy river with good salmon, sometimes excellent sea trout early in the summer and consistently good fly fishing for trout. It is interesting that the Earn has the best of the sea trout in the system. Tay itself used to run quite reasonable numbers of sea trout up to Islamouth and a little beyond, but these fish have been in decline for some seasons. They may return, of course. Sea trout graphs vary a bit on most rivers.

The stillwaters in the area offer fishing on some of the largest lochs in Scotland, Loch Tay, Loch Earn and Loch Garry, but it is not in these that you will find the best trouting. Smaller lochs on the fertile lower valley of the Tay, below the Highland line at Dunkeld or close to it, offer some nice fat fishing. Some interesting new fisheries like Butterstone should be tried and some older fisheries, now freely available to visitors like Carsbreck, near Gleneagles, should be visited. In general, however, it is not an area of prolific loch fishing, but what there is varies the enormous amount of river and stream fishing and should be tried.

METHODS FOR TAY SALMON

Spring: Sinking lines and large waddingtons – Garry Dog, Willie Gunn, Orange and Black – Sizes 3 ins. used in the coldest waters, but usually one and a half to two inch waddingtons. Late spring salmon: Use floating line from mid-April on or sink-tip line with 1 in. black tube flies, or mixed yellow and black. The Tay does not respond well to small Dee flies on floating line. Err on the larger size, even in warm weather.

Summer: See late spring.

Autumn: Large flies, slow sinking lines or sink-tips. Doubles size 6 or our favourite waddingtons and medium sized tube flies should be used.

METHODS FOR TAY TROUT

> The dark olives of spring are well imitated by size 12 (occasionally size 10) Dark Greenwell, fished dry. Similarly, March Brown, but if fished wet use Hare Lug nymph. The Iron Blue Duns appear in April and may be fished dry or wet. Blae and Black is also popular up to the end of April.

> In May and June smaller dry flies, Greenwell Spider, Black Spider, Woodcock and different bodies – quill, Yellow or mixed colour. Wet flies, Greenwells, Olives and Black Spiders.

LOCAL OPINION

Let's leave aside the well known salmon fishing of Tay for a moment and think of it as an outstanding spring trout fishery and a good autumn grayling fishery. I have seen the dry fly fishing – mostly Dark Olives and March Browns – of the middle and end of April being quite outstanding. Bags of five trout on dry fly, where the best fish is in excess of two pounds are memorable, but they are not uncommon in the Dunkeld, Caputh and Stanley areas.

Tay System
Rivers Dochart and Lochay

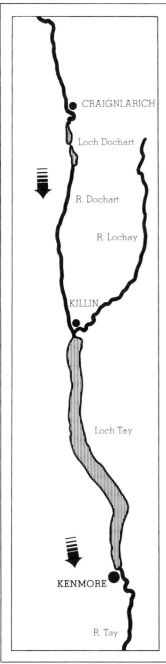

River Dochart. Brown Trout. **P.** D & S Allan, Fishing Tackle Shop, Main Street, Killin. Tel: Killin 362. £1 per day: £5 per week.

River Lochay. Trout. **P.** D & S Allan, Fishing Tackle Shop, Main Street, Killin. Tel: Killin 362. £1 per day: £5 per week.

 Tay System
Upper River Tay and Tummel

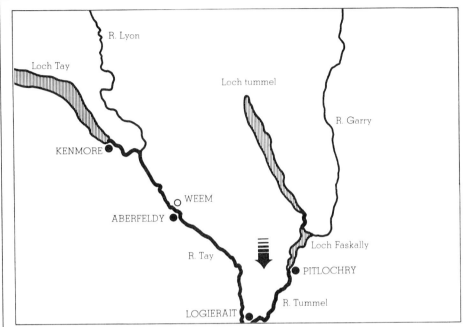

River Tay. <u>Salmon, Trout.</u> **P.** Weem Hotel by Aberfeldy, Perthshire. Tel: Aberfeldy 381.
£5 per rod per day.

River Tay. <u>Salmon, Trout, Grayling.</u> **P.** Logierait Hotel, Ballinluig. Tel: Ballinluig 253.
From £5 per rod per day. From £15-£70 per week. Boat and ghillie £15 per day plus VAT.

River Tay. <u>Salmon, Brown Trout, Grayling.</u> **P.** Grandtully Hotel, Strathtay, Perthshire. Tel: Strathtay 207.
£7.50 - £15 per day. One boat available.

River Tay. Fyndynate, Cloichfoldich, Edradynate, Derculluch and Grandtully beats. <u>Salmon.</u> **P.** Renton Finlayson, Estate Office, Aberfeldy. Tel: Aberfeldy 20234.
Cost on application.

River Tay, Farleyer Beat. <u>Salmon.</u> **P.** Major Neil Ramsay & Co., Farleyer, Aberfeldy, Perthshire. Tel: Aberfeldy 540.
By arrangement mainly weekly lets.

River Tay, Aberfeldy. <u>Brown Trout.</u> **P.** Jamieson's Sports Shop, Dunkeld Street, Aberfeldy.
50p per day: £2 per week: £5 per season.

River Tay. Trout. **P.** Post Office, Dunkeld and Birnam.
R. Scott Miller, Tackle Shop, Atholl Street, Dunkeld. Tel: Dunkeld 556.
50p per day: £1.50 per week.

River Tay, Dunkeld. River Braan, Loch Clunie, Loch Freuchie. Trout. **P.** R. Scott Miller, The Top Shop, Tackle Dealers & Sports Shop, Atholl Street, Dunkeld.
£1 per day: £4 per week. Permit covers both rivers and lochs.

River Braan. Girron Burn. Brown Trout. P. Amulree Hotel, Amulree, By Dunkeld. Tel: Amulree 218.
£1 per day, free to hotel guests.

River Ericht. Salmon, Brown Trout. **P.** Bridge of Cally Hotel, Blairgowrie, Perthshire. Tel: Bridge of Cally 231.
Salmon: £3-£4 per day. Trout: 75p-£1 per day.

River Ericht, Craighall Water (2 miles). Salmon, Trout. **P.** Mr. P. Rattray, Craighall, Blairgowrie. Tel: Blairgowrie 2678.
Cost on application.

River Ericht 4½ miles. Salmon, Trout. **P.** J. Crockart & Son, Gunmakers, 26 Allan Street, Blairgowrie.
R. Jackson, High Street, Blairgowrie.
Shotcast, Whitehall Crescent, Dundee.
Salmon: £8 per day, £25 per season. Trout: 50p per day, £2 per week.

Dean Water and Lower Isla. Brown Trout, Grayling. **P.** Strathmore Angling Improvement Association: J. Christie, 51 Broadford Terrace, Broughty Ferry, Dundee.
Meigle & Meigle Hotel, Meigle.
J. R. Gow and Sons, 12 Union Street, Dundee.
Shotcast, Whitehall Crescent.
Fagan's Stores, 38 Union Street, Dundee.
£1 per day: £6 per season: Membership £4 per year.

Dean Water. Glamis to Castle grounds on east and from Gas Works Bridge downstream including Dunkenny, Cookston, and Castleton Estates. Brown Trout. **P.** Canmore Angling Club: E. Mann, 44 Sherriff Park Gardens, Forfar, Angus.
20p per day: 50p per week.

River Ardle, Kirkmichael. Perthshire. Salmon, Trout. **P.** The Log Cabin Hotel, Glen Derby. Tel: Strathardle 288.
Cost on application.

River Ardle, Blairgowrie. Perthshire. Salmon, Trout. **P.** Corriefodly Hotel, Bridge of Cally. Tel: Bridge of Cally 236.
Cost on application.

River Ardle. Salmon. **P.** Bridge of Cally Hotel, Bridge of Cally, Perthshire. Tel: Bridge of Cally 231.
Salmon: £3-£4 per day. Trout: 75p-£1 per day.

River Tay. <u>Salmon.</u> **P.** Dunkeld House Hotel, Dunkeld, Perthshire. Tel: Dunkeld 243.
Salmon: £12. Residents' bank fishing free (5 rods).

River Lyon, North Chesthill beat. <u>Salmon.</u> **P.** Gregor Cameron, Keeper's Cottage, Chesthill, Glen Lyon. Tel: Glen Lyon 207.
Cost on application.

River Lyon, Roro beat. <u>Salmon.</u> **P.** Mrs. J. Bickerton, Roroyere, Glen Lyon. Tel: Bridge of Balgie 216.
Cost on application.

River Lyon (6 miles). <u>Salmon, Brown Trout.</u> **P.** Fortingall Hotel, Fortinghall. Tel: Kenmore 367.
Salmon from £5: Trout from £1.

River Tummel. <u>Salmon, Trout.</u> **P.** Mr. John Wildblood, Y.M.C.A. Bonskeid House, Pitlochry, PH16 5NP, Perthshire. Tel: Killiecrankie 208.
Cost on application.

River Tummel. Port-na-Craig Stretch below Pitlochry Dam. (South Bank). <u>Salmon.</u> **P.** Pitlochry Angling Club, c/o Pitlochry Tourist Office, 28 Atholl Road, Pitlochry, Perthshire PH16 5DA.
R. Gardiner, Esq.
Tel: Pitlochry 2157 5.30-6.30 p.m.
South Bank 3 rods per day – £8 per rod. April-June £15 per rod.

River Tummel. Port-na-Craig Stretch below Pitlochry Dam (North Bank). Salmon, Sea Trout. P. The Pine Trees Hotel, Pitlochry. Tel: Pitlochry 2121.
Cost on application. 3 rods per day Mar.-Apr. Boats available.

River Tummel. Port-na-Craig Stretch (North Bank). <u>Salmon, Sea Trout.</u> **P.** Mrs. Mohamed, 20 East Barnton Gardens, Edinburgh. Tel: 031-336 1379.
Apr.-Jun. £20 per day (weekly tickets only). Other months £15 per day (daily tickets available). 3 rods maximum.

River Tummel, Kinloch Rannoch. <u>Salmon, Brown Trout.</u> **P.** The Manager, West Tempar Estate, Kinloch Rannoch, Perthshire. Tel: Kinloch Rannoch 338.
£3 per day. £15 per week.

River Tummel. Moulinearn to Ballinluig. <u>Salmon, Sea Trout.</u> **P.** R. Gardiner, Esq., Pitlochry Angling Club, c/o Pitlochry Tourist Office, 28 Atholl Road, Pitlochry. Tel: Pitlochry 2157.
£6 per day.

River Tummel. <u>Salmon.</u> **P.** Sport in Scotland, 6A High Street, Dunfermline. Tel: Dunfermline 22765.
£15-£40 per day.

River Tummel. Kinloch Rannoch Weir to Tummel Bridge. <u>Brown Trout.</u> **P.** E. Beattie, Esq., 2 Schiehallian Place, Kinloch Rannoch. Tel: Kinloch Rannoch 261.
£1 per day.

River Tummel. Clunie Dam to Falls of Tummel, both banks. <u>Brown Trout.</u> **P.**
Pitlochry Tourist Office.
P. D. Malloch, Sports Shop, Atholl Road, Pitlochry.
Secretary, Pitlochry Angling Club, 28 Atholl Road, Pitlochry.
75p per day: £2 per week: £5 per season.

River Garry. <u>Brown Trout, Rainbow Trout.</u> **P.** Tilt Hotel, Blair Atholl.
Highland Guns & Tackle, Blair Atholl.
Atholl Arms Hotel, Blair Atholl.
Cost on application.

River Gaur. <u>Brown Trout.</u> **P.** Moor of Rannoch Hotel, Rannoch Station,
Perthshire. Tel: Bridge of Gaur 238.
Free to hotel guests: £1 per day to others.

River Braan. Girron Burn. <u>Brown Trout.</u> **P.** Amulree Hotel, Amulree,
Perthshire. Tel: Amulree 218.
Free to hotel guests: £1 per day to others.

River Tilt and Garry as indicated on permits. One pond. <u>Brown Trout,
Rainbow Trout.</u> **P.** Atholl Angling Club.
The Tilt Hotel, Blair Atholl.
Blair Castle Caravan Site, Luckenbooth, Blair Atholl.
Highland Guns & Tackle, Blair Atholl.
Atholl Arms Hotel.
50p-£2.50 per day.

River Tummel. Port-na-Craig footbridge to Ballinluig. Both banks. <u>Brown
Trout, Grayling.</u> **P.** Pitlochry Tourist Information Centre.
Peter Malloch, Sports Shop, Atholl Road, Pitlochry.
Milton of Fonab Caravan Site.
Ballinluig Post Office.
£1 per day: £4 per week: £10 per season.

River Tay. 2½ **miles.** Aberfeldy Angling Club water. <u>Trout.</u> **P.** L. Jamieson,
Sports Shop, Dunkeld Street, Aberfeldy.
50p per day.

Tay System
Middle Tay and Tributaries

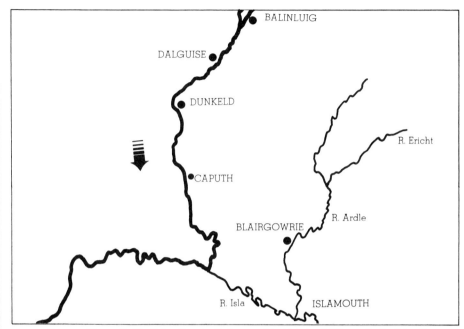

River Tay, Ballathie Beat. <u>Salmon</u>. **P.** Estate Office, Ballathie Farms, Balmains, Stanley, Perthshire. Tel: Melkleour 250.
Cost on application.

River Tay. <u>Salmon, Trout.</u> **P.** Dunkeld House Hotel, Dunkeld, Perthshire. Tel: Dunkeld 243.
Salmon: £12 per day. Trout: £2 per day. Free bank rods to hotel residents Jan.-March.

River Tay (private beats). <u>Salmon.</u> **P.** Sport in Scotland, 6A High Street, Dunfermline. Tel: Dunfermline 22765.
£15-£40 per day.

Tay System
Lower Tay and Tributaries

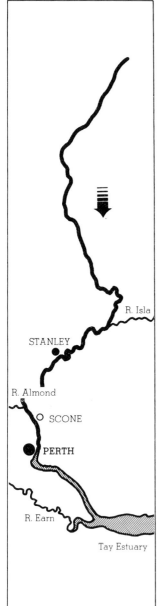

River Tay. Salmon, Brown Trout, Sea Trout. **P.** Ballathie Estate Office, Ballathie Farms, Near Stanley, Perthshire. Tel: Meikleour 250.
Salmon from £42 per rod. Boats and ghillies available.

River Tay. Salmon, Trout. **P.** Director of Finances Offices, Perth, Perthshire.
£3 per day. £8 per week.

River Tay, within boundaries of City of Perth. Salmon, Brown Trout, Sea Trout. **P.** Director of Finance, Perth and Kinross District Council, 1, High Street, Perth. Tel: Perth 21161.
Day permits available for non-residents. Bookable in advance.

Kerock & Delvine Beats. Salmon, Trout. **P.** Kinloch House Hotel, Dunkeld House Hotel, Dunkeld Road, Blairgowrie, Perthshire. Tel: Essendy 237.
Salmon £30-£70 per rod per day.

River Tay. Salmon. **P.** Messrs. P.D. Malloch (Field Sports) Ltd. Tackle Manufacturers, 24 Scott Street, Perth.
Cost on application.

River Tay estuarial water. Salmon, Sea Trout. **P.** Dundee District Council, Parks & Recreation Dept., 17 King Street, Dundee. Tel: Dundee 23141.
No charge. Bank fishing only.

Tay System
River Earn

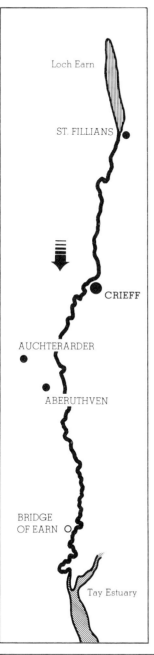

River Earn. <u>Salmon Trout.</u> **P.** Mrs. Lindsay, Loanhead Farm, Aberuthven. Tel: 2687.
£1.50 per rod per day until 1 Sept. £3 per rod per day Sept./Oct.

Allan Water. Greenloaning. <u>Salmon, Brown Trout, Grilse.</u> **P.** Allanbank Hotel, Greenloaning. Tel: Braco 205.
From £2 per rod per day.

River Earn, near Bridge of Earn. <u>Salmon, Sea Trout, Brown Trout.</u> **P.** Managed Estates, 18 Maxwell Place, Stirling. Tel: Stirling 62519.
Cost on application.

River Earn. (Crieff Angling Club water). <u>Salmon, Sea Trout, Brown Trout.</u> **P.** W. Cook & Son, Tackle Dealer, High Street, Crieff. Perthshire. Tel: Crieff 2081.
From £3-£5 per day. From £12.50-£25 per week.

River Earn. <u>Salmon, Sea Trout, Brown Trout.</u> **P.** St. Fillans and Loch Earn Angling Association: J. Macpherson Rannoch, 4 Earn View, St. Fillans, Perthshire. Tel: St. Fillans 219.
Loch Earn Post Office. Tel: Loch Earn 201.
St. Fillans Post Office. Tel: St. Fillans 220.
Cost on application.

Forteviot (Broomhill fishings). <u>Salmon, Sea Trout.</u> **P.** David Black, Hobby and Model Shop, New Row, Dunfermline. Tel: Dunfermline 22582.
£4-£6 per day.

River Earn (small beat). <u>Salmon, Sea Trout, Brown Trout.</u> **P.** Earnbrook House Hotel, Bridge of Earn, Perthshire. Tel: Bridge of Earn 2360.
Free to hotel guests.

Hilton Beat. <u>Salmon, Sea Trout, Brown Trout.</u> **P.** Bob Sime, 57 South Methven Street, Perth.
£2 per day.

Tay System – Stillwaters

Loch Bhac. Brown Trout, Rainbow Trout, Brook Trout. **P.** Airdaniar Hotel, Atholl Road, Pitlochry. Tel: Pitlochry 2266.
Pitlochry Angling Club Secretary.
£2 per day (bank), £8 per boat (2 rods).

Butterstone Loch Fishing by Dunkeld. Rainbow Trout, Brown Trout. **P.** The Bailiff, Lochend Cottage, Butterstone Loch, by Dunkeld, Perthshire. Tel: Butterstone 238.
£9 per boat (3 rods).

Carsebreck, including Upper and Lower Rhynd Reservoir. Brown Trout. **P.** Blackford Farms, Dunblane. Tel: 0786 824000.
£11.50 per day per boat (2 adults).

Castlehill Reservoir, Glendevon. Brown Trout, Rainbow Trout. **P.** The Boathouse, South end of Reservoir. Tel: Muckhard 357.
£4 per person. Boat £5.

Loch Clunie. Trout. **P.** Miller, Tackle Dealer, Atholl Street, Dunkeld.
Cost on application.

Crombie Country Park. Brown Trout. **P.** Monikie Angling Club Bailiff. Tel: Newbigging 300.
Cost on application, 3 boats.

Loch Dubh. Canadian Brook Trout. **P.** Moor of Rannoch Hotel, Rannoch Station. Tel: Bridge of Gaur 238.
£5 pe rod per day.

Dunalastair Loch. Brown Trout. **P.** Dunalastair Hotel, Kinloch Rannoch 323. Mr. Stratton, Lassintulloch House, Kinloch Rannoch. Tel: Kinloch Rannoch 238.
Dunalastair Estate, Kinloch Rannoch (residents of holiday homes only).
Bank: £1 per day. Boat: £8 per rod (2 rods).

Loch Earn. Salmon, Brown Trout. **P.** St. Fillans and Loch Earn Angling Association, J. MacPherson, Rannoch, 4 Earn View, St. Fillans, Perthshire. Tel: St. Fillans 219.
Loch Earn Post Office.
St. Fillans Post Office.
Cost on application.

Loch Eigheach. Trout. **P.** J. Brown, Esq., The Square, Kinloch Rannoch. Tel: Kinloch Rannoch 331.
Moor of Rannoch Hotel, Rannoch Station. Tel: Bridge of Gaur 238.
£1 per day, £3.50 per week, £7 per season.

Loch Faskally. Salmon, Trout. **P.** P. Williamson, Boathouse, Loch Faskally, Pitlochry. Tel: Pitlochry 2919 or 2612.
Bank: £2 per day, £1.50 per ½ day. Boat: Cost on application.

Loch Finnart. Trout. **P.** J. Brown, Esq., The Square, Kinloch Rannoch. Tel: Kinloch Rannoch 331.
£5 per day inc. boat.

Loch Frandy. Brown Trout. **P.** Mr. Jack, Regional Water Engineer, Fife Regional Council, Glenrothes. Tel: Glenrothes 76541.
Bank: £1.70 per ½ day.

Loch Garry. Char and Brown Trout. **P.** Airdaniar Hotel, Atholl Road, Pitlochry. Tel: Pitlochry 2266.
Pitlochry Angling Club Secretary, Mr. Clair, 7 Leslie Place, Pitlochry.
50p per day bank only.

Glendevon Upper Reservoir and Glanfarg Reservoir. <u>Brown Trout.</u> **P.** Mr. Jack, Regional Water Engineer, Fife Regional Council, Glenrothes. Tel: 756 541.

Glenquey Reservoir. <u>Brown Trout.</u> **P.** Wightman Booksellers, Dollar or Castle Hotel, Glendevon.
Cost on application.

Loch Kinardochy. <u>Brown Trout.</u> **P.** Airdaniar Hotel, Atholl Road, Pitlochry. Tel: Pitlochry 2266.
Pitlochry Angling Club Secretary.
£8 per boat inc. 2 rods. £2 per day from bank.

Kingsmyre Trout Fishings (secluded 16 acres stank lock). <u>Brown Trout, Rainbow Trout.</u> **P.** Mr. Meldrum, The Keeper's House, Taymount Estate, Stanley. Tel: Stanley 289.
Day ticket £8 per boat (2 rods). Evening £10 per boat (2 rods).

Loch Laich. <u>Brown Trout, Rainbow Trout.</u> **P.** Gleneagles Hotel. Tel: Auchterarder 2231.
Hotel guests only, permit £3.

Loch Laidon. <u>Brown Trout.</u> **P.** Moor or Rannoch Hotel, Rannoch Station, Perthshire. Tel: Bridge of Gaur 238.
Bank £1 per day. Boat £10 per day incl. 2 rods.

Meikleour Private Loch. <u>Rainbow Trout, Brown Trout.</u> **P.** Estates Office, Ballathie Farms, Balmains, Stanley. Tel: Meikleour 250.
£10 plus VAT per boat per day, 2 rods.

Loch Monochan. <u>Trout.</u> **P.** J. Brown, Esq., The Square, Kinloch Rannoch. Tel: Kinloch Rannoch 331.
£5 per day incl. boat.

Loch Monzievaird Ochtertyre By Crieff. <u>Brown Trout, Rainbow Trout.</u> **P.** Mr. A. Calquhoun, Loch Monzievaird Ltd., Dalchonzie, Comrie. Tel: Comrie 273.
Cost on application.

Loch Rannoch. <u>Brown Trout.</u> **P.** Dunalastair Hotel.
Bunrannoch Hotel.
Moor of Rannoch Hotel.
Bridge of Gaur Post Office.
Loch Rannoch Hotel.
Warden, Forestry Commission, Campsite, Carie, Loch Finnoch.
E. Beattie, Esq., 2 Schiehallion Place, Kinloch Rannoch (block bookings only).
J. Brown, Esq., The Square, Kinloch Rannoch.
£1 per day, £1.50 from Bailiff, £4 per week, £10 per season.

Loch Rannoch, Dunalastair Reservoir. <u>Brown Trout.</u> **P.** Dunalastair Hotel, Kinloch Rannoch, Perthshire. Tel: Kinloch Rannoch 323.
6 boats, £6 per boat per day.

Loch Rescobie. <u>Brown Trout, Rainbow Trout.</u> **P.** The Bailiff, South Lodge, Resvallie, Forfar. Tel: Letham (Angus) 384.
Cost on application.

Loch Tay. <u>Salmon, Trout.</u> **P.** Ardeonaig Hotel, Ardeonaig by Killin, Perthshire. Tel: Killin 400.
Non-residents: boat plus permit £20 per day. Residents: boat plus permit £18 per day. Ghillie: £11 per day, £10 per half day.

Loch Tay. <u>Salmon, Trout</u>. **P.** The Clachaig Hotel, Killin, Perthshire. Tel: Killin 270/565.
Residents free after 3 days. Non-residents £14 per day incl. boat and outboard.
Loch Tay. <u>Salmon, Trout</u>. **P.** Killin Hotel, Killin, Perthshire. Tel: Killin 296.
£7 per day. Boat £10.50 incl. outboard.
Loch Tay. <u>Salmon, Trout</u>. **P.** Ben Lawers Hotel, by Aberfeldy, Perthshire. Tel: Killin 436.
1 boat – £10 per day, with outboard £15 per day for fishing and boat.
Loch Tay. <u>Trout</u>. **P.** D. & S. Allan, Tackle Dealers, Main Street, Killin. Tel: Killin 362.
£1 per day. £5 per week.
Loch Tay. <u>Brown Trout</u>. **P.** Loch Tay Guest House, Kenmore, Perthshire. Tel: Kenmore 236.
Free to guests only. Boats available locally to hire.
Loch Tummel. <u>Brown Trout</u>. **P.** Port-an-Eilean Hotel, Strathtummel. Tel: Tummel Bridge 233.
Free to hotel guests. Boat £4 per day, outboard £4 extra per day.
Loch Turret By Crieff. <u>Brown Trout</u>. **P.** The Director of Finance, Central Scotland Water Development Board, 30 George Square, Glasgow. Tel: 041-248 5855.
W. Cook & Sons, 19 High Street, Crieff. Tel: Crief 2081.
Boat £2.40 per day. Outboard £2.10. Bank fishing £1.40 per day, 70p per ½ day, £3.60 per season.

Angus and The Mearns

AN INTRODUCTORY NOTE

The area of Angus and The Mearns lies north and east of Dundee and Montrose and provides us with two interesting salmon and sea trout rivers which drain south east from the high hills behind, flowing in their lower reaches through rich agricultural land and entering the north sea within a few miles of each other. The South Esk enters the sea at Montrose with its loch-like tidal basin, while the more Highland North Esk has its estuary a few miles to the north.

Both rivers carry spring salmon and good summer runs of both sea trout and salmon. The North Esk, however, is the better river for early fish although the South Esk has some spectacular individual beats for spring salmon. Both rivers have excellent runs of sea trout and grilse and they have indigenous stocks of brown trout also. The South Esk has a splendid glen at its head called Glen Clova, while the North Esk has magnificent gorges near Edzell and a high moorland and hill glen, Glen Esk. The inland area of both rivers is fine Highland scenery and well repays a visit.

LOCAL OPINION

In this comment I want to concentrate on the good sea trout fishing we have on the South Esk. From late May onwards, with a peak about the end of June (according to water) we have first class night fly fishing to offer. A bit of local knowledge helps, but this is available.

Angus and the Mearns
South Esk System

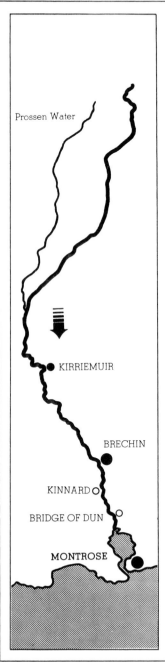

Prossen Water

KIRRIEMUIR

BRECHIN

KINNARD ○

BRIDGE OF DUN ○

MONTROSE

River Lunan. <u>Brown Trout, Sea Trout, Finnock.</u> **P.** T. Clark & Sons, 274 High Street, Arbroath. Tel: Arbroath 73467.
£1 per day, £5 per season.

Noran Water. <u>Brown Trout.</u> **P.** Canmore Angling Club, Mr. E. Mann, 44 Sheriff Park Gardens, Forfar; C. Kerr, 1 West High Street, Forfar.
20p per day, 50p per week.

South Esk River. <u>Salmon, Sea Trout, Brown Trout.</u> **P.** The Secretary, Kirriemuir Angling Club, 13 Clova Road, Kirriemuir. Tel: Kirriemuir 3456.
£4 per day, £20 per week.

River Westwater. <u>Salmon, Sea Trout, Brown Trout.</u> **P.** Glenesk Hotel, Edzell, Angus. Tel: Edzell 319.
£2 per day.

Dean, Kerbert, Lunan, Noran, Lemo Waters, Alrney-four Rescobie Loch, Glenogil Res., Forfar Loch. <u>Trout.</u> **P.** C. Kerr, 1 West High Street, Forfar; Secretary, Canmore Angling Club, 44 Sheriff Park Gardens, Forfar.
Rivers 20p per day. Glenogil Res. £1 per day, £1 for boat. Other prices on application.

South Esk River (6 miles). <u>Salmon, Sea Trout.</u> **P.** Secretary Kirriemuir Angling Club, 13 Clova Road, Kirriemuir. Tel: Kirriemuir 3456.
£4 per day, £20 per week.

Lintrathen Reservoir (Lintrathen Angling Club Water). <u>Brown Trout</u> (stocked). **P.** Water Services Dept., 10 Ward Road, Dundee. Tel: Dundee 21164.
£8 per boat per session. 2/3 rods.

Monikie Country Park, North and Island Ponds. <u>Brown Trout</u> (stocked). **P.** Mr. A. Colquhoun, Loch Monzievaird Ltd., Dalchonzie, Comrie. Tel: Comrie 273.

Loch Saugh. <u>Rainbow Trout, Brown Trout.</u> **P.** Sports Shop, Brechin; Ramsay Arms Hotel; Drumfochty Arms Hotel.
£2 per day.

Westwater (north bank). <u>Salmon, Sea Trout, Brown Trout.</u> **P.** Sports Shop, High Street, Brechin.

Angus and the Mearns
North Esk System

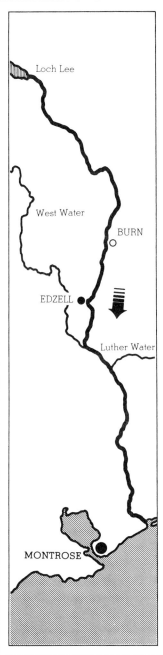

North Esk River, from Marykirk Railway Viaduct north or left bank 2 miles down stream to Den Mouth of Morphie. Salmon, Sea Trout Brown Trout. **P.** Joseph Johnston & Sons, 3 America Street, Montrose. Tel: Montrose 2666.
£3-£15 per rod per day.

North Esk River, from lower North Water Bridge both banks 1½ miles up-stream to Den Mouth of Morphie. Sea Trout, Brown Trout. **P.** Joseph Johnston & Sons, 3 America Street, Montrose. Tel: Montrose 2666. Permits Free.

North Esk, Gallery Hatton Beats. Salmon, Sea Trout, Grilse. **P.** Links Hotel, Montrose. Tel: Montrose 2288. Cost on application.

North Esk, Canterland Salmon, Sea Trout. **P.** Joseph Johnston & Sons, 3 America Street, Montrose. Tel: Montrose 2666.
£3-£16 per day plus VAT.

Luther Water. Salmon, Brown Trout, Sea Trout. **P.** Mr. J. Mowat, 111 High Street, Launrencekirk. Tel: Laurencekirk 319.
£2.50 per day, £5 per week.

North Esk, Morphie. Trout, Finnock. **P.** Joseph Johnston & Sons, 3 America Street, Montrose. Tel: Montrose 2666.

Lunan Water. Sea Trout, Brown Trout. **P.** T. Clark & Sons, 274 High Street, Arbroath.
Cost on application.

West Water. Salmon, Sea Trout. **P.** Brians, 5 Lordburn, Arbroath.
Cost on application.

Bervie Water, from Mondynes Bridge to Arbuthnott Estate. Salmon, Brown Trout, Sea Trout. **P.** Mr. J. Mowat, 111 High Street, Laurencekirk. Tel: Laurencekirk 319.
£2.50 per day, £5 per week.

Luther Water, from Blackiemuir Bridge to approx. Luthermuir. Salmon, Sea Trout, Brown Trout. **P.** Mr. J. Mowat, 111 High Street, Laurencekirk. Tel: Laurencekirk 319.
£2.50 per day, £5 per week.

Loch Saugh. Brown Trout, Rainbow Trout. **P.** Drumtochty Arms Hotel, Auchenblac. Tel: Auchenblac 210; Ramsay Arms Hotel, Fettercairn. Tel: Fettercairn 334.
Cost on application.

Loch Lee

West Water

BURN

EDZELL

Luther Water

MONTROSE

The Dee and Don Areas

AN INTRODUCTORY NOTE

The Aberdeeshire Dee is possibly the most famous and most productive salmon river in Scotland. It is also, in the opinion of many anglers, the most beautiful of waters – a bold claim to make. The Dee flows east from the massive Cairngorm mountains, carrying very clear water over a shallow rocky bed to the sea at Aberdeen. It offers over fifty miles of first class salmon fishing from the lively streams at Braemar and Invercauld down through beats whose names are legend in salmon and fly fishing – Cambos o' May, Glen Tannar, Dinnet, Aboyne, Carlogie and Ballogie, and down to Durris, through Banchory to the lower river and Aberdeen. It is a first class spring river with fish in its waters throughout from the beginning of February and although recent March fishings have been slow, the river has a great reputation for bringing in excellent April fish and, in the cream of its season, May, it provides superb fishing with small flies on a floating line, which has few parallels anywhere. The summer on Dee can be patchy according to the weather, but good years, like 1983 can produce outstanding grilse and summer salmon sport right through June and July and, in the lower river, can see fine fresh fish coming in right to the end of September.

In contrast, the Don, in the next valley north, is widely known as a fine trout stream, offering some of the best river trouting in Scotland, especially in spring. It does have a spring run of salmon, but not a large one. Its main salmon run is in late spring and early summer, followed by a good run in summer, bringing large fish into the lower river in autumn. It is a river which has recovered from heavy pollution in the course of this century and, indeed, is still carefully watched and has been the subject of recent court actions. As a salmon river, it will never have the calibre of its neighbour, the Dee, but it can provide good sport in its lower reaches early and late in the season and in its middle and upper reaches throughout the spring and the summer.

LOCAL OPINION

The two rivers are so different. Dee is marvellous as a spring salmon water, peaking in May. Don is not so good as a salmon water in spring, but has fine heavy fish in the back end. Dee is not recognised as a trout water; Don is the April and May trout river par excellence. I would rate its early May dry fly trouting in the Alford area as the best trout fishing in Scotland.

AGENCY

We handle weekly or daily permits
on the River Dee.

We are the letting Agents for the
Lower Cassley.

SHOP

We carry a large range of fishing
rods, reels and accessories.

We have our own fly tier who will
make special patterns to order.

We are now in new premises
(opposite the East Church)

74-76 Station Road, Banchory
Kincardineshire AB3 3YJ

Agency Tel: **(03302) 3022**
Shop Tel: **(03302) 2855**

River Dee

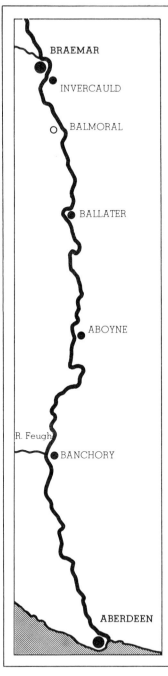

Mar Lodge. <u>Salmon.</u> **P.** Mar Lodge Hotel, Braemar. Tel: Braemar 216.
£30 + VAT per day.

Braemar. <u>Salmon.</u> **P.** Invercauld Arms Hotel, Braemar. Tel: Braemar 605.
From £60-£110 + VAT per week per rod. Max. 4 rods.

River Dee. <u>Salmon, Sea Trout.</u> **P.** Macsport Ltd., St. Nicholas House, 68 Station Road, Banchory. Tel: Banchory 3343.
Cost on application.

Banchory. <u>Salmon, Sea Trout.</u> **P.** Banchory Lodge Hotel, Banchory. Tel: Banchory 2625.
Cost on application.

Crathes Castle, Crathes, Banchory. <u>Salmon, Sea Trout.</u> **P.** Pelett Administration Ltd., 68 Station Road, Blanchory. Tel: Blanchory 3343.
From £100-£350 + VAT per week per rod.

Ardoe Beat, Blairs. <u>Salmon, Sea Trout.</u> **P.** Ardoe House Hotel, Blairs, By Aberdeen. Tel: Aberdeen 867355.
£10 per rod per day – early/late season. Mid-season £5 per day.

Middle Drum. <u>Salmon.</u> **P.** Bell Ingram, 7 Walker Street, Edinburgh. Tel: 031 225 3271.
£35-£154 per week.

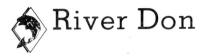

River Don

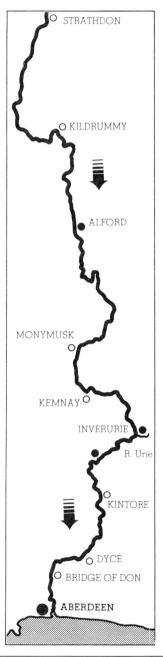

STRATHDON

KILDRUMMY

ALFORD

MONYMUSK

KEMNAY

INVERURIE

R. Urie

KINTORE

DYCE

BRIDGE OF DON

ABERDEEN

Glenkindie. <u>Salmon, Brown Trout</u>. **P.** Glenkindie Arms Hotel, Glenkindie, Strathdon. Tel: Glenkindie 288.
Salmon £6 per day, Trout £3 per day.

Kintore. 2½ miles on right bank, 3½ miles on left bank. <u>Brown Trout, Salmon.</u> **P.** Kintore Arms Hotel, Kintore. Tel: 32216.
J. Copland, Newsagent, 2 Northern Road, Kintore. Tel: 32210.
£3-£4 per rod per day.

Kildrummy Estate Water, Kinclune Beat and Ley Beat, by Glenkindie. <u>Salmon, Brown Trout</u>. **P.** Kildrummy Castle Hotel, Kildrummy, Near Alford. Tel: Kildrummy 288.
Salmon £7 per day, Trout £2.50 per day.

Alford. <u>Salmon, Brown Trout</u>. **P.** Forbes Arms Hotel, Bridge of Alford. Tel: Alford 2108.
Cost on application.

Glenkindie. 2¼ miles. <u>Salmon, Trout</u>. **P.** Bell Ingram, 3 Rubislaw Terrace, Aberdeen. Tel: Aberdeen 644272.
From £20 per week + VAT.

Forbes Estate. <u>Salmon, Brown Trout</u>. **P.** Forbes Estate, Estate Office, Whitehouse, by Alford. Tel: Whitehouse 224.
£20-£40 per rod per week + VAT, £10 + VAT per day when available.

Upper Parkhill, by Dyce and Lower Parkhill. <u>Salmon, Sea Trout, Brown Trout.</u> **P.** Jas. Somers & Son, 40 Thistle Street, Aberdeen. Tel: Aberdeen 639910.
£5 per day, £15 per week.

Upper Fintray. <u>Salmon, Brown Trout</u>. **P.** Jas Somers & Son, 40 Thistle Street, Aberdeen. Tel: Aberdeen 639910.
£5 per day, £15 per week.

Monymusk. <u>Salmon, Brown Trout, Sea Trout</u>. **P.** Grant Arms Hotel, Monymusk. Tel: Monymusk 226.
£5-£7 per day, £25-£35 per week.

Inverurie, 2 miles Polinar Burn downstream to junction of River Urie on North Bank. <u>Salmon, Brown Trout, Sea Trout</u>. **P.** J. Duncan, 4 West High Street, Inverurie. Tel: 20310.
P. McPherson, Ironmonger, 49 Market Place Inverurie. Tel: 21363.
£3-£4 per day, £12 per week, £25 per season.

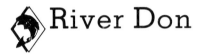 # River Don

Manar Beat, above Burgh water 1.6 miles left bank only. <u>Salmon, Brown Trout.</u> **P.** J. Duncan, 4 West High Street, Inverurie. Tel: 20310.
£5 per rod per day, max. 8 rods.

Luib Bridge and Bridge of Buchat. 9 miles North bank. <u>Brown Trout.</u> **P.** Coquhonnie Hotgel, Strathdon. Tel: Strathdon 210.
From £3.50 per day.

Tornashean Water. 3 miles. <u>Salmon, Brown Trout</u>. **P.** E & D Smith, The Square, Dufftown.
T V Services, The Square, Dufftown.
J A & I A Ferguson, Fife Street, Dufftown.
Cost on application.

The Moray-Buchan Waters

AN INTRODUCTORY NOTE

The great north eastern shoulder of Scotland lying between Aberdeen and Moray is sometimes called the Moray-Buchan area and it is dominated by the River Spey. In our Guide we have dealt with the Spey valley as a separate entity and have grouped the remaining Moray-Buchan waters together in this section.

Two small waters of this area lie immediately to the north of Aberdeen – the Ythan and the Ugie. The Ythan is of particular note since it has a well-known estuary in which some excellent fly fishing for sea trout is available. Following the district round to the north we meet the Deveron, a salmon, sea trout and trout water with some spring sport and good summer and autumn sport with salmon and sea trout. Its brown trout fishing around Rothiemay is exciting and produces some fine fish in late spring.

The other main water, this time north-west of the Spey is the Findhorn. Its lower half has some good spring fishing for salmon and after June its upper half comes into play. It is a beautiful water with spectacular timbering on its banks at Darnaway and a memorable gorge at Logie. Above, the Findhorn takes on the character of a shingly, rather thin river, typical of a wide Highland glen. Further up still, it becomes a moorland stream widening among its mountains. It is a spate river in its style and it can both rise and fall with great rapidity. Its salmon and sea trout, in the right conditions can be excellent.

The Moray-Buchan area is not noted for its lochs, but some exist and where they do they are often good. It is, however, a fine unspoiled region of rivers and burns with all three game fish present in good numbers throughout.

Moray–Buchan Area

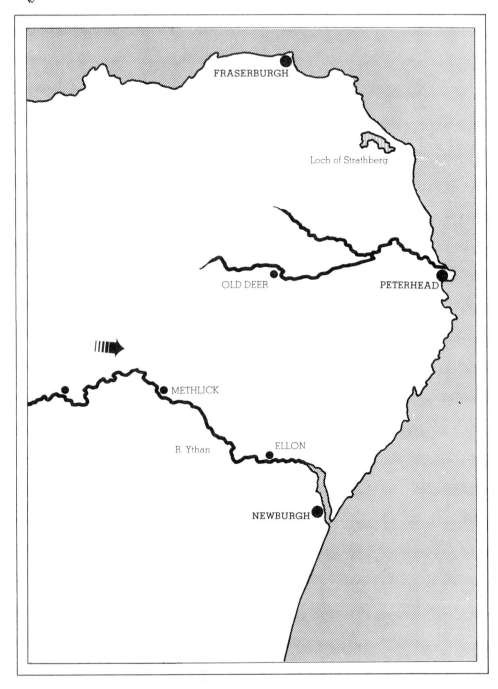

FRASERBURGH

Loch of Strathberg

OLD DEER

PETERHEAD

METHLICK

R. Ythan

ELLON

NEWBURGH

Moray–Buchan Area

River South Ugie, Old Deer. <u>Salmon, Sea Trout, Rainbow Trout, Brown Trout.</u> **P.** A. Drever, Rangers Cottage, Aden Country Park, Mintaw. Tel: 2857. No charge.

River Ugie (Pitfour Fishings), Peterhead. <u>Salmon, Sea Trout, Brown Trout.</u> **P.** Dicks Sports, 54 Broad Street, Fraserburgh; G. Milne, Esq., Newsagent, 3 Ugie Road, Peterhead.
£3 per day, £10 per week. Season – £10 tidals only, £25 whole river.

River Ugie, 1 mile north of Petershead extending westward. <u>Salmon, Sea Trout, Trout.</u> **P.** Robertson Sports, 1-3 Kirk Street, Peterhead. Tel: 2584.
Cost on application.

River Ythan, at Fyvie, north bank 3 mile stretch. <u>Salmon, Sea Trout.</u> **P.** Bank House, Fyvie; Vale Hotel, Fyvie; Spar Shop, Fyvie; Ythan Bar and Sheiling Tor Cafe.
£1.50 per rod per day. Oct. £2 per rod per day.

River Ythan, Ellon. <u>Salmon, Trout, Finnock.</u> **P.** Buchan Hotel, Ellon. Tel: 20208.
£2 per rod per day.

River Ythan, Newburgh. <u>Salmon, Sea Trout, Finnock.</u> **P.** Mrs. Forbes, 3 Lea Cottages, Newburgh. Tel: 297.
Cost on application.

River Ythan, Methlick (south bank from Waterloo Bridge to Tangland Bridge). <u>Salmon, Sea Trout.</u> **P.** Estate Office, Haddo House, Methlick. Tel: Tarves 664; S. French & Sons, Methlick. Tel: 213.
60p-£6 per rod per day.

River Ythan, Newburgh. <u>Salmon, Sea Trout, Finnock.</u> **P.** Mrs. Forbes, 3 Lea 40 Thistle Street, Aberdeen. Tel: Aberdeen 639910.
£5 per day, £15 per week.
Loch of Strathbeg. <u>Sea Trout, Brown Trout.</u> **P.** Brown & McRae, Solicitors, Frithside Street, Fraserburgh. Tel: 4761.
£4 plus VAT–1 rod, £5 plus VAT–2 rods, £6 plus VAT–3 rods.

Loch Red, 3 miles south of Fraserburgh. <u>Brown Trout, Rainbow Trout.</u> **P.** Pet Shop, Cross Street, Fraserburgh.
£2 per rod per day.

Moray–Buchan Area
River Deveron

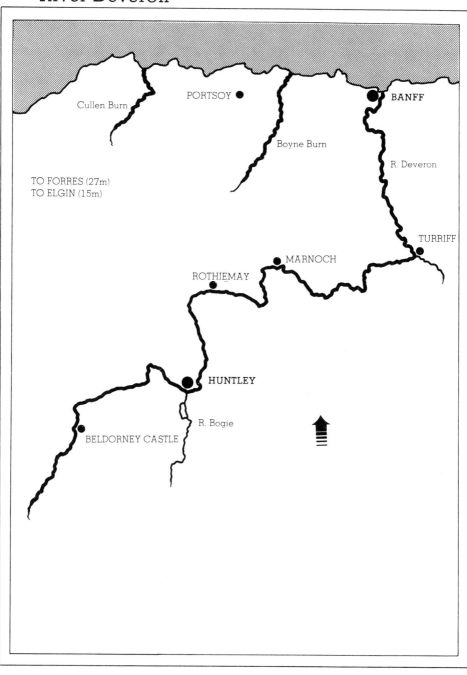

PORTSOY ●

Cullen Burn

BANFF ●

Boyne Burn

R. Deveron

TO FORRES (27m)
TO ELGIN (15m)

TURRIFF ●

● MARNOCH

ROTHIEMAY
●

● HUNTLEY

R. Bogie

● BELDORNEY CASTLE

Moray–Buchan Area

River Deveron

Boyne Burn, by Portsoy. <u>Trout, Sea Trout, Grilse.</u> **P.** Seafield Estate Office, Cullen, Buckie, Banffshire.
Cost on application.

Carron, Stonehaven. <u>Brown Trout.</u> **P.** David Sports Shop, 31 Market Square, Stonehaven. Tel: Stonehaven 62239.
£1 per day, £2 per week, £3 per fortnight.

Cowie, Stonehaven. <u>Salmon, Sea Trout, Brown Trout.</u> **P.** David Sports Shop, 31 Market Square, Stonehaven. Tel: Stonehaven 62239.
£1 per day, £2 per week, £3 per fortnight.

Cullen Burn. <u>Trout, Sea Trout, Grilse.</u> **P.** Seafield Estate Office, Cullen, Buckie, Banffshire.
Cost on application.

Muckle Burn, by Forres. <u>Salmon, Sea Trout, Brown Trout.</u> **P.** Moray Estates Development Co., Estate Office, Forres, Moray.
£1.15 per rod per day.

River Bogie, Bridge at Gartly Station downstream to south of the meeting of the waters. <u>Salmon, Sea Trout, Grilse, Brown Trout.</u> **P.** J. Christie, Esq., 27 Duke Street, Huntly. Tel: 2291; G. Manson, Sports Shop, Gordon Street, Huntly. Tel: 2482.
£4 per rod per day, £14 per week.

River Deveron, Banff. <u>Salmon, Sea Trout, Brown Trout.</u> **P.** Jay-Tee Sports Shop, Low Street, Banff. Tel: 5821; L. Smith (River Bailiff), 54 Barrymuir Road, Macduff.
Cost on application.

River Deveron, by Huntly. <u>Salmon, Sea Trout, Grilse, Brown Trout.</u> **P.** J. Christie, Esq., 27 Duke Street, Huntly. Tel: Huntly 2291; G. Manson, Sports Shop, Gordon Street, Huntly. Tel: 2482.
£4 per day, £14 per week.

River Deveron, Huntly. <u>Salmon, Sea Trout, Brown Trout</u> **P.** Castle Hotel, Huntly. Tel: Huntly 2696.
Hotel Residents only, £5.50 per rod per day.

River Deveron, Rothiemay. <u>Salmon, Sea Trout, Brown Trout, Grilse.</u> **P.** Forbes Arms Hotel, Rothiemay. Tel: 248.
£8 per rod per day plus VAT.

River Deveron, right hand bank between the Turriff Burn and the Deveron Bridge. <u>Salmon, Sea Trout.</u> **P.** Ian Masson Sports Ltd., Main Street, Turriff. Tel: 2428.
£1 per day, 2 permits each week only.

River Deveron, various beats. <u>Salmon, Sea Trout, Grilse, Brown Trout.</u> **P.** G. Manson, 45 Gordon Street, Huntly. Tel: Huntly 2482.
£5-£15 per rod per day.

River Deveron, Turriff. <u>Salmon, Sea Trout, Brown Trout</u> **P.** Ian Masson Sports Ltd., Main Street, Turriff. Tel: 2428.
Cost on application.

River Deveron, Beldorney Castle. <u>Salmon.</u> **P.** Bell Ingram, Durn, Isla Road, Perth.
Weekly bookings only—£55 per rod per week.

River Deveron, Huntly Lodge. <u>Salmon.</u> **P.** Bell Ingram, Durn, Isla Road, Perth.
Weekly bookings only—£75 per rod per week.

River Deveron, Nr. Bridge of Marnoch. <u>Salmon, Sea Trout, Trout.</u> **P.** Mr. & Mrs. A. Murray, Euchries Farm, Bridge of Marnoch, By Huntly. Tel: Bridge of Marnoch 337.
£9 per rod per day.

Turriff Burn, east bank to Old Mill Lade. <u>Brown Trout.</u> **P.** Ian Masson Sports Ltd., Main Street, Turriff. Tel: 2428.
£1 per day.

Bishopmill Trout Fishery. <u>Rainbow Trout.</u> **P.** Bishopmill Trout Fishery, Spynie Churchyard Road, Bishopmill, Elgin.
£3.50 per day.

Moray–Buchan Area
Rivers Findhorn, Lossie

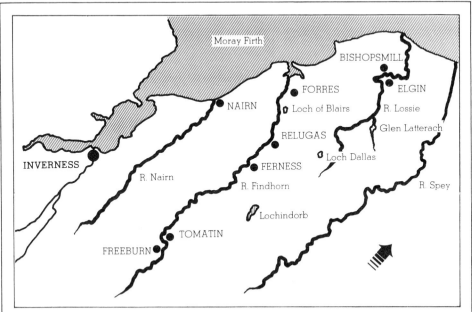

River Findhorn by Forres. Salmon, Grilse, Sea Trout, Finnock. **P.** G. Lilley, The Tackle Shop, 97b High Street, Forres. Tel: 72936.
£25-£35 per week.

River Lossie. Salmon, Sea Trout, Finnock, Brown Trout. **P.** Lossiemouth Angling Association, Homecrafts, 16 Queen Street, Lossiemouth; La Caverna, Clifton Road, Lossiemouth; Elgin Angling Centre, Moss Street, Elgin; The Tackle Shop, High Street, Elgin.
£1 per day, £3 per week.

Findhorn Estuary. Sea Trout. **P.** Post Office, Findhorn; Kimberley Inn, Findhorn; Crown & Anchor Hotel, Findhorn.
50p per day, £2 per week, £3 per season.

Loch Blairs, 2 miles south of Forres. Rainbow Trout, Brown Trout (stocked). **P.** Moray District Council, Department of Recreation, 30-32 High Street, Elgin. Tel: Elgin 45121; G. Lilley, 97b High Street, Forres. Tel: 72936.
Cost on application.

Loch Dallas. Brown Trout. **P.** Pat MacKenzie, 79 High Street, Forres.
Cost on application.

Lochindorb. Brown Trout. **P.** G. Lilley, The Tackle Shop, 97b High Street, Forres. Tel: 72936.

Loch of Loirston, Nigg. Rainbow Trout. **P.** Jas. Somers & Sons, 40 Thistle Street, Aberdeen. Tel: Aberdeen 639910.
£5 per day, £15 per week.

The Spey and its Waters

AN INTRODUCTORY NOTE

The Spey is one of our longest, most diverse and most productive waters in Scotland. It flows for more than fifty miles from Loch Insh down through Grantown, Aberlour, and Fochabers to its mouth on the Moray Firth, providing some magnificent salmon fishing focused mainly on spring and summer. The river also has excellent sea trout again providing good sport well upstream almost to Loch Insh. It is also a good trout water and although its spring fly fishing has declined somewhat in recent years, it has still some wonderful sport to offer and with care and with the excellent management brought by a preservation order, may restore the river to its former glories as far as trouting goes.

The high waters of Spey wind for many miles through the moorlands between Newtonmore and Laggan and some nice trout fishing can be had in this region. The Truim joins the main river near Newtonmore and for some miles the river winds among boggy banks, with canal-like reaches which hold good trout but are not to everyone's taste for fly fishing. Loch Insh, with trout, some sea trout and salmon marks the end of this sluggish section of the Spey and below this, down through Aviemore district, being increased by the waters of the Feshie, the river becomes more and more productive. This upper region can be good for night fly fishing for sea trout and in certain reaches, for salmon from April on. There are good club waters at Boat of Garten, Nethybridge and, outstandingly, in the Grantown-on-Spey area, which has possibly the best salmon fishing available in the UK, on a visitor's ticket basis on the Spey and the Dulnain. In Grantown there are excellent fishing hotels, some of them with good fishing courses and access to private beats of the river.

From Grantown down, through Castle Grant, Tulchan and Ballindalloch you will find the finest fly fishing of the middle Spey. The Avon (pronounced A'an) joins at Ballindalloch, itself a nice sea trout and salmon stream flowing crystal clear from the hills to the east. A succession of famous waters marks the river between Ballindalloch and Aberlour, including Carron Elchies and Aberlour itself.

It is a fine heavy broad river which flows down through Craigellachie, past Rothes and through the almost sacred beats of Arndilly and Delfur, followed by Orton and the Brae water at Forchabers. These are legendary places, very highly productive in most years, but, like many salmon waters in Scotland, suffering a decline in stocks in recent years, and particularly suffering a loss of spring sport.

The Spey valley is spectacularly beautiful with fine wooded lower lands backed by excellent forests and heathery hills. Behind it all lies the massive Cairngorm range, snowcovered for much of the year and providing good spring water for the river. It is not a region very rich in lochs but various trout lochs exist, some for example Vaa and Dallas, stocked with rainbows. If salmon prove to be difficult in low waters in summer, remember that the Spey provides, in its middle and upper middle reaches, some of the best night sea trout fishing you will find in Scotland. It is best from mid-June to early August. Recent numbers of sea trout and weights, have shown a firm upward trend.

LOCAL EXPERT KNOWLEDGE

Mr G. Mortimer, Tackle Maker, Grantown on Spey: The Spey is one of the most impressive river systems in Scotland. It can produce spring salmon from early February, followed by good late spring runs of fish and fine grilse and summer salmon to follow. There has been a dropping off of spring catches recently, however, and important steps have been taken in the management of the river to try to restore the runs. For example, a special arrangement relating to the closed netting times was introduced in 1984 and it is hoped that this will ensure good summer stocks initially, with spring stocks of salmon building up.

As far as sea trout are concerned, the Spey is on the up-and-up. Sea trout arrive in the Grantown area in April but are not caught in any numbers until about mid-May. June is perhaps the peak of the night fishing and fish up to six pounds are taken in night fishing. Good stocks of smaller sea trout run throughout the summer months also, making this a very important sector of our annual sport.

I would like to say that the Spey was also a good trout river. It was once noted for its good trout in May and June, but in recent years stocks have dropped and I cannot honestly say that its trout fishing is better than average now. Discussions are in hand to try to remedy this, but that is for future seasons.

The Grantown area is, of course, one of the best areas for holiday fishing and touring anywhere in the Highlands. Good local advice is available and good salmon fishing courses are run locally each spring.

The Spey
Loch Insh and Aviemore to Grantown

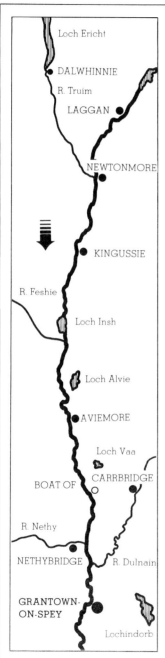

Loch Alvie, River Spey. <u>Salmon, Trout.</u> **P.** Lynwilg Hotel, Loch Alvie, Aviemore, Inverness-shire. Tel: Aviemore 810602.

Kinrara Estate Office, High Street, Grantown on Spey, Moray.

Boats £1-£5 per boat. Fishing £5 per day on River Spey, £30 per week.

Avielochan. <u>Brown Trout, Rainbow Trout.</u> **P.** Mrs. M. McCook, Avielochan, Aviemore, Inverness-shire. Tel: Aviemore 810450.

G. G. Mortimer & Son (Fishing Tackle), 61 High Street, Grantown-on-Spey, Moray. Tel: Grantown-on-Spey 2684.

10 a.m.-6 p.m. £2.25 per rod plus VAT: 6 p.m.-10 p.m. £1.75 per rod plus VAT. Bank fishing only.

Loch Cuaich. <u>Brown Trout.</u> **P.** Badenoch Angling Association. Local Tackle shops in Kingussie.

Keeper's House, Cuaich, Dalwhinnie, Inverness-shire. £1 per day: £5 per week: £8.50 per season. Boats £2 per day.

Loch Dallas, Loch Vaa. <u>Brown Trout, Rainbow Trout.</u> **P.** G. G. Mortimer & Son, High Street, Grantown-on-Spey, Moray. Tel: Grantown-on-Spey 2684.

Mrs. M. McCook, Avielochan, Aviemore. Tel: Aviemore 810450.

2 rods per boat £7 per day.

Loch Ericht. <u>Brown Trout.</u> **P.** Badenoch Angling Association. Grampian Hotel, Dalwhinnie.

Loch Ericht Hotel, Dalwhinnie.

£1 per day: £5 per week: £8.50 per season. Boats available.

Loch Mor, Loch Pityoulish. <u>Brown Trout, Rainbow Trout.</u> **P.** G. G. Mortimer, 61 High Street, Grantown-on-Spey, Moray. Tel: Grantown-on-Spey 2684.

Boat £6 per day.

Spey Dam. <u>Trout.</u> **P.** Badenoch Angling Association, Secretary, Mrs. J. Waller, 39 Burnside Avenue, Aviemore.

A. MacDonald, 6 Gergask Avenue, Laggan, Inverness-shire.

£1 per day; £5 per week; £8.50 per season. Boat available.

The Spey
Loch Insh and Aviemore to Grantown

River Spey, whole of left bank and most of right bank from Spey Dam to below Kingussie. Salmon, Trout, Sea Trout. **P.** Badenoch Angling Association, 39 Burnside Avenue, Aviemore.
Local Tackle shops in Kingussie and Newtonmore.
£1 per day: £5 per week: £8.50 per season.

River Spey. Salmon, Sea Trout, Brown Trout. **P.** Osprey Fishing School, Aviemore Centre, Aviemore.
Tel: Aviemore 810767/810911.
From £3 per day: £8 per week.

River Spey. Salmon, Sea Trout, Brown Trout. **P.** Kelmans Stores, Boat of Garten, Inverness-shire.
Kelmans Caravans. Tel: Boat of Garten 205.
£3 per day: £10 per week.

River Spey (6 miles both banks). Salmon, Sea Trout, Brown Trout. **P.** The Boat Hotel, Boat of Garten, Inverness-shire. Tel: Boat of Garten 258.
£3 per day: £10 per week.

River Spey, Feshie, Loch Insh. Salmon, Brown Trout, Sea Trout. **P.** Invereshie House Hotel, Kincraig, by Kingussie, Inverness-shire. Tel: Kincraig 332.
1 boat Loch Insh—£7 per rod per day.

River Spey, River Truim, 7 Highland lochs. Salmon, Sea Trout, Brown Trout. **P.** Silverfjord Hotel, Kingussie, Inverness-shire. Tel: Kingussie 292.
Cost on application.

River Spey, River Dulnain (7 plus 12 miles both banks respectively). Salmon, Sea Trout, Brown Trout. **P.** Strathspey Angling Association, G. G. Mortimer, 61 High Street, Grantown-on-Spey. Tel: Grantown-on-Spey 2684.
£12 per week.

Spey, Feshie Lochs. Salmon, Brown Trout, Sea Trout. **P.** The Osprey Fishing School, The Fishing Centre, Aviemore Centre, Aviemore.
Spey River from £2.50 per day: £7 per week.

Spey River, Calder River, Loch Ericht, Loch Laggan, Loch Cuaich. Salmon, Trout. **P.** Mains Hotel, Main Street, Newtonmore, Inverness-shire. Tel: Newtonmore 206.
Fishing £1 per day.

River Truim. Salmon. **P.** Badenoch Angling Association, J. Dallas, 9 High Street, Kingussie.
Daily bookings £1 only.

The Spey
Grantown To The Sea

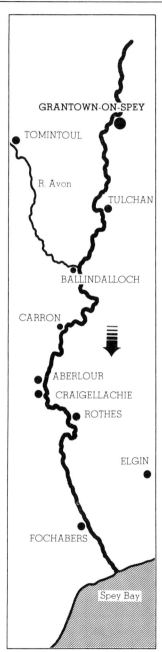

GRANTOWN-ON-SPEY

TOMINTOUL

R. Avon

TULCHAN

BALLINDALLOCH

CARRON

ABERLOUR

CRAIGELLACHIE

ROTHES

ELGIN

FOCHABERS

Spey Bay

River Spey, Aberlour. Salmon, Grilse, Sea Trout, Brown Trout. **P.** J. A. J. Munro, 95 High Street, Aberlour. Cost on application.

River Spey, Carron Estate (2 beats). Salmon, Sea Trout. **P.** Bell Ingram, Durn, Isla Road, Perth. Tel: 0738-21121.
Cost on application.

River Spey, Fochabers. Salmon. **P.** Gordon Arms Hotel, Fochabers. Tel: 0343 820 508/9.

River Spey, various private beats. Salmon, Sea Trout, Brown Trout. **P.** Dowans Hotel, Aberlour.
£4 per day.
J. A. J. Munro, 95 High Street, Aberlour.
Private fishing from £100-£350 per week plus VAT. Local water £4 per day.

Invernessshire Waters

AN INTRODUCTORY NOTE

Inverness-shire covers the largest land mass of any region in Scotland and within it lie a great variety of east and west-flowing rivers, together with a very wide range of large and small lochs. The area is very clearly divided into waters of the Ness and the Great Glen – the basins of Loch Ness, Loch Oich and, to the west, Loch Lochy. The Ness is a short, heavy river with salmon running it from the earliest spring to the late autumn. Many of the spring fish appear in the Moriston River, or go through to the head of Loch Oich to run the Garry. Fish are caught in Loch Ness, but normally by trolling. Good fly fishing can be had in the river itself, however, and summer runs can be prolific.

The western end of the Great Glen drains from Loch Lochy to the river of the same name and it takes the waters of the Spean (and Roy) and much of the water from Loch Laggan. A hydro scheme blocks migratory fish from Loch Laggan, but salmon run the Spean and the Roy. The Lochy is an excellent salmon river with a club at Fort William fishing its lower waters. It is best in wet summers and autumn.

To the north west of Fort William lies the peninsula of Ardgour running out to Ardnamurchan. Loch Shiel divides the landscape and provides, at its western end particularly (Archaracle) interesting sea trout and some salmon fishing on the loch. Dapping is a favourite approach for its sea trout, which are good from the end of June onwards. Sea trout and salmon run up into Loch Doilet, reached from Strontian, but this can be a dour water.

Further north, following the Fort William to Mallaig road, Loch Eilt and the Ailort are reached and above them, Loch Morar. Both lochs have a name for good sea trout fishing from late June on. There are many trout lochs in this area and inland, in the Cluanie, Affric valleys and further north lie some of the best trout lochs in the county. Loch Quoich, reached via Invergarry, is famous for large trout and good numbers. Inverness and its immediate neighbourhood to the north also embraces two salmon rivers of some note, the Beauly and the Conon, excellent waters from late spring onwards. Both rivers run sea trout from May onwards and the hills up both valleys have a wide variety of trout lochs available.

Inverness and The Great Glen

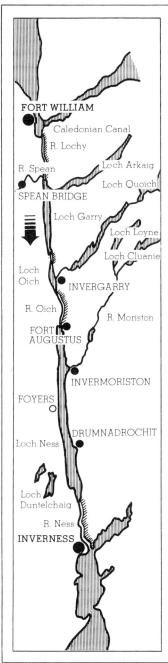

FORT WILLIAM

Caledonian Canal

R. Lochy

R. Spean   Loch Arkaig

     Loch Quoich

SPEAN BRIDGE

Loch Garry

    Loch Loyne

     Loch Cluanie

Loch Oich   **INVERGARRY**

R. Oich   R. Moriston

FORT AUGUSTUS

INVERMORISTON

FOYERS

DRUMNADROCHIT

Loch Ness

Loch Duntelchaig

R. Ness

INVERNESS

Loch Dochfour. Caledonian Canal. <u>Brown Trout</u>. **P.** The Factor, Dochfour Estate Office, by Inverness. Tel: Dochgarroch 218 or 230.
£1.25 per day: £3.50 per week, £8 per season.

River Enrick. Loch Meiklie. <u>Salmon, Trout</u>. **P.** Kilmartin Hall, Glenurquhart. Tel: Glenurquhart 269.
Free to residents.

Loch Meiklie. <u>Brown Trout</u>. **P.** Eurecosse Agencies, 7 Greenhill Street, Dingwall, Ross-shire. Tel: Dingwall 62462.
Cost on application.

Loch Meiklie. <u>Brown Trout</u>. **P.** Martin Rock Chalets, Kilmartin Farm, Glenurquhart. Inverness-shire.
Free to residents.

Glenmoriston. 22 Hill lochs. <u>Brown Trout</u>. **P.** Glenmoriston Estate Office, Glenmoriston, Inverness-shire. Tel: Glenmoriston 51202.
£1.80 per rod per day. £8 per boat inc. VAT.

Knockie, Bran Lochs, Ruthven and Tarff Ness. <u>Salmon, Brown Trout</u>. **P.** Whitebridge Hotel, Stratherrick, Inverness-shire. Tel: Gorthleck 272.
£5 per boat per day.

Loch Ruthven. <u>Brown Trout</u>. **P.** Estate Office, Brin Estate, Flichty. Tel: Farr 211.
Cost on application.

River Moriston. Torgoyle to river mouth, both banks. <u>Salmon, Trout</u>. **P.** Glenmoriston Estates Office, Glenmoriston, Inverness-shire.
Estuary beat £5.50-£8.60 per day, limit 6 rods. Dundreggan beat £3 per day. Combined beats, Trout £1.80 per day.

Loch Ness. <u>Salmon Trout</u>. **P.** Mrs. J.M. Tilford, 'Point Clair', Invermoriston, Inverness-shire.
£45-£85 per week inc. accommodation.

Loch Ness, Loch Farraline, Loch Garth, Loch Bran, Loch Mhor. <u>Salmon, Brown Trout</u>. **P.** Foyers Hotel, Foyers, Inverness-shire. Tel: Gorthleck 216.
Free to residents. £4 per day non-residents. £10 per day for ghillie with boat and tackle.

Loch Ness. <u>Salmon, Trout</u>. **P.** Inchnacardoch Lodge Hotel, Fort Augustus, Inverness-shire. Tel: Fort Augustus 6258.
2 boats inc. ghillie – £20 per day.

Inverness and The Great Glen

Loch Ness. <u>Salmon Trout.</u> **P.** Glenmoriston Estates Office, Glenmoriston, Inverness-shire. Tel: Glenmoriston 51202.
Boat and outboard £8.60 per day.

River Ness. <u>Salmon, Sea Trout.</u> **P.** Inverness Angling Club, J. Fraser, 33 Hawthorn Drive, Inverness, and local tackle shops.
£2.50 per day: £10 per week.

Loch Liath. <u>Brown Trout.</u> **P.** Glenmoriston Estates Office, Glenmoriston, Inverness. Tel: Glenmoriston 51202.
Cost on application.

Loch Ma Stac. <u>Brown Trout.</u> **P.** Glenmoriston Estates Office, Glenmoriston, Inverness. Tel: Glenmoriston 51202.
Cost on application.

Loch A'Choire. <u>Brown Trout.</u> **P.** Estate Office, Brin Estate Flichty, Inverness-shire. Tel: Farr 211.
Cost on application.

River Oich. <u>Salmon. Brown Trout.</u> **P.** A. MacDonald, Craigphadrig, Fort Augustus. Tel: Fort Augustus 6230. Glendoe Beat £6 per day, Aberchalder Beat £2 per day. Trout only £2 per day.

Loch Oich. <u>Brown Trout.</u> **P.** Glengarry Castle Hotel, Invergarry, Inverness-shire. Tel: Invergarry 254.
Cost on application.

Loch Benevean. <u>Trout.</u> **P.** J. Graham & Co. Ltd., 27 Union Street, Inverness. Tel: Inverness 33178.
Boat fishing only – £3.75 per day, 2 rods.

Northern Inverness-shire

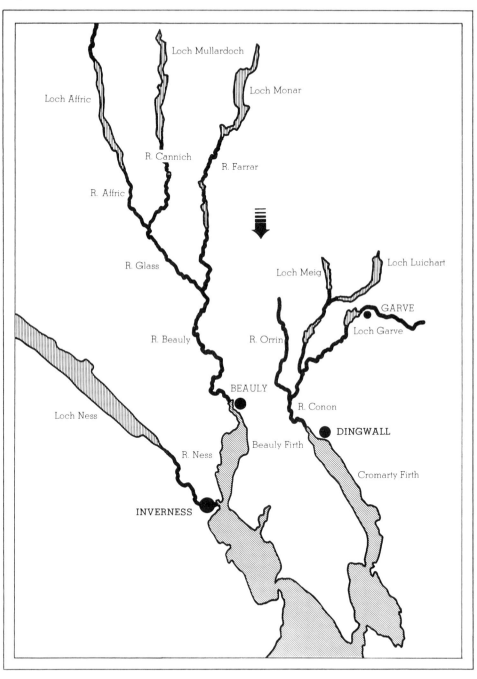

Northern Inverness-shire

River Conon. <u>Salmon, Brown Trout, Sea Trout.</u> **P.** Loch Achonachie Angling Club, C. Pieroni, Ravenscroft Guest House, Strathpeffer, Ross and Cromarty. Tel: Strathpeffer 403.
70p-£6.25 per day.

River Conon, New Pool, Morrison Pool, Bridge Pool. <u>Sea Trout.</u> **P.** Dingwall and District Angling Club. Secretary, H. A. Macleod, 27 Mackenzie Place, Maryburgh, Conon Bridge, Ross and Cromarty.
A. Shanks, Jun. Sports Stores, High Street, Dingwall, Ross and Cromarty.
£1.25 per day: £4 per week: £10 per month.

Cuil Na Caillich Loch. <u>Brown Trout.</u> **P.** Aigas Field Centre, Beauly, Inverness-shire. Tel: Beauly 2443.
£1 per day inc. boat plus £1 per rod. Bank fishing £1 per day.

Loch Mullardoch. <u>Brown Trout.</u> **P.** Glen Affric Hotel, Cannich, Inverness-shire. Tel: Cannich 214.
Cost on application.

Affric Hill Lochs. <u>Rainbow Trout, Brown Trout.</u> **P.** Forestry Office, Cannich, Inverness-shire. Tel: Cannich 272.
Bank fishing £2 per day plus VAT. Boat on one loch at £3 per day plus VAT plus £2 per rod.

Loch Aigas. <u>Brown Trout.</u> **P.** Forestry Office, Cannich, Inverness-shire. Tel: Cannich 272.
£1 per rod per day plus VAT.

River Beauly. <u>Salmon, Sea Trout, Brown Trout.</u> **P.** Lovat Estate Office, Beauly. Tel: Beauly 782205.
Cost on application.

Loch Benevean. <u>Brown Trout.</u> **P.** Glen Affric Hotel, Cannich, Inverness-shire. Tel: Cannich 214.
£5 per day for 2 rods inc. boat and outboard motor.
Grahams, 71 Castle Street, Inverness. Tel: 233178.
£4 per day for 2 rods inc. boat and outboard motor.

River Glass. <u>Salmon, Brown Trout.</u> **P.** Glen Affric Hotel, Cannich, Inverness-shire. Tel: Cannich 214.
Cost on application.

Loch Monar. <u>Brown Trout.</u> **P.** Glen Affric Hotel, Cannich, Inverness-shire. Tel: Cannich 214.
Cost on application.

Fort William
Lochaber and Ardnamurchan

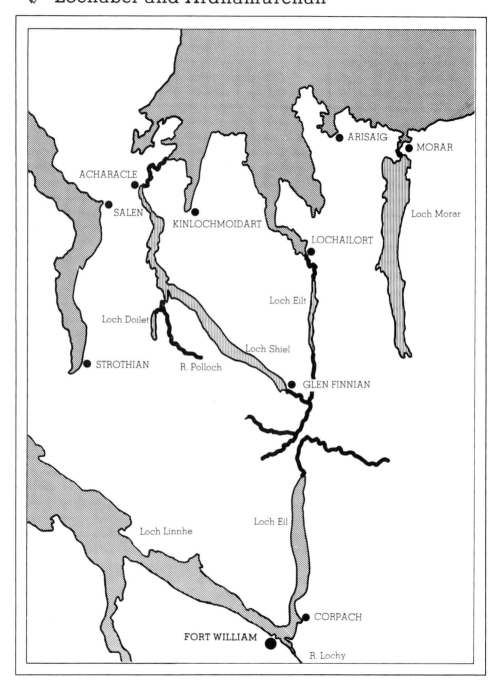

ARISAIG

MORAR

ACHARACLE

SALEN

Loch Morar

KINLOCHMOIDART

LOCHAILORT

Loch Eilt

Loch Doilet

Loch Shiel

STROTHIAN

R. Polloch

GLEN FINNIAN

Loch Eil

Loch Linnhe

CORPACH

FORT WILLIAM

R. Lochy

Fort William
Lochaber and Ardnamurchan

Loch Cluanie. <u>Brown Trout.</u> **P.** Dochfour Estate Office, Dochgarroch, by Inverness. Tel: Dochgarroch 218/9.
Boat £5 per day, 2 rods. Boat plus outboard £6 per day. Bank fishing £1 per day.

Loch Eilt, Loch Ailort. various hill lochs. <u>Salmon, Sea Trout, Brown Trout.</u> **P.** Lochailort Inn, Lochailort, Inverness-shire. Tel: Lochailort 208.
Cost on application.

Loch Garry, Loch Inchlaggan. <u>Rainbow Trout, Brown Trout.</u> **P.** Garry Gualach Ltd., Invergarry, Inverness-shire. Tel: Tomdoun 230.
Tomdoun Hotel, Invergarry, Inverness-shire. Tel: Tomdoun 218.
£1 per day: £6 per week: £15 per month. Boats available £4 per day inc. fishing.

River Garry (upper). <u>Brown Trout.</u> **P.** Garry Gualach Ltd., Invergarry, Inverness-shire. Tel: Tomdoun 230.
£1 per day: £6 per week: £15 per month. Boats available £3.50 per day inc. fishing.

Loch Morar. <u>Salmon, Sea Trout, Brown Trout.</u> **P.** Morar Hotel, Mallaig.
Morar Motors, Morar.
3 boats, £40 per boat.

Loch Morar, An Nostarie Loch, A Ghillie Ghobaich Loch and other hill lochs. <u>Salmon, Brown Trout, Sea Trout.</u> **P.** Morar Fishings, 'Allt and Loan', Morar, nr. Mallaig, Inverness-shire.
Tackle Shop, Mallaig.
Morar Motors, Morar.
£1 per day: £5 per week until 31 May: £2 per day, £10 per week thereafter.

Loch Quoich. <u>Trout.</u> **P.** J. Sabin, Lovat Arms Hotel, Fort Augustus, Inverness-shire. Tel: Fort Augustus 6206.
Bank fishing: £2 per day: £6 per week: £18 per month.
Boats £3 per day, 2 rods.

River Scaddle. <u>Salmon, Sea Trout.</u> **P.** Ardgour Hotel, by Fort William. Tel: Ardgour 225.
£5 per rod per day.

Loch Shiel. <u>Salmon, Sea Trout, Brown Trout.</u> **P.** Strontian Angling Club, Strontian, Argyll.
3 boats: £12 per day with engine. Fishing £5 per day.

Loch Shiel. <u>Salmon, Sea Trout.</u> **P.** D. Macaulay, Dalilea Farm, Archarcle, Argyle. Tel: Salen 253.
Cost on application.

Loch Shiel. <u>Salmon, Sea Trout.</u> **P.** The Creel Fishing Facilities Co., Creel Cottage, Archarcle, Argyle. Tel: Salen 281.
Boat £10 per day. Outboard £2 per day.

Loch Shiel. <u>Salmon, Trout, Sea Trout.</u> **P.** Ben View Hotel, Strontian, Argyll. Tel: Strontian 2333.
3 boats, £12 per day.

Loch Shiel, River Finnan. <u>Salmon, Sea Trout</u>. **P.** Glenfinnan House Hotel, Glenfinnan, Inverness-shire. Tel: Kinlocheil 235.
3 boats, £10 per day.

Loch Shiel. <u>Salmon, Sea Trout, Brown Trout</u>. **P.** Stage House Inn, Glenfinnan, Inverness-shire. Tel: Kinlocheil 246.
7 boats from £8.

River Spean. <u>Salmon, Sea Trout.</u> **P.** Spean Bridge Hotel, Spean Bridge, Inverness-shire. Tel: Spean Bridge 250.
Cost on application.

Strontian, Polloch River, Loch Diolet and Loch Shiel. <u>Salmon, Brown Trout, Sea Trout</u>. **P.** Loch Sunart Hotel, by Acharcle, Strontian, Argyll. Tel: Strontian 2231/2471.
£6 per day: £30 per week. Boats: Loch Doilet £6, Loch Shiel £7.

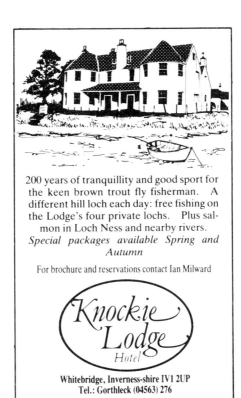

Easter and Wester Ross

AN INTRODUCTORY NOTE

There is a considerable contrast between Easter and Wester Ross. The lands to the east of the county, bordering the North Sea are fertile, gentle and strangely un-Highland in their appearance. As you travel west, up the Conon valley to Garve you drive into an area of high hills with narrow valleys and attractively set lochs. The shorter rivers drain to the west, through beautiful West Highland territory strewn with hill lochs and laced with burns. A particular area of great fishing interest is Loch Maree, one of the outstanding sea trout lochs of Scotland. It is fed by the Kinlochewe River at its southern end and gathers waters from hills to the west and east before flowing through its own short outlet river the Ewe to join the sea at Poolewe.

To the West of Maree lies Torridon and Shieldaig, with small spate rivers and systems of sea trout and trout lochs. The outlook from some of these Wester Ross hill waters is remarkable, with seascapes and vistas of hill and glen. The views of Raasay and Skye are sometimes unforgettable.

If you travel north from Garve to Ullapool you again enter an area of short rivers and systems of lochs backing them in the hills. You can branch west from the Ullapool road to meet the Dundonnel river and strike some good trout lochs on the way to Gairloch, or you can continue north through Ullapool and fish sea trout and trout lochs near Achiltibuie. The Polly lochs and river and the renowned Loch Sionascraig, a trout loch of great beauty, lie just to the north of this. In all, this area is astonishingly rich in trout lochs, has some nice sea trout fishing to offer and has good summer salmon fishing in loch and river provided the water levels are right after summer rain.

Wester Ross is a delightful west Highland county of lochs, burns and the varied, weathered hills and seascapes we think of as typical of the North west Highland coast. It is an area of hill and moor with magnificent lochs, such as Loch Maree, lying in its beautiful glens. Thee is a vast amount of hill loch trout fishing in Wester Ross and an introduction can do little more than say that it is available everywhere through hotels and local estates. There is also some good summer salmon and sea trout fishing available. It is very dependent on water and in a warm summer can be at a standstill for weeks, except on large waters like Maree. Even there, wind is essential, but summer afternoon thermals can transform the day from dead calm into highly productive drifting for sea trout.

This is an excellent area for touring and fishing with many western beaches to visit, a good supply of hotels and other accommodation and memorable views of mountains, shores and islands. It is therefore a good choice for the angler split between a family holiday and fishing.

Ross and Cromarty–Easter Ross

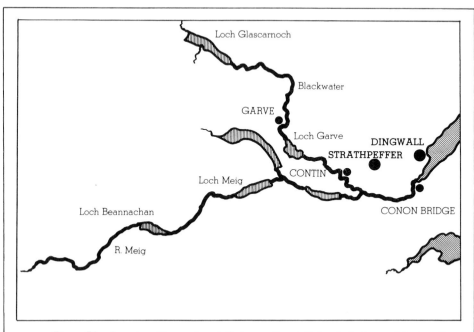

River Blackwater, Upper beat. <u>Salmon, Trout.</u> **P**: Loch Achonachie Angling Club, C. Pieroni, Ravenscroft Guest House, Strathpeffer, Ross and Cromarty. Tel: Strathpeffer, Strathpeffer 403.
£2.50 per day.

River Blackwater. <u>Salmon, Trout, Sea Trout.</u> **P**. Craigdarroch Lodge Hotel, Craigdarroch Drive, Contin, by Strathpeffer, Ross-shire. Tel: Strathpeffer 265.
£2 per boat. Trout: £2 per day. Salmon: £6-£15 per day.

River Carron. <u>Salmon, Sea Trout.</u> **P**. Renton Finlayson, Estates Office, Bonar Bridge, Sutherland.
Cost on application.

Loch Catrine. <u>Brown Trout.</u> **P**. Inveroykel Lodge Hotel, Strathoykel, by Ardgay, Sutherland. Tel: Rosehall 200.
Cost on application.

Loch Meig. <u>Trout.</u> **P**. Loch Achonachie Angling Club, C. Pieroni, Ravenscroft Guest House, Strathpeffer, Ross and Cromarty. Tel: Strathpeffer 403.
£1.10 per day from bank. £3.15 per day from boat (2 rods).

Loch Meig, Beannacharian Loch, Meig River. <u>Brown Trout.</u> **P**. East Lodge Hotel, Strathconon. Tel: Strathconon 222.
Boat — £3.50 per day (2 rods). Loch Beannacharain, £3.15 per day (2 rods). Loch Meig. Bank fishing — £1.50 per day. River fishing — £1.50 per day.

Ross and Cromarty – Wester Ross

Loch Sionascraig

Loch Badagyle

Loch Lurgain

Loch Strath Kanaird

ULLAPOOL

Loch Damph

R. Dundonnel

Loch Maree

Loch Glascarnoch

R. Torridon

Ross and Cromarty – Wester Ross

Balmacara Estate Lochs. <u>Brown Trout.</u> **P.** Balmacara Hotel, by Kyle of Lochalsh, Ross & Cromarty. Tel: Kyle of Lochalsh 283.
£2 per day.

Rivers Garvie and Polly. <u>Salmon, Sea Trout, Brown Trout.</u> **P.** Royal Hotel, Ullapool, Ross-shire. Tel: Ullapool 2181.
Cost on application.

Loch Glascarnoch. <u>Trout.</u> **P.** Aultguish Inn, by Garve, Ross & Gromarty. Tel: Aultguish 254.
£1 per day: £3 per week: £7.50 per month. Boat £3 (2 rods).

River Kerry, Loch Black Lady, Loch Garbaig. <u>Salmon, Sea Trout, Brown Trout.</u> **P.** Mr. Harold Davis, Creag Mor Hotel, Gairloch, Wester Ross. Tel: Gairloch 2068.
Trout: £1 per day. Salmon: £5 per day. Boats on lochs £4, sea boat £8.

Loch Maree. <u>Salmon, Sea Trout, Trout.</u> **P.** Shieldaig Lodge Hotel, Gairloch, Ross & Gromarty. Tel: Badachro 250.
Cost on application.

Loch Maree. <u>Salmon, Brown Trout, Sea Trout.</u> **P.** Loch Maree Hotel. Tel: Loch Maree 200.
£68 per week inc. boat.

Loch Maree. <u>Salmon, Sea Trout, Brown Trout.</u> **P.** Kinlochewe Hotel, Kinlochewe, by Achnasheen, Ross & Cromarty. Tel: Kinlochewe 253.
Cost on application.

Polly Lochs, top, middle and lower. <u>Salmon, Sea Trout.</u> **P.** J. McDonald, Inverpolly, Ullapool, Ross & Cromarty. Tel: Lochinver 252.
£3-£5 per day incl. boat.

Lochs Sionascaig, Lurgain and Badagyle. <u>Salmon, Sea Trout, Brown Trout, Ferrox.</u> **P.** Royal Hotel, Ullapool, Ross & Cromarty. Tel: Ullapool 2181.
Cost on application.

Loch Strath Kanaird. <u>Brown Trout.</u> **P.** Highland Coastal Estates (Rhidorroch) Offices, Shore Street, Ullapool, Ross and Cromarty.
Cost on application.

River Torridon, Loch An Iascaigh, River Baigy, Loch Damph. <u>Salmon, Brown Trout, Sea Trout.</u> **P.** Loch Torridon Hotel, Torridon, by Achnasheen, Ross-shire. Tel: Torridon 242.
Loch An Iascaigh £4-£7 per boat, max. 2 rods. Loch Damph £10 per boat and engine incl. 1 rod. £5 per extra rod.

River Ullapool. <u>Salmon, Sea Trout, Brown Trout.</u> **P.** Highland Coastal Estates (Rhidorroch) Offices, Shore Street, Ullapool, Ross & Cromarty.
Cost on application.

River Dundonnel (Eilean Darach Beat). <u>Salmon, Sea Trout.</u> **P.** Dundonnell, by Garve, Ross & Cromarty. Tel: Dundonnel 204.
£10 per day.

Loch Maree–Wester Ross

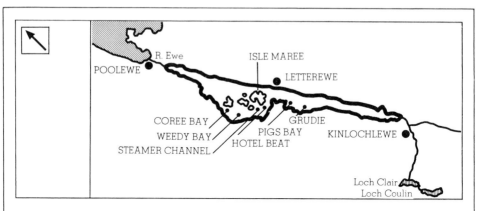

AN INTRODUCTORY NOTE

Loch Maree is one of those excellent waters in Scotland which lie on a south-west to north-west fault and provide us with some of the best sea trout fishing in the country. It is a large body of water drained to the north-west by a short river into the sea at Poolewe. As with other waters lying on this angle and drained by short rivers it is particularly famous for its trout runs, although the water also has salmon, brown trout and a few char.

Maree brings in its first runs of sea trout with the salmon which come into the loch about the middle of May, but this early run of sea trout is not much fished for, even if it contains some of the very largest sea trout of the year. The salmon run of late spring and early summer is fished for in the River Ewe and was once sought by trolling in the Loch Maree Hotel beats, with some success, but it has not been very popular recently. Equally, there were often good salmon catches at Kinlochewe around the third week of May and into the beginning of June, but again, these have not had the attention they deserve in recent years.

The main sport on Maree is in the high summer months from mid-June to the end of the season in October. Perhaps the best sport is July and August. Maree, with its wonderful Highland setting – high hills on either side and a fine array of islands – gives the long windswept drifts which make dapping successful. It is possibly the most successful and most interesting dapping water in Scotland. Loch Maree has, in the past twenty years or so, produced sea trout of up to nineteen and a half pounds, but in the last ten both sizes and numbers have dropped off. Since 1980, however, there are distinct signs that stocks are again on the increase and heavier fish are again being taken in good numbers. There is no doubt that this remarkable water remains in the forefront of sea trout fishing in Scotland and has tremendous potential for recovery from cyclic reduction in stocks.

The River Ewe, a short full river entering the sea at Poolewe has excellent night sea trout fishing in June and has good day salmon fishing from May to October. Fishings on loch and river can be organised through local hotels in Poolewe, Gairloch, Loch Maree and Kinlochewe. Fishings are also arranged on Lochs Clair and Coulin above Kinlochewe, which fish best late in the season.

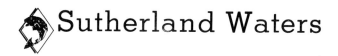# Sutherland Waters

AN INTRODUCTORY NOTE

Sutherland is a magnificent place for fly fishing. It has everything one would want – salmon rivers and lochs, good sea trout, excellent and wild scenery and west, offering spring fishing on the east coast and summer fishing on both east and west coast in such measure that it almost qualifies for the perpetual fishing county.

It is useful to divide the county into sections, more or less related to the access roads. The road from Inverness takes you over the Kyle of Sutherland at Bonar Bridge. There you will cross the very interesting, tidal joint estuary of the Shin, Oykel, Cassely and Ross-shire Carron which joins at Ardgay. There is extensive and unusual fly fishing available on this Kyle. The rivers which flow into the Kyle of Sutherland include the Shin, still with a spring run and some summer fish but affected by the Hydro electric dam near Lairg. The Oykel is a spring and summer river with some excellent sport available in the right conditions of weather and water. The Cassely equally has a long reputation of sport, given conditions which suit it. Loch Shin above, near Lairg, is a water which can be first class for brown trout, and has occasional very large fish as well as good numbers of fish around the pound mark. Its tributary the Tirry can also fish well after rain. Numerous small lochs are to be found in this sector of Sutherland also.

Following the Wick road up the east coast, you will come to two famous and interesting river systems, the Brora and the Helmsdale. The Brora can be thought of as two rivers – the upper river which drains into Loch Brora (which is in three separate parts) and the lower Brora which drains the loch. The earliest spring fishing for salmon (February and March) is enjoyed on the lower river. The upper fishes from mid-March onwards and can be splendid in April and May. Indeed, the Brora system can, with the right water, go on fishing throughout the summer, bringing fresh fish in to river and loch right to the end of September. There are some fine runs of sea trout and finnock also and the loch enjoys good sport with these in summer. Access to the upper waters is by estate lease only but there is access to the lower river through local hotels in Brora and to the loch above. There is also a Brora angling club which has a boat on the loch and certain access to the lower river.

The Helmsdale above is a fine salmon river, but is largely preserved. The angling club, however, based on Helmsdale itself has the lower beat of the river and visitors might be able to fish this water. This beat fishes well in spring and early summer and can be good for sea trout on summer evenings. At the head of the Helmsdale there is a rich array of lochs available for trout fishing. This is tremendous trouting country, with large and small waters, some well worth the walk over the hill to get to them. Centred on the Badanloch estate or on Forsinard, you have not just a full holiday of fishing available but enough for a lifetime.

Further west, the preserved river Naver drains the loch of the same name where there is access to salmon and sea trout fishing. The attractive River Mudale, a tributary of the system has good salmon and brown trout fishing in early summer. Lochs abound in the hills around Altnaharra and it is usually from here that anglers drive to Loch Hope in northern Sutherland for its good sea trout fishing. Nearby lie the good lochs and streams around Tongue, including Loch Loyal and the Berriedale River.

Sutherland seems endless. To the north west of the county lies the fine Durness river draining to the north and bringing salmon and sea trout up in numbers to its remote loch in the hills above. There is the Cape Wrath peninsula for the adventurous, and trout lochs in plenty.

South of this, in a valley which connects to the east with Loch Shin and Lairg, lie Loch Stack, a famous sea trout and salmon loch and Loch More above it. Stack was a fabulous sea trout water but reverted to salmon some fifteen years ago. It is now showing strong signs of recovery and promises well for the years ahead. Further South again, in a land of innumerable lochs and streams, lies the River Inver and Loch Assynt, centred on Lochinver, and the River Kirkaig. The Inver has splendid summer salmon and good sea trout, as has Loch Assynt above. The Kirkaig has good summer and late summer salmon in specactular settings but its salmon do not reach the Fionn Loch above where trout fishing can be outstanding.

Further south again lie the vast loch fishing resources of Scourie, a huge area of trout lochs, some of no particular merit but many with excellent trout and sea trout fishings. Local advice is the only way to plan a trip here, although almost every water will give you sport. This part of Sutherland reminds the angler of the huge natural resources of Scotland and the virtually endless prospect of new waters, new mountain vistas and good sport.

LOCAL EXPERT OPINION

Rob Wilson of Brora, a well known angling authority and tackle maker reminded me that 'Sutherland has been called the half-pound county'. It is a place of many lochs, often with more waters than you could name, and certainly more than you could visit in a lifetime. It is a county with great family fishing possibilities, with marvellous walks to chains of hill lochs and fabulous vistas of mountains and hills to range your eye over. In the valleys run innumerable burns and waters, many of which have good stocks of trout, excellent for picnic walking and fishing.

But Sutherland has also its excellent salmon and sea trout fishing. The rivers flowing east into the Kyle of Sutherland – the Shin, the Oykel (and Cassley) and the Carron (technically in Ross) have spring and summer fishing to offer. The Brora has good spring and often outstanding summer salmon, with good runs of sea trout from June onwards, some of which are caught in the loch. The Helmsdale is first class and over to the west the famous Naver and a group of smaller rivers – Halladale, Borgie, Hope and Dionard, all offer salmon and sea trout sport. These fishings, chosen from a list of so many different waters, characterise a county with something to offer for everybody, from the expert salmon fisher to the family mixing fishing with just enjoying the beauties of Sutherland.

The Kyle of Sutherland and Lairg Districts

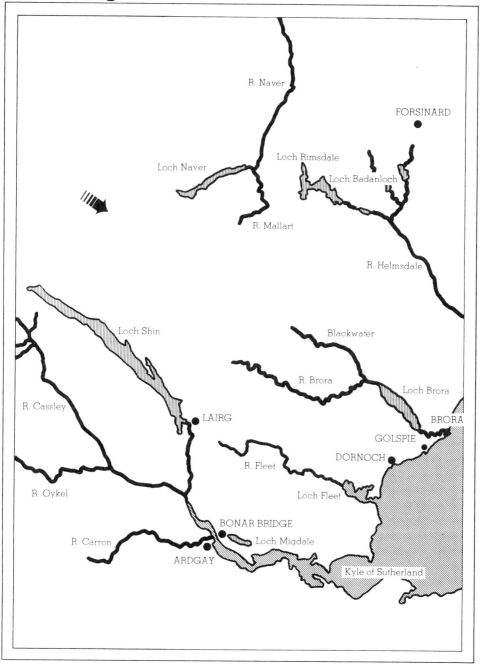

The Kyle of Sutherland and Lairg Districts

Loch Beannach. <u>Brown Trout.</u> **P.** Sutherlands Arms Hotel, Lairg, Sutherland, Tel: Lairg 2291.
Boat £4.50 per day inc. VAT.

Fuarloch. <u>Brown Trout.</u> **P.** Sutherland Arms Hotel, Lairg, Sutherland. Tel: Lairg 2291.
Boat £4.50 per day inc. VAT.

Loch Ghriama. <u>Brown Trout.</u> **P.** Overscaig Hotel, Overscaig by Lairg, Sutherland. Tel: Merkland 203.
Free to residents, boats and ghillies available.

Kyle of Sutherland, Migdale Loch. <u>Brown Trout, Sea Trout.</u> **P.** Invershin Hotel, Invershin, Lairg, Sutherland. Tel: Invershin 202.
2 boats: £6 per day.

Kyle of Sutherland. <u>Sea Trout.</u> **P.** Inveroykel Lodge Hotel, Strathoykel, by Ardgay, Sutherland. Tel: Rosehall 200.
Cost on application.

Loch Migdale. <u>Brown Trout.</u> **P.** Inveroykel Lodge Hotel, Strathoykel, by Ardgay, Sutherland. Tel: Rosehall 200.
Cost on application.

Loch Migdale. <u>Brown Trout.</u> **P.** Dornoch Hotel, Dornoch. Royal Golf Hotel, Dornoch.
1 boat: £2 per day. Fishing: £2 per day.

Loch Migdale. <u>Trout.</u> **P.** W. A. McDonald, Castle Street, Dornoch, Sutherland.
Boats: £3 per day. Banking fishing: 50p per day.

Loch Merkland. <u>Brown Trout.</u> **P.** Overscaig Hotel, Overscaig by Lairg, Sutherland. Tel: Merkland 203.
Free to residents, boats and ghillies available.

Lochan Ochtow. <u>Brown Trout.</u> **P.** Inveroykel Lodge Hotel, Strathoykel, by Ardgay, Sutherland. Tel: Rosehall 200.
Cost on application.

River Oykel. <u>Salmon, Sea Trout.</u> **P.** Renton Finlayson, Estates Office, Bonar Bridge, Sutherland.
Cost on application.

River Oykel. <u>Salmon, Sea Trout.</u> **P.** Inveroykel Lodge Hotel, Strathoykel, by Ardgay, Sutherland. Tel: Rosehall 200.
Free to residents.

Loch Shin. <u>Brown Trout, Ferox.</u> **P.** Lairg Angling Club. Sutherland Arms Hotel.
Boat £3 per day (inc. permit): Outboard motors £4 per day plus VAT.

Loch Shin. <u>Brown Trout.</u> **P.** J. M. Ross, Secretary, Lairg Angling Club, Post Office House, Lairg, Sutherland. Tel: Lairg 2010.
Lairg Pharmacy and local hardware fishing tackle shop, or Club Warden, club hut at lochside beyond Lairg Dam.
£1 per day: £4 per week: Boats: £7 per day (3 rods).

Loch Shin. <u>Brown Trout</u>. **P.** Overscaig Hotel, Overscaig by Lairg, Sutherland. Tel: Merkland 203.
Free to residents. Boats and ghillies available.

Loch Urigill. <u>Brown Trout, Rainbow Trout</u>. **P.** Inveroykel Lodge Hotel, Strathoykel, by Ardgay, Sutherland. Tel: Rosehall 200.
Cost on application.

River Brora. ¾ mile tidal water. <u>Sea Trout, Finnock, Brown Trout</u>. **P.** None required.
(Free.)

Loch Brora. <u>Salmon, Sea Trout, Brown Trout.</u> **P.** Estate Offie, Gordonbush, Brora, Sutherland. Tel: 323.
£5 per day: £30 per week: £120 per month, VAT extra (including boat).

Forsinard and Badanloch Areas

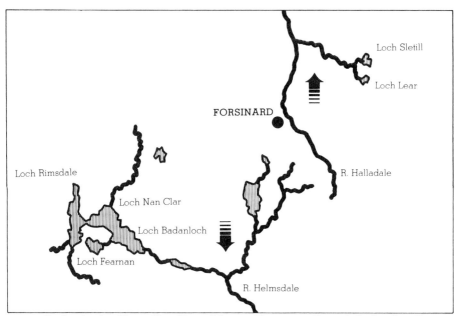

Badanloch, Clar, Cor Nam Mang, Fearnan, Rimsdale Lochs. Brown Trout. **P.** Navidale House Hotel, Helmsdale, Sutherland. Tel: Helmsdale 258. Polson MacKenzie, Badaloch, Kinbrace.
Cost on application.

River Halladale, Loch Slethill, Loch Lear, Loch Talaheel, Crosslochs, Loch Clach, Bad Bothian. Salmon, Sea Trout, Canadian Brook Trout, Brown Trout. **P.** Forsinard Hotel, Forsinard, Halladale. Tel: Halladale 221. 6 boats: £4.60 per boat. Residents free. Fishing charges: River £10, £4.60 per boat, £2 bank. Residents free.

River Helmsdale. Salmon, Sea Trout. **P.** Helmsdale River Board, Fishery Office, Strathnaver, Kinbrace, Sutherland. Tel: Strathnaver 201.
Weekly tickets from A. Jappy & Sons Ltd., Shore Road, Helmsdale. Cost on application.

The Naver and Borgie Districts

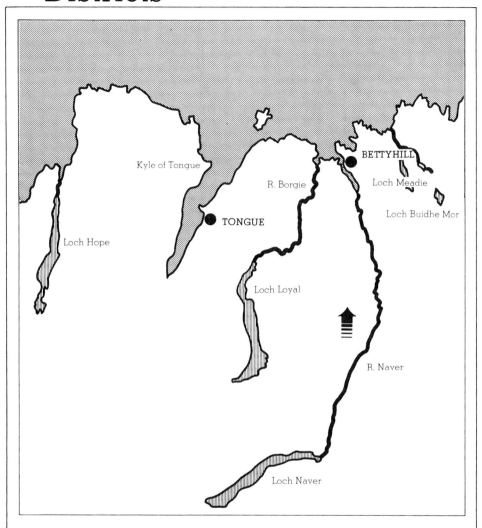

Loch Craggie. <u>Brown Trout.</u> **P.** Ben Loyal Hotel, Tongue, Sutherland. Tel: Tongue 216.
£3 per week: 75p per day. Boat £2 per day.

Lochs Craggie, Ailsh. <u>Rainbow Trout, Brown Trout, Sea Trout.</u> **P.** Oykel Bridge Hotel, by Lairg, Sutherland.
Cost on application. 6 boats available.

Loch Hakel. <u>Brown Trout.</u> **P.** Ben Loyal Hotel, Tongue, Sutherland. Tel: Tongue 216.
75p perday: £3 per week. Boat £3 per day.

The Naver and Borgie Districts

Kyle of Tongue. <u>Sea trout.</u> **P.** Ben Loyal Hotel, Tongue, Sutherland. Tel: Tongue 216.
No charge.

Maovally. <u>Brown Trout.</u> **P.** Ben Loyal Hotel, Tongue, Sutherland. Tel: Tongue 216.
75p per day: £3 per week. Boat £2 per day.

Meadie, Mor, Kirktomy, Caol, Nan Loagh, Craite Lochs, Duinte, Girdh Creagan Lochans. <u>Brown Trout.</u> **P.** Bettyhill Hotel, Bettyhill, Sutherland. Tel: Bettyhill 202.
2 boats: £3 per day, outboards £3 per day. Fishing free to residents: Brown trout lochs 50p per day.

Loch Modsarie. <u>Brown Trout.</u> **P.** Ben Loyal Hotel, Tongue, Sutherland. Tel: Tongue 216.
75p per day: £3 per week. Boat £2 per day.

River Mudale. (and various lochs in areas). Salmon, Brown Trout. **P.** Angling Centre, Altnaharra Fishings, Altnaharra, by Lairg, Sutherland. Tel: Altnaharra 225.
Cost on application.

Loch Loyal. <u>Brown Trout.</u> **P.** Ben Loyal Hotel, Tongue, Sutherland. Tel: Tongue 216.
75p per day: £3 per week. Boat £2 per day.

Kylesku, Lochinver and Inchnadamph

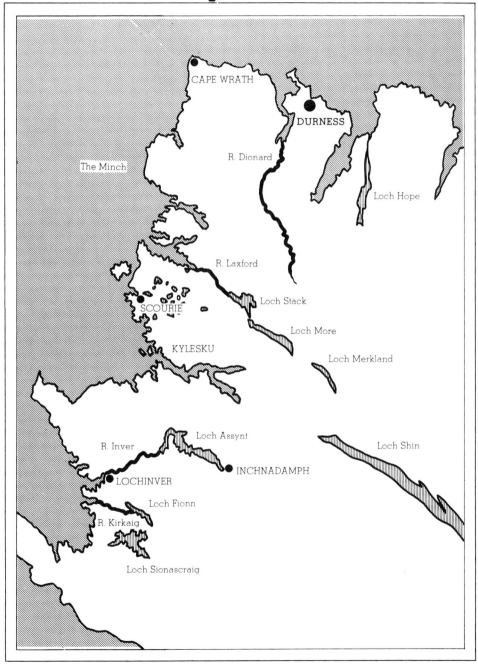

Kylesku, Lochinver and Inchnadamph

Loch Assynt. Salmon, Brown Trout. **P.** Inchnadamph Hotel, Inchnadamph, Sutherland. Tel: Assynt 202.
Cost on application. Boats available.

Assynt. (34 lochs). Brown Trout. **P.** Assynt Angling Club. Secretary, S. M. McClelland, Baddidarroch, Lochinver, Sutherland. Tel: Lochinver 253.
Culag Hotel, Lochinver.
M. Turnbull, Newsagent, Lochinver.
Locality Offices, Lochinver. Tel: 214.
I. Yates, 114 Achmelvich, Lochinver.
D. MacLeod, Hillhead, Lochinver.
Drumbeg Hotel. Tel: Drumbeg 236.
Kylesku Hotel. Tel: Kylestrome 200.
M. MacLeod, Achmelvich Caravan Site.
W. Hutchinson, Inverkirkaig.

Loch Drumbeg. (20 lochs near hotel). Brown Trout. **P.** Drumbeg Hotel, Assynt, by Lairg. Tel: Assynt 236.
£1.50 per day: £4 per week. 6 boats: £1.60 per day. Free to hotel residents.

Loch Gillaroo. Brown Trout. **P.** Inchnadamph Hotel, Inchnadamph, Sutherland. Tel: Assynt 202.
Free to hotel residents. Charges on application to non-residents.

Loch Letteressie. Salmon, Brown Trout. **P.** Inchnadamph Hotel, Inchnadamph, Sutherland. Tel: Assynt 202.
Free to hotel residents. Charges on application to non-residents.

River Kirkaig, Loch Culag, Loch Fionn, Loch Assynt, Cul Fraoich Loch, Loch Claise, Loch Crocach, Loch Beannach. Salmon, Brown Trout, Sea Trout, Rainbow Trout. **P.** Culag Hotel, Lochinver, Sutherland. Tel: Lochinver 209/255.
Boats: £8 per day. Loch fishing £1.20 (bank); £17 for River Kirkaig per day.

Scourie Lochs, and Lochans over an area of 15,000 acres. Salmon, Brown Trout, Sea Trout. **P.** Scourie Hotel, Scourie, by Lairg, Sutherland. Tel: Scourie 2396.
12 boats: £1.50 per day, free to residents.

Loch Stack, Loch More and Loch Merkland

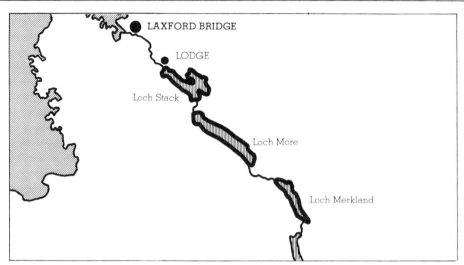

Loch Stack lies at the head of the short Laxford River near Laxford Bridge in western Sutherland. It is a magnificently set water nestling between high hills to the south and the north. Above Loch Stack and on the same system lies Loch More. This system was until about 1975 predominantly a sea trout fishery with good summer salmon on the river Laxford, but changes of a cyclic nature took place and the loch for some years turned into something approaching a salmon loch with some sea trout. It has again started to show a return to its former glories as a sea trout water with dapping and wet fly fishing producing bags of good quality in summer and autumn. The first fish arrive with the high tides in mid-June but the main runs are in July and August. Salmon come in mid-June also.

The fishing are let by Westminster Estates through their local estates offices but various local hotels have boats on Lochs Stack and More. The latter water fishes best late in the season in September and October.

Hotels with access to boats on Stack and More include Overscaig Hotel, which lies at the head of Loch Shin west of Lairg.

Loch Stack. <u>Salmon, Sea Trout.</u> **P.** Overscaig Hotel, Merkland, by Lairg, Sutherland. Tel: Merkland 203.
From £15 day to £30 day (boat). (Ghillie extra if required.)

Loch More. <u>Salmon, Sea Trout</u>. **P.** Overscaig Hotel, Merkland, by Lairg, Sutherland. Tel: Merkland 203.
Average £20 per boat/day, varying with season. Best late summer/autumn.

Loch Merkland. <u>Trout.</u> **P.** Overscaig Hotel.
Costs on request.

Loch Shin (upper). <u>Trout and occasional salmon</u>. **P.** Overscaig Hotel.
Costs on request.

Loch Hope

This interesting loch lies in the north west of Sutherland draining through the short River Hope into the Pentland Firth on the northern coast of Scotland. It is one of those very interesting waters with a largish loch lying above a short river, offering easy access for salmon and sea trout in season. The loch is fished from Altnaharra Hotel and through local estates and both lets and hotel fishing can be arranged. It fishes well in late spring for salmon, although, like many northern lochs, it is neglected as a fishery during this period. The first sea trout run in late June (in any significant numbers) and continue to run until the autumn, providing very attractive sport to dapping and wet fly.

Information about Loch Hope and bookings can be made through:

Altnaharra Hotel, by Lairg, Sutherland. Tel: Altnaharra (054981) 222.

The Angling Centre, Altnaharra by Lairg, Sutherland.

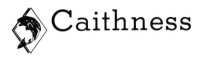 # Caithness

AN INTRODUCTORY NOTE

Caithness is sometimes called the lowlands beyond the Highlands. It is the county lying on the extreme north of the mainland of Scotland, looking over at Orkney on one of its sides. This plain beyond the highlands is a most interesting fishing area. The geology of the area owes a great deal to the ice ages which deposited lime-enriched boulder clay on the Caithness lowlands and this has helped to form excellent shallow lochs with rich beds. A good example of this is Watten in the middle of the county. Further north, there are excellent lochs near the coast in the Thurso and Dunnet areas where the lochs lie directly over shell sand, providing a very rich environment for the trout. In these waters, growth rates are impressive and fish quality is high.

The rivers of Caithness include the well-known Thurso, flowing north west from the moors around Altnabreac, forming lochs en route and winding its way through moorland scenery to the sea at Thurso. This river can be an early opener, and it is a spring river of some note later in the season, in April and May. In the last decade it has shown its best catches, however, in summer with some astonishing grilse and small summer runs which have provided some wonderful sport in recent years. The Thurso is a rather slow-flowing river over much of its length but its waters can be sporting and productive when wind and flow are right. Its upper reaches have fine streams.

The Wick river, flowing north east into the sea at the town of Wick is a moorland water with streams on its middle and lower reaches. It fishes best in summer after rain but can produce grilse and sea trout, giving good sport.

In its upper reaches, around Altnabreac in wild grouse moor country, lie excellent moorland lochs, some with reputations for large fish (Loch Glutt for example). This is fine walking and fishing country far from care and it has an unforgettable quality.

River Thurso, whole river. <u>Salmon, Sea Trout</u>. **P.** The Secretary, Thurso Fisheries Ltd., Thurso East, Thurso, Caithness. Tel: Thurso 63134.
£100-£275 per week incl. accommodation, depending on season.

River Berriedale. <u>Salmon, Sea Trout.</u> **P.** Portland Arms Hotel, Lybster, Caithness. Tel: Lybster 208.
From £14 per rod per day plus VAT.

Melvich Hill Lochs. <u>Brown Trout.</u> **P.** Melvich Hotel, Melvich, by Thurso, Caithness. Tel: Melvich 206.
£2 per rod per day (guests), £3 per day non-residents.

Ulbster Estates, 12 hill lochs. <u>Brown Trout</u>. **P.** Ulbster Arms Hotel, Halkirk, Caithness. Tel: Halkirk 206/641.
£3.50 per day.

Loch Watten. <u>Brown Trout.</u> **P.** Loch Watten Hotel, Watten, Caithness. Tel: Watten 232.
£4 per day incl. boat for residents. £4.50 per day non-residents.

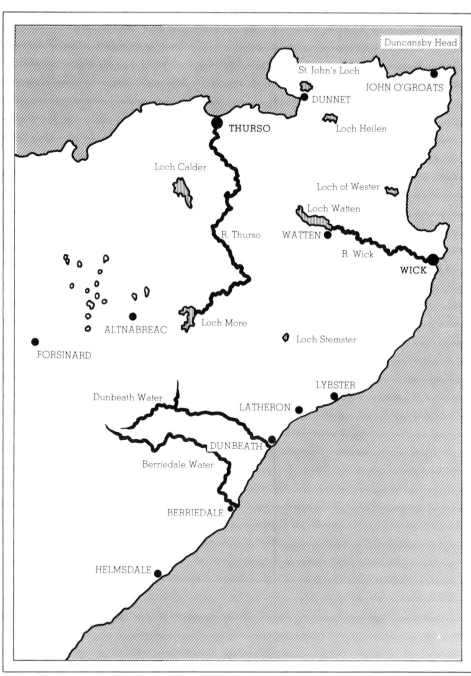

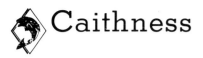 # Caithness

Loch Watten, Loch Calder, St. John's Loch. <u>Brown Trout.</u> **P.** St. Clair Hotel, 15 Sinclair Street, Thurso, Caithness. Tel: Thurso 3730.
4 boats. £4 per day, £2 per evening.

Loch Watten. <u>Brown Trout.</u> **P.** Harpers Fly Fishing Services, Drill Hall, Thurso. Tel: Thurso 3179.
The Tackle Shop, Francis Street, Wick. Tel: Wick 4284.
Loch Watten Hotel, Watten, Caithness. Tel: Watten 232.
D. Gunn, Watten Lodge, Watten. Tel: Watten 217.
J. A. Barnetson, Lynegar, Watten. Tel: Watten 205.
Cost on application.

Loch St. John's. <u>Brown Trout.</u> **P.** The Northern Sands Hotel, Dunnet, Caithness. Tel: Barrock 270.
Cost on application.

Loch Heilen. <u>Brown Trout.</u> **P.** H. Pottinger, Greeland Mains, Castletown. Tel: Castletown 210.
Cost on application.

Loch Stemster. <u>Brown Trout.</u> **P.** J. Doull, Estate Office, Lybster. Tel: Lybster 246.
Cost on application.

Loch Airigh Leathaid. <u>Brown Trout.</u> **P.** Ulbster Arms Hotel, Halkirk. Tel: Halkirk 206.
Cost on application.

Loch of Wester. <u>Brown Trout, Sea Trout.</u> **P.** A. Dunnet, Auchorn Farm, Lyth. Tel: Keiss 208.
Cost on application.

Garbh Loch. <u>Brown Trout.</u> **P.** Ulbster Arms Hotel, Halkirk. Tel: Halkirk 206.
Cost on application.

Loch Caol. <u>Brown Trout.</u> **P.** Ulbster Arms Hotel, Halkirk. Tel: Halkirk 206.
Cost on application.

Loch an Ruathair. <u>Brown Trout.</u> **P.** Factor, Langwell Estate Office, Berriedale, Caithness. Tel: Berriedale 237.
Cost on application.

LOCAL OPINION

When you come to fish Caithness, think of unspoiled lochs in open rolling moors. Watten can be excellent and some of the Altnabreac hill lochs are superb for that great holiday activity, walking and fishing. The Caithness lochs are peaty, windswept and productive – first class for summer fly fishing.

YOU MAKE THE CHOICE

but we suggest you should consider the unspoilt fly-only waters of the THURSO RIVER catchment.

For well managed waters where the angler really matters and where fair play and attention to detail count you cannot choose better than salmon on the Thurso or trout fishing on one of a dozen hill lochs all under the management of:

THURSO FISHERIES LTD.
THURSO EAST
THURSO, CAITHNESS
Telephone: Thurso (0847) 63134

And if you choose the Thurso you should also choose

THE ULBSTER ARMS HOTEL
HALKIRK, CAITHNESS
Telephone: Halkirk (084783) 641 or 206 where the needs and wishes of anglers are specially catered for from an efficient drying room for wet clothes to flexible meal times. Write now for further information.

YOU CAN FISH ALL NIGHT ON THE CAITHNESS HILL LOCHS IN JUNE
catching the fighting wild brown trout for which they are famous . . .

Argyll Waters –Mainland only

AN INTRODUCTORY NOTE

The former county of Argyll, now largely part of Strathclyde Region, is rich in game fishing waters. It is Highland in its character, with some of the larges Inner Hebrides included in the Region. In our Guide, however, we have dealt only with mainland waters.

This area forms many small districts, but it can be seen broadly as falling into two. Firstly, the Oban and Awe area which lies to the north-west of the county. Morvern, the mountainous promontary north of Oban is best thought of as a western extension of the Fort William Area, since it is best reached by road from Ardbour (near Fort William). The largest stillwater in the area is Loch Awe which is drained by the short and once very heavy river Awe, but since the hydro-electric dam was erected at the exit from the loch, the flow of the river has decreased, and while it still brings in good runs of salmon from the sea and provides migratory fish for the loch above and for the Orchy and its loch, the Awe is only a slimmed down version of its former self.

Salmon run the Awe mainly in summer, although early fish still come in in small numbers. It is a good grilse river and in the past has had the name of producing some very heavy summer fish. It has good finnock and sea trout in July and August also. Salmon are only occasionally taken from Loch Awe, although they are seen there regularly, especially towards the head where the Orchy joins it. The Orchy is a nice middle-sized Highland river which comes into play if there is rain and can produce good salmon in the Glen.

Oban is backed by a multitude of lochs, most of them good for trout, but several with nice summer runs of sea trout and occasional salmon. The area south of Oban, which is the second large area we identify, has some nice small spate rivers in it, including the Add and a wide variety of trout lochs. Below this, down the leg of Kintyre to Campbelltown, there are many lochs and various small spate streams which, if in play, can provide good summer sea trout and salmon fishing. I have in mind the Fyne, the Aray (both near Inveraray) and, further down the Kintyre, the Carradale and, at Campbell-town, the Lussa.

Argyll Waters –Mainland only

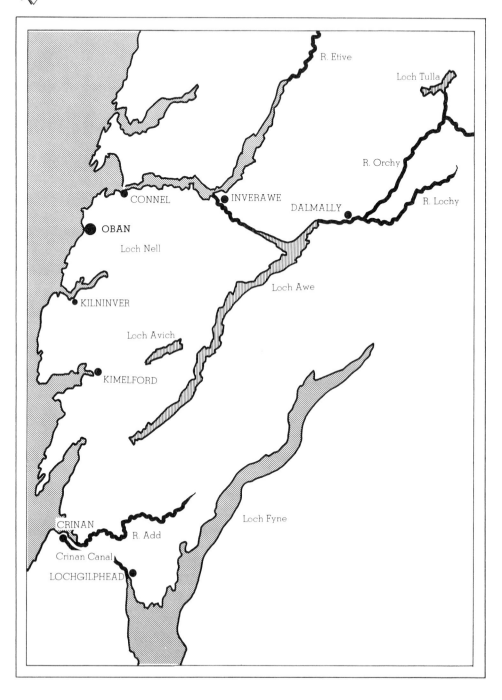

R. Etive

Loch Tulla

R. Orchy

CONNEL

INVERAWE

DALMALLY

R. Lochy

OBAN

Loch Nell

KILNINVER

Loch Avich

Loch Awe

KIMELFORD

Loch Fyne

CRINAN

R. Add

Crinan Canal

LOCHGILPHEAD

Cam Loch and Inverliever Hill Lochs. <u>Brown Trout.</u> **P.** Ford Post Office. Tel: Ford 054 681 271; A. Campbell, Inverliever Lodge, Ford.
£1.

Gleann A'Bhearradch Loch. <u>Brown Trout.</u> **P.** Cologin Homes Ltd., Lerags, by Oban. Tel: Oban 4501; The Barn Bar, Cologin, Lerags, by Oban.
2 boats available £3 per day, residents free. Fishing £1 per day, residents free.

Loch Nell. <u>Salmon, Sea Trout, Brown Trout.</u> **P.** Tackle Shop, Airds Place, Oban; David Graham, Combie Street, Oban.
Cost on application.

Loch Gleann A'Bhfarraidh. <u>Trout.</u> **P.** The Barn Bar, Cologin, Lerags, by Oban; Cologin Chalets, Lerags. Tel: Oban 64501.
Cost on application.

Loch Scammadale. <u>Salmon, Sea Trout, Brown Trout.</u> **P.** Mrs. MacCorkindale, Scammadale.
£1.50 per rod, £2 per boat.

Loch Seil and Loch Dhu. <u>Brown Trout, Sea Trout.</u> **P.** Major J. T. P. Mellor, Barndromin Farm, Knipoch. Tel: Kilninver 273.
£2.50 per day with use of boat.
Inverawe Fishing Centre (River, stocked ponds and lochs). <u>Rainbow Trout,</u> Salmon, Sea Trout. **P.** Inverawe Fisheries, Taynuilt, Argyll. Tel: 08662 262.
Cost on application.

30 Hill Lochs, Oban & Lorn Angling Club waters. <u>Brown Trout.</u> **P.** Tackle Shop, Airds Place, Oban; David Graham, Combie Street, Oban; Sports Shop, Benderloch; Post Office, Kilmelford; Melfort Motor Inn, Arduaine; Dunstaffnage Arms Hotel, Connel; Further information from: Dr. John Mauchline, Tel: Oban 62244.
Cost on application.

Loch Nell, Loch Oudh, Hill Lochs, Dubh Mor A'Chreaghain, Dubh Bheag A'Chadruim, An Daimh. <u>Brown Trout.</u> **P.** Tackle Shop, Railway Pier, Oban.Cost on application.

Loch Scammadale. <u>Salmon, Sea Trout, Brown Trout.</u> **P.** Mrs. Mary McCorkindale, Scammadale, Kilninver, by Oban.
Cost on application.

River Add. <u>Salmon, Sea Trout.</u> **P.** Poltalloch Estate Office, Argyll.
Cost on application.

River Aray (Castle Section). <u>Salmon, Sea Trout, Brown Trout.</u> **P.** Argyll Estates Office, Cherry Park, Inveraray; Ardbrecknish House Hotel.
Cost on application.

Carradale. <u>Salmon, Sea Trout.</u> **P.** E. Martindale, Kennels, Argyll.
Cost on application.

Loch Tarsan. <u>Brown Trout.</u> **P.** Dunoon and District Angling Club: J. G. Lindsay Pate, Hon. Secretary, 160 Argyll Street, Dunoon. Tel: Dunoon 2631.
85p per day, £2.75 per week, £12 per season.

River Cur. <u>Salmon, Sea Trout, Brown Trout.</u> **P.** Dunoon and District Angling Club; J. McKinnell, Merchant, Strachur, Argyll; Purdie's Tackle Shop, Queen's Hall Buildings, Dunoon. Tel: Dunoon 3232; Whistlefield Hotel, Strachur.
Cost on application.

Eachaig (upper and lower beach). <u>Salmon, Sea Trout.</u> **P.** Mr. Carter, Estate Office, Ballochmyle Estate, Sandbank, by Dunoon. Tel: Sandbank 206.
Cost on application.

Little Eachaig (4 miles from Dunoon) <u>Salmon, Sea Trout.</u> **P.** Mr. Murray, Orchard Farm, Kilmun. Tel: Sandbank 207; Mr. Manuel, Ballachmyle by Sandbank. Tel: Sandbank 352.
Cost on application.

River Fyne (tidal water). <u>Salmon, Sea Trout.</u> **P.** Arkinglas Estate Office, Cairndow, Argyll. Tel: Cairndow 217; Cairndow Estate Office, Cairndow, Argyll. Tel: Cairndow 284.
Cost on application.

Glendaruel (River Rue). <u>Salmon, Sea Trout, Brown Trout.</u> **P.** Mr. W. Hume, Post Office, Glendaruel. Tel: Glendaruel 271.
Cost on application.

River Ruel. <u>Salmon, Sea Trout, Brown Trout.</u> **P.** Glendaruel Hotel, Glendaruel; W. Hume, The Post Office, Glendaruel. Tel: Glendaruel 271.
Cost on application.

Loch Glashan. <u>Brown Trout.</u> **P.** Lochgair Hotel, by Lochgilphead, Argyll. Tel: Lochgair 233.
£1.50 per day, boat £6, engine £3.

Auchalochy, Crosshill, Lochruan. <u>Brown Trout.</u> **P.** Kintyre Fish Protection and Angling Club, Secretary, Mr. J. M. B. Anderson, 101 Ralston Road, Campbeltown; A. P. McGrory & Co., Main Street, Campbeltown; David Livingstone, Longrow, Campbeltown.
Cost on application.

Hill Lochs on Argyll Estates. <u>Brown Trout.</u> **P.** Argyll Estates Office, Cherry Park, Inveraray, Argyll.
Cost on application.

Loch Lussa (Campbeltown). <u>Brown Trout, Rainbow Trout.</u> **P.** J. M. B. Anderson, 101 Ralston Road, Campbeltown; A. D. McGrory & Co., Main Street, Campbeltown; R. Armour & Sons, Longrow, Campbeltown; David Livingstone, Longrow, Campbeltown.
Cost on application.

Lochain Ghleann, Locha, Mudle Loch. <u>**Brown Trout, Sea Trout.**</u> **P.** Kilchoan Hotel, Ardnamurchan, Argyll. Tel: Kilchoan 200.
£5 per day.

Loch Lussa. <u>Trout.</u> **P.** J. M. B. Anderson, 101 Ralston Road, Campbeltown; A. D. McGrory & Co., Main Street, Campbeltown; R. Armour & Sons, Longrow, Campbeltown; David Livingstone, Longrow, Campbeltown.

River Awe. <u>Salmon, Sea Trout.</u> **P.** Loch Awe Hotel.
Cost on application.

River Ochy. <u>Salmon.</u> **P.** Dalmally Hotel, Dalmally, Argyll; W. A. Church, Croggan Crofts, Dalmally, Argyll.

River Euchar, one mile. <u>Salmon, Sea Trout.</u> **P.** J. T. P. Mellor, Barndromin Farm, Knipoch, by Oban, Argyll. Tel: Kilninver 273.
£3 per rod per day.

River Euchar, Lagganmore, 1 mile both banks. <u>Salmon, Sea Trout, Brown Trout.</u> **P.** Lieut-Col. P. S. Sandilands, Lagganmore, Kilninver, by Oban, Argyll. Tel: Kilninver 200.
£2 per rod per day.

Loch Avich. <u>Brown Trout.</u> **P.** Chief Forrester, Forestry Commission, Dalavich, Taynuilt.
Boats £5 per day, £6 extra with outboard plus £1 per rod inc. VAT. Fly fishing only, £1-£4 per week.

Loch Awe. <u>Salmon, Brown Trout, Sea Trout.</u> **P.** Portsonachan Hotel, by Dalmally, Argyll; A. Campbell, Keeper, Forestry Commission, Inverleiver Lodge, Ford, Argyll; Ford Hotel, Ford, Argyll;

Loch Lomond and Associated Waters

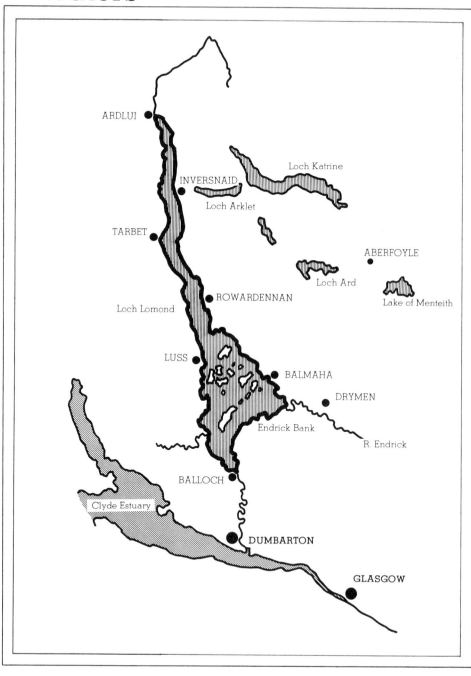

Loch Lomond and Associated Waters

AN INTRODUCTORY NOTE

Loch Lomond is among the largest inland waters of the British Isles and it lies spectacularly over the Highland line. Thus, its south eastern is a lowland loch, with broad reaches of shallow water such as the Endrick Bank and with many picturesque islands over its waters. To the north west lie the first Highland hills, with Ben Lomond principal among them. The loch lies narrower here from Luss and Rowardennan up to Ardlui and the head of the loch where Glen Falloch brings down the water of that name. The Highland end of the loch is deep, has few driftable bays and is far less productive than the shallower water to the south where Balmaha and Balloch lie.

The Endrick is the main in-flowing tributary and it runs down from the hills above Fintry to Drymen, below which it joins the loch making a fine bank of silt off its mouth where salmon and sea trout fly fishing can be splendid in summer. Salmon are also caught on fly on drifts out from Balmaha between the islands and along the attractive northern shore to Rowardennan. The loch fishes well with wet fly for sea trout and salmon, and the dap can do well in July and August with some of the sea trout running to eight pounds or over. Other tributaries of the loch are less well established as fisheries than the Endrick. The Fruin, for example, brings good sea trout in to its waters in August and September, but it is the Endrick which provides the best of the river fishing in the district. From the end of July onwards, according to water conditions, excellent fish run its waters. Salmon have been in a minority recently, but are now returning in greater numbers. But there is a good run of large sea trout up to ten pounds into the Endrick and they can be taken in the right water conditions, providing great sport.

The Loch drains into the Firth of Clyde by way of the River Leven. There is not much flow in this river and for a good part of its short course it flows through fairly well built up territory. It does produce some good salmon and sea trout fishing, however, since it carries Loch Lomond's whole stock up to the fishery above.

River Endrick. Salmon, Sea Trout, Brown Trout. **P.** Loch Lomond Angling Improvement Association. R. A. Clement & Co., C.A., 224 Ingram Street, Glasgow.
Cost on application.

River Falloch, Fruin (up to Strathclyde Boundary). Salmon, Sea Trout, Brown Trout. **P.** Loch Lomond Angling Improvement Association, R. A. Clement & Co., C.A., 224 Ingram Street, Glasgow.

River Leven. Salmon, Brown Trout, Sea Trout. **P.** Loch Lomond Angling Improvement Association, R. A. Clement & Co., C.A., 224 Ingram Street, Glasgow.
Weekly permits from: Messrs. Peter Ewing Ltd., 188 Main Street, Alexandria.
Cost on application.

Loch Lomond. Salmon, Sea Trout, Brown Trout. **P.** Loch Lomond Angling Improvement Association, R. A. Clement & Co., C.A., 224 Ingram Street, Glasgow, and various tackle shops.
Cost on application.

Loch Lomond (Ardlui). <u>Salmon, Sea Trout, Brown Trout</u>. **P.** Ardlui Hotel, Ardlui, by Arrochar. Tel: Inveruglas 243.
Cost on application.

Loch Lomond, River Leven. <u>Salmon, Sea Trout</u>. **P.** Inverbeg Inn, Near Luss, Dunbartonshire. Tel: Luss 678.
Free to hotel residents of 3 nights or more.

Loch Lomond, River Leven. <u>Salmon, Sea Trout, Brown Trout</u>. **P.** Rowardennan Hotel, by Drymen. Tel: Balmaha 273.
Free to residents: Non-residents £3.16 per day, £8.20 per week. Boat £7.50 per day with engine.

LOCAL OPINION

It is remarkable to have Loch Lomond, with its big sea trout and its salmon, right on the doorstep of greater Glasgow. It is a water which repays those who study it. It has fine island reaches and long windswept shorelines and its summer sea trout fishing can produce fish of eight to ten pounds to wet fly and dap. Not many major conurbations have this recreational asset on their doorstep.

The Clyde and its Tributaries

AN INTRODUCTORY NOTE

The River Clyde has a long course in the hills, where it is a splendid, clear trout water, long before it reaches the industrial belt of Scotland from Motherwell to Glasgow and where until recently, its waters were polluted and unfishable. The contrast is extreme. The high waters from Crawford John and Abington down through Lamigton and Howford offer first class fly fishing for trout and grayling. It is in these high reaches that the tradition of Clyde fly fishing, with its small very sparsely dressed flies will be found. The water holds some magnificent trout and they test the best fly fisher.

In the hills, in addition to the burns and waters which join the Clyde, are numerous reservoirs and lochs, among them the Daer Reservoir, in which some nice trout fishing can be had.

Recent sterling work in cleaning up the Clyde, and its main lower tributary the Kelvin, has produced the exciting prospect of a river on the mend. Not only is the available trout fishing extending downstream to provide good sport in the Motherwell and Bothwell areas and below, but the first salmon to be seen in the Clyde for perhaps a century were reported in 1984. They are the first fruits of a good river purification policy and we all hope that it will not be long before the Clyde and possibly also the Kelvin are listed by the Guide as salmon waters.

River Clyde and Tributaries

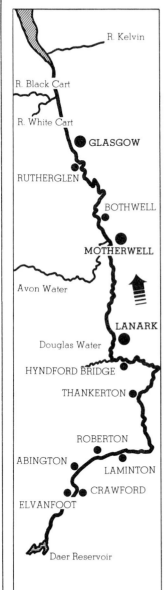

River Clyde (and main tributaries except Lanark and Lamington Angling Club water). <u>Brown Trout.</u> **P.** United Clyde Angling Protective Association, R. C. Sharp, 20 Cunningham Street, Motherwell; and most tackle dealers in Glasgow.
Cost on application.

River Clyde (Roberson to Thankerton). <u>Brown Trout.</u> **P.** Lamington and District Angling Improvement Association, P. D. McAndrew, Old Station House, Symington, Biggar; H. Bryden, Newsagent, High Street, Lanark., and local Bailiff.
Cost on application.

River Clyde (Lanark). <u>Brown Trout.</u> **P.** Lanark and District Angling Club, 89 Rhybor Ave, Lanark. Tel: 3525.

River Clyde. <u>Brown Trout, Grayling.</u> **P.** Upper Clyde Angling Protective Association Ltd., Mr. J. Quigley, 15 Auchter Road, Cambus Court, Wishaw. Tel: Cambusnethan 382 479; and most tackle shops and local bailiffs.
£2 per day, annual permit £5.

River Clyde and Douglas Water from Kirkfield bank to Sandilands. <u>Brown Trout, Grayling.</u> **P.** Lanark & District Angling Club, Secretary, Mr. W. Frood, 89 Rhybor Avenue, Lanark. Tel: Lanark 3525; Mr. E. Wilson, Watchmakers, St. Leonards Street, Lanark; The Sports Shop, High Street, Lanark; Mrs. Brown, Hyndfordbridge, Lanark.
£1.50 per day, £4 per season.

River Avon. <u>Brown Trout.</u> **P.** Upper Clyde Angling Protective Association, J. Quigley, 15 Auchter Road, Cambus Court, Wishaw; and most tackle shops.
£2 per day, £5 annual permit.

Camps Reservoir, Daer Reservoir, Craford, Logan Reservoir, Lesmahagow, Peden Reservoir. <u>Trout.</u> **P.** Strathclyde Regional Council Water Department, Regional Office, Hamilton, ML3 0AL. Tel: 0698/282828 ext. 313.
No charge.

South-West Scotland
Ayrshire, Galloway and Dumfries-shire

AN INTRODUCTORY NOTE

THe south west of Scotland is a most attractive rural and hill area bounded on the west and south by the sea and on the east by the valley of the river Nith. Think of it, firstly, as a gentle basin draining the Ayrshire rivers from low green hills into the Firth of Clyde. The rivers Ayr, Doon, Girvan and Stinchar are the main waters in this Ayrshire section of the area. These are trout and salmon waters with the best trout being in the Ayr and the best salmon and sea trout being in the Stinchar, which is the furthest south of the Ayrshire rivers. All four rivers are short and bring their migratory fish in after summer and autumn spates. The Doon has fish as early as April in its waters, but should be thought of as a grilse and autumn water with some good runs. The Girvan, further south is smaller than the Doon, producing a few salmon in the late spring, but largely thought of as a summer sea trout and salmon river. These three rivers, Ayr, Doon and Girvan are somewhat outclassed by the Stinchar, however. This fast, interesting water, rising in the hills between Straiton and Newton Stewart, can produce remarkable sport after summer floods. Unfortunately these floods are unpredictable and are of short duration and some luck is required to find the water just right. There is some nice night fishing for sea trout available in July and August and there can be good runs of grilse and small summer salmon. Autumn can bring in larger salmon.

The rivers of the area which flow south and south west include the Cree, a small hill and lowland river with both spring and summer salmon, the little spate streams of Galloway, including the small Fleet, the Dee, which has some good brown trout in it but is not generally spoken of as a place for migratory fish. The little river Urr can be productive in summer and autumn (it has an extended season) and there are many hill waters and burns throughout the region which offer interesting trouting in fine wild hilly country.

The Nith is a river with a fine history, involving resurrection from near loss through pollution to become again a significant salmon and sea trout river with a good autumn profile. There are private and club waters available, but the latter are often unpleasantly crowded. Club waters on Nith are also heavily wormed and spun, to their detriment. Many other beats, however, yield splendid June and July sea trout fishing at night and when the 'grey backs' of autumn arrive in September and October, fish well into the teens and twenties of pounds appear and can give good sport. The Nith season is extended to the end of November to cover this sport.

The south west of Scotland is a kind of mini-highlands in its interior. There are heather-clad hills and well-forested valleys. Stillwaters abound, varying from small hill lochs to well tended reservoirs. Some of the lochs in the furthest south west are thought to be reducing their sport through acid rain, but careful monitoring and study is under way. Loch Doon, the largest stillwater in the Ayrshire area holds only small trout, however, and has done as long as I can remember. Migratory fish do not reach Loch Doon in any numbers, although there is a fish pass where the river leaves the loch.

South-West Scotland
Ayrshire, Galloway and Dumfries-shire

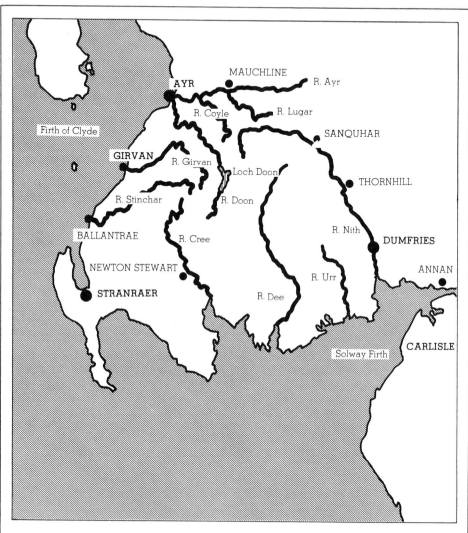

LOCAL OPINION

The area is a gentle one compared with the Highlands, but it has a great range of trout fishing to offer and some nice summer and autumn sport with sea trout, grilse and the heavier salmon which come in September and October. The rivers are small, in national terms, and they do require rain. Given the right kind of summer, however, sport can be exceptional, right over the range.

Rivers Ayr, Doon, Girvan and Stinchar

River Ayr. Salmon, Sea Trout, Brown Trout. **P.** Director of Finance, Town Buildings, Ayr.
Arthur Allen, 25 Kyle Street, Ayr.
Gamesport, 60 Sandygate, Ayr.
85p pe day, £2.15 per week.

River Ayr. Salmon, Sea Trout, Brown Trout. **P.** Auchinleck Angling Association, J. McColm, Secretary, 21 Milne Avenue, Auchinleck, Ayrshire. Tel: Auchinleck 219535.
£1.50 per day.

River Ayr. Salmon, Sea Trout, Brown Trout. **P.** Linwood & Johnstone, Newsagent, The Cross, Mauchline, Ayrshire.
Mr. & Mrs. Preston, Post Office, Main Street, Ochiltree.
£1.50 per day Mon.-Fri., £2 Saturday, £5 per week.

River Ayr. Salmon, Sea Trout, Brown Trout. **P.** Director of Finance, Kyle & Carrick Buildings, High Street, Ayr.
£1.20 per day, £3 per week.

River Coyle. Brown Trout, Grayling, Occasional Salmon. **P.** Sundrum Castle Hotel, Sundrum, by Ayr. Tel: Joppa 253.
Residents free.

River Coyle. Brown Trout, Grayling. **P.** Drongan Youth Group Angling Club, A. Kennedy, Treasurer, 1 Craig View, Coylton, Ayrshire.
50p per day.

River Doon. Salmon, Sea Trout, Rainbow Trout, Brown Trout. **P.** Hollybush House Hotel, Hollybush, Ayrshire. Tel: Dalrymple 214.
£2 per day residents free.

River Doon. Salmon, Sea Trout, Brown Trout. **P.** Drumgrange and Keir's Angling Club, Mr. M. MacDonald, Palace Bar, Waterside Stores, Dunaskin, Ayrshire. Tel: Patna 204/545.
£2 per day, £4 per season.

River Doon. Salmon, Sea Trout, Brown Trout. **P.** Mr. Dale, Linlayston Farm, Dalrymple/Maybole Road, on B742.
£1.50 per day.

River Lugar. Salmon, Sea Trout, Brown Trout. **P.** Auchinleck Angling Association, J. McColm, Secretary, 21 Milne Avenue, Auchinleck, Ayrshire. Tel: Auchinleck 21953.
£1.50 per day.

River Lugar. Salmon, Sea Trout, Brown Trout. **P.** Linwood & Johnstone, Newsagent, The Cross, Mauchline, Ayrshire.
Mr. & Mrs. Preston, Post Office, Main Street, Ochiltree.
£1.50 Mon.-Fri., £2 Saturday, £5 per week.

River Girvan. Salmon, Sea Trout. **P.** J. H. Murray, 3 Dalrymple Street, Girvan. Tel: 0465 2039.
W. Prentice, Keeper, Kilkerran Estates.
£1.50 per day, £3 per week.

River Stinchar. <u>Salmon, Sea Trout.</u> **P.** The Jolly Shepherd's Hotel, Barr.
Commercial Hotel, Barrhill.
King's Arms Hotel, Barr.
J. Stewart at Laigh, Alticane Farm, Pinwherry.
£3 per day.

Loch Bradan. <u>Brown Trout.</u> **P.** Mr. R. Heaney, Talaminnoch, Straiton,
Ayrshire. Tel: Straiton 617.
5 boats available – 1 person £2.50 per day, 2 or more persons £3.50 per day.
Fishing £1.25 per day.

Loch Breckbowie. <u>Brown Trout.</u> **P.** R. Heaney, Talaminnoch, Straiton,
Ayrshire. Tel: Straiton 617.
1 boat available – 1 person £2.50 per day, 2 or more persons £3.50 per day.
Fishing £1.25 per rod.

Loch Skelloch. <u>Brown Trout.</u> **P.** Mr. R. Heaney, Talaminnoch, Straiton,
Ayrshire. Tel: Straiton 617.
£1.25 per rod per day, £4.50 per rod per week. 1 boat – 1 person £2.50, 2 or
more persons £3.50 per day.

Rivers Cree, Dee, Urr, Fleet and Nith

Loch Cally. <u>Trout.</u> **P.** Cally Hotel, Gatehouse-of-Fleet, Kirkcudbrightshire. Tel: Gatehouse 341.
£1.50 per day, £9.50 per week, £30 per month. 2 boats – free to residents.

River Cree, River Bladnoch, Loch Pibble, Loch Newton (private lochs). <u>Salmon, Brown Trout, Rainbow Trout</u>. **P.** Corsbie Villa Guest House, Newton Stewart, Wigtownshire. Tel: Newton Stewart 2958.
2 boats available. £8 & £6 per day per rod on lochs. £7.50 per week on rivers.

Dalbeattie Reservoir. <u>Loch Leven Trout, Rainbow Trout</u>. **P.** Dalbeattie Angling Association, N. Parker, Ticket Secretary, 30 High Street, Dalbeattie, Kirkcudbrightshire.
Cost on application.

Loch Dee. <u>Brown Trout</u> (stocked). **P.** Galloway Deer Museum, Clatteringshaws, New Galloway & Talnotry Caravan Park, Newton Stewart.
£1.25 per rod per day, £5.50 per rod per week.

River Ken, Lochs Stroan & Clatteringshaws. <u>Salmon, Trout.</u> **P.** Ken Bridge Hotel, New Galloway, Kirkcudbrightshire. Tel: New Galloway 211.
Fishing free to residents only.

Loch Kirrieroch. <u>Trout.</u> **P.** Newton Stewart Angling Association, R. W. McDowall, 4 Arthur Street, Newton Stewart, Wigtownshire. Tel: Newton Stewart 2163.
£1 per day.

Knockguassen Reservoir. <u>Brown Trout.</u> **P.** Stranraer & District Angling Association, c/o 90 George Street, Stranraer, Wigtownshire. Tel: Stranraer 2705.
and hotels, sports shops, ironmongers and camping sites in Stranraer & District.
£2 per rod per day, £7 per week.

River Minnoch. <u>Salmon, Grilse.</u> **P.** Newton Stewart Angling Association, R. W. D. McDowall, 4 Arthur Street, Newton Stewart. Tel: Newton Stewart 2163.
£1 per day, £5 per week. .

River Nith, Tidal stretch at Dumfries and short stretch above weir. <u>Salmon, Grilse, Sea Trout, Brown Trout.</u> **P.** Director of Finance, Municipal Chambers, Dumfries, Dumfriesshire. Tel: Dumfries 3166.
£6.90 per week, £20.70 per season.

River Nith, and tributaries Kello, Crawick, Euchan and Mennock Waters. <u>Salmon, Sea Trout, Brown Trout.</u> **P.** Upper Nithsdale Angling Club, William Forsyth, Secretary, Solicitor, Sanquhar, Dumfriesshire. Tel: Sanquhar 241.
£4 per day, £20 per week, £45 per season.

River Nith, Thornhill. <u>Salmon, Sea Trout, Brown Trout.</u> **P.** R. W. Coltart, Secretary, Mid-Nithsdale Angling Association, c/o A. Coltart & Son, Shoe Shop, Thornhill, Dumfriesshire. Tel: Thornhill 464.
£6 per day, £25 per week.

River Nith. <u>Salmon, Sea Trout, Brown Trout, Grayling</u>. **P.** Mennockfoot Lodge hotel, Sanquhar, Dumfriesshire. Tel: Sanquhar 382.
Cost on application.

Loch Ochiltree. <u>Trout</u> (stocked). **P.** Newton Stewart Angling Association, R. W. McDowall, 4 Arthur Street, Newton Stewart, Wigtownshire. Tel: Newton Stewart 2163.
£1 per day. Boat available.

River Urr. <u>Salmon, Sea Trout, Brown Trout.</u> **P.** Tommy's Sports Shop, 20 King Street, Castle Douglas, Kirkcudbrightshire.
£3 per day, £10 per week.

River Urr. <u>Salmon, Trout.</u> **P.** Caldow Lodge, Corsock, Castle Douglas. Tel: Corsock 286.
Cost on application.

Loch Whinyeon, River Cree, River Fleet. <u>Salmon, Rainbow Trout, Brown Trout, Sea Trout.</u> **P.** Murray Arms Hotel, Gatehouse-of-Fleet, Kirkcudbrightshire. Tel: Gatehouse 207.
5 boats available. Charges on application.

100 acre Reservoir surrounded by the North Yorkshire Moors. Graduated depth 92 feet. Fishing ticket available in adjacent car park. Food available Fearby Village, $2\frac{1}{2}$ miles.
1985 SEASON: Saturday, April 6th–Sunday, October 13th.
CHARGES: Season £150.00, Day £7.00, Evening £4.00, (Under 14 and Disabled $\frac{1}{2}$ Day ticket)
DAY LIMIT: 6 fish. EVENING LIMIT: 4 fish.
RESTRICTIONS: No wading, fly fishing only.
STOCKING POLICY: Rainbow—twice weekly, Brown—annually. A proportion of fish up to 10lbs included in all weekly stocking.
AVERAGE DAILY CATCH RATE PER ROD: 2 fish.
RECOMMENDED FLIES: Early season—Baby Dolls, Dog Nobblers. Mid and late season—Sedges, Muddlers, Daddy Longlegs.

Annan, Border Esk and Tributaries

AN INTRODUCTORY NOTE

The two main rivers of this area – the Annan and the Border Esk – are Solway waters, draining the Scottish lands to the north east and east of the English border. For part of its lower course, the Border Esk runs through English territory. The Annan is a gentle, medium sized lowland river with some fine pools on its lower and middle sections. It collects the flow of the Moffat Water in its upper reaches and it reacts quickly to rain in the high grassy and heathery hills behind. It has good brown trout in its waters (and a few big chub), but from early summer onwards, has good runs of sea trout and finnock in its waters. The sea trout fishings in the middle section of the Annan, near Hoddom can be excellent for night fly sport.

During the summer also, the Annan has runs of grilse and good summer salmon, and as summer changes to autumn, the river attracts more and more larger fish into its pools. It is one of the rivers of the South West of Scotland with runs of 'grey backs' – large salmon often in excess of twenty pounds which come into Solway and Ayrshire rivers from September onwards. The season is extended in many of these rivers to cater for the sport they produce.

The Border Esk is thought of principally as a sea trout river, but, like the Annan, it has salmon in its waters from late spring onwards and it too can bring in large autumn fish. As a sea trout and finnock (herling) river it has a well deserved reputation. The fish appear early and in large numbers, normally by the first week of June, but building up in numbers through July. The finnock arrive in July and August. The pools of the Esk around Canonbie and up through various beats to Langholm provide excellent night fishing for sea trout and double figure bags are not uncommon if the fish are on.

There is good club water available at Langholm and above and if one manages to avoid the local worming brigade good fly fishing will be enjoyed. The numbers of fish in the clear pools is fascinating. A few fish may be tempted by day, especially if the water is up and has some colour in it, but most bags are made in the dusk and dark. The upper reaches of the Esk, both White and Black, have some delightful sea trout sport to offer to the night fly in summer. The Liddle, a tributary of the Esk, also has good sea trout sport from June onwards.

LOCAL OPINION

The aspect of the area which makes the greatest impact is the sea trout fishing. The fish which run the Esk and its tributaries are marvellous early summer fly fishing and the area from Canonbie to Langham is outstanding for dusk and dark fly fishing, providing double figures on a good night. Annan has similar sport with heavy autumn salmon to add to it.

Annan, Border Esk and Tributaries

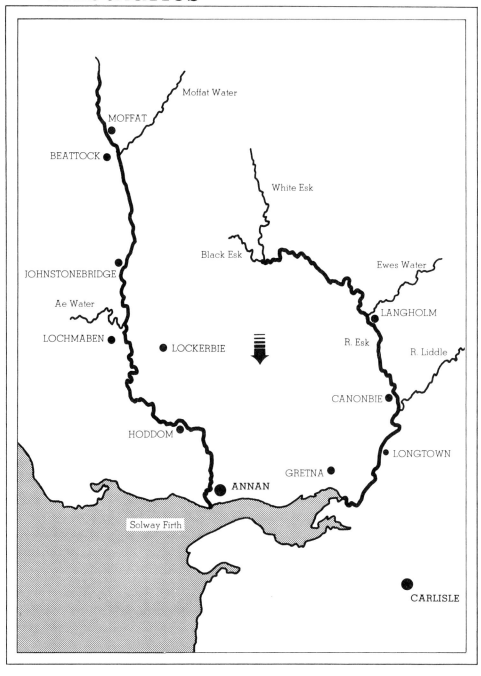

Moffat Water

MOFFAT

BEATTOCK

White Esk

Black Esk

Ewes Water

JOHNSTONEBRIDGE

Ae Water

LANGHOLM

LOCHMABEN   LOCKERBIE   R. Esk   R. Liddle

CANONBIE

HODDOM   LONGTOWN

GRETNA

ANNAN

Solway Firth

CARLISLE

River Annan. Salmon, Sea Trout, Brown Trout. **P.** Messrs. McJerrow & Stevenson, Solicitors, Lockerbie, Dumfriesshire. Tel: Locherbie 2123.
£10 per week, £50 per season.

River Annan. Salmon, Sea Trout, Brown Trout. **P.** Red House Hotel, Wamphray, Moffat, Dumfriesshire. Tel: Johnstone Bridge 214.
£1.50-£2 per day.

River Annan and Moffat Water. Salmon, Sea Trout, Brown Trout. **P.** Upper Annandale Angling Association, J. Black, 1 Rosehill Grange Road, Moffat, Dumfriesshire. Tel: Moffat 20104.
Salmon: £1 per day, £5-£7 per week. Trout: £1 per day, £5 per week.

River Annan, Kinnel, Dryfewater (Applegarth Estate). Salmon, Sea Trout, Grilse. **P.** Smiths Gore, 64 Warwick Road, Carlisle. Tel: Carlisle 27586. A. Wright, Clock House Cottage, Mill House Bridge, Lockerbie.
£12 per week, £30 per season plus VAT.

River Annan. Brown Trout, Salmon. **P.** Manse Country Guest House, Wamphrey, Dumfriesshire. Tel: Johnstone Bridge 367.
Free to residents.

River Annan. Salmon, Sea Trout, Grilse, Brown Trout. **P.** Mrs. Clark, Newbie Mill, Annan. Tel: Annan 2068.
Cost on application.

River Annan, Hoddom. Salmon, Sea Trout, Brown Trout, Herling. **P.** P. Helm, Dumhelm, Ecclefechan. Tel: 220.
Cost on application.

River Annan, Newbie Estates. Salmon, Sea Trout, Brown Trout, Herling. **P.** T. Nelson, Nembie Mill, Annan. Tel: 2608.
Cost on application.

River Annan. Salmon, Sea Trout, Brown Trout, Grilse. **P.** Newbie Estates, Hoddom, Mr. P. Helm, 22 Fernlea Cres., Annan. Tel: Annan 2922. Castlemilk Estate Office, Norwood, Lockerbie. Tel: Kettleholm 203.
Cost on application.

Applegarth Water, Annan Water, Kinnel Water and Dryfe. Salmon, Sea Trout, Brown Trout, Grilse. **P.** Mr. Graham, The Smithy, Millhousebridge. Tel: Lochmaben 397.
Red House Hotel, Whampray. Tel: Johnstonebridge 214.
Cost on application.

River Annan, Moffat Water, Little Annan. Salmon, Sea Trout, Brown Trout. **P.** Beattock House Hotel, Beattock.
The Secretary, Mrs. Harkness, Grocer, High Street, Moffat.
T. Porteous, Sports Centre, High Street, Moffat.
Wm. Fraser, Orchard, Beattock.
Red House Hotel, Whampray. Tel: Johnstonebridge 214.
T. R. Jackson, 59 High Street, Lockerbie.
S. B. McCall, High Street, Lockerbie.
Beattock Caravan Park, Beattock.
Cost on application.

Purdiestone Reservoir (Hoddom and Kinmount Estate). <u>Brown Trout.</u> **P.** Mr. P. Helm, 22 Fernlea Crescent, Annan. Tel: Annan 2922.
Cost on application.

River Esk. <u>Salmon, Sea Trout, Grilse.</u> **P.** The Esk and Liddle Fishery Association, Secretary, Mr. J. B. Hill, Solicitor, Langholm. Tel: Langholm 80428.
Cost on application.

Black Esk Reservoir. <u>Brown Trout.</u> **P.** The Esk and Liddle Fishery Association, Secretary, Mr. J. B. Hill, Solicitor, Langholm. Tel: Langholm 80428.
£5 per day, boat fishing. £3 after 6 p.m.

River Esk, Canonbie ticket. <u>Salmon, Sea Trout, Brown Trout, Herling.</u> **P.** The Esk and Liddle Fishery Association, Secretary, Mr. J. B. Hill, Solicitor, Langholm. Tel: Langholm 80428.
P. Little, 19 Rownburn, Canonbie, Dumfriesshire. Tel: Caonbie 279.
£9-£18 per week, £46 per season.

River Esk and Liddle (all waters ticket). <u>Salmon, Sea Trout, Brown Trout, Herling.</u> **P.** The Esk and Liddle Fishery Association, Secretary, Mr. J. B. Hill, Solicitor, Langholm. Tel: Langholm 80428.
J. Irving Wylie, River Watcher, Byreburnfoot, Canonbie. Tel: Canonbie 279.
P. Lillie, 19 Rownburn, Canonbie. Tel: Canonbie 279.
£25-£50 per week, £140 per season.

River Esk, Langholm ticket. <u>Salmon, Sea Trout, Brown Trout, Herling.</u> **P.** The Esk and Liddle Fishery Association, Secretary, Mr. J. B. Hill, Solicitor, Langholm. Tel: Langholm 80428.
J. Irving Wylie, River Watcher, Byreburnfoot, Canonbie. Tel: Canonbie 279.
£9-£18 per week, £46 per season.

Canonbie, Liddle, Lower Liddle ticket. <u>Salmon, Sea Trout, Brown Trout, Herling.</u> **P.** The Esk and Liddle Fishery Association, Secretary, Mr. J. B. Hill, Solicitor, Langholm. Tel: Langholm 80428.
J. Irving Wylie, River Watcher, Byreburnfoot, Canonbie. Tel: Canonbie 279.
£5-£11 per week, £28 per season.

River White Esk, Ewes, Wauchope, Tarras Water (tributaries ticket). <u>Salmon, Sea Trout, Brown Trout, Herling.</u> **P.** The Esk and Liddle Fishery Association, Secretary, Mr. J. B. Hill, Solicitor, Langholm. Tel: Langholm 80428.
J. Irving Wylie, River Watcher, Byreburnfoot, Canonbie. Tel: Canonbie 279.
P. Lillie, 19 Rownburn, Canonbie. Tel: Canonbie 279.
£2-£4 per week, £10 per season.

GLENMORANGIE

10 YEARS OLD
SINGLE HIGHLAND MALT
SCOTCH WHISKY

2. ARCHIE MURDOCH arrives at the malting shed shortly after sun-rise. A maltman of 19 years' standing,
he can judge the quality of the barley *(grown on wind-swept estates in the glens of Ross-shire)*
by sifting the grain through his hands. Once he has satisfied himself that nature, and the harvesters,
have done their job, only then can the day's distilling begin.

Handcrafted by the Sixteen Men of Tain.

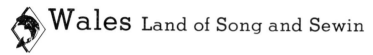

Wales Land of Song and Sewin

Sewin fishing is not a sport in Wales, it is a religion, followed by its native anglers, to almost the exclusion of any other fishing.

Having made a marked recovery after the scourge of the salmon disease in the seventies, these sea trout, peculiar to Wales (Salmon, Trutta) move up river in twos and threes, in the early summer, frequently reaching eight to ten pounds in weight. Later in July, the smaller fish shoal in the Foxglove season and are branded locally as 'holiday fish', attributable to the hoards of visiting rods which they attract.

Sewin fishing, one must realise, is very definitely neither second-grade salmon fishing nor up-market trout fishing with a nocturnal handicap; it is a sport if not a craft in its own right. Here is a lively sporting fish which fights pound for pound like a Trojan and bears a charm often misjudged by the impatient and inefficient. Success with this fish requires concrete planning and the observance of certain pre-requisites.

Sewin, unlike wild brown trout move around within a river system, having entered the bar of the estuary on a combination of tide and surge from the source. The first rule therefore, for the visiting angler, is to locate the fish before the proposed night's fishing. Many an angler has fished all night in a pool containing not a single fish. Watch the pools in the day-time; listen to the reports from the locals. This may, though heaven forbid, involve a recce of the local pub.

Having located a shoal, stick with it. There is little 'chuck and chance' about night sewin fishing with the fly. Speed and depth of presentation are the two decisive factors to success. Quite often a thronging pool of sewin with the appetites of barracuda on hunger strike, will only take the fly at a specific depth and with an appropriate movement through the water. It is all important to get the offering down to that level in the most effective way.

Sea trout flies are as varied as salmon and trout flies, however, the reservoir angler would not find his fly box an undue handicap. But he should be prepared to vary his offerings in both size and hue.

South East Wales

It's hard to appreciate that in 1834, when George Agar Hansard toured Wales on his most memorable trip, he described the rivers of the South East as 'abounding with salmon and sea trout'. The industrial revolution was hot on his heels since when, these waters have run 'Bible black' for a century. It is now comforting to learn of the annual laundering of these waters and although it would be unfair to direct the visiting angler to these banks as yet, another decade could provide a hint of their 19th century grandeur.

This of course does not apply to the Usk, which is, without doubt, one of the best wild brown trout rivers in the U.K. The Usk fishes well from the first to the last day of the season, though the mayfly of early June provides the most activity for the dry fly. A water steeped in salmon and trout history.

Many small reservoirs were built to quench the thirst of industry in this area, some of which have become important fisheries and are now managed by the Welsh Water Authority. These reservoirs can provide surprising sport within this industrial overgrowth.

The resevoirs of the Taff division are stocked from a purpose-built hatchery, adapted from an old filter house by local fishery officer John Davies. This had proved an excellent innovation – the old filter beds hold fry, which are introduced to local reservoirs on a trickle basis, thus reducing stocking costs dramatically. Though generally centred on an environmentally neglected area, some of the Taff lakes have quite beautiful surroundings. The Neuadd reservoirs are especially worth a visit.

The capital Cardiff boasts two reservoirs within the city; Lisvane and Llanishen. It is true that they, like Eglwys Nunydd reservoir in Port Talbot are concrete bowls, but every effort has been made to offset the surroundings by the quality of the fishing. A concerted effort is being made by the Welsh Tourist Board to attract holidaymakers to this area. Quite a task.

The Usk valley rescues the cosmetic deficiencies of this region with its Llndegfedd and Talybont reservoirs. Two very attractive waters, with quality fish in pastoral settings. The brown trout here have gained quite a reputation for themselves during the last few seasons and have attracted a flood of visiting fishermen.

Beacon Reservoir

STOREY ARMS, Tel: Cardiff 399961 or Merthyr Tydfil 5457.
Brecon Beacons. Proprietor: Welsh Water Authority.

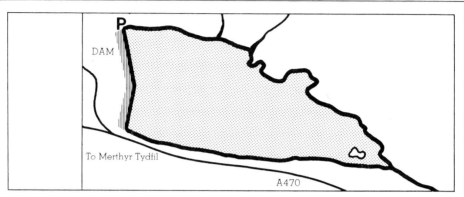

Beacon Reservoir is a very shallow upland reservoir of 52 acres stocked with brown and rainbow trout. It is popular with local anglers for its fine quality brown trout. A fishery of tranquil charm.

Facilities:	Self-issuing permit vending machine at Llwynon, four miles down valley. Toilet and car parks on site.
Season:	21st March–17th October. Hours: 8.00 am to one hour after sunset.
Rods per day:	Unlimited.
Charges:	Season £80, Day £3.50. Concession for OAP, Juniors and Disabled: Season £54, Day £2.50.
Day limit:	6. Boats: None available.
Restrictions:	Fly only.
Stocking policy:	Regular stocking throughout the season.
Annual catch per rod:	Unquantified.
Recommended flies:	
April:	Ace of Spades, Black Lures, Butcher, Alexandra, Peter Ross, Soldier Palmer.
May:	Black Lure, Baby Doll, Red Tag, Worm Fly, Wickham's Fancy, Muddler.
June:	Coch-a-bon-ddu, Invicta, Peter Ross, Coachman, Hare's Ear.
July:	Sedge patterns, Butcher, Black Pennel, Zulu, Appetizer, Buzzers.
August:	Dunkeld, Whisky, Worm Fly, Mallard & Claret, Grenadier, Crane Flies.
September:	Crane Flies, Grenadier, Black Spider, Hare's Ear, Corixa.
Local knowledge:	The Beacon is a well-loved, challenging reservoir for the hardier locals who tackle this remote water. Modern reservoir techniques seem to have largely replaced the age-old small fly on a floating line. But purists like Jack Harris still bag their limits here with the traditional approach.

Cantref Reservoir

NORTH CWM TAFF,   Tel: Merthyr 5457.
Merthyr Tydfil.   Proprietors: Welsh Water Authority.

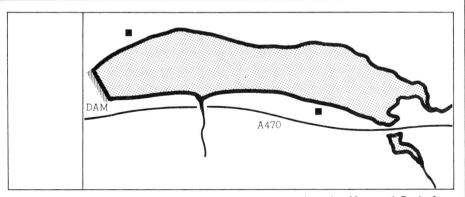

Cantref Reservoir is a 42 acre fishery situated in the National Park. It is stocked with brown and rainbow trout to a very high standard, in a trickle stocking system and is fly only and therefore popular with discerning anglers.

Facilities:	Self-issuing permit booth at Llwynon Filter Works, which is two miles downstream. Toilets and car park.
Season:	21st March–17th October. Hours 8.00 am until one hour after sunset.
Rods:	Unlimited.
Charges:	Season £80, Day £3.50. Concessions: OAP, Juniors and Disabled: Season £54, Day £2.40. Rod Licence: Welsh Water Authority.
Day limit:	6 fish. Boats: none.
Restrictions:	Fly fishing only, no fishing from dam or overflow.
Stocking policy:	Regular stocking policy on trickle system to meet demand.
Annual catch per rod:	Unquantified.

Recommended flies:

March:	Black & Peacock Spider, March Brown, Black Lure,
April:	Black Lure, Baby Doll, Mallard & Claret, Dunkeld,
May:	Invicta, Nymph, Muddler, Mallard & Claret, Coch-a-bon-ddu.
July:	Sedges, Longhorns, Grenadier, Dunkeld, Butcher, Zulu, Blae & Black.
August:	Crane Flies, Silver Invicta, Soldier Palmer
September:	Teal & Green, Soldier Palmer, Invicta, Muddler, Black & Peacock.
October:	Black Lure, Baby Doll, Whisky, Dognobbler, Mallard & Claret, Crane Flies.
Local knowledge:	Humbert Gwynne is an angler who takes a keen interest in fishery administration. He likes Cantref for its quality trout and favours the fairly traditional approach of three-fly cast worked some 10 to 15 yards out and the bob fly 'hop-scotching' along the surface in an enticing manner. A delightful way to take fish.

Clwywedog Reservoir

LLANDILOES, POWYS.
Proprietors: Llandiloes Angling Association.

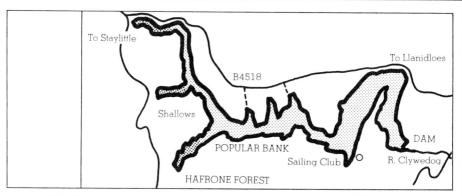

This 615 acre upland fishery is a great favourite with mid Wales anglers and offers miles of empty bank spaces for those who are prepared to walk. The browns and rainbows move well to a small fly bobbed along the surface.

Facilities:	Permits from tackle shops in Llanidloes.
Season:	18th March–30th November.
Rods per day:	Unlimited.
Charges:	Season £45, Day £3.50.
Day Limit:	8 fish.
Boats:	8 boats.
Restrictions:	Fly only.
Stocking Policy:	Four or five times during the season.

Recommended flies:

March:	Sweeny Todd, Black & Peacock Spider, Viva, Peter Ross.
April:	Muddlers, Buzzers, Butcher, Alexandra.
May:	Pheasant Tail, Black Nymph, Zulu.
June:	Coch-a-bon-ddu, Invicta.
July:	Zulu, Heather Moth, Muddler, Alexandra.
August:	Crane Flies, Muddlers, Dunkeld.
September:	Crane Flies, Jersey Herd, Whisky, Mallard & Claret, Alexandra.
Local knowledge:	Emyr Lewis is Water Bailiff with the Welsh Water Authority and spends a lot of time fishing in Clywedog. His is a very traditional approach with light tackle and small flies. He takes many of his fish on the small nymph that he devised many years ago. This is quite a deep water which can turn extremely cold. A sinking line is therefore a must early and late on in the season.

Dolygaer Reservoir

PENT-TWYN TAF-FECHAN, Tel: Cardiff 300061 or Merthyr 5457.
Nr Merthyr Tydfil. Proprietor: Welsh Water Authority.

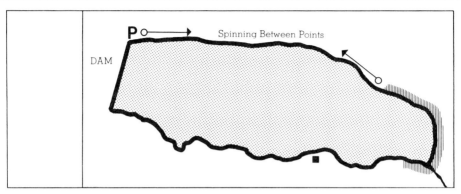

Dolygaer Reservoir is a shallow 96 acre water in the upper Taff valley with partly wooded banks. It is stocked with brown and rainbow trout and is connected with Pontsticill reservoir.

Facilities:	A self issue permit vending machine is available at the Pontsticill Filter House. Toilets and Car parks available on site.
Season:	21st March–17th October. Hours: 8.00 am until one hour after sunset.
Rods per day:	Unlimited. Boats: none.
Restrictions:	Fly fishing only with the exception of the dam. Spinning permitted on West Bank.
Stocking:	Well stocked at beginning of season only.
Annual catch per rod:	Unquantified.
Recommended flies:	
March:	Black Lure, Black Muddler, Ace of Spades, Black & Peacock, Spider, Zulu.
April:	Black Lure, Muddler, Black & Peacock, Mallard & Claret, Greenwell.
May:	Ace of Spades, Muddler, Black Pennel, Mallard & Claret, Red Tag.
June:	Buzzers, Brown & Green Nymph, Muddler, Viva, Baby Doll, Dognobbler.
July:	Muddler, Sedges, Grenadier, Wickham, Red Tag, Soldier Palmer.
August:	Crane Flies, Claret & Mallard, Silver Invicta, Soldier Palmer, Baby Doll.
September:	Crane Flies, Jack Frost, Black Lure, Green Nymph, Pheasant Tail.
October:	Muddlers, Black Lure, Mallard & Claret, Invicta
Local knowledge:	Each reservoir has its regular clientele and Dolygaer is no exception. Most of the regulars favour lures, scaled down to rather smaller sizes and fished with normal bank tactics. Generally there are ample angler-free spaces on the banks to enable keen fishermen the freedom to search for feeding trout.

Eglwys Nunydd Reservoir

PORT TALBOT, WEST GLAM. Phone: Port Talbot 883161, ext. 3368.
Proprietor: British Steel Co.

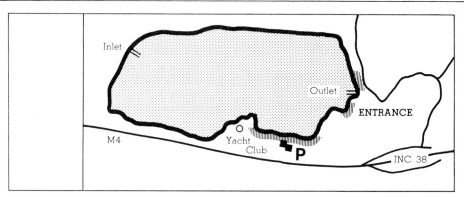

Eglwys Nunydd is one of the most productive fisheries in Wales. Sadly its 260 acres are some of the least aesthetically appealing in Wales; being sandwiched between the steel jungle of the Margam Steel works and the pounding motorway traffic. In this impossible environment anglers catch large brown trout and the locals have produced a home-made fishery of great potential. A new hatchery and a modern club house are just two of their achievements.

Facilities:	Fishing lodge on banks of reservoir.
Season:	3rd March–30th September. Hours: Sunrise to one hour after sunset.
Rods per day:	Unlimited. Licence: Welsh Water Authority.
Charges:	Season £30.50. Day permit £4, Weekly £12.
Day limit:	6 fish.
Restrictions:	Fly only.
Stocking:	From own hatchery on banks of reservoir. Varies from season to season but has been known to be as many as 50,000.
Annual catch per rod:	Unknown. Average weight: 1 lb plus.
Recommended flies:	
March:	Black Lure, Ace of Spades, Jack Frost, Dognobbler
April:	Black Lure, Zulu, Black Buzzer, Black & Peacock
May:	Invicta, Dognobbler, Black Lure, Buzzers, Green & Brown Nymph.
June:	Pheasant Tail Nymph, Shrimp, Damselfly Nymph,
July:	Sedges, Invicta, Longhorns, Black Pennel, Mallard & Claret, Muddler.
August:	Crane Flies, Muddler, Black & Peacock Spider,
September:	Viva, Muddlers, Black & White, Invicta.
Local knowledge:	The anglers visiting this fishery in the early months should go deep and slow with bigger black lures. Yet Keith Snook, the captor of the best brown trout to come from Eglwys Nunydd, which weighed over nine pounds, will tell you that after the water has warmed up, small buzzers and nymphs will take good quality trout when fished on a floating line.

Llandegfedd Reservoir

PONTYPOOL, GWENT. Phone: Pontypool 55122.
Proprietor: Welsh Water Authority.

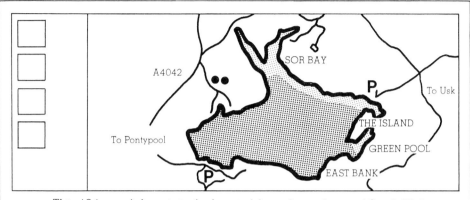

This 434 acre fishery is in the heart of the industrial area of South Wales, just two miles from Panteg Steelworks, ten miles north of Newport and near the new town of Cwmbran; yet it has retained its rural and tranquil nature being tucked into the rich farmland and wooded slopes of the Gwent countryside. The water quality is good, having been pumped from the river Usk and supports rich aquatic life.

Facilities: Permits available at self-issue booths (locations indicated 'P' on the map). Boat booking has to be made at the Sluvad Treatment works or by phoning Pontypool 55122.

Season: 20th March–17th October. Hours: 6.00 am until 11.30 pm (depending on month).

Charges: Day permit £4. Boat (rowing) £5 a day, £2.50 after 4.00 pm. Motor boats £10, £5 after 4 pm. Licence: Welsh Water Authority.

Daily limit: 6 fish.

Boats: Rowing boats – 18; motor boats – 2.

Restrictions: Size limit 12 in. No chest waders. Fly fishing only. Only two persons per boat.

Stocking policy: Total of 16,500 per season. Generally stocked 3 to 4 times per month.

Recommended flies:

March: Black Lure, Ace of Spades, Baby Doll, Muddler,

April: Jack Frost, Viva, Black Lure, Sweeny Todd, Brown & Green Nymphs.

May: Invicta, Dognobbler, Black Buzzer

June: Shrimp, Pheasant Tail Nymph, Black Lure

July: Mallard & Claret, Invicta, Whisky, Nymphs and Buzzers.

August: Baby Doll, Viva, Black Chenille, Crane Flies

September: Muddlers, Green Nymph, Pheasant Tail Nymph

October: Dognobbler, Jack Frost, White Lure, Black Lure,

Local knowledge: The wardens of Llandefedd are extremely helpful and very considerate to the disabled. They recommend boat fishing with lures on sinking lines in the early season and scaling the flies down from June onwards.

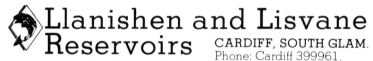

Llanishen and Lisvane Reservoirs
CARDIFF, SOUTH GLAM.
Phone: Cardiff 399961.

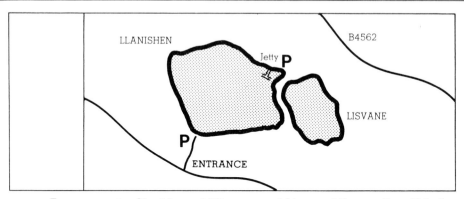

Two reservoirs: Llanishen of 59 acres and Lisvane 19 acres lie within the boundaries of the Welsh capital. The water quality is good and the stocked trout are always in super condition.

Facilities:	Self-issue permit vending machine.
Season:	21st March–17th October (for brown trout). Hours: 8.00 am to one hour after sunset. 21st March–28th February (for rainbow trout).
Rod:	Unlimited.
Licence:	Welsh Water Authority.
Charges:	Season £100, Day £4.50. Concession for OAP, Juniors, Disabled: Season £67, Concession £3.
Day limit:	4 fish. Boats: Clubs membership only (Cardiff Reservoirs Fly Fishing Club).
Restrictions:	Fly fishing only.
Stocking policy:	Trickle stocking to meet demand. Many fish stocked in excess of 2 lbs, some up to 12 lbs.

Recommended flies:

March:	Sweeny Todd, Black Lure, Baby Doll.
April:	Ace of Spades, Muddler, Black & Peacock.
May:	Mallard & Claret, Coch-a-bon-ddu.
June:	Dunkeld, Viva, Sedge.
July:	Invicta, Green Nymph.
August:	Viva, Crane Flies, Shrimp.
September:	Jack Frost, Black & Peacock, Sweeny Todd.
October:	Dog Nobbler, Pheasant Tail.
Local knowledge:	Ken Bowring arguably bags more fish than anyone in the principality, fishing as he does each day of the season. He believes in keeping the line in the water and will quickly change from a lure on a fast sink – to a small nymph on floating line – as conditions dictate on Llanishen and Lisvane.

Llwyn-On Reservoir

CWM TAFF,   Phone: Cardiff 399961 Merthyr 5457.
Merthyr Tydfil, Mid Glam.   Proprietor: Welsh Water Authority.

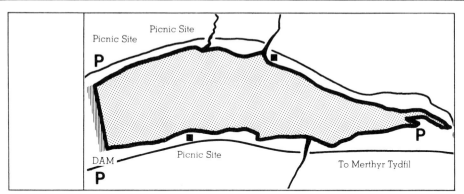

A 150 acre water some 800 feet above sea level, set in the Brecon Beacons. Llwyn-on is surrounded by mature coniferous forest and is a multimethod fishery.

Facilities:	Self issue permit vending machines on site. Toilets and car parks.
Rods per day:	Unlimited.
Charges:	Day £3.50, Concession £2.50.
Season:	21st March–17th October. Hours 8.00 am until one hour after sunset.
Day limit:	6 fish. Boats: none.
Restrictions:	No fly fishing on dam or overflow.
Stocking policy:	Regular trickle stocking to meet demand.
Annual catch per rod:	Unquantified.

Recommended flies:

March:	Ace of Spades, Baby Doll, Black & Peacock Spider, Mallard & Claret.
April:	Black Lure, Muddler, Wickham, Claret & Mallard, Blae & Black.
May:	Soldier Palmer, Butchers, Teal & Green, Mallard & Claret, Hawthorn.
June:	Coch-a-bon-ddu, Wickham, Dunkeld, Soldier Palmer, Sedge, Buzzers.
July:	Coch-a-bon-ddu, Worm Fly, William's Favourite, Muddler, Whisky.
August:	Crane Flies, Whisky, Dunkeld, Peter Ross, Pheasant Tail Nymph.
September:	Crane Flies, Black & Peacock, Dunkeld, Jersey Herd.
October:	Black Lure, Butcher, Dunkeld, Blae & Black, Worm Fly, Baby Doll.
Local knowledge:	A multi-method fishery can at times be very rewarding to the fly angler as the fish are not too familiar with the artificial fly. One of the more successful fly fishers of Llwynon generally makes for the far bank and the more remote spots. A team of small wet flies fished on light tackle can be rewarding.

Lower Neuadd Reservoir

TAF FECHAN VALLEY,   Phone: Cardiff 399961, Merthyr 5457.
Merthyr Tydfil, Mid. Glam. Proprietor: Welsh Water Authority.

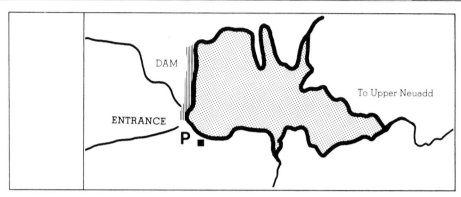

A small 12 acre reservoir, stocked with very large rainbow trout in the five to eight pounds range. This is the premier fishery in the principality for larger fish.

Facilities:	Self-issue permit vending machine on site.
Season:	21st March–17th October. Hours: 8.00 am until one hour after sunset.
Rods per day:	Unlimited. Licence: Welsh Water Authority.
Charges:	Season: none. Day £4. No concessions.
Day limit:	6 fish. Boats: none.
Restrictions:	Fly fishing only.
Stocking:	Trickle stocking with top quality fish.
per rod:	Unquantified.

Recommended flies:

March:	Dognobbler, Baby Doll, Black Lure, Ace of Spades, Jack Frost, White Lure.
April:	Black Lure, Ace of Spades, Black Matuka, Viva, Zulu, Brown Nymph.
May:	Invicta, Pheasant Tail, Shrimp, Black Buzzers, Green Nymph.
June:	Dunkeld, Whisky, Silver Invicta, Worm Fly, Black & Peacock, Claret & Mallard.
July:	Coch-a-bon-ddu, Sedges, Invicta, Baby Doll, Muddler, Shrimp.
August:	Crane Flies, Dunkeld, Whisky, Worm Fly, Viva, Jack Frost, Black Pennell.
September:	Crane Flies, Muddlers, Pheasant Tail Nymph, Baby Doll, Viva.
Local knowledge:	Hubert Gwynne, the Secretary of the Welsh Anglers Council, loves this fishery with its jumbo rainbow trout. The full range of reservoir techniques are used to take the big fish in Lower Neuadd, but a small nymph on a floating line in high summer, is the pinacle of reservoir fishing. Sunk line and lures take the majority of the fish and the black attractors seem to be the most effective.

Pontsticill Reservoir

TAF-FECHAN　　　　Phone: Cardiff 399961 or Merthyr 5457.
Proprietor: Welsh Water Authority.

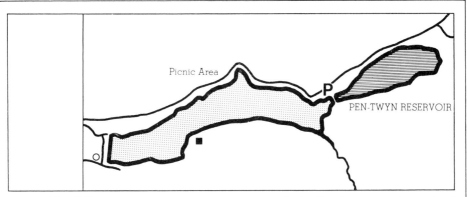

Picnic Area

P

PEN-TWYN RESERVOIR

This 253 acre reservoir set in an attractive wooded valley, is managed as a mixed fishery, with brown and rainbow trout and coarse fish. The coarse fishing takes place between October 1st and the last day of February.

Facilities:	Self permit issuing machine. Toilets and car parks on site. There is also a small-gauge steam railway adding extra interest.
Season:	Brown trout 21st March to 28th February.
Hours:	8.00 am until one hour after sunset.
Rods per day:	Unlimited.
Charges:	Season £60, Day £2.50. Concessions: OAP, Juniors and Disabled: Season £40, Day £2.00.
Day limit:	6 fish. Boats: none.
Restrictions:	Fly-fishing not permitted on dam face.
Stocking policy:	Stocked with brown and rainbow trout throughout the season. Best brown trout 14 lbs, best rainbow 5 lbs.

Recommended flies:

March:	Black & Peacock, Blae & Black, March Brown, Ace of Spades.
April:	Muddler, Black Lure, Black & Peacock, Butcher, Buzzers, Pheasant Tail.
May:	Hawthorn, Viva, Jack Frost, Muddlers, Wickham, Zulu,
June:	Sweeny Todd, Viva, Wickham, Zulu, Coch-a-bon, Soldier Palmer.
July:	Sedges, Green & Brown Nymph, Buzzers, Wickham, Dunkeld, Whisky.
August:	Crane Flies, Wickham, White Lure, Dog Nobbler, Black & Peacock.
September:	Crane Flies, Greenwell, Black Lure, Ace of Spades,
October:	Crane Flies, Blae & Black, Viva, Jack Frost, Sedges, Pheasant Tail.
Local knowledge:	One of the most consistently successful anglers on Pontsticill uses a sinking line almost exclusively, with a mini version of a Black Lure. He attributes his success to his mobility along the ample bank space – casting a few dozen times in each location, then moving on.

River Severn

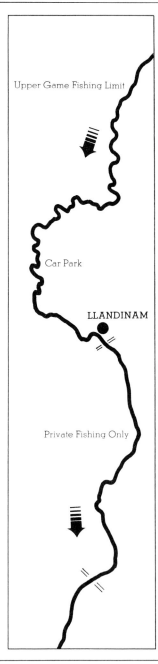

Upper Game Fishing Limit

Car Park

LLANDINAM

Private Fishing Only

The River Severn is the longest river in England and Wales. It rises in Powys and flows in an Easterly and Southerly direction for 180 miles into the Bristol Channel. Trout and grayling fishing is best in the mid and upper reaches.

Facilities: Dinam Estate at Llandinam offers good trout and grayling fishing with day and season permits available.
Licence: Severn & Trent Angling Association.
Season: 18th March–30th September for trout. Hours: 8.00 am to one hour after sunset.
Permit: Season £55. Day £2.80.
Rods per day: 30.
Day limit: 4 trout plus 4 grayling.
Restrictions: Fly only.
Stocking policy: Approximately 3,000 brown and rainbow trout stocked at fortynightly intervals; trout of $3/4$ lb to 2 lbs stocked.

Site 1: Dinam Estuary Fishery. This is approximately four miles of super 'brown' water managed by the Severn & Trent Water Authority. The Severn at Llandinam is of ideal dimensions for wet fly fishing, which can prove superb in April and May. The stocked fish make for very interesting fishing in ideal surroundings.

Site 2: Lion Hotel Water. Permits at Hotel in Caerhowell, Powys.

Site 3: Red House Farm Water. Permits at Red House Farm, Halfway, Montgomery.

Site 4: Captains Bridge Water, Abermule. Permits from Welshpool Angling Association, trout fishing.

Site 5: Maesmawr Hall Hotel. Permits available from Maesmawr Hall, Caersws, Powys. Trout fishing.

Site 6: Caersws Water on river Carno, tributary of Severn. Permits available Bob's Tackle Shop, Newtown Powys.

Recommended flies: Wet flies: Hare's Ear, Mallard & Claret, Snipe & Purple Butcher, Peter Ross, Greenwell's Glory. Dry flies: Imperial, Black Gnat, Greenwell, Sedges, Blue Dun, Wickham's Fancy, Hawthorn.

Local knowledge: Contrary to popular opinion, the Severn **can** offer good trout fishing with the fly. The Llandinam stretch is fly only and very exciting. Regular stocking also ensures sport on the most dour days. Wet fly does well in March and April – then the dry takes over.

Talybont Reservoir

TALYBONT ON USK,
NR. BRECON, POWYS. Proprietor: Welsh Water Authority.

To Merthyr Tydfil

A40

Nant Tarthwyni

View Point

To Talybont
and Brecon

This 318 acre reservoir straddling the 600 foot contour line, is set in a wooded valley in the Brecon Beacons National Park. The water quality is of high pH and thus produces large wild brown trout. Anglers are expected to pay particular heed to the country code, as certain areas of the water are designated as Nature Reserves.

Facilities: Permits available from the Usk Division, Station Building, Newport, Gwent.

Season: 20th March–17th October. Hours: 6.00 am till 9.30 pm–11.30 pm depending on month.

Rods per day: Unlimited. Licence: Welsh Water Authority.

Charges: Season £60, Day £3.

Day Limit: 6 fish. Boats: none.

Restrictions: Fly fishing only, except for spinning in one restricted area.

Stocking policy: Monthly stocking of browns and rainbows.

Annual catch
per rod: 1.2 fish

Recommended flies:

March: Black & Peacock Spider, Mallard & Claret

April: Black & Peacock Spider, Silver Invicta, Sweeny Todd

May: Greenwell, Invicta, Baby Doll, Green & Brown Nymphs, Wickham.

June: Dry Grey Duster, Wickham, Mallard & Claret, Sedge

July: Sedges, Dry Black Gnat, Invicta, Peter Ross, Stick Fly.

August: Alder, Crane Flies, Sedges, Invicta, Butchers, Dunkeld.

September: Crane Flies, Sedges, Wickham, Invicta, Sweeny Todd.

October: Black Lure, Baby Doll, Peter Ross, Green Nymph

Local knowledge: Dave Cole, the secretary of the Talybont Fly Fishers Association regards the Talybont reservoir as one of the most beautiful in Wales, especially when the wooded valley is illuminated at sunset. He considers the sedge time (late June and July) as the best of the season and many wild brown trout in the one and a half pound class are taken. The sedge fishing in 1983 was superb and anglers took a good number of three pound wild browns just as the light was fading.

Upper Neuadd Reservoir

TAF FECHAN VALLEY,   Phone: Cardiff 399961 or Merthyr 5457.
Nr. Pontsticill.   Proprietors: Welsh Water Authority.

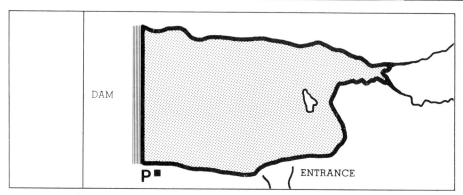

A most picturesque reservoir of 57 acres set under Pen-y-fan, the highest point of the Brecon Beacons. The angler will find solitude and quiet pleasure in this remote water. A good American Brook trout fishery.

Facilities:	Self-issue permit machine available at the Pontsticill Filter House at the entrance to the valley. Toilets and car park on site.
Season:	21st March-17th October. Hours: 8.00 am to one hour after sunset.
Rods per day:	Unlimited. Rod licence: Welsh Water Authority.
Charges:	Season £80, Day £3.50.
Day limit:	6 fish. Boats: none.
Restrictions:	Fly fishing only, no fishing from dam.
Stocking policy:	Regular stocking on trickle basis

Recommended flies:

March:	Black Lure, Ace of Spades, Baby Doll, Muddler, Black & Peacock.
April:	March Brown, Mallard & Claret, Grenwell, Baby Doll, Ace of Spades.
May:	Red Tag, Mallard & Claret, Baby Doll, Ace of Spades, Wickham, Invicta.
July:	Sedges, Coch-a-bon-ddu, Wickham, Butcher, Dunkeld; Green Nymph.
August:	Buzzers, Nymphs, Mallard & Claret, Whisky, Muddlers, Ace of Spades.
September:	Crane Flies, Muddlers, Mallard & Claret, Black Pennel, Invicta.
October:	Jack Frost, Muddlers, Black Lure, Mallard & Claret, Wickham.
Local knowledge:	Catching fish would seem to be an almost unnecessary bonus in such a picturesque setting as Upper Neuadd. But catch fish they do, in good quantities and locals are convinced that in the colder days and, at 1,000 feet above sea level it can be very cold, the sinking line does well. The American Brook Trout lke the bob fly on the surface and afford interesting and exciting fishing.

Usk Reservoir

BETWEEN LLANDOVERY AND BRECON.

Phone: Llandovery 20422.
Proprietors: Welsh Water Authority.

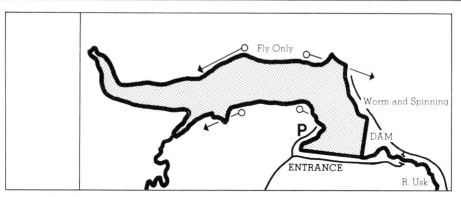

This 280 acre fishery is located in attractive wooded uplands. The pure water produces some quality trout. As it is some 1000 feet above sea level the weather can be severe, but still produces good fly life especially in June and July.

Facilities:	Self-issue permit booth, car parks, toilets and picnic area.
Season:	20th March–17th October. Hours: 8.00 am until 9.00 pm-11.30 pm (depending on month).
Rods per day:	Unlimited. Licence: Welsh Water Authority.
Charges:	Season £80, Day £3.50. Evening permit: not available.
Day limit:	6. Boats: none.
Restrictions:	Fly fishing allowed on whole reservoir. Worming and spinning allowed on certain defined sections.
Stocking policy:	Two to three stockings a month. Total of 11,000 fish stocked 1983 season.
Catch per rod:	1.4.

Recommended flies:

March:	Black & Peacock Spider, Mallard & Claret, Black Lure
April:	Mallard & Claret, Muddler, Butcher, Muddler, Blae & Black.
May:	Black Quill, Mallard & Claret, Muddler, Butcher, Muddler, Dunkeld.
June:	Coch-a-bon-ddu, Wickham, Silver Invicta, Claret & Mallard, Dunkeld.
July:	Sedges, Wickham, Invicta, Black & Peacock, Mallard & Claret.
August:	Crane Flies, Dunkeld, Mallard & Claret, Coch-a-bon-ddu.
September:	Crane flies, Viva, Baby Doll, Pheasant Tail, Invicta
Local Knowledge:	Ken Watkins has been the warden on the Usk Fishery for many years and his knowledge is duly extensive. The Usk presents fly anglers its best fishing in the warmer days of June and July when insect life is most prolific. The upper reaches of the reservoir are ideal for the fly-fisher who uses delicate tackle and a small wet fly fished in traditional style.

Wentwood Reservoir

PENHOW,
GWENT.

Phone: Penhow 400213.
Proprietor: Welsh Water Authority.

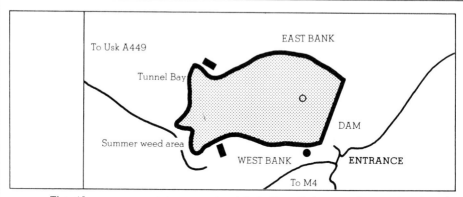

This 41 acre reservoir is approximately half a mile long and a quarter of a mile wide. At 450 feet above sea level, it is a typical lowland reservoir with a high pH factor, making it a very productive water. The Wentwood forest, with its panoramic views extending to the Bristol Channel, adds considerably to the aesthetic appeal of the fishery.

Facilities: Self issue permit booth.

Season: 20th March–17th October. Hours: 8.00 am until 9.30 pm or 11.30 pm (depending on month).

Rods per day: Unlimited. Licence: Welsh Water Authority.

Charges: Season £80, Day £3.50.

Day limit: 6. Boats: none.

Restrictions: Fly Fishing only.

Stocking policy: Two stockings per month. Brown & Rainbows. Total of 3650 fish stocked in 1983 season.

Annual catch per rod: 1.4

Recommended flies:

March: Ace of Spaces, Black Lure, Sweeny Todd, Muddler, Green Baby Doll.

April: Black & Peacock, Baby Doll, Sweeny Todd, Alexandra, Butcher.

May: Peter Ross, Invicta (Silver), Jack Frost, Pheasant Tail.

June: Dunkeld, Peter Ross, Mallard & Claret, Gold Ribbed Hare's Ear, Greenwell.

July: Buzzers, Grey Duster, Black Quill, Greenwell

August: Whiskey, Dunkeld, Claret & Mallard, Wickham

September: Crane Flies, Dunkeld, Black Lure, Green-Back Baby Doll.

October: Ace of Spades, White Lure, Muddler, Alexandra

Local Knowledge: The fluctuating water levels of Wentwood confuse even the regulars who confess it to be a difficult water to know. Fish average one and a quarter pounds and are taken with a traditional small fly and floating line. Nymphs and Buzzers on light leaders are favoured in the summer. Lures work well on the deep areas from the mound.

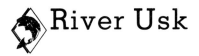

River Usk

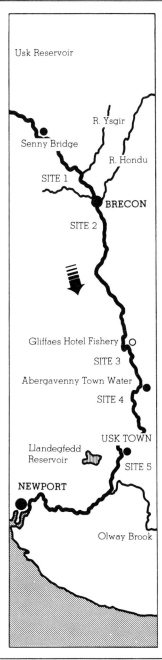

The River Usk is one of the finest trout rivers in the Principality. It flows from Carmarthen Fan some 2,500 ft. above sea level, in a somewhat erratic path through limestone country giving the water its high pH and thus enticing the aquatic life and stocks of wild brown trout. It is not easy to secure permits to fish the river, but the visiting angler would do well to remember that the Usk tributaries also offer good trout fishing.

Facilities: These vary immensely but the fly fishing on the whole of the river Usk is well preserved.
Licence: Welsh Water Authority.
Season: Trout 3rd March–30th September. Salmon 20th March–17th October.
Permit prices vary immensely and in some sites it is on application.

Site 1: Sunny Bridge Association Water, generally at very reasonable prices.

Site 2: Brecon Fishery Association and Brecon town water. Permits at Watergate Newsagents, Brecon. Secretary of the Association is Leslie Peters, the doyen of Usk fly-fishers. Early season: wet fly down river and then from end of April the dry olives do well. Permits reasonably priced.

Site 3: Gliffaes Hotel Water. Residents at the Hotel have the use of the Hotel water and up to eight rods fish for trout daily and four for salmon. Hotel water is divided into two beats. Tackle and equipment may be hired from the Hotel, which is a truly excellent retreat for fishermen. Fly fishing only for trout.

Site 4: Abergavenny Town Water: Permits from Town Council, Monk St, Abergavenny.

Site 5; Usk Town Water Fishery. Two miles, both banks up stream of Llanbadoc Church. Permits from Sweet, The Tackle Shop, in the town of Usk. Permit prices on Usk Town Water: Season £36, Weekly £10, Daily £3.50. Fly only with 9 inch size limit. No salmon permits are available.

Recommended flies: Early season for trout: Dark and Medium Olive, March Brown, Stone Fly Nymphs
Mid season: Black Gnat, Light and Dark Sedge, Coch-a-bon-ddu, Evening Dun, Red Spinner, Pheasant Tail

Local knowledge: Leslie Peter of Brecon has fished the river Usk for over 60 years. He uses the wet fly on the cold days of early season, March Brown, Snipe and Purple and Olives. Later he prefers the dry fly with patterns of olives again serving him well.

River Wye – Upper Reaches
Powys

Arguably one of the finest coarse rivers in England, the Wye has also traditionally been considered as one of the leading salmon rivers in England and Wales. Both Walton and later Cobbett applauded it. Yet these days few fish are taken on the fly; though many purists pursue the salmon this way, the bait fisherman is generally the only one with a full creel.

The upper reaches of the Wye and its tributaries however offer demanding trout fishing to the discerning angler. From Plynlimon, in its early stages, it rushes as a boulder-strewn brook, brimming with modest wild browns. Down from Rhayader it slowly matures, with the trout increasing in size and the salmon, albeit autumn fishing, assumes importance. The tributaries Irfon, Dulais and Edw, each a valuable water, join the main river here.

Below Builth Wells, coarse fishing predominates, although good quality trout haunt the lower reaches. The serious trout hunters however look to the Monmow, Lugg, Garron and Trothy; small challenging waters with fine quality fish.

For the adventurous who would seek the salmon with a fly, the stretch up river from the junction of the Llyfni is probably best. The grilse put in a welcome mid-summer appearance here also.

Facilities: Although the Wye has large stretches of private water, there are several beats available for visitors; permits are available from Angling Associations or Hotels. Hotel residents often have their fishing fee include in the weekly or daily terms.

Licence: The Welsh Water Authority licence covers the whole of the river, despite its lower reaches being in England. The salmon licence is £21.65 per season. £10.00 for 14 days and £3.25 per day. The trout licence is £6.20 for the season, £1.50 for 14 days. The salmon season is from January 26th to October 25th. (Below Llanwrthwl Bridge the season closes on 30th September). The trout season is March 1st to September 30th.

The River Wye divides itself into two reaches:

Site 1: Three stretches in this area are Hendre Water; tickets available from Plynlimon Guest House in Llangurig. Clock faen Estate Waters; permits from Glansevern Arms, Llangurig and the Marteg tributary, which is managed by the Rhayader Angling Association; permits from tackle shops in Rhayader. Best fishing in this area is in May and June, with the much valued Coch-a-bon-ddu beetle putting in an appearance in July. Permit prices very reasonable.

Site 2: Three miles up river of Rhayader Bridge runs another stretch managed by Rhayader Angling Association, also offering good trout fishing. Permits from The Pharmacy and Garth House in Rhayader.

River Wye – Lower Reaches
Powys–Bristol Channel

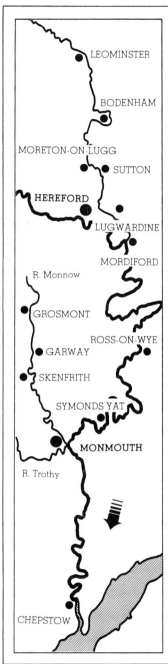

The River Wye from Builth to Chepstow is made up of large bends and loops, with the pace of the water being far more leisurely and slow. The trout fishing deteriorates except for the tributaries where there is good early season activity. Immediately south of Builth Wells lie some of the best salmon stretches.

Site 1: The Ford Bridge Water, one mile of left bank; permits from Ford Farm, Ford Bridge, Nr. Leominster.
Rectory Water, on the Lugg tributary, just up river of Mordiford Bridge; permits from the Old Rectory, Mordiford.
The Lugg Mill stretch, down river of the Lugg Bridge; permits from the Lugg Bridge House, Lugwardine.
Moreton Beat: Three quartes of a mile down river of Moreton-on-Lugg; permits available at Green Bank, Stoke Lacy, Bromyard.
Bodenham; large stretches of the river Lugg are managed by the Birmingham Anging Association and between Bodenham and Sutton lie a few miles of scattered fishing, available on the purchase of BAA permits.

Site 2: Ross-on-Wye. The BAA own the Wilton fishery just below Wilton bridge. A good site for both trout and salmon.

Site 3: Symonds Yat. Below the café at Symonds Yat, the BAA has one mile of Wye, for trout and salmon fishing.

Site 4: Monmouth: A stretch at Monmouth is also owned by the BAA and extends half a mile down river of junction with the Mally Brook. Few trout but interesting for salmon.

Site 5: River Monnow: one of the best tributaries of the Wye for trout. The Monnow has no salmon however.
The Glenmonnow Estate: managed by the BAA for half a mile down river of Garway Mill.
The Priory Water, this stretch is up river of the Priory Motel at Skenfrith; applications for permits should be made to the Motel.
Malthouse Farm, Skinfrith has a small stretch and permits available from the farm.
Grosmount Stretch: Three quarters of a mile on a right hand bank down river of Grosmount Village. Application for permits to Tresenny Farm at Grosmount.

Recommended flies: In the upper reaches the smaller, wet flies do well and traditional patterns cannot be bettered. Flies such as Greenwell's Glory, Pheasant Tail, various Olives and March Browns do well, fished wet in the early days of the season. The best standard dry flies are Kite's Imperial, Grannom, Vicer Powell's Doctor and Baby Sun Fly, Caperer and Black Gnat.

Favoured salmon flies in recent years have been mainly the hair-wing varieties taking the place of the old favourites like Thunder and Lightning, Silver Wilkinson and Shrimp Fly. As on most other rivers the tube has become popular.

Ynysyfro Reservoir

HIGH CROSS, NEWPORT, Phone: Newport 59886
GWENT. Proprietors: Newport Reservoir Fly Fishing Assoc.

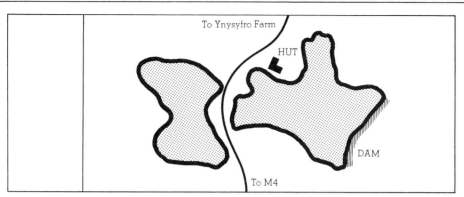

The Ynysyfro Reservoirs are two small waters of 10 and 16 acres. The smaller is stocked primarily with rainbow trout, the larger with brown. Spinning is allowed from the dam wall on the big water for O.A.P.'s and the disabled; otherwise it is all fly only. The fishery is managed by an Association, hence the friendly atmosphere, with Association members always around to help visitors. Ynysyfro has prolific hatches of Longhorn sedges and midges and holds a good head of sticklebacks.

Facilities:	Angler's hut and toilet.
Season:	March 20th–17th October. Hours 7.00 am-until darkness.
Rods per day:	Unlimited. Licence: Welsh Water Authority.
Charges:	£3.50 per day. Reduction for O.A.P.'s and the Disabled.
Day limit:	6 fish. Boat: Two for use by members at £1 per session of half day.
Restrictions:	Size limit 9". Only three rainbow from top lake.
Stocking policy:	1983 figures: 2370 Browns, 9"-12". 2000 rainbows, 10"-18".
Catch per rod:	.63, average weight 0.74lb. Total catch 1318 browns, 1438 rainbows, Best Brown: 4lb, 8ozs.
Recommended flies:	
April:	Black lure, Black Muddler, Ace of Spades, Baby Doll.
May:	Midge pupa, Peppermint Doll, Black Lure, Black Muddler, Pheasant Tail.
June:	Mallard & Claret, Sedge pupa, Pheasant Tail
July:	Dry: Grey Duster, Invicta, Mallard & Claret
August:	Damsel Fly Nymph, Crane flies, Invicta, Grenadier
September:	Small Lure, Grenadier, Midge buzzers.
Local Knowledge:	Paul Jenkins, the Secretary of the Newport Reservoir Fly Fishers, manages the reservoir and he seldom misses a day on the water. His is a delicate approach using a floating or a sink tip line. The big hatches of midges and sedges tend to favour the angler who uses small flies. During high summer it is possible to stalk the trout near the edges as they feed on the sticklebacks. Paul finds that the hotspots change weekly depending on the direction of the wind.

Ystradfellte Reservoir

GLYNNEATH,
WEST GLAM.

Phone: 0639 720337
Proprietor: Glynneath Association.

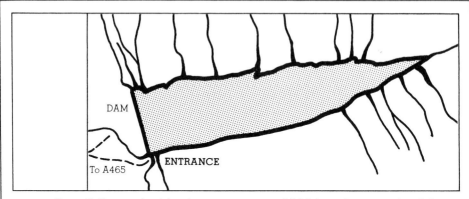

Ystradfellte is a highland reservoir some 1200 feet above sea level. It is a remote fishery nesting in the Brecon Beacons, accessible by a two mile road. It is of some 70 acres, being fairly rectangular in shape and three quarters of a mile long.

Facilities:	Two boats available. A fishing lodge.
Season:	3rd March–30th September. Hours: 8.00 to two hours after sunset.
Rods per day:	Unlimited. Licence: Welsh Water Authority.
Charges:	Day permit £2.50, Juniors, O.A.P. £2.00, A family permit for father and one or two sons is available at reduced rates. Boats: Two £3 per day.
Day limit:	6 trout.
Restrictions:	Fly and worm only.
Catch per rod:	Approximately 2 fish.
Recommended flies:	
March:	March Brown, Black & Peacock, Blae & Black.
April:	Alder, March Brown, Blae & Black.
May:	Greenwell, Black Gnat, Mallard & Claret, Peter Ross.
June:	Coch-a-bon-ddu, Connermara Black, Olives, Sedges.
July:	Sedges, Black Buzzers, Hare's Ear & Gold.
August:	Crane Flies, Small Muddlers.
September:	Crane Flies.
Local Knowledge:	Lynn Williams in addition to being one of the prime administrators of Ystradfellte Reservoir is also a keen angler. He likes to fish the water in the early part of the season and up until June. The fishery is best covered with smallish flies. Lynn's favoured method is to drift down-water in a boat and take trout on a floating line. He is especially happy that his association has been able to cement relations with the towns of Vienne in the South of France, Udine in Northern Italy and Essligen in West Germany, which has allowed European anglers special rates on the fishery.

South West Wales

A mere glance through the classified section of any angling journal would credit the south west with attracting more fishermen than any other region of England or Wales. Its wealth of hotels and guests houses offer fishing for residents on often highly exclusive waters. This combination of prime sewin fishing combined with a surfeit of accommodation attracts the family fisherman who can spend the daytime with the children and evenings with the fly box. The still waters are a bonus for the holidaymaker when the rivers are out of condition.

The three principal rivers in the Aberyswyth area are managed in the main by local angling clubs, from which permits are usually available on a daily or weekly basis.

The Rheidol produces portmanteau sewin, the best last year topping 12 lb. The Ystwyth, an ever improving river, has good late runs of salmon and sea trout, most of which are taken on the fly. The Aeron, running into the sea at Aberaeron is the smallest of the three rivers and yet can produce quite astounding runs of fish throughout the season.

The Taff and the Cleddau are the two great waters dominating the old county of Pembrokeshire. The Taff at Saint Clears and Whiteland, though not easy to fish with the fly, offers very reasonable day permits and contains good stocks of salmon and brown trout. The eastern and western Cleddau offers extremely attractive fishing up river of Haverfordwest. Both are sewin waters and fish best in the summer months.

The Teifi is the prestige river of the south west. Described as the 'Queen of the fly waters', its upper reaches offer wet and dry fly fishing for brown trout; the lower reaches, before meeting the sea at Cardigan support good stocks of salmon and sea trout. The sewin fishing peaks in June and July; the salmon in October. Most of the Teifi salmon are taken on bait, however, the opportunity for the fly fishermen is there, more so after heavy autumn rains.

The river Towy generally produces sewin from the first day of the season. It is an ideal fly water, with its open banks and gentle flow. The reservoir on the upper reaches controls potential surges and floods and eases the strain of night fishing. The salmon runs are usually confined to late August and September, although earlier fish have been taken.

River Aeron
Ceredigion-North Dyfed

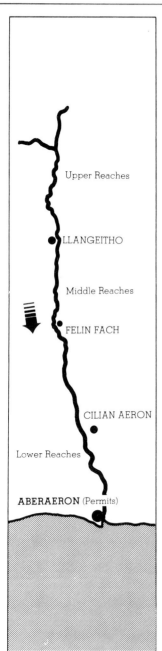

Upper Reaches

LLANGEITHO

Middle Reaches

FELIN FACH

CILIAN AERON

Lower Reaches

ABERAERON (Permits)

River Aeron is a comparatively small river running from the hills of mid Ceredigion into the sea at Aberaeron. For most of its course it is owned by local farmers, from whom permission to fish is not too difficult to obtain. The lower section (by far the best for fly fishing) is managed by Aberaeron Angling Club, who offer day and season permits. Unfortunately, the lower Aeron is not blessed with many pools, which creates a little overcrowding on the bank when the sewin are running.

Facilities: Permits obtainable at local tackle shop in the town of Aberaeron.

Licence: Welsh Water Authority. Season: 20th March–17th October.
Trout: 3rd March–30th September.

Permits: Season £30, Day £3, week £15.

Upper reaches: Some small trout fishing available – good fun on dry fly. Sadly most stretches now overgrown. Sewin move into this area in the late weeks of the season.

Middle reaches: Some good pools and runs; ideal for sewin, especially at night. Daytime fishing in this section is confined to the time when the river is running-down after flood.
The lower section, near the town of Aberaeron, has some pools which are very well stocked with sewin. Anglers lucky enough to catch the right conditions can easily reach the limit of ten, which is the club rule.

Recommended flies: Upper reaches for trout: Mallard & Claret, Partridge & Orange, Snipe and Purple, Butcher.
Sewin flies: Butcher, Silver March Brown, Medicine, Black Pennal, Squirrel, Teify Terror, Dai Ben.

Local knowledge: Dan Evans is one of the ablest sewin anglers in the whole of the principality. He takes approximately 200 sewin annually and is a master at spinning and fly-fishing. His two favourite flies are Butcher and Silver March Brown in sizes eight and ten.

Eastern Cleddau

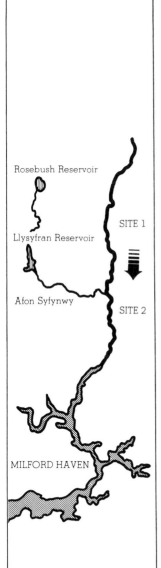

Rosebush Reservoir

Llysyfran Reservoir

SITE 1

Afon Syfynwy

SITE 2

MILFORD HAVEN

The Eastern Cleddau is a controlled river, with its headwaters impounded by the Llyfyran dam. From the Llyfyran it flows some fifteen miles in a South Westerly direction and into the sea at Milford Haven. It holds trout, sewin and salmon. The sewin run up river in June and July and offer good fly fishing, especially during the hours of darkness.

Facilities: Fishing Hut at Red House in the middle reaches.
Fishing Hut at Slebech Estate Beat in lower reaches.
Fishing Hut to be positioned in upper beat at Trwynt Farm.

Licence: Welsh Water Authority.

Season: Trout 3rd March to 30th September.
Sewin and salmon 20th March to 17th October.

Permit prices: Day £6, evening £4.50, week £40.

Limit on rods: 6 per day. Hours: twenty-four hours.

Restrictions: Fly only, except in high water on Slebech and Trwynt Farm beats. No restrictions on Red House water.

Site 1: Upper reaches Trywynt Farm. Managed by Pembrokeshire Fly Fishers. This is fly fishing only and has trout fishing in the early months. Sewin fishing at best later in the season.

Site 2: Red House beat. Managed by the Pembrokeshire Fly Fishers. All method fishery. Charges above.

Site 3: Slebech beat, this is tidal and contains fresh sewin for most of the season.

Site 4: Permits from Thomas, Llandre-Egremount, Clynderwen. Has two miles of private fishing.

Recommended flies: Early season for trout: March Brown, Butcher, Peter Ross, Greenwell, Olives.
For sewin: Silver Doctor, Dai Ben, Dunkeld, Bloody Butcher.
Late Season for sewin: Elverine Fly, Blue Fly, Invicta, Silver Doctor, Butcher.
Dry fly: March Brown, Black gnat, Pheasant tail, Tupps Indispensable, Oliver, Kite's Imperial, Grey Wulf at Mayfly time.

River Cothi
Carmarthen–Dyfed

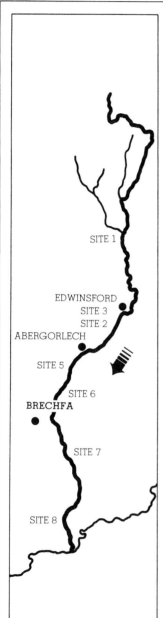

The Cothi was one of the most productive rivers in the principality and it was absolutely astounding the number of sewin that ran in late July and August. Recently, the figures have been down on the sixties and early seventies. However, for a small river it is still very good.

Licence: Welsh Water Authority.
Season: Migratory fish 20th March–17th October.
Permit prices: Vary from stretch to stretch but most association permit prices are extremely reasonable.

Site 1: Cothi Vale Water. Permits available from Clwb Godre'r Mynydd Du. One and a half miles of both banks up river of Bailey Bridge.

Site 2: Disgwylfa Water. Permits available to fish half a mile down river of Abergorlech Bridge. Water owned by New Quay Angling Association and season tickets available from Davies, Minyrafon Abergorlech.

Site 3: Bryn Cothi Water. Managed by Swansea Amateur Anglers Association. One and a half miles of both banks from Bryncothi Lodge to Ynyscniw. Tickets available for friends of Association members only.

Site 4: Tyrycae and Ynys Rhyd. Up stream of Brechfa Bridge, permits are available from Forest Arms Brechfa. Day permits £5.

Site 5: Gwau-cae-gurwen Water. Some three quarters of a mile up river of Pontynyswen to Brechfa Road. Weekly and season tickets on application to Jones, 6a Glyn Road, Brynaman, Amanford.

Site 6: Brechfa Lodge Water. Some three miles of left bank of river Cothi down river of Darren Swing Bridge. Tickets from Brechfa Fishing Lodge.

Site 7: Cross Hands Angling Association Water. Day permits £3.50, apply to V. Jones, 157 Penygroes Road, Blaeanu Amanford.

Site 8: Carmarthen & District Angling Club Water. Down river of Pontargothi. Permits available at tackle shops in Carmarthen or from H. Evans, 25 Maple Crescent, Carmarthen.

Recommended flies: Dai Ben, Blue Squirrel, Peter Ross, Teal Blue & Silver, Teal & Black, Butcher, Muddler.

Local knowledge: The Cothi is best fished at night if using a fly. A short line is often necessary and up river casting in overgrown areas can be rewarding.

Elan Valley Reservoirs

ELAN VILLAGE,   Phone: Rhayader 810449.
RHAYADER.   Proprietor: Welsh Water Authority

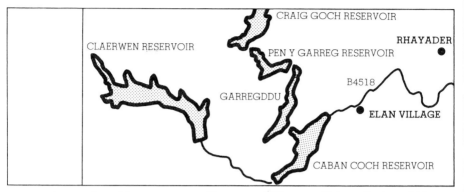

A complex of five reservoirs, Claerwen 650 acres, Caban Coch and Garreg Ddu 500 acres, Penygarreg 124 acres and Graig Goch 217 acres. Each with the exception of Claerwen is lightly stocked during the season. Claerwen is a natural wild brown trout water which fishes well in mid summer. The stocking is done from the feeder streams.

Facilities:	Permits from Elan Estates Office in Elan Village with tackle, food and accommodation available at Rhayader.
Season:	20th March–17th October. Hours:
Rods:	Unlimited.
Charges:	Season £25, Day £1. Licence: Welsh Water Authority.
Day limit:	6 fish.
Restrictions:	Fly only on Claerwen.
Stocking policy:	See above.
Annual catch per rod:	Unquantified.
Recommended flies:	
March:	Black Spider, Cochlenlas, Silver March Brown.
April:	Claret & Mallard, Butcher, Black & Peacock, Teal & Green.
May:	Hawthorn, Mallard & Claret, Wickham.
June:	Coch-a-bon-ddu, Hawthorn Fly, Black & Peacock, Dunkeld, Peter Ross.
July:	Sedges, Pheasant Tail, Green Peter.
August:	Crane Flies, Dunkeld, Wickhams, Green Nymph.
September:	Crane Flies, Zulu, Cochenlas, Blae & Black.
Local knowledge:	Peter Medlicot is the Captain of the Welsh Fly Fishing team and a regular Elan Valley visitor. He is a surface of the water angler, using a floating line exclusively. Smallish flies with light tackle, is the key to success with these wild brown trout. A team of three of four flies worked near the surface in a good breeze brings a quick response from the free rising fish of Claerwen.

Editor's note: The management of waters other than Claerwen has, as we go to print, been aquired by a newly-formed, local angling association. Ask Welsh Water Authority for details.

Llanllawddog Lake

CARMARTHEN, DYFED. Phone: 026784 436.
Proprietors: Mr & Mrs Olive.

Feeder Stream

HOME FARM

A two-and-a-half acre horseshoe-shaped lake in a beautiful, sheltered valley. Built as a fishery some 12 years ago, it has a rich aquatic life with an abundance of fly life especially nymphs and buzzers. Fish are free-rising and average some two to two and a half pounds. The best in 1983 went to over ten pounds.

Season:	21st February–30th November. Hours 9.00 am–9.00 pm.
Rods per day:	9.
Charges:	Day £7.50, Evening £4.00. Licence: Welsh Water Authority.
Day limit:	Four fish. Evening two. No boat fishing.
Restrictions:	Fly fishing only. No wading. No radios or dogs.
Stocking policy:	Daily to match catches. Rainbows.
Annual catch per rod:	2.7 Average weight 2.2 lbs.
Recommended flies:	
March:	Black Pennel, Black & Peacock Spider, Alexandra,
April:	Blae & Black, Pheasant Tail Nymph, Mallard & Claret,
May:	Sedge Flies and Sedge Pupas, Pheasant Tail Nymph,
June:	Black Pennel, Dunkeld, Midge Pupa, Pheasant Tail Nymph, Invicta.
July:	Dry, Grey Duster, Sedge Pupa, Black Pennel, Mallard & Claret, Crane.
August:	Sedges, Black Pennel, Mallard & Claret, Pheasant Tail Nymph, Dry Olive.
September:	Blae & Black, Crane Flies, Green & Brown Ivans' Nymphs, Invicta.
October:	Black Lure, Orange Nymph, Baby Doll, Pheasant Tail Nymph.
November:	Baby Doll, Black Lure, Black & Peacock Spider,
Local knowledge:	John Mercer is a prominent local lawyer who finds his angling pleasure on Llanllawddog fishery. He is consistently successful with small flies fished on or near the surface. Dark flies more often then not bring results and John favours the same quiet and gentle approach, which he applies to his sewin.

Llysyfran Reservoir

NR. MAENCLOCHOG,   Tel: Maenclochog 273.
Haverfordwest.   Proprietors: Welsh Water Authority.

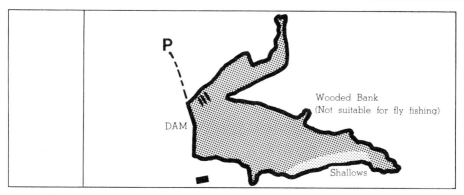

This is an ideal family water offering good brown and rainbow trout fishing. The rainbows move well after stocking and a good head of wild browns adds to the interest. It is a pleasant retreat with attractive walks and nature trails adding to its appeal.

Facilities:	Picnic tables, cafe, boat launching facilities for own boat. Ticket booth on site and toilets.
Season:	1st April–30th September. Hours: 8.00 am until roughly one hour after sunset.
Charges:	Season £80, day £3.50. Juniors, OAP and Disabled: Season £54, Day £2.40.
Day limit:	6 fish. Boats £5.00, five boats available.
Restrictions:	Fly fishing only from boats. No trolling.
Stocking:	Approximately 10,000 per season at fortnightly intervals.
Annual catch per rod:	1.2 in 1983. Total of 8,100 in 1982.
Recommended flies:	
April:	Black & Peacock, Black Lure, Zulu, Mallard & Claret.
May:	Mallard & Claret, Viva, Black Spider.
June:	Hawthorn, Mallard & Claret, Dunkeld, Wickham, Blackie.
July:	Invicta, Sedge, Longhorns, Black Pennel, Wickham.
August:	Dunkeld, Whisky, Baby Doll, Zulu, Mallard & Claret.
September:	Crane Flies, Wickham, Zulu, Dunkeld, Mallard & Claret.
Local knowledge:	Malgwyn Lewis is a regular visitor to Lysyfran and more successful than most. He sticks generally to traditional patterns in smaller sizes – 12s or 14s. Boat fishing here is reasonably priced and provide access to the otherwise too wooded East bank.

Rosebush Reservoir

CLYNDERWEN,
DYFED.

Phone: Maenclochog 507.
Proprietor: Stuart Askew.

```
                    BLAENPANT ●
        Worm Fishing Area        ⌁ ENTRANCE
                                              B4313
  DAM

       S.E. Bank (wooded)
```

Rosebush is a 39 acre reservoir, sided by a step valley, in the picturesque hills of Preseli. Its water quality encourages quite rich aquatic life. It is a tranquil fishery with wild brown trout adding to the pleasure of the traditional fly fisher.

Facilities: Meals and packed lunches available at the local Post Office, also accommodation. Caravan park nearby, reservations made on above number.

Season: March 20th – 17th October. Hours: daylight.

Rods per day: Unrestricted.

Charges: Season £35, Day £2.50, Evening £2.00, Week £10.00. Season £30, Day £2.00, Evening £1.50, Week £10.00 (concession for disabled).

Day limit: 4 fish. Boats: Two rowing boats available, boat price included in the permit price for fly fisherman.

Restrictions: Fly only. A small section of bank open for worm anglers.

Stocking policy: Regular stocking of rainbow trout of around the pound mark. Brown trout stocked three or four times a season.

Annual catch per rod: Approximately one trout per visit. Average weight 1 lb.

Recommended flies:

March: Blae & Black, Black Pennel, Mallard & Claret

April: March Brown, Mallard & Claret, Peter Ross, Black Pennel, Butcher.

May: Invicta, Mallard & Claret, Teal & Black, Teal & Green.

June: Coch-a-bon-ddu, Dry Grey Duster, Invicta, Sedge flies in evenings.

July: Coch-a-bon-ddu, Black nymphs, Peter Ross, Butcher

August: Crane flies, Dunkeld, Mallard & Claret, Teal & Green.

September: Crane flies, Mallard & Claret, Butcher, Dunkeld

Local knowledge: Peter Ward is one of the local anglers at Maenclochog and is able to take advantage of the fishery at its best. He favours the smaller flies and the floating line to get his fish. Both Peter and his father favour the brown trout at Rose bush, in preference to the stocked rainbows – and both ended the 1983 season with impressive catches.

River Taf
Pembroke–Dyfed

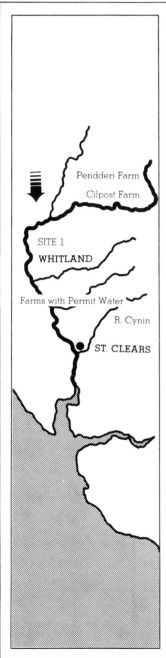

The River Taf flows off the Prescelly mountains in North Pembrokeshire in a south westerly and later a south easterly direction to Carmarthen Bay, near the mouth of the Towy. It carries the reputation of holding good sewin, as well as salmon and brown trout. Some areas are stocked annually with brown trout. The River Taf has extensive stretches of private fishing, but there are two important Angling Associations at St Clears and Whitland, which issue permits to visitors.

Licence: Welsh Water Authority.
Season: Trouth 3rd March–30th September.
Salmon 20th March–17th October.

Site 1: Some six miles of good fishing on the River Taf is controlled by the Whitland Angling Club and permits for visitors can be obtained from the garage at the Station Road. There are a number of farms up-river of Whitland that issue day permits which cost around £2. Contact: Cilpost Farm, Water-Lewis, Whitland. Penderi Farm Water: Mr Lloyd, Penderi Farm, Llanfallteg, Whitland.

Site 2: St Clears Angling Association in addition to having waters on the River Taf itself, also has stretches on the Cowin, an excellent tributary of the Taf. Also on the Rivers Dewi Fawr and Cynin – two other Taf tributaries. Permits and advice on St Clears Fishery can be obtained from David Bryan, Madras House, Laugharne, Dyfed. There are a number of smaller stretches for which the visitor can obtain permits by approaching fishery owners directly. Two such farms are Clogn Water, permits from Mr Evans, Clogyfran, Whitland and Maes-y-llan Farm water, permits from Mr Llewellyn, Maesyllan Farm, Login, Whitland. The Carmarthen & District Angling Club has one mile of fishing on the Taf and permits and advice can be obtained from Hon Sec Herbert Evans, 25 Maple Crescent, Carmarthen.

Recommended flies: For Trout: Greenwell's Glory, Butcher, Peter Ross, Iron Blue Dun, Snipe & Purple, Black Spider.
For sewin: Teal, Blue & Silver, Dai Ben, Teify Terror, Muddlers, Black Lure, Squirrel, Teal Series in Number Six.

Local knowledge: David Bryan knows the River Taf better than most and has been concerned with its administration for many years. Early season the trout fishing is quite good especially in the stocked areas with the sewin providing the best sport after June.

Teifi Pools

PONTRHYDFENDIGAID,
Ystrad Meurig, Dyfed.

Phone: 09745 201.
Proprietor: Teifi Pools Anglers Association.

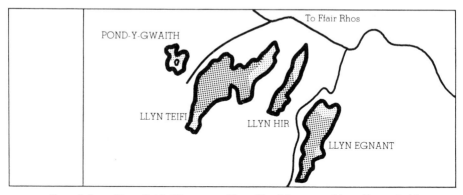

Four lakes, Llyn Teifi 61 acres, Llyn Hir 12 acres, Llyn Egnant 44 acres, Pond-y-gwaith 8 acres. An upland fishery in a wild rugged environment. Contains some good wild brown trout which are most active during the sedge period in mid July. A fishery far from the madding crowd, yet quite easily accessible.

Facilities:	Tackle and permits can be bought and hired at the Post Office at Pontrhydfendigaid and lunches available at the hotels at Pontrhydfendigaid.
Season:	20th March–17th October. Hours: 8.00 am until one hour after sunset.
Rods:	No limit.
Charges:	Season £25, Day £3, Boat £4. Permits from Post Office Pontrhydfendigaid. Welsh Water Authority Licence.
Day limit:	Six fish.
Boat:	One boat on Llyn Egnant.
Restrictions:	Fly only on Llyn Egnant and Llyn Hir. Llyn Teifi and Pond-y-gwaith open to all legal methods.
Stocking policy:	Llyn Teifi stocked with rainbow every fortnight. Llyn Hir and Llyn Egnant stocked three to four times a season. Total stocking per annum: 5,000.
Recommended flies:	
March:	Blae & Black, Peacock Spider, Ace of Spades
April:	Zulu, Blae & Black Lure, Green & Black Nymph,
May:	Claret & Mallard, Invicta, Coch-a-bon-ddu, White Lure,
June:	Sedge patterns, Hawthorn, Harry Tom
August:	Muddlers, Poacher, Crane Flies, Harry Tom
September:	Crane Flies, Black & Peacock, Pheasant Tail, Zulu,
October:	Muddlers, Black Lure, Baby Doll, Claret & Mallard, Silver Invicta.
Local knowledge:	Evan Jones from Llanilar is a keen local angler. Most of his fishing is done on Llyn Egnant and he favours using a sinking line early in the season and a floater as the water warms up in late May. Summer is slow coming to Teifi Pools. Llyn Teifi provided Evan with good bags in 1983 but most of the pleasure was had in August when the brown trout in Llyn Egnant really moved well.

River Teify
North Dyfed

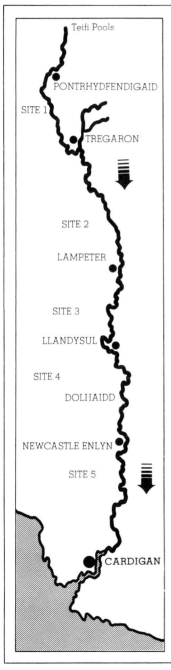

River Teify flows generally in a south-westerly direction, from the hills of Mid-Wales and from the Teify Pools to the famed nature reserve of Caron Bog, and through Tregaron, Lampeter, Llandysul, Newcastle, Emlyn and on to Cardigan Bay below Cardigan town. In its upper water trout predominate, with salmon and sewin dominating the lower reaches. It has numerous tributaries which offer interesting trout fishing. Permission for fishing tributaries is usually obtained from riparian owners and these waters are ideal for dry fly or up-river wet fly.

Facilities: Although much of the water of the Teify is in private hands, there are long stretches controlled by Angling Associations which issue fishing permits on a day or season basis at reasonable charges. The Licence required for the River Teify is the Welsh Water Authority licence obtainable at tackle shops and Post Offices.

Season: March 3rd to September 30th for trout.
March 20th to October 17th for migratory fish.

Site 1: Pontrhydfendigaid; Upper reaches; trout fishing with dry fly in May, June and September being good. This stretch is of a typical quick-running 'pool and rifle' nature.
Tregaron; The River Teify here is of a more matronly decorum, having flown through the Caron Nature Reserve. Wet fly fishing good in March and April with the dry fly coming into its own after the Grannom hatches in early May. Llanddewi; The Teify here is still of ideal size for wet and dry fly fishing. The running stretches are more productive than the slow glides and flies of a bushy nature are preferred, both by local fishermen and trout. Permits to fish 15 miles of upper Teify can be purchased at local shops. Water controlled by Tregaron & District Angling Association. Day permit approximately £3, season £25.

Site 2: Llanybyther Angling Association Water Permits at Lloyds Bank, Llanybyther. Trout and sewin fishing.

Site 3: Llandysul Angling Association: Controls some 12 miles of water on lower Teify. Its upper stretches contain good trout, with a few grayling on one particular stretch. Day tickets available at Alma Boot Stores in main street of Pontrhydfendigaid. Advisable to book before visit.

Site 4: Newcastle Emlyn on lower Teify. Sewin and salmn are the main quarry in this area. Tickets on this stretch available at Teify Trout Association, in Emlyn Boot Store ('phone 0239 710415), Newcastle Emlyn.

River Teify
North Dyfed

Site 5: Dolhaidd Isaf. Three quarters of a mile of river for residents at the cottages. Fishing and accommodation let together, with free fishing for residents. Approximately three rods per day. Good fly fishing for salmon at its best in September and October.

Local knowledge: The regional author has fished the Teify for some forty years and enjoys good sport the season through with wet and dry fly. Night fly-fishing for sewin in high summer is, however, the cream of the Teify fishing. Early season the Pheasant Tail, Snipe & Purple and Greenwell do well, fished in the traditional downriver style, and the Imperial Dogsbody and Doctor, fished dry in May and June give good returns. For sewin fishing, Muddlers, Teify Terror and Teal Blue and Silver will suffice to tempt the fish during the hours of darkness.

River Towy

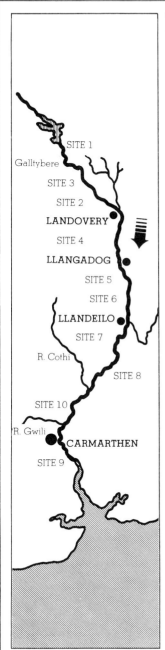

The River Towy flows from the Brianne Reservoir, which was constructed to supply the industrial thirst of South Wales and has been blamed for many of the ills of the water. The Towy runs southwards from the hills of mid Wales through Llandovery and Llandeilo and into the sea south of Carmarthen. It is the premier sewin river in Wales and has the unique distinction of having fresh fish running in March. Smaller sewin run in June and July. It does contain some trout worthy of the fly fishers attention, yet few seek them. There are a good number of permit waters accessible to the visitor, although about 50 per cent of the fishing rights are in private hands. Visitors are advised to check availability of permits before trip as availability of fishing rights can change dramatically overnight.

Licence: Welsh Water Authority.
Season: Trout: 3rd March–30th September. Migratory trout: 20th March–17th October.
Hours: Unlimited. Rods: Unlimited. Permit prices: Vary but association charges reasonable.

Site 1: Gallt-y-Bere Water in upper Towy. Permits from Williams, Gallt-y-Bere Farm, Rhandirmwyn, Llandovery. Permit approximately £2.50 daily. Caravans and accommodation available.

Site 2: Llandovery Angling Association Water. Enquiries: M. Davies, Cwm Rhudden Lodge, Llandovery. Five miles on Towy, one mile on Gwydderig and one mile on Bran. Permits on daily, weekly and seasonal basis available. Very reasonable.

Site 3: Approximately one mile of fishing above A40 road bridge. Enquiries: Mr Thomas, Tonn Farm, Llandovery. Permits approximately £3.50.

Site 4: Cross Hands & District Angling Association Water. Enquiries to: Mr Thomas, 71 Cae Glas, Cross Hands. Season tickets £25.

Site 5: Llangadog Angling Association Water. Enquiries: Sec. Mr Slaymaker, Bryn awelon, Llangadog. Approximately two miles of premier water in four stretches on the Towy. Permits from Red Lion Hotel, Llangadog. Day: £3.50. Season: £30.

Site 6: Gwaun-cae-gurwen Angling Association Water. Near two miles on Towy. Enquiries to Sec: Mr Jones, Cysgod Y Glyn, Bryn Aman.

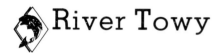 # River Towy

Site 7: Llandeilo Angling Association Water. Eight miles of fishing including both banks on Towy, three miles of Cennen Brook and two miles on Dulais. Tickets from Towy Sports, Llandeilo. Enquiries from visiting anglers to secretary, Dilwyn Richards, Ffair Fach, Llandeilo.

Site 8: Cawdor Estate Fishery. Season tickets on Estate water must be applied for, to: The Estate Office, Llangathen, Carmarthen, SA32 8AE. Season tickets around £200 each.

Site 9: Carmarthen & District Angling Club Water. This angling club has extensive stretches of water on Towy, Gwili, Gothi and Taf. Permits available from tackle shops in Carmarthen. Visitors advised to contact sec.: Mr Evans, 25 Maple Terrace, Carmarthen.

Site 10: Carmarthen Amateur Angling Association Water. This association has extensive stretches on the Towy, Gothi and the Gwili but visitors advised to contact sec.

Recommended flies: For sewin and salmon: Dai Ben, Teify Terror, Topper, Blue Squirrel, Peter Ross, Teal, Blue & Silver, Muddler, Allrounder, Black Lure, Logie, Doctor series, Silver Doctor, Black Doctor, Black & Silver Tube Flies.

North East Wales

Perhaps devoid of the anglers which it deserves, this area is dominated by the River Dee; a premier water, famed for its salmon and sea trout, and around Bala and Corwen, for its grayling stocks, which have increased significantly in recent seasons.

The Dee rolls off the Aran mountains of mid Wales, flowing through Bala, Crowen, Llangollen and Chester, eight miles from where it joins the sea. Salmon are fishable all along the Dee, but the fly angler should concentrate on the upper reaches above Llangollen, where the wild brown trout abound. Bala, or Llyn Tegid, is the largest natural lake in Wales, holding no less than 14 species of fish, some of which are impressively large trout; 10 lb was last season's record. Bala and three other still waters in the Dee Valley, ensure constant flows along the river down to Chester. The Dee tributaries, Aled and Alwen, though small, also offer good dry fly fishing.

The Clwyd and its tributary, the Elwy, are two under-estimated rivers with good runs of migratory fish and native brown trout. The sewin dominates these waters but small fighting brown trout rise well to the dry fly in the upper reaches, where the quality of the water enhances their stocks.

Still water fishing abounds in the north east, with Brenig, the major Welsh reservoir, boasting a fleet of 40 boats available for chasing its large rainbows and American brook char. Strong tackle is advised by the locals.

A number of small fisheries have opened up in recent years ion the north west and are seemingly thriving. The size of their stock however is often reflected in the permit price and £12.00 to £14.00 is not uncommon for a day ticket. They are, however, popular and must therefore be providing value for money.

This is generally an exciting area for fishing with a variety of waters and species.

Alwen Reservoir

CERRIG-Y-DRUDION, NR. CORWEN, CLWYD.

Phone: Cerrig-drudion 463. Proprietor: Welsh Water Authority.

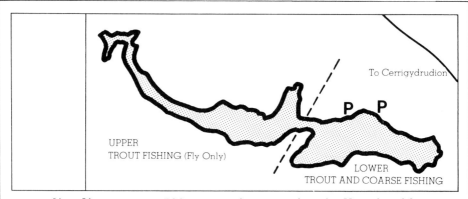

UPPER
TROUT FISHING (Fly Only)

To Cerrigydrudion

P P

LOWER
TROUT AND COARSE FISHING

Llyn Alwen is some 500 acres and is situated on the Hiraethog Mountains some 1200 feet above sea level. The lake is surrounded by spruce forest and heather moorland. The Alwen bank is full of empty spaces affording the angler mobility. Fly hatches are not prolific and early evening offers the best opportunities. Alwen is a water for the delicate angler who likes to use small flies and light tackle.

Facilities:	Nil on bankside but everything at the nearby Brenig Information Centre.
Season:	1st April–17th October Hours: 8.00 am until one hour aftersunset.
Rods per day:	Unlimited. Licence: Welsh Water Authority.
Charges:	Season £25, Day £2.
Restrictions:	Lake is zoned for fly, spinning and worm methods.
Catch per rod:	Approximately one per visit. Average weight: 10-12 oz.

Recommended flies:

April:	Blae & Black, Black & Peacock Spider, Butcher, Black Pennel.
May:	Greenwell's Glory, Black Pennel, Sooty Olive, Muddler, Midge Pupa.
June:	Sedge Pupa, Stick Fly, Greenwell, Soldier Palmer, Coch-a-bon-ddu.
July:	Zulu, Stick Fly, Sedge Flies, Coch-a-bon-ddu, Haul-a-gwynt, Bongoch.
August:	Crane Flies, Mallard & Claret, Invicta, Black Pennel, Greenwell.
September:	Crane Flies, Stick Flies, Invicta, Wickham Fancy, Midge Pupa.
Local knowledge:	An article written by Chris Boase and Steve Dann on Alwen, which they described as the Jewel on the Welsh Moors, outlined their love for this isolated and tranquil fishery. They recommended longish leaders with buzzers and sedge pupas on floating and sink-tip lines. Their approach, as is advisable on so many Welsh lakes, is to be mobile. The abundance of open spaces encourages and rewards the bank fisher.

Llyn Brenig

CERRIG-Y-DRUDION,   Phone: Cerrig-y-drudion 463.
Nr. Corwen, Clwyd.   Proprietor: Welsh Water Authority.

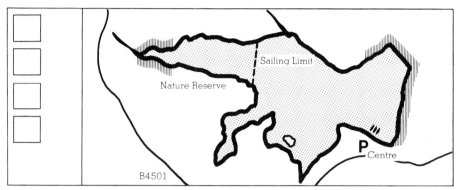

Llyn Brenig is a massive 919 acres, situated on Hiraethog mountain. It is the major fly fishery in Wales, supporting over thirty boats and selling about 15,000 permits annually. Situated in an area of great natural beauty, Brenig is a highland fishery about 1,400 feet above sea level. Anglers must be prepared for variable and sometimes severe weather. It holds a good head of wild brown trout.

Facilities:	Tea rooms and tackle shop at lakeside.
Season:	1st April–17th October. Hours: 8.00 am until one hour after sunset.
Charges:	Season £100, Day £4, Evening £2.80.
	Boat charges: Motor: Wed–Fri £8.50. Sat & Sun £10 Rowing: Wed–Fri £5.50. Sat & Sun £5.50
	Family day ticket: One adult and two or three children – £7
	Couple evening ticket plus boat – £9
Day limit:	Six. Boats: 30 plus available.
Restrictions:	Two no-go areas for boat anglers; nature reserve and dam.
Stocking policy:	Put and take, an average of 16,000 stocked annually of brown, rainbow and brookies.
Catch per rod:	1.5.

Recommended flies:

April:	Black Lures, Ace of Spades, Muddler, Blae & Black
May:	Baby Doll, Black Lure, Invicta, Green Peter, Butcher,
June:	Muddlers, Coch-a-bon-ddu, Mallard & Claret, Olives
July:	Small Gold Muddlers, Invicta, Peter Ross
August:	Crane flies, Whisky, Baby Doll, Small dry flies
September:	Muddlers, Black Lure, Viva, Mallard & Claret
Local knowledge:	Mike Green from Corwen is one of the regulars on Llyn Brenig. Being a fly dresser of considerable expertise, he believes that his small flies are the most successful presented to the Brenig trout when they are on the surface. On the days when they go low then the larger lures have to be used. Mike prefers his small Gold Muddlers and Invictas in the warm days of June and July.

Llyn Celyn

BALA, GWYNEDD.

Phone: Bala 520368.   Proprietor: Welsh Water Authority.

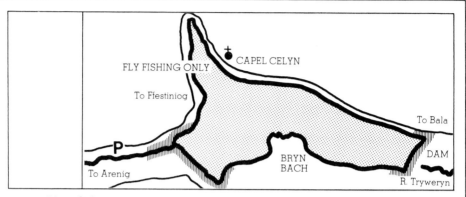

Llyn Celyn is an 800-acre-mountain reservoir set in picturesque country-side, a multi-method fishery with spinning and worming allowed. It is a water with plenty of open spaces and fly fishers are able to stalk their trout by walking good distances along the banks. Celyn has some nice wild brown trout but the quality of the water does not encourage stocked fish. It is a quiet fishery affording much pleasure to the discerning angler.

Facilities:	Permits available from Post Office at Frongoch and tackle shops in Bala.
Season:	1st March–17th October. Hours: 7.00 am until one hour after sunset.
Rods per day:	Unlimited. Licence: Welsh Water Authority.
Charges:	Season £60, Day £3, Evening £2.
Day limit:	6 fish. Boats: Nil.
Restrictions:	Size limit of 10 in.
Stocking policy:	5,500 of brown and rainbows per annum, stocking on a monthly basis.
Catch per rod:	1.57 Average weight: 15 oz.
Recommeded flies:	
March:	Black & Peacock, Black Pennel, Blae & Black, Claret & Mallard.
April:	Greenwell, Capel Celyn, March Brown, Black Pennel.
May:	Greenwell, Mallard & Claret, Butcher.
June:	Pheasant Tail Nymph, Mallard & Claret, York's Special.
July:	Coch-a-bon-ddu, Sedges, Rhwyfwr Cochddu Mawr.
August:	Crane Flies, Mallard & Claret, Bongoch, Bibio, Zulu, Harry Tom.
September:	Mallard & Claret, Crane Flies, Muddlers, Coch-a-bon-ddu.
Local knowledge:	Norman Davies is one of the ablest of the many fly-fishers in the delightful town of Bala. Another of the traditional anglers of Wales, using small dark flies on a floating line, he likes to walk and work for his rewards. Norman believes in keeping his line wet and advocates that all anglers fishing Celyn should fish hard.

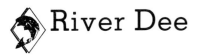

River Dee

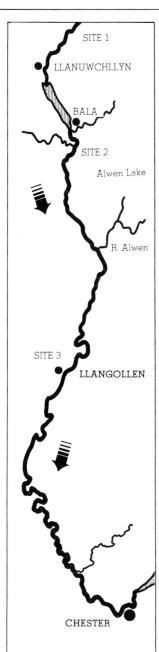

SITE 1

LLANUWCHLLYN

BALA

SITE 2

Alwen Lake

R. Alwen

SITE 3

LLANGOLLEN

CHESTER

The river Dee rises on the Aran Mountains in Mawddwy Gwynedd and flows northwards through Bala and thence eastwards through Corwen, Llangollen, Overton and finally to Chester. The trout anglers' main preserves are up-river of Llangollen, while the salmon anglers find their sport along the whole length of the river, if the water level permits. The river Dee from Bala, through Corwen and down to Llangollen, is of ideal proportion and topography for wet and dry fly fishing for trout. The pools and runs here offer the angler ideal venues to present his flies either wet or dry.

Facilities: Although strictly preserved for much of its length, there are certain stretches which can be fished by day permits.
Licence: Welsh Water Authority.
Season: Trout 3rd March–30th September.
Salmon 26th January–17th October. Permits vary in prices but not too expensive on waters controlled by associations.

Site 1: Above Bala Lake is controlled by Llanuwchllyn Angling Association. The association offer permits on rivers Dee, Twrch and Lliw, with all legal fishing permitted.

Site 2: Bala Angling Association. This association controls over 20 miles of river fishing for trout, salmon and grayling. This represents the most reasonably priced fishing in the whole of the principality. Permit prices: week £5.50, season £16.50, day £2.00. A limit of six trout per day.
Restrictions: No maggot fishing on rivers. Permits – tackle shops in Bala.

Site 3: Llangollen. Approximately 6½ miles of fishing on the river Dee is controlled by the Llangollen Association. Fishing methods for trout restricted to fly and worm only. The water is stocked twice annually from own stock pond. There are other stretches available on daily permits especially on the tributaries Alwen and Alun.

Recommended flies: Trout: March Brown, Pheasant Tail, Iron Blue, Greenwell's Glory, Butcher.

Local knowledge: Mike Green from Corwen is one of the most successful of the Dee anglers and is one of the leading fly dressers in the principality. In the early days of the season, his approach is wet fly, on a floating line, down river. This also works well with the grayling, which are in abundance in the Corwen area. Mike also takes salmon on the fly at the latter end of the season.

River Rheidol
Ceredigion–North Dyfed

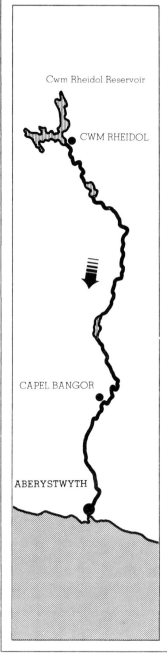

Cwm Rheidol Reservoir

CWM RHEIDOL

CAPEL BANGOR

ABERYSTWYTH

The Rheidol flows quickly off the Plynlimon Mountain and after a very short course meets the sea at Aberystwyth. It runs generally in a westwardly direction and is controlled, to some extent, by the Nantymoch and Dinas reservoirs, whose waters are used to generate electricity. It is thus subjected to variations in flow and temperature. The River has those pools and deep glides, ideal for fly-fishing sewin and salmon. The fishing on the Rheidol is traditionally with wet fly.

Facilities: Practically all the Rheidol is managed by the Aberystwyth Angling Association, which issues permits obtainable from local tackle shops in Aberystwyth town. The licence required is the Welsh Water Authority licence.
Season: Brown trout 3rd March–17th October.
Sewin and salmon 20th March–17th October.
Charges: Aberystwyth water (eleven miles): Season £70, Week £30, Day £7.50.

Upper reaches: Good sewin run up this section in late May and early June. There are a number of deep pools and good runs, ideal for night fishing. The temperature in this section during generating can be down on normal water, but the added level is an aid to fishing.

Middle reaches: Has long glides which are admirably suited to wet fly sewin fishing day or night. The fish in this area are always of fairly modest proportions and respond well to a fly fished deep on coldish nights. As the generating increases the water level periodically, the sewin are constantly kept on the move.

Lower reaches: Generally hold the smaller fish which swim in with the tide. These are taken in good numbers in July and August.

Local knowledge: Local dentist Illtyd Griffiths, is a regular sewin fisher on the Rheidol. His terrain is the upper reaches where the elusive, large fish lie. Armed with both floating and sinking line, for temperature change, Illtyd takes several fish in excess of 10 lbs each season. His 1983 record was 12 lb 4 oz.

 Lake Vyrnwy

LLANWDDYN, VIA Phone: 069 173 244.
OSWESTRY. Proprietors: Mrs. R.I. Muir and Co. Sir John Baynes

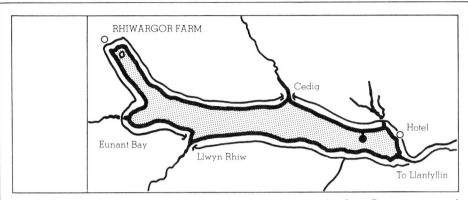

Lake Vyrnwy is 1,121 acres of magnificent water in the Aran Berwyn range of mountains some 800 feet above sea level. It is a challenging water, a fishery for genuine anglers and not for fishmongers. The splendid masonry dam was built in 1889 to hold back the waters of river Vyrnwy to quench the thirst of the Liverpudlians. Vyrnwy, is a long narrow lake of four and a half miles, with a rather bare, rocky bank providing little feed for the trout.

Season: 1st March–15th October. Hours: 8.30 am until 10·00 pm.

Rods: Maximum 26 (two per boat). Licence not required on lake.

Charges: All fishing on Vyrnwy is from boats. Boat fishing is free to residents at the Hotel. Day visitors: 1st April–14th July £4 Rest of season £3. Evening boat: £2.50 and £2.00.

Restrictions: Fly only. Boat fishing only on lake.

Stocking policy: Around 2,000 per annum stocked from February until June.

Limit: 8 fish.

Catch per rod: 1.8 per visit. Average weight 12 oz-1 lb.

Recommended flies:

April: Sweeny Todd, Butcher, March Brown, Blae & Black

May: Black Pennel, Sweeny Todd, Green Peter, Zulu, Greenwell.

June: Black & Peacock Spider, Mallard & Claret, Sedges, Coch-a-bon-ddu.

July: Sedges, Black Chenille, Mallard & Claret, Peter Ross

August: Heather Fly, Bibio, Invicta, Bongoch, Crane Flies, Olives.

September: Peter Ross, Muddler, Black Pennel, Mallard & Claret.

Local knowledge: This is a water for true fishermen. Managed as it is with care and experience, the hotel has retained enough 'old world charm' to complement any fishing trip with its consideration. Drifting downwind in a boat on Vyrnwy with smallish flies hop-scotching the surface is not far from Heaven. Balmy June/July evenings here amid these wild Welsh hills can provide idyllic sport. Another Jewel of a fishery.

North West Wales

This most picturesque top corner with its rugged mountains and natural lakes is not only welcoming to visitors but dependent on them for the maintenance of its fishing. Fishing hotels and facilities are therefore abundant.

Short, quick flowing sewin rivers criss-cross the whole area, which extends from the Dovey above Aberystwyth, up and around the coast of North Wales to the mouth of the Conway. Both the Dovey and the river Conway are famed for sewin, which can exceed eight pounds in weight. These fish need strong tackle to hold them and many are lost by visitors underestimating their strength and weight.

In the north near Caernarfon the Seiont, Gwyrfai and Llyfni, fish well in high summer and produce a few salmon for interest later in the season.

The Dwyfawr, Glaslyn and Erch flow south from the Lleyn Penninsular and attract fish of astounding quality. 10 lb sewin are common annually. Bank space can become a little scarce when the fish are running well, however, the visitor will have the advantage of hours over the local, who will inevitably have to earn his daily bread at some juncture.

The abundant mountain lakes of the north west vary significantly in quality. Recently, acid rain has become more apparent and it is advisable to check up on a water before embarking on a trip. Though the indigenous brown trout can sustain quite high acid levels, the stocked fish suffer badly.

Llyn Alaw

LLANERCHYMEDD, ANGLESEY.
Phone: 040788 762 (Llanfaethlu). Proprietor: Welsh Water Authority.

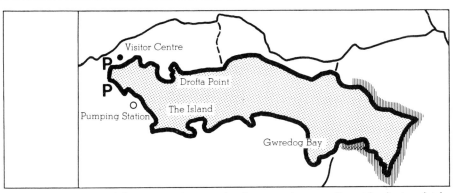

A 777 acre lake, some three miles long and one mile wide, being fairly shallow with numerous interesting bays. Has impressive hatches of sedges and buzzers. The shallow banks allow for wading. It is a rich lake with an abundance of aquatic life. Little problem with weed growth.

Facilities:	Three car parks within close proximity of lake. A visitors centre plus toilets nearby. Vehicle access to lake for disabled anglers.
Charges:	Day £4, Evening £3, Weekly £20.
Season:	20th March–31st October.
Hours:	One hour before sunrise to one hour after sunset. Evening ticket from 4.00 pm until one hour after sunset.
Day limit:	6 fish. Boats: none for hire.
Restrictions:	No fishing in bird sanctuary at top end of lake. This is a multi-method lake but no maggots, sweet corn or any ground baiting allowed.
Stocking policy:	Stocked every fortnight. Total stock for 1983: 4,000 Browns and 7,000 Rainbows.
Annual catch per rod:	.98 1983, 1.01 1982. Average weight: 1.2 lbs.
Recommended flies:	
April:	Buzzers, Zulu, Dunkeld, Butcher, Peter Ross.
May:	Buzzers, Pheasants Tail Nymph, Mallard & Claret
June:	Buzzers, Invicta, Green Peter, Wickhams Fancy
July:	Buzzers, Sedges patterns.
August:	Buzzers, Invicta, Butcher, Mallard & Claret, Hare's Ear.
September:	Zulu, Pheasant Tail Nymph, Butcher, Dunkeld
October:	Crane Flies, Green Peter, Butcher Nymph patterns.
Local knowledge:	John Thomas from Newborough is a member of the Welsh Fly Fishing team and as expected, favours fly on Llyn Alaw. He fishes as fine as conditions will allow and uses many of the old Welsh traditional patterns. His small lightly dressed flies work well especially in the evenings. A team of three wet flies or nymphs fished on a floating or slow sink line serves the angler well.

River Conway
Gwynedd

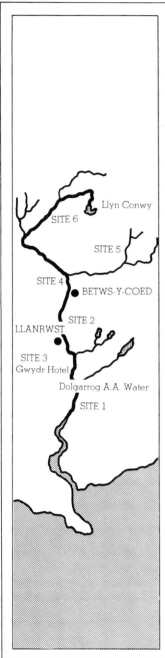

The River Conway has earned its reputation for being the large sewin river and the quality of the fish is indeed outstanding. Trout fishing is practised in the upper regions and salmon also come up river in late season. The river runs off the hills of Carnarfonshire, northwards through Betws Y Coed and Llanrwst and into the sea north of Conway. There are many stretches available to the visiting angler from both angling associations and from private riparian owners who provide a limited number of permits. These smaller beats, let by hotels and local owners, are more expensive but provide a good opportunity to take fish, because of less pressure on the water.

Licence: Welsh Water Authority.
Season: Trout: 3rd March–30th September.
Migratory fish: 20th March–17th October.
Prices of permits vary considerably from stretch to stretch.

Site 1: Dolgarrog Angling Association water. This stretch, in the lower reaches of the Conway, fishes best in late season. All enquiries to Corrie, 3 Taylor Avenue, Dolgarrog. The association also offers fishing on two lakes in the area.

Site 2: Llanrwst Angling Club water. This is an excellent fishing station for both sewin and salmon, when the water is in good condition. Approximately three miles of water managed by the club and enquiries should be to Thomas, Hon. Sec., Erw Las Llwyn Brith, Llanrwst.

Site 3: Gwydr Hotel water. This hotel has extensive stretches on the river Conway which is mainly reserved for guests at the hotel. Head Keeper Roy Jones is there to advise anglers. Enquiries should be made in good time to: Miss Smith, Gwydyr Hotel, Betws-y-coed. The hotel also has the fishing rights on Llyn Elsi.

Site 4: Betws-y-coed Anglers' Club waters. Good water on Conwy and Llugwy with best fishing from May to October. Permits from Sec.: Mr. Jones, 25 Bro Gethin, Betsw-y-coed.

Site 5: Dolwyddelan Fishing Association Waters. Permits available on this water, enquiries to Sec.: Mr. Jones, Dolawel, Dolwyddelan. The migratories particularly the salmon, fish best from August onwards.

Site 6: National Trout water. Both banks are open from Conway Falls to Rhydlanfair Bridge. Permits are very reasonably priced. Application to National Tourist Office, Dinas, Betws-y-coed.

River Conway
Gwynedd

Recommended flies: Peter Ross, Black Pennel, Huw Nain, Blue Squirrel, Zulu, Conway Red, Conway Blue.

Local knowledge: Roy Jones is the head keeper on the Gwydyr Hotel water and is therefore in a position to know most of the secrets of the Conway river. A former Captain of the Welsh Fly Fishing team, Roy favours small flies, but goes bigger for the jumbo sewin that travel the Conway. He also favours a floating line and works his flies across the river slowly and in mid water. The use of maggott on the fly is a valued ploy to help the angler; this however is extremely dubious fly-fishing.

Dinas Reservoir

CAPEL BANGOR,   Phone: Capel Bangor 667.
Aberystwyth, Dyfed.   Proprietors: Central Electricity Generating Board.

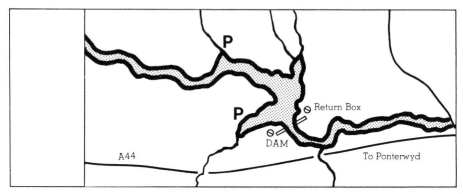

This 65 acre fishery is a highly organised 'put and take' lake. It works its own hatchery and the brown trout are of a good quality. Despite the fact that it is a multi method fishery, fly fishers have ample room to stalk about.

Facilities:	Local hotel at Ponterwyd caters for anglers, and local caravan parks are available. Permits from tackle shops at Aberystwyth and local garage at Ponterwyd.
Season:	1st April–30th September. Hours: 8.00 am to sunset.
Rods per day:	Unlimited.
Charges:	Day permit £3.50, weekly £15. OAP, Juniors and disabled: £2.20 daily, £10 weekly. Licence: Welsh Water Authority.
Day limit:	6 fish. Boats: none.
Stocking policy:	Once or twice weekly in accordance to catches and demands. It is generally stocked to a high density.
Catch per rod:	Between one and two fish per visit. Average weight: 14 oz.

Recommended flies:

April:	Blae & Black, Black Peacock, Mallard & Claret, Zulu, Butcher.
May:	Mallard & Claret, Black Spider, Zulu, Black & Peacock Spider.
June:	Coch-a-bon-ddu, Claret & Mallard, Haul & Gwynt, Invicta, Butcher.
July:	Sedges, Rhwyfwr Cochddu Mawr, Claret & Mallard, Invicta, Butcher, Zulu.
August:	Crane Flies, Butcher, Claret & Mullard, Wickham, Butcher.
Local knowledge:	Although a smallish water, Dinas supports some two hundred visitors weekly. Because it is a multi method fishery, it pays the fly angler to use small flies, and this is especially important when the weather warms up around late May and June. Finding secluded spots and working small, black flies back slowly in the upper layer of the waters, is the recipe for success.

River Dovey
Mid Wales

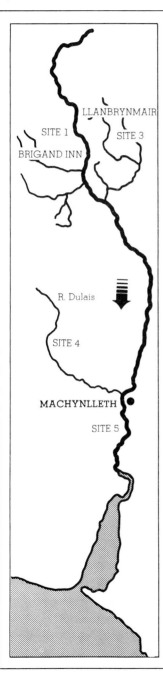

The river Dovey rises on the Aran Mawddwy mountains to flow some 30 miles in a south to south-westerly direction to the area of Aberdovey. It is one of the premier sewin rivers of Wales and carries a fair run of salmon in late season. The trout fishing is confined to the upper reaches and the tributaries.

The New Dovey Fishery Association owns most of the fishing on the river and permits are not easy to obtain. Applications to Secretary of the Association for season permits. Visitors must stay in local hotels. Permits on upper reaches of the Dovey can be obtained from farms and hotels.

Licence: Welsh Water Authority.
Season: Trout 3rd March-17th October.
  Migratory fish 20th March-17th October.
Restrictions: Fly only except in high water for the New Dovey Fishery Association Water and no Sunday fishing. Other waters open to all methods.

Site 1: Brigand's Inn Waters on Rivers Dovey and Cleifion. Approximately two and a half miles on river Dovey and is reserved mainly for hotel guests. Up to eight rods per day. Application to the Brigand's Inn Water, Mallwyd, Machynlleth.

Site 2: A considerable amount of water is controlled by Prince Albert Angling Association and application for permits must be made to Mr. Sparks, High Lodge, Upton, Macclesfield, Cheshire. These stretches are over a wide area and offer some very interesting and varied fishing.

Site 3: Llanbrynmair Angling Club. This association has water on the river Twymyn, which holds good sewin and is stocked with brown trout. A delightful up river fishery. Permits from D. Evans, Garage at Cemmaes – Llanbrynmair.

Site 4: River Dulais – tributary of Dovey. Permits from Mr. Maelor, Stoes Corris. Best time August to October. Reasonable priced permits.

Site 5: New Dovey Fishery Association, permits very limited, visitors must confirm before visit.

Recommended flies: Trout: for upper reaches; Greenwell's Glory, Butcher. Sewin and Salmon: Haslam.

Local knowledge: Emyr Lewis is a water bailiff on the River Dovey and is an expert fly angler. He favours the upper reaches where he can fish for the brown trout the season through, using small flies.

The River

The River Dovey, rushing on the wild and rugged Arran Mawddwy and flowing down through the beautiful Dovey Valley, is a classic example of the very best in Sea-Trout and Salmon fishing to be found in Wales. Many would argue that the Dovey is without Peer and the numbers and high weights caught each year would certainly support this. Last year we had three Sea-Trout in excess of 10 lb. the heaviest being almost 12 lb.

The Inn

The Brigands Inn dates back to the 15th Century and is one of the country's oldest and best known fishing Inns. A well known guide to Wales printed in 1875 describes it as "a capital place for fishing and the gathering of fisherfolk" and we like to think that this still applies today.

Briefly the Inn has 14 letting bedrooms, some with private bath, a large beamed Residents lounge with open fire, large dining room, T.V. room, all for the private use of residents. We have a set evening meal with additional a la carte choices and a very comprehensive bar snack menu. Meal times are spread to allow maximum time for fishing and packed lunches etc. are available.

There is ample parking and most beats are easily walked to from the Inn.

The Fishing

We have some $2\frac{1}{2}$ miles of mainly double bank on the Dovey together with $\frac{3}{4}$ mile of double bank on the Cliefion, a major tributary. This includes a stretch below the Pen-y-Bont falls in the form of a deep rocky gorge which is reserved for bait fishing.

The remainder is fly only and there are some 12 named pools together with good holding water connecting them, fast running at normal and above water heights. Casting is clear and there are no problems fishing from the bank. Wading is not normally necessary and in some areas not advisable.

The clear areas are best appreciated when night fishing, when the chances of success are at their greatest.

Best Times: Salmon   May, June, September, October
Sea-Trout   May to September

Mallwyd, Machynlleth, Powys SY20 9HJ
Tel: (STD 06504) 208 Reception. (STD 06504) 351 Visitors
Proprietors: Peter & Shirley Huntington.

River Dysynni
Mid Wales

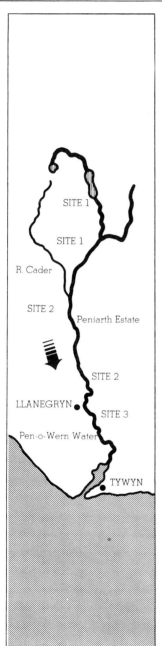

The River Dysynni rises in Llyn Cau on the steep south side of Cader Idris and after a short rapid journey, falls into the picturesque Tal-y-llyn. From this lake it flows westwards as a small upland river. Below Abergynolwyn it moves slower and deeper and joins the sea some distance above the town of Towyn. Dysynni holds trout, sewin and salmon. Trout are to be found in most of the stretches; the sewin come up-river mostly in the summer months. The salmn are not very plentiful and fly-fishing for more is very difficult indeed.

Facilities: Although many stretches are in private hands, permits can be obtained for a few beats. Some sections of the river can be fished by seeking permission of the local farmers.
Licence: Welsh Water Authority.
Season: Trout 3rd March–30th September.
Migratory fish 20th March–17th October.
Hours unlimited.

Site 1: Estamaner Angling Association. Permits from tackle shop at Tywyn. The association owns the stretch on the tributary, the river Cader. It also has seven miles on the upper Dysynni. Both are all-method fisheries and although the trout are small they offer good sport.

Site 2: Tickets for this Peniarth Estate Water are available from the tackle shop at Tywyn. This is approximately some four miles of fishing and the sewin can be good from July onwards.

Site 3: Some farms give permission or charge a nominal permit price as does Pen-o-wern Farm at Bryncrug. The sewin fishing here is mainly in August but most local anglers fish here for mullet in the tidal water.

Recommended flies: For trout: Hare's Ear, Partridge & Orange, Blue Dun, Butcher, Greenwell, Peter Ross, Black Pennel, Pheasant Tail, March Brown. For migratory fish: Peter Ross, Blue Squirrel, Connemara Black, Mallard & Claret, Black & Silver.

Local knowledge: Emyr Lewis, the local water bailiff is well placed to know the fishing secrets of this area. He is a purist and favours small flies.

River Erch
Nr. Pwllheli-Gwynedd

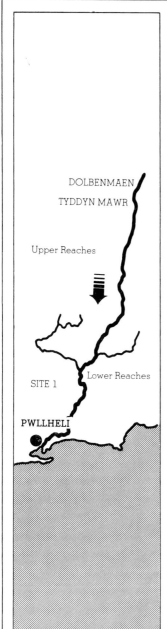

The River Erch runs down the mountains of the Lleyn Peninsular and into the sea near Pwllheli. Approximately 10 miles of the river is managed by the Pwllheli & District Angling Association. The Erch is a narrow tumbling river in its upper reaches; in places it is less than six feet wide. This grows to a good 35 feet in the lower reaches. Fishing varies considerably due to nature of river and the season.

Licence: Welsh Water Authority.
Season: 3rd March–31st October.
Charges: Season permit £10, Week £5, Day £2. No limit on fish caught.

The fishing on the river Erch is chiefly divided between brown trout and sewin, with the occasonal salmon being taken. The brown trout fishing can be quite good, with stocked browns put in to supplement the natural wild fish. The stocked fish are generally of ¾ lb in weight and provide decent fishing before the migratory trout arrive.

Site 1: Migratory fish, in the form of small sewin, arrive in the latter part of August and the fishing is really good in September. The best stretches for fly fishing lie in the lower sections just above Pwllheli.

Recommended flies: For trout: Pheasant Tail, Snipe & Purple, Partridge & Orange, Blue Dun, Greenwell, Spiders, March Brown, Dogsbody Imperial. For sewin: Butcher, Teal & Black, Medicine, Huw Nain, Torby Coch, Black Pennel, Conway Red, Harry Tom.

Local knowledge: Geraint Pritchard, Secretary of the Pwllheli and District Angling Association, is well respected on his local waters for his expertise with the wet fly. Early season sport on the Erch is provided by the brown trout and Geraint uses a cast of two, or sometimes three, of the above wet flies. When the sewin arrives, he uses the same tactics with larger flies.

River Glaslyn
Portmadog-Gwynedd

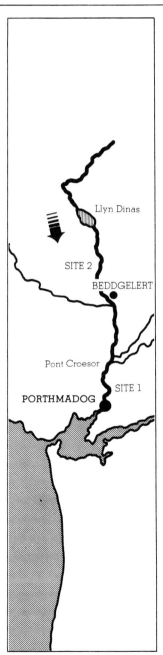

Rises in Llyn Conwy and travels through three lakes to Beddgelert. From Beddgelert, it flows through the Aberglaslyn pass and along the valley floor to Portmadog, where it flows through sluice gates. It is the only river in Wales where April is the best month for sewin. The trout fishing is at its best in the upper reaches. The Glaslyn is a unique river in many respects and its early sewin fishing is a bonus in that it lengthens the season. Although most stretches lie in private hands, there are opportunities for visitors to obtain day permits on some sections.

Season: Trout 3rd March–30th September.
Migratory fish 20th March–17th October.
Licence: Welsh Water Authority. Permits reasonably priced on association waters.

Site 1: Glaslyn Angling Association water. This is an extensive stretch of river from Portmadog to Beddgelert, with only a few private stretches being unavailable. Enquiries: Hon. Sec. Mr. Pierce, 1 Bron Alltwen, Penmorfa, Portmadog. Access to fishery off main road from Portmadog to Penrhyndeudraeth and from Brenteg to Beddgelert.

Site 2: Dinas Fishery Beddgelert. Dinas Lake is of some 25 acres offering good sewin fishing. Fishery also includes both banks above lake to first bridge and some distance of right bank down river of lake.

Recommended flies: Trout: Greenwell's Glory, Butcher, Black Pennel, Hare's Ear, Partridge & Orange, Peter Ross.
Sewin: Muddler, Butcher, Teal Blue & Silver, Mallard & Claret, Black Lure.

Local knowledge: W. J. Williams of Blaenau, is one of the chief administrators of angling in North Wales and has the interest of the river Glaslyn close to his heart. The early running big sewin, he maintains, will, given the water, speed up to the Beddgelert area, creating exciting sport in perfect surroundings.

◆ River Gwyrfai

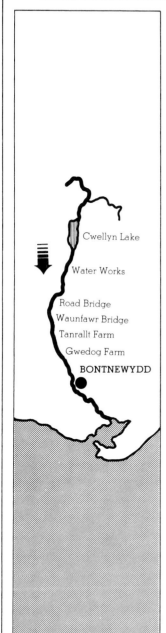

Cwellyn Lake

Water Works

Road Bridge
Waunfawr Bridge
Tanrallt Farm
Gwedog Farm
BONTNEWYDD

The river flows northwards from Llyn-y-Gadair to the Menai Straits. It is predominantly a river of migratory fish, the sewin having become more numerous in recent seasons. The Gwyrfai is mainly controlled by the Seiont, Gwyrfai and Llyfni Anglers' Association, which issue permits on a daily, weekly and seasonal basis. These permits are unlimited. Gwyrfai is quite a pleasant river to fish with pool and run topography making it ideal for the fly fisher. The trout tend to be small, but, in quick running water, they give good account of themselves.

Facilities: Most of the river managed by the Seiont, Gwyrfai and Llyfni Anglers' Association.
Licence: Welsh Water Authority.
Permits: Season £35, Week £20, Day £6.
Season: Migratory fish 20th March–17th October.
Trout 3rd March–30th September.

Site 1: From Llyn-y-Gadarr to Llyn Cwellyn.

Site 2: Down river from Llyn Cwellyn to Waunfawr Bridge. This is a good stretch for the fly fisher especially when the sewin start to run.

Site 3: From Waunfawr Bridge to Bontnewydd Bridge is mostly owned by the above association with the exception of a few private stretches. From Bontewydd to the sea the association owns the fishing on Foryd Farm.

Recommended flies: Early season: Hare's Ear, Blue Quill, Blae & Black, Greenwell's Glory, Grouse & Green, March Brown, Snipe & Purple, Mallard & Claret, Butcher, Peter Ross & Dunkeld.
Late season: Coch-y-bon-ddu, Wickhams Fancy, Mallard & Claret, Mallard & Yellow, Greenwell's Glory, Grouse & Green, Black Gnat, Snipe & Purple, Butcher, Peter Ross, Dunkeld, Black & Peacock spider.
Specially recommended casts of three flies: Mallard & Claret, Greenwell's Glory and Coch-y-bon-ddu. Butcher, Peter Ross and Dunkeld.

Local knowledge: Hugh Hughes is the secretary of the Seiont, Gwyrfai and Llyfni Anglers' Society and is a traditional Welsh angler favouring the gentle approach with small flies and light tackle. Visitors would do well to heed his style and approach.

River Llyfni
Caernarvon-Gwynedd

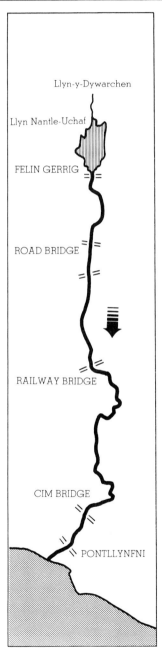

Llyn-y-Dywarchen

Llyn Nantle-Uchaf

FELIN GERRIG

ROAD BRIDGE

RAILWAY BRIDGE

CIM BRIDGE

PONTLLYNFNI

The river Llyfni rises in Llyn Dywarchen about one mile north of Rhyd-ddu and runs through Llyn Nantlle and on to the sea. The Seiont Gwyrfai & Llyfni Anglers' Society controls extensive stretches – more so the lower reaches. The Llyfni has some very rapid running water – presenting a massive handicap in keeping in touch with the cast. Hugh Hughes is the secretary of the asociation and believes that Llyfni fishes best when it is running high.

Facilities: Extensive stretches managed by Seiont Gwyrfai & Llyfni Anglers' Society – day, week and season permits are available to the visitor.
Licence: Welsh Water Authority obtainable from tackle shops in Caernarvon.
Season: Trout: 3rd March–30th September.
Migratory fish: 20th March–17th October.
Permit prices: Season £35, Week £20, Day £6.

Four road bridges cross the Llyfni providing good access to the river; Llanllyfni Road Bridge, Rail Bridge, Pont-y-Cim and Pontllyfni Road Bridge. Stretches vary according to season and water level.

Recommended flies: For early season: Hare's Ear, Blue Quill, Blae & Black, Greenwell's Glory, Grouse & Green, March Brown, Snipe & Purple, Butcher, Peter Ross, and Dunkeld. Mid season onwards: Coch-a-bon-ddu, Wickham Fancy, Mallard & Claret, Mallard & Yellow, Greenwell's Glory, Partridge & Orange, Black Gnat, Snipe & Purple, Butcher, Peter Ross, Dunkeld, Black & Peacock Spider. The Association recommends the following combinations for anglers fishing three fly casts: Mallard & Claret, Greenwell's Glory and Coch-a-bon-ddu. Butcher, Peter Ross and Dunkeld.

Nantymoch Reservoir

CAPEL BANGOR,   Phone: Capel Bangor 667.
Aberystwyth, Dyfed.   Proprietors: Central Electricity Generating Board.

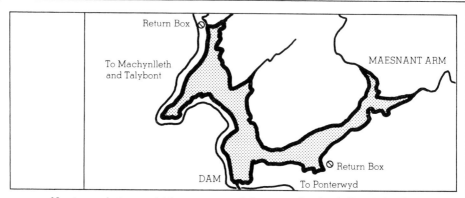

Nantymoch is a wild brown trout fishery in the foothills of the Plynlimon mountains. It has a wealth of interesting bays, allowing the anglers to work stealthily along the bank to stalk these mountain trout. It abounds with small, free-rising, wild trout, which offer sport at a very modest price. It pays the angler to be mobile.

Facilities:	Permits are available at tackle shops in Aberystwyth and Evan's garage in Ponterwyd. The local hotel at Ponterwyd caters for visiting anglers.
Season:	1st April–30th September.
Rods per day:	Unlimited.
Charges:	Day permit £1, Season permit £13.
Stocking:	None.
Catch per rod:	Approximately 3-4.
Recommended flies:	
April:	Small Black Flies, Blae & Black, Black Pennel, Greenwell.
May:	Black Spider, Greenwell, Hawthorn, Mallard & Claret, Peter Ross.
June:	Coch-a-bon-ddu, Black Gnat, Mallard & Claret, Greenwell.
July:	Sedges, Bongoch, Coch-a-bon-ddu, Pheasant Tail, Green Nymph.
August:	Crane Flies, Mallard & Claret, Greenwell.
September:	Crane Flies, Invicta, Black Spider, Red Tag.
Local knowledge:	Nantymoch is a fishery for the old fashioned fly angler who would measure the success of his day in other ways than by the weight of the creel. Wild brown trout fisheries are not common and they offer very satisfactory sport, especially on warmish days in summer. It is best to avoid cold weather on the highland fisheries in Wales in general; the dog days of high summer, however, can be very rewarding.

Penrhyncoch Lakes

ABERYSTWYTH,
DYFED.

Phone: Aberystwyth, 828433.
Proprietors: Aberystwyth Angling Association.

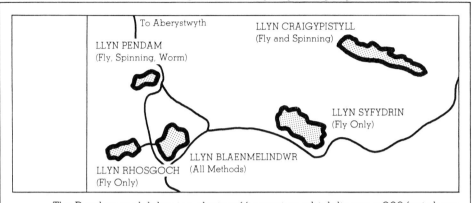

The Penrhyncoch lakes is a cluster of five waters which lie some 900 feet above sea level. Although today they appear as natural lakes they were in fact man-made during the last century, to provide water for the local lead mines. They are principally wild brown trout fisheries, some of them providing trout of over a pound. The average size is about 6-12 inches. The near proximity of the five lakes allows the angler to change venue quickly adding variety to a day's fishing.

Facilities:	Permits available from the tackle shops at Aberystwyth.
Season:	20th March–17th October. Hours: Daylight.
Rods per day:	Unlimited.
Charges per season:	Season £70, Day tickets £7.50, weekly £30.
Day limit:	No limit on four lakes, Llyn Craigypistyll, Llyn Syfydrin, Llyn Pendam, Llyn Blaenmelindwr. Limit of four fish on Llyn Rhosgoch.
Restrictions:	Fly only on Rhosgoch and Syfydrin.
Stocking policy:	Lakes stocked on selective basis from time to time.
Recommended flies:	
March:	Blae & Black, Mallard & Claret, Black Pennel, Silver March Brown.
April:	Greenwell, Peter Ross, Zulu, Mallard & Claret.
May:	Soldier Palmer, Greenwell, Dry Hawthorn.
June:	Sedges, Dry Grey Duster, Greenwell.
July:	Sedges, Rhwyfwr Mawr, Coch-a-bon-ddu, Butcher Dunkeld.
August:	Crane Flies, Greenwell, Grouse & Green, Peter Ross.
September:	Crane Flies, Invicta, Butcher, Black Pennel, Peter Ross.
Local knowledge:	This miniature lake-land in the hinterland of Aberystwyth, offers interesting fishing from May onwards. Anglers have their personal preferences but the more mobile should give each lake a couple of hours to enjoy the change of scenery and tactics. It is advisable to give Rhosgoch the evening session, especially in June and July and to fish the sedge as a dry fly. Acid rain has recently become apparent on some of the lakes and experimental liming has been conducted on Llyn Pendam.

Llyn Trawsfynydd

TRAWSFYNYDD,
Gwynedd.   Proprietors: Prysor Angling Association

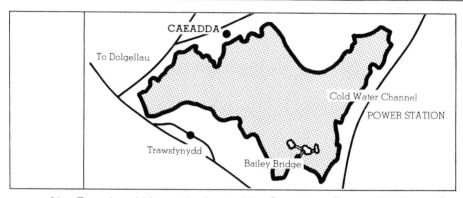

Llyn Trawsfynydd lies at the heart of the Snowdonia Park and is three miles long, its width varying from a quarter of a mile to two miles. The water is some six degrees warmer than normal as it is discharged from the power station, having cooled the nuclear reactors. This warm water provides good feed and hence good angling conditions in February and March.

Facilities:	Tackle shop and permits obtainable in the village.
Season:	1st October–17th October. Hours: 8.00 am to one hour after sunset.
Charges:	Season £30, weekly £14, daily £3. Boat: £4 daily.
Day limit:	6 fish. Boats: 30 rowing boats.
Restrictions:	Hook size limit 10″.
Stocking policy:	Fish reared in own hatchery and are stocked weekly according to demand.
Annual catch per rod:	In 1982 a total of 26,000 visiting anglers took 31,200 fish which is an average of 1.20 fish per visit. Average weight: 15 oz.

Recommended flies:

February:	Black Lure, Ace of Spades, Baby Doll
March:	Black Lure, Black & Peacock Spider, Black Pennel
April:	York's Special, Green Peter, Dunkeld, Bibio
May:	Greenwell, Green Nymph, Yorkie, Mallard & Claret
June:	Bibio, Soldier Palmer, Coch-a-bon-ddu, Invicta
July:	Muddler, Baby Doll, Whisky, Mallard & Claret, Yorkie.
August:	Crane Flies, Small Dry Flies, Green & Brown Nymphs.
September:	Crane Flies, Mallard & Claret, Lake Olives
Local Knowledge:	Arthur Owen is one of the most popular anglers in Wales, and was the recent captain of the Welsh Fly Fishing team. On Llyn Trawsfynydd he is supreme and invariably wins most of the competitions held there. His technique is simple, generally using a boat and a floating or sink tip line. His casts are short with a combination of Mallard & Claret, York's Special and Green Peter or sometimes a Bibio, he drifts along the shallow bays. The Trawsfynydd rainbow trout react well to a bob fly ripped along the surface.

Trisant Lakes

NEAR TRISANT,   Phone: Aberystwyth 828433.
DYFED.   Run by Aberystwyth Angling Assoc.

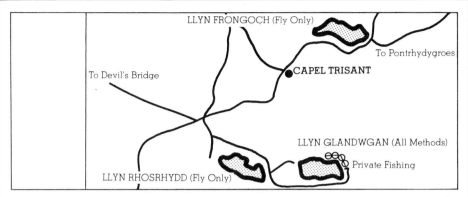

A trio of lakes just outside the village of Trisant. Llyn Frongoch, by the road side, is a good boat fishery with two six-berth caravans for hire. Fishing is reserved for the caravan tenants on Monday, Tuesday, Thursday and Friday of each week. Llyn Rhosrrhydd holds big brown trout, which are very partial to the large sedge that hatches in late June. Llyn Glandwgan some ¼ mile downstream of Rhosrhydd is a multi-method fishery. All parts of this lake may be fished except for the sector marked by the white posts which is private.

Facilities:	Permits from tackle shops in Aberystwyth.
Season:	20th March–17th October.
Rods per day:	Unlimited.
Charges:	Season £70. Day Ticket £7.50 Weekly £30.
Day limit:	4 fish.
Boats:	Two on Frongoch and one each on Rhosrhydd and Glandwgan.
Restrictions:	Fly only on Rhosrhydd and Frongoch.
Stocking policy:	On a selective basis with browns and rainbows. In some instances fish are taken from mountain streams to supplement stocking and to retain a good head of wild brown trout.

Recommended flies:

March:	Black lure, Black & Peacock spider, Blae & Black
April:	Peter Ross, Zulu, Black Pennel, Mallard & Claret, Red Tag.
May:	Greenwell, Black Pennel, Soldier Palmer.
June:	Sedges, Rhwyfwr Mawr Cochddu, Black Pennel, Mallard & Claret.
	Dry flies: Grey Duster & Sun Fly.
July:	Sedges, Coch-a-bon-ddu, Whickham's Fancy, Butcher,
August:	Crane flies, Greenwell, Grouse and Green, Peter Ross.
September:	Crane flies, Black Pennel, (Silver) Dunkeld, Butcher.
Local Knowledge:	These three lakes offer challenging fishing for the discerning angler. In May and June when the trout are at their best a small dry or wet fly fished on the surface film will do well. A day with a stiffish breeze is best and the late evening is the time for the large trout to come on stage.

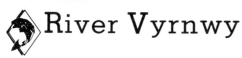 River Vyrnwy

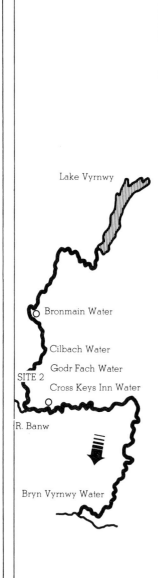

The River Vyrnwy runs from Lake Vyrnwy in the north of Powys through Dolanog and Myfod and down to Llandrinio. It is a major river for the Midland anglers, offering trout and salmon fishing, with some excellent coarse fishing.

Season: Trout 18th March–30th September.
Salmon 2nd February–30th September.
Licence: Severn & Trent Water Authority.
Facilities and restrictions vary with each site.

Site 1: Bryn Vyrnwy Water: One mile down river from Llansantffraid Village. Permit from D. Williams, Bryn Vyrnwy, Llansantffraid. Best time for trout (which average about 10 ozs) April and May.

Site 2: Cross Keys Inn Water: Cross Key Inn, Llansantffriad, Gwern-y-cilau, Powys. Best period for fly fishing in May and June.

Site 3: Godr Llansantffraid. Permits from A. Murgatroyd, Godr, Llansantffraid. Access: A495 Llansantffraid-Meifod road.

Site 4: Cilbach Water. Permits from Goulding, Cilbach, Meifod.

Site 5: Bronymaen Water. Permits from James, Bronymain, Meifod. This is one and a quarter miles o both banks. Access A495 Llansantffraid-Meifod road.

Site 6: Dyffryn Water. Permits from J. R. Wilkinson, Dyffryn, Meifod. Best time in April and May.

Site 7: Neuadd Water on the Banwy – a tributary of the Vyrnywy. Permits from Edwards, Neuadd Bridge Farm, Caravan Park, Llanfair Caereinion, Nr. Welshpool.

Recommended flies: Early season: Snipe & Purple, March Brown, Iron Brown Dun, Pheasant Tail, Partridge and Red, February Red.
Mid-season flies: Coch-a-bon-ddu, Hawthorn, Black Gnat, Olives, Sedges, Grannom.

River Ystwyth
Ceredigion–North Dyfed

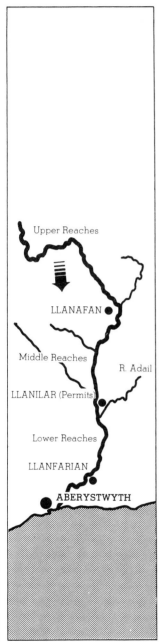

Upper Reaches

LLANAFAN ●

Middle Reaches

R. Adail

LLANILAR (Permits) ●

Lower Reaches

LLANFARIAN ●

● ABERYSTWYTH

The River Ystwyth runs off the hills of mid-Wales and after a comparatively short course, into Cardigan Bay at Aberystwyth. It is an excellent sewin river presenting good wet/dry fly sport both during the day and night, when the conditions are right. It is a fairly fast-running river, with long runs, but somewhat lacking in big pools. When the river is running down after a flood, the cautious angler, fishing the runs carefully with a wet fly, has every opportunity of taking some prime sewin.

Facilities: River Ystwyth is mainly managed by the Llanilar Angling Association, permits for which are available on a seasonal and daily basis.
Licence: Welsh Water Authority.
Both licence and permit available at local Post Office. Permit: £5 per day. Queries in respect of permits to Mark Hamblin, Delwar, Llanilar, near Aberystwyth. (Secretary of Llanilar Angling Association.)

Site 1: Upper reaches: The sewin are slightly staler and more readily to move to smaller flies. This sction needs a fair flow to get the fish out into the runs during the day. Night fishing can be productive using small flies in the pools.

Site 2: This section contains some notable pools, which, with local knowledge, can be fished successfully at night. The tail ends of these pools are the important areas to concentrate on in low water conditions.

Site 3: Sewin in this area are far fresher having just come off the tide. Good stretches for fly fishing in water thinning down after a flood.

Site 4: Below the village of Llanfarian lie some good pools for salmon but unfortunately they are too small for the fly to be fished well, except when the river is high. The fly does not account for a large percentage of salmon on the River Ystwyth but there are encouraging signs that the late-running salmon are showing an interest and have been taken on sewin flies.

Recommended flies: Sewin flies in all sizes take fish on the river Ystwyth. There would appear to be a definite link between the length of time that the sewin has been in the river and the size of the fly. In the upper reaches the smaller flies – Butcher and Peter Ross do well. In the lower reaches, larger sizes of Teal Blue and Silver and tube flies are favoured. Normal sewin patterns used on the Ystwyth include: Squirrel, Jack Frost, Viva, Haslam.

Index of Advertisers

A.C.A., 18
Anglia Water, Cambs., 119
Arundel Arms, Devon, 47
Barn Book Supply, Wilts., 102
Bev Harper-Smith, E. Sussex, 141
Bewl Bridge Reservoir, Kent, 106
Black Monk Trout Lakes, Worcs., 157
Brigands Inn Hotel, Powys, 340
Bristol Waterworks, Avon, 28
Calderbrook Lakes, Lancs., 28
C.E.G.B., Liverpool, 148
Corsemalzie House Hotel, Wigtownshire, 165
Countryman Prints, London W6, 12 .
Craigdarroch Lodge Hotel, Rosshire, 247
Cross Keys Hotel, Roxburghshire, 193
David A. H. Grayling, Cumbria, 215
Debretts Peerage Ltd., London SW6, 59
Dunalastair Hotel, Perthshire, 203
Farlows of Pall Mall, London SW1, 17
The Field, London EC4, 6, 24, 38
Fishermans Feathers, Worcs., 88
Forsinard Hotel, Sutherland, 255
Glenmorangie, IFC, 14, 172, 287
Gliffaes Hotel, Powys, 306
Hutchinsons Publishers, London, 148
Jimmy Robertson, Northumberland, 203
Knockie Lodge Hotel, Inverness, 244
Lake Vyrnwy Hotel, Salop, 334
Lanarth Hotel, Cornwall, 47
Lechdale Trout Farm, Glos., 88
Leighton Reservoir, N. Yorks., 282
Llanllawddog Lake, Dyfed, 324
Loch Maree Hotel, Ross-shire, 247
Mackays Hotel, Ross-shire, 247

Macsport Ltd., Kincardine, 219
Mount View Hotel, Invernessshire, 334
Osprey Fishing School, Invernessshire, 334
Pemba Channel Club, 5
Peter Stone, Wolverote, Oxford, 102
Portsonachan Hotel, Argyll, 271
Profeits Hotel, Aberdeenshire, 222
Rams Head Inn, Devon, 76
Ringstead Grange, Trout Fishing, Northants., 119
Rottal Lodge, Angus, 215
Royal Oak Hotel, Dolton, 76
Safari Scotland, Perth, 177
Salmon & Trout Assoc., London, 23
Severn Arm Hotel, Powys, 310
Sinnigton Trout Farm, Yorks., 28
Smythson of Bond Street, London, 141
Speciality Leisure, Hants., 239
Spey Valley Hotel, Moray, 334
Tara Designs, Norfolk, 165
The Lake Hotel, Powys, 306
The Sportsman's Lodge, Northampton, 119
The Swan Hotel, Glos., 157
Tom C. Saville Ltd., Nottinghamshire, 141
Town Mills Hotel, N. Devon, 76
Ulbster Arms, Caithness, 266
Vince Lister Agent, Essex, 55
Wessex Fly Fishing Schools, Dorset, 76
Wessex Water Authority, Somerset, 28
Woodburn House Hotel, Selkirk, 181
Woodford Bridge Hotel, 1BC